AT A JOURNAL WORKSHOP

This Inner Workbook is
part of a series that explores
psyche and spirit through writing,
visualization, ritual, and
imagination.

Other books in this series include:

The Artist's Way
BY JULIA CAMERON

The Adult Children of Divorce Workbook
BY MARY HIRSCHFELD, J.D., PH.D.

Following Your Path
BY ALEXANDRA COLLINS DICKERMAN, M.F.C.C.

The Inner Child Workbook
BY CATHRYN L. TAYLOR, M.A., M.F.C.C.

A Journey Through Your Childhood
BY CHRISTOPHER BIFFLE

Pain and Possibility
BY GABRIELE RICO

The Path of the Everyday Hero
BY LORNA CATFORD, PH.D., AND MICHAEL RAY, PH.D.

Personal Mythology
BY DAVID FEINSTEIN, PH.D., AND STANLEY KRIPPNER, PH.D.

The Possible Human
BY JEAN HOUSTON

The Search for The Beloved
BY JEAN HOUSTON

Smart Love
BY JODY HAYES

True Partners
BY TINA TESSINA, PH.D., AND RILEY K. SMITH, M.A.

Your Mythic Journey
BY SAM KEEN AND ANNE VALLEY-FOX

AT A JOURNAL WORKSHOP

*Writing to Access the Power
of the Unconscious and
Evoke Creative Ability*

Ira Progoff, Ph.D.

Jeremy P. Tarcher/Putnam
a member of
Penguin Putnam Inc.
New York

Most Tarcher/Putnam books are available at special quantity
discounts for bulk purchases for sales promotions, premiums,
fund-raising, and educational needs. Special books or book
excerpts also can be created to fit specific needs.
For details, write Putnam Special Markets
375 Hudson Street, New York, NY 10014

Jeremy P. Tarcher/Putnam
a member of
Penguin Putnam Inc.
375 Hudson Street
New York, NY 10014
www.penguinputnam.com

Library of Congress Cataloging in Publication Data

Progoff, Ira.
    At a journal workshop : writing to access the power of the unconscious
    and evoke creative ability / Ira Progoff.
        p.   cm.
    Includes bibliographical references and index.
    (pbk.)
    1. Diaries—Therapeutic use.   2. Psychotherapy.   I. Title.
    RC489.D5P74   1992
    158 ' .1—dc20   91-36435
                                                              CIP

Design by Tanya Maiboroda

Intensive Journal® is a registered trademark of Dr. Ira Progoff and is used
under license by Dialogue House Associates, Inc.

Originally published by Dialogue House as two separate volumes, *At a
Journal Workshop* (1977) and *The Practice of Process Meditation* (1980).

Manufactured in the United States of America

30 29 28 27 26 25 24 23 22 21

Contents

Introduction   viii

Part 1   *PREPARING FOR YOUR JOURNAL WORK*   1

1. The Scope of Personal Renewal   2

2. Seeking the Elan of Life:
   The Dimensions of Private Journal Work   19

3. The Atmosphere of a Journal Workshop   33

Part 2   *FIRST STAGES OF YOUR JOURNAL WORK*   45

4. Positioning Yourself in the Present: The Period Log   46

5. Twilight Imagery and Life Correlation   57

6. The Daily Log   65

Part 3   *THE LIFE/TIME DIMENSION*   73

    Introduction to the Life/Time Dimension   74

7. The Steppingstones   76

8. The Steppingstone Periods in the Life History Log   90

9. Intersections: Roads Taken and Not Taken   102

10. Time-Stretching: Backward and Forward   108

Part 4   *THE DIALOGUE DIMENSION*   123

      Introduction to the Dialogue Dimension   124

11.   Dialogue with Persons   127

12.   Dialogue with Works   141

13.   Dialogue with the Body   154

14.   Dialogue with Events, Situations, and Circumstances   167

15.   Dialogue with Society   182

Part 5   *THE DEPTH DIMENSION*   195

      Introduction to the Depth Dimension   196

16.   The Dream Log: Beginning to Work with Our Dreams   198

17.   Twilight Dreaming: Using Dream Enlargements
      and Imagery Extensions   209

Part 6   *THE MEANING DIMENSION*   222

      Introduction to the Meaning Dimension   223

18.   Meditation Log I: Entrance Meditations   225

19.   Meditation Log II: Spiritual Positioning   232

20.   Meditation Log III: Inner Process Entries   241

21.   Connections I: The Cycles of Connective Experience   247

22.   Connections II: Gatherings   257

23.   Connections III: Spiritual Steppingstones
      and Inner Wisdom Dialogue   267

24.   Connections IV: Re-Openings of Spiritual
      Roads Not Taken   286

25.   PDE: Peaks, Depths, and Explorations   300

26.   Modalities for Next Experience   312

27.   Mantra/Crystal Experiences   328

28. Testament 350

29. Now: The Open Moment 359

Part 7 *CONTINUING YOUR JOURNAL WORK* 364

30. Resource and Continuity 365

APPENDICES

Appendix A: Entrance Meditations 383

Appendix B: Mantra Crystals from the Workshop Floor 392

Appendix C: Spiritual Steppingstones 397

Appendix D: The Registered *Intensive Journal* Workbook 402

Other Books by Ira Progoff 411

Index 412

About the Author and The *Intensive Journal* Program 421

Introduction

This new one-volume edition of *At a Journal Workshop* and *The Practice of Process Meditation* has a two-fold purpose. Primarily it is to make available, in one volume in a condensed form, the essence of the two volumes that have served as the texts for the *Intensive Journal* process. The second provide an updated version of the Journal sections and exercises that accompany them.

The book is designed so that you can give yourself an *Intensive Journal* workshop wherever you are, whatever your situation, whenever you are in the mood to work in your life. And you can also use it as a reference volume to add to your experience at, or after, an *Intensive Journal* workshop.

A sequence has established itself in the more than twenty-five years since the *Intensive Journal* process was offered to the public. The order of the exercises is an integral part of the success of the work. First you feed the data of your life into your workbook. You do this mainly while you are learning the ways of using the Journal sections as you carry out the exercises. Then, as you reread the entries you have made, you feed the data back into those Journal sections in which something further is trying to be formed. In this is the simple way we find the *Journal Feedback* leads that point us to the next development in our life. It is the follow-up that occurs naturally after each of your workshop experiences.

Those who have already used the *Intensive Journal* process know that it is not limited to making daily entries in the style of a daily diary. It is an open-ended means of gaining a perspective on where you are in the movement of your life. You are carrying out the active exercises in private, and you are exploring the possibilities of your future in the context of your whole life.

Since it carries a process of continuous life experience, this is not a book to be read through at a sitting or two but to be worked with a step at a time. When you have carried out all the exercises, allowing them to stretch over as long a period as they require, an exciting awareness like the breaking of dawn will come to you. It will be the cumulative impact both of seeing your life set itself in perspective and recognizing the elusive process by which your Journal Feedback exercises have been working for you.

The experience of recognition that will come to you then will be very much like learning to play a musical instrument. After slow and stumbling beginnings, you suddenly realize that you now comprehend not only the keyboard as a whole but the infinite possibilities for combining the keys creatively. From that point onward, the instrument is accessible to you with all its potentials.

The same is true of learning to use the *Intensive Journal* method. First you must begin slowly, even arduously, to learn the nature of the instrument and its techniques. Once you have learned how to use it, however, the *Intensive Journal* process will always be available to you. You can then call upon it as you need it, not only to help you through the crises that may recur in the cycles of your life but also to give you access to depths of creative resources within yourself.

You will perceive as you work with it that this is not a book of pat answers nor advice for quick success. It does not espouse any particular doctrine or belief. It does, however, describe a method that persons of all ages and levels of education coming from the most diverse cultures have been able to use effectively in clarifying their lives and developing their own beliefs.

You may glean some of my personal philosophy as you read, but the purpose of this book is not to set forth any beliefs. It is to explain a method of working privately at the inner levels of your life. You may agree with my personal philosophy, or you may not. That will not matter. What *is* important is that you use these techniques to help you become your own person and find a way of living that will validate itself to you both in terms of your inner sense of truth and the reality of your outer experience.

Part 1

PREPARING FOR YOUR JOURNAL WORK

The Scope of Personal Renewal

Suppose all the Bibles of the world were burned, what would befall civilization?

When I returned to civilian life after my army service in World War II, I often lost myself in unhappy contemplation of the destructive events of recent history. In one decade from 1935 to 1945, civilization had come precariously close to destroying itself. I found myself especially reflecting on the massive burning of books that had taken place during the Hitler era. Again and again I asked myself what would have happened to civilization if the ritual Nazi burnings of the books had been continued until all the recorded wisdom of humankind had been destroyed.

I answered that question in two parts. The sciences, I concluded, would be retained in the technology of the engineers. Science would be preserved, although in a stunted form, if only because science is necessary for making weapons of war and for producing commodities to sell. But what of the sacred scriptures, I asked. Suppose all the Bibles of the world were burned, the Old and the New Testaments, the Tao Teh Ching, the Upanishads, the Koran, and all the others. If that happened, what would befall civilization?

I used to lie awake wondering what the human race would do if all its sacred scriptures were destroyed. Finally one night the answer was given to me. It came as a simple practical statement spoken in everyday tones. We would, the voice said, simply draw new spiritual scriptures from the same great source out of which the old ones came.

In that moment I became aware of how vast and self-replenishing are the resources of the human spirit. The fires of Hitler could burn the sacred books, but they could not destroy the abiding depths out of which those scriptures had emerged. I heard also the words of the Polish rabbi chanting as he was being buried alive: "Green grass lives longer than Nebuchadnezzar." God's smallest creations will outlast the power of tyrants. And this is because, as Walt Whitman knew, the simple leaves of grass come from the same infinite, re-creative source as the depths of the human spirit, from which the wisdom and the strength of civilization also come.

A great difficulty of Western society is the belief that major revelations are no longer possible because the gift of prophecy was taken away.

That understanding opened a new range of hope for me. Humankind would not be destroyed. No matter what foolish, destructive acts people would perpetrate on the physical level, new fountains of life would continue to rise from reservoirs deep within. Recognizing that there are indeed infinite dimensions to our universe, the immortality of life began to be a fact for me.

Soon another realization arose in me. If mankind has the power to draw additional spiritual scriptures out of the depth of itself, why do we have to wait for a tyrant to burn our Bibles before we let ourselves create further expressions of the spirit? If it is indeed true that each human soul contains a Bible within itself, may it not be that each person contains the possibility of new spiritual events and awarenesses taking place in his and her own experience? Perhaps there are new Bibles, many new Bibles, to be created as the sign of spiritual unfoldment among many persons in the modern era. It may indeed be that the creation of multiple spiritual scriptures, and especially the extension of old scriptures, is an event that needs to happen in our time as part of the further qualitative evolution of our species.

This thought led me to additional explorations concerning the Bibles of the world. I soon realized that each of the Bibles of mankind is a spiritual source book for the civilization it serves. As the scripture for its society, a Bible is not a book that comes into existence by means of a single individual. It is the product of many experiences and numerous lives. It reflects the experiences of many persons as they reach toward a contact with divinity in the midst of the harsh social and economic facts of history. Each Bible expresses the social and spiritual struggles that formed the life of its civilization through the centuries.

The Bibles of the world provide a tradition and a wisdom from which those who are attuned to them can draw sustenance for their lives.

The Bibles of each of the major civilizations are connections to the past. They do not restrict us to the past, but they link us to it. They give us a sense of continuity so that each generation can be reminded that the present moment has been preceded by many that have gone before. No matter how intense our own experience may be, we are not the first who feel it. We are not the first to be groping and leaping our way toward the truth. We need therefore to be aware of what has taken place in earlier times so that we can live our present experiences in an organic relationship with the past.

In addition, the major Bibles of the world contain the profound wisdoms that have been achieved by or been revealed to the great historical persons. The texts express, sometimes in obscure esoteric and symbolic forms, perceptions of the mysteries of human existence as well as profound philosophic guidance for the conduct of life.

Bibles are teachers of the various meanings and possibilities in human life. Consequently, when individuals come to crossroads of decision or to points in their lives where they are tested by adversity, they can find not only a deep source of guidance but the energy of reinspiration in the pages of the great scriptures. The Bibles take the form of books, but they are more than books. They are teachers of persons because they are carriers of ageless wisdom in forms that can speak to the condition of individuals at the particular time and place of their existence. Thus they have the capacity to renew the lives of individuals. And that is one reason why the Bibles of all civilizations are venerated as *holy* scriptures.

Because they each contain the profound teachings that carry the wisdom of their civilization, the Bibles of the world are indeed worthy of being regarded as *holy,* of being revered and lovingly preserved by those who are devoted to them. In all their forms, as oral traditions and as written texts, they are the composite record of the major moments in history when chosen individuals, in caves and on mountain tops, in desert retreats or casually going about their chores, were touched by a power greater than their own personalities and given directions that were meaningful to a large part of their society as well as to themselves.

Bibles express the spiritual and cultural life of entire civilizations and periods of history, but the inner experience by which their meaning can be known is individual. For that reason, the work of re-establishing contact with the Bibles of the past and extending their meaning in the present is a work with large social implications, but it is a work that can be done only person by person. Spiritual contact, the awareness of the profounder meanings of life and the experience of its symbols, is an individual endeavor that can be carried through only in the silence of privacy. It is a work that each person has to do alone, but it is helpful to know that many of us are working alone together. It is helpful also to understand that we do not all have to hold the same beliefs in order for us each to contribute an atom of spirit to the human atmosphere. It seems important that as many persons as possible do their private inner work as deeply as they can. For that we require a methodology that can be used by individuals whatever their faith or lack of faith, and whatever their level of intellectual development and personal interest. Such a process is what I seek to provide in this book.

Spiritual contact is the awareness of the profounder meanings of life which can only be experienced in the silence of privacy.

The Intensive Journal Program

When I appreciated the dimensions of the spiritual need confronting this period of history, I set myself on a path of exploration to see if I could discover or develop, primarily for myself, a viable means of access to the sources out of which the Bibles of the world have been drawn. More than three decades have passed since then, with much trial and error, testing and expanding. Eventually, out of my personal searching and my professional research, first in the historical study of society and then in depth psychology, a set of underlying principles took shape. From these there evolved the *Intensive Journal* system of thought and practice.

The *Intensive Journal* concept was first formulated in 1966. Since that time it has been the subject of considerable research that has led to substantial extensions and applications. The pace of this development was accelerated in 1975 by the first publication of *At a Journal Workshop,* the book that has served as the basic text and reference manual for the *Intensive Journal* system. As the method came to be more widely known and used, the National Intensive Journal Program was formed to make *Intensive Journal* workshops available throughout the United States, and more recently in other countries. By means of the national program it has become possible to offer to the general public a sequence of *Intensive Journal* workshops with a standard, carefully organized curriculum of exercises taught by consultants specifically trained for each module of the work. By standardizing the curriculum of the workshops, it has become possible for individuals to focus on the particular areas of experience that seem most appropriate, or urgent, at a given time in their lives. And they can do that special focusing within the context of their life as a whole, thanks to the *Intensive Journal* system.

The basic instrument for the national program is the *Intensive Journal* workbook. It has been described as deceptively simple. I agree. If you examine it apart from the program in which it is used, the *Intensive Journal* workbook may seem to be nothing more than a notebook with twenty-five colored dividers. In practice, however, it turns out to be a highly specific structure of interrelated moving parts based on the various *hypotheses of process,* each of the Journal sections being a channel for a particular inner process of personal life. Each section is used with specific active procedures that serve to evoke the contents of a person's life without analysis or diagnosis, but in such a way as to stimulate additional inner perceptions and movements of many kinds. The sections tend to cross-fertilize and activate one another, releasing new energies and bringing about new combinations of ideas and feelings. Even in short periods of use, the process carried by the *Intensive Journal* structure is able to build a cumulative energy that often has a transforming and redirective effect upon a person's life. (A complete *Intensive Journal* workbook as it is currently used is printed in this book as an Appendix.)

A special value of the *Intensive Journal* approach is that it enables individuals to break through situations of stalemate where their lives had seemed to have reached a dead end. It achieves this in part because its non-analytic approach generates a movement of inner energies. The progressive, interrelated continuity of exercises within the *Intensive Journal* program has the effect of evoking new ideas and opening contexts of understanding. The inner activity that it stimulates leads to new courses of action, and the newly built momentum of energy provides the strength to set them into motion. These are the specific steps by which the *Intensive Journal* program functions non-analytically to set people into motion on the track of their lives.

The sequence of inner events by which this takes place can be very energizing, and therefore it may sometimes build strong enthusiasms.

But the *Intensive Journal* program provides protection against making and carrying out errors of judgment that may arise while we are seeking to re-establish our lives. The wholeness of its structure establishes a perspective for the movement of one's life, so that the past, present, and future are included in a single, comprehensive framework. The fullness of this context is a protection against acting on momentary enthusiasms, a danger that is often very great when people feel their lives to be in crisis.

Too often, when we are trying to help ourselves in times of desperation, our actions only prove the truth of the old adage, "Out of the frying pan into the fire." The *Intensive Journal* structure is a protection against this because it sets the sequence of its exercises in such a way that the contents of a life can be experienced in perspective. Over-reactions to adversity or over-enthusiasms of hope can then equally be set in context and brought into balance in the course of the journal exercises in the continuity of the process.

Context and continuity are two basic aspects of the work that the *Intensive Journal* structure makes possible, enabling us to draw our lives into focus at a given moment in the midst of the pressures of a crisis so that we can resolve the immediate issues. Then, at a later time, we use additional journal sections and exercises in order to reconsider the situations of our lives from additional vantage points as we move through new circumstances and events. In this way the *Intensive Journal* program serves as a vehicle that carries people through the difficult and confusing transitions of their lives. In addition to providing perspective, it acts as a self-adjusting compass, seeking the true north, the special meaning and direction of each individual life.

Process Meditation: A Source of Inner Wisdom

As it brings an inner self-guidance for life's problems, the *Intensive Journal* approach has also produced an interesting, if unexpected extra. In the course of its work it deepens the level of experience, and this draws an individual into contact with the profound sources of inner wisdom. Many persons have found that as they involved themselves in the *Intensive Journal* process to resolve the immediate problems of personal life, they have inadvertently opened awarenesses that are transpersonal in scope. Without intending it, they find that they are drawn beyond themselves in wisdom to levels of experience that have the qualities of poetry and spirit.

The reason that this takes place is fundamental to understanding why and how the *Intensive Journal* process has been helpful to so many persons. And it is the key to Process Meditation. The source of it lies in the *Intensive Journal* structure, for it is the structure that gives the method its capacity to generate new energy. Through the relation of the Journal sections to each other, an inner dynamic is built, and this dynamic moves in two directions. One is outward toward the activities of the world. The other is inward. Both are integral to the process as a whole, but it is by the progressive and cumulative deepening of the inward movement that the new energy is built. This is true whether you are at a Journal workshop with many other persons or are working alone. The process of the method draws you systematically inward until it establishes an atmosphere of quietness and depth in which the refocusing and then the reintegration of the life can take place.

It is apparent that this inward movement has an inherently meditative quality. During the early years of this work it was common for people to comment, often in surprise, that the feelings stirred in them at *Intensive Journal* workshops reminded them of profound prayer or of deep meditation. And yet they also observed that the process was dealing factually with the nitty-gritty of their lives and that it was not prescribing for them any particular religious philosophy.

The *Intensive Journal* work is indeed a type of prayer and meditation, but not in isolation from life and not in place of active life involvement. Rather, it is meditation in the midst of the reality of our life experiences. It draws upon the actualities of life for new awarenesses, and it feeds these back into the movement of each life as a whole. The fact is that the fundamental *process* in Process Meditation is each life itself.

At the surface of our life we are conscious of the many pressing problems that beset us, the conflicts, the anxieties, the angers, the decisions that we feel we must urgently make. But one reason that the *Intensive Journal* method has been effective for many people is that it practices an *indirect* approach to solving our life problems. Rather than move head-on to encounter problems in the external form in which they appear in our lives, we step back and move inward to meet them at a deeper level.

Over the years my personal experiences as well as my observations had led me to question whether we solve our life problems best by reacting directly to the pressures they place upon us. Eventually I discovered that the *Intensive Journal* structure makes possible an alternate strategy, an indirect strategy. The first step is to acknowledge the problems of our life as we find them, to observe them and describe them as objectively as we can. That gives us a reference point in outer reality, but we do not establish our position there. We draw back. We move away from the surface of things. We move inward in order to return with a greater resource to use in reapproaching the situation.

It is basic to this inward phase of the work that we begin by setting the movement of our lives in a full perspective. Once we have established our life context we have parameters within which we can move deeper and deeper to explore the contents and resources of our life. The purpose and style of that exploration is neither to diagnose nor to judge, but to enable our life to disclose to us what its goals and its meanings are. In doing this, we each find different meanings, different directions for our lives. But we discover that, regardless of the diverse conclusions we may reach, we are all impressed by the quality of experience that comes to us as individuals when our attention is focused inwardly in this way, especially when our inwardness has established an atmosphere of depth and stillness of being. The atmosphere of inward attention seems to possess a profound validity that dwarfs any particular opinions, or any particular anxieties we may hold about the details of our existence.

The set of procedures to which I have been alluding is the means by which we build the inward dynamic of the *Intensive Journal* work. It is called *progressive deepening*. The years of using this essentially psychological procedure to draw personal lives into focus have demonstrated a truth of more than psychological significance. When our attention is focused inwardly at the depth of our being in the context of the wholeness of our life, resources for a profound knowledge of life become accessible to us.

Process Meditation enables us to work actively and systematically at this inner level, reaching toward an experience both of personal meaning and of a meaning in life that is more than personal. It is in one sense an outgrowth of the *Intensive Journal* concept and in another sense a fulfillment of it. The practice of Process Meditation makes it possible to work tangibly with the dimension of spiritual meaning in the specifics of our individual life history. To this degree it also fulfills the fundamental vision that was stated many years ago as a goal of Holistic Depth Psychology: to provide an integrative method by which the psychological and the spiritual can be experienced as two sides of a single coin. It may be that all psychological work has been implicitly seeking this ever since William James and C. G. Jung recognized that there is no lasting personal healing without an experience of meaning at the depth of one's being.

Process Meditation first became part of the *Intensive Journal* program in 1970, when the principles underlying Process Meditation were sharply enough defined to enable me to use at least some of its techniques in *Intensive Journal* workshops. Some of the procedures and certain aspects of the concept behind the method were still in an exploratory stage, however, and I did not feel ready to include them in *At a Journal Workshop* when I published it in 1975 as the basic textbook for the *Intensive Journal* method. The Process Meditation methodology was thus not described in that book.

Since that time, however, I have been able to take substantial strides in developing the underlying conception of Process Meditation and in working out the details of its procedures. For one thing, the increased public participation in the *Intensive Journal* program as a whole has provided me with extended opportunities for gathering empirical data regarding the various Process Meditation procedures. It has enabled me to explore and test new principles and techniques.

As an outcome of this extended exploration, a full Process Meditation component containing five separate sections for active inner work has been added to the *Intensive Journal* workbook since *At a Journal Workshop* was published. In this edition, the Process Meditation sections are all encompassed under the term *Meaning Dimension* which is the fourth dimension of the *Intensive Journal* workshop. By now they are well established as a functional part of the total structure of the *Intensive Journal* method.

How to Use This Book

Since this is a method for carrying out a program of inner work, portions of the text are designed to lead into the actual exercises. When these sections appear, it will do no good for you to remain a merely passive reader. It will be necessary for you to at least begin your inner work by participating in the exercises as we proceed. Working in the exercises may slow down your reading time, but you will find that as you carry out the exercises you are filling in the structure of the process with your own experiences. The concepts and principles that are involved in the *Intensive Journal* method will thus become more meaningful to you as you proceed because they will be made specific by the contents of your own life and especially by your own ongoing inner experience. Step by step, as you work with each of the sections, you will be setting the process of your inner life into motion, deepening it, evoking new experiences and generating an interior energy as you proceed.

To help in carrying out the exercises, I shall describe the sequence of the steps to be followed much as we do at a workshop, setting the atmosphere and leading into the experience. I shall also discuss here the additional steps and the variations that may be drawn upon in continuing your journal after a workshop. My desire is to provide a sufficient store of information with respect both to the theoretical and the practical aspects of the *Intensive Journal* process so that you can use it as an ongoing spiritual discipline largely under your own direction once you have learned it. It may thus serve as a background book to be referred to as you proceed in your work, and also as a direct guide to working in the exercises that build your own experience.

Do not content yourself with reading the descriptions and merely thinking about what you would write *if* you did the exercises. Thinking about what you would write is not the same as actually writing it. The act of writing in the atmosphere that is created by the journal process at work and that builds cumulatively as you follow the format of its exercises seems to evoke depths in us that mere thinking does not reach. You will find that the act of carrying out the steps of the work and actually recording them in written form has the effect of stimulating a movement within you that draws forth awarenesses you would not have thought of in advance.

To get the benefit of this method it is necessary actually to use it and to do so in writing. Thinking about it and figuring it out is not enough, because that gives us the illusion that we understand it conceptually when we cannot in fact understand how the dynamic of its principles operates without working with it over a period of time. We should not place ourselves in the position of talking *about* a process that we do not actually know as facts of our inner experience, for that

The Intensive Journal process seeks to achieve on the practical level a goal that C.G. Jung held dear—for individuals to fulfill their seed possibilities.

leads to intellectual chatter rather than to spiritual reality. The *Intensive Journal* process gives each person a means of taking whatever meaningful experiences they have already had in their lives—whether large and dramatic or small and inconspicuous experiences—and reopens them by re-entering them, allowing them to serve as starting points for new, and often unpredictable inner events. We shall see step by step how this works.

Once you have learned how to use it, the *Intensive Journal* method becomes like a musical instrument you can play; and its melodies are the themes and the intimations of meaning in your life. Going to great heights and to great depths, the life music that persons find themselves playing upon their *Intensive Journal* instrument is often startling. They did not expect to find in themselves sounds of such strength or such sweetness, such sensitivity in the midst of pain, such capacities for harmony or such inner vision.

Quite often as I sit at workshops, listening to persons read the experiences that have been evoked in them during their *Intensive Journal* exercises, I find myself reflecting that the words that were spoken to me (or within me) years ago are being fulfilled now in ways I could not have imagined at the time. Individuals, working in their own lives and in the depths of their own being, do in fact activate spiritual knowledge they did not know they possessed. They did not know how wise they were, nor the power and range of their visionary capacities. Nonetheless it comes from within them undirected, evoked in the spontaneity of their experience by the *Intensive Journal* process. Bibles are indeed being renewed and extended in the depth of individual experience. It must be that, as we work in our personal depths, we make contact each in our own way and in varying degrees with the same inexhaustible sources out of which the old Bibles came. Whenever an individual touches those sources, regardless of the language or the doctrine or the symbols in which the experience comes, new sparks of divinity enter the world. And these sparks ignite fires that give warmth and light but do not consume.

For many people the *Intensive Journal* process has evolved into a spiritual discipline that fulfills the creative role of awakening and extending the Bibles that have been sleeping in their souls. In the discussions and experiences that follow, it will be good if we can bear in mind this large frame of reference as the background and purpose of what we do. In the practice of the *Intensive Journal* method we are reaching back through our heritage as civilized persons to the inner source of that heritage in order to touch the power by which it originally came to be. And we seek to give that old reality a new life through our individual experiences.

Many persons have already had experiences in which they have sensed the presence of an underlying reality in life, a reality which they have recognized as a personal source of meaning and strength. It may have come to them in a brief, spontaneous moment of spiritual exaltation, or it may have come as a flash of awareness in the midst of darkness and pain. They came very close then to a deep, unifying contact, but it slipped away from them because they had no means of holding it and sustaining the relationship. Some could not break through because of their inherited overlay of religious doctrines or other intellectual concepts. Others missed their opportunity because they had so low an opinion of themselves that it did not occur to them that there could be depth and meaning in the experiences of their lives.

The *Intensive Journal* workbook is specifically designed to provide an instrument and techniques by which persons can discover within themselves the resources they did not know they possessed. It is to enable them to draw the power of deep contact out of the actual experiences of their lives so that they can recognize their own identity and harmonize it with the larger identity of the universe as they experience it. Where they had negated themselves, they can, by means of their *Intensive Journal* work, give their lives full value.

The specific means of achieving this contact with the inner resources of one's life is by the regular and disciplined use of the *Intensive Journal* with its progressive exercises. The effective principle operating in this is that when a person is shown how to reconnect himself with the contents and the continuity of his life, the inner thread of movement by which his life has been unfolding reveals itself to him by itself. Given the opportunity, a life crystallizes out of its own nature, revealing its meaning and its goal. This is the self-integrating principle of life which the journal procedures make available to us.

The *Intensive Journal* method has been described as a method that is beyond psychotherapy because it takes a transpsychological approach to what had been thought of as psychological problems. Here the word *transpsychological* means a process that brings about therapeutic effects not by forcing an individual to passively accept so-called treatment, but by providing active techniques that enable an individual

The Journal workbook is an instrument with techniques by which persons can discover within themselves the resources they did not know they possessed.

The Scope of Personal Renewal 13

to draw upon his inherent resources for becoming a whole person. It systematically evokes and strengthens the inner capacities of whole persons by working from a nonmedical vantage point and proceeding without analytic or diagnostic categories. It establishes a person's sense of his own being by enriching his inner life with new experiences of a creative and spiritual quality. Since these experiences happen to him and are recorded in his *Intensive Journal* workbook while they are actually taking place, each person accumulates a tangible and factual validation of his personal growth as it is happening.

As an individual works in the continuity of the *Intensive Journal* process, the past experiences of his life gradually fit into place—times of exultation and times of despair, moments of hope and anger, crises and crossroads, partial failures and successes. As we use them over a period of time, the procedures of the *Intensive Journal* method make it possible for all the events and relationships of our life to show us what they were *for,* what their purpose was in our lives, and what they wish to tell us for our future. Thus we gradually discover that our life has been going somewhere, however blind we have been to its direction and however unhelpful to it we ourselves may have been. We find that a connective thread has been forming beneath the surface of our lives, carrying the meaning that has been trying to establish itself in our existence. It is the inner continuity of our lives. As we recognize and identify with it, we see an inner myth that has been guiding our lives unknown to ourselves.

In the course of the gradual and cumulative work by which an individual recognizes the nonconscious guidance that has been directing his personal life involvements, he perceives that the peaks and the valleys are of equal importance. All are necessary, for the high is not possible without the low. In a more fundamental sense, he recognizes that the essence lies not in the events of his life in themselves, not in the things that have happened to him, but in his inner relationship to those events. At the moment when they were actually taking place, his relation to them may have been inadequate because of many small fears and limited understanding. For that, he may feel guilty, angry, and negative toward himself. As the larger perspective opens through the journal work, however, a new quality of relationship can be established to the events of the past. The continuity of life renews itself, and we have a fresh opportunity. In the light of our new recognition of the inner movement and meaning of our lives, it actually seems that we can now begin our life anew. That is what the ageless symbolism of rebirth has been trying to say to people since the beginning of religion.

One of the most significant realizations that has come to me in the course of this work has been the observation of the extra increment of meaning that is added to an individual's awareness as the *Intensive Journal* procedures reopen the possibilities of life. As the events of a life set themselves in order, giving perspective for the past and guidance for the future, *something additional* happens. It is as though previously untapped knowledge is activated so that a person is brought face-to-face with the ultimates, and the meaning of his personal existence. It is there before him, collected in his own handwriting in his *Intensive Journal* workbook. We often find that the experience of this deep opening in a person's life spontaneously expresses itself in the language of the spirit, regardless of the individual's religious background. Many of the entries written in the journal at such moments of realization have the style of natural poetry or personal prophecy, the language of the self discovering itself.

Experiences of this kind take place in the midst of the *Intensive Journal* work regardless of the social or economic level on which a person is living. To reintegrate and renew one's life perspective has a transforming and spiritually renewing effect on every person in whom it takes place, whether young or old, wealthy or impoverished, intellectual or unlettered. Observing this has served to strengthen the social use of the *Intensive Journal* method. It has fortified the central concept of renewing society by renewing individuals, specifically by giving all individuals, wherever they are in the culture, an opportunity to contact their deep sources by reconstructing the inner continuity of their lives.

The process of using the *Intensive Journal* workbook can fairly be described as a method for all seasons in a person's life. We may use it actively and intensely during times of conflict and difficulty; we may use it softly and slowly when our life is more relaxed, letting that be the time for philosophic deepening. At certain points in the cycle of our experience, we may let it fall into temporary disuse. Sometimes we use it at a Journal Workshop in the company of others; sometimes we use it by ourselves; and sometimes we use it in the one-to-one relationship with a qualified Journal Consultant. The essence of the work, however, and its capacity to bring about personal growth, lies in the continuity of the process by which the Journal is used in a diversity of modes.

Experience with the *Intensive Journal* process over the past several years has demonstrated that the most effective way to begin its use is by attending a Journal Workshop. After that, the Journal Feedback procedures can be used in privacy and may have various kinds of emphasis. But the Journal Workshop is the basic first experience. This is the experience we are now preparing ourselves for, and in which we shall participate with the exercises and experiences described in this book.

There are two main achievements to which you can look forward when you attend your first Journal Workshop. One is the experience of drawing the present situation of your life into focus in a broad perspective that includes both past experiences and future potentials while it opens deeper contact with spiritual and creative sources. The second is to learn, while you are thus engaged in *positioning* yourself in the movement of your life, the numerous techniques of the Journal Feedback method so that you will know how to use the *Intensive Journal* workbook continuously as an effective personal instrument after the workshop is over.

The first purpose in attending a basic Journal Workshop is indeed important. It is to enable us to experience in a full and open-ended perspective the movement of our lives as a whole. Through the Journal Feedback process, we establish a large overview in which we can recognize the cycles of change, of development and diminution, that comprise our life history. This gives us the *context of continuity* in which we can perceive our individual existence, and within this context we *position* ourselves between our past and our future. The composite of entries and exercises which we record in the course of a Journal Workshop places us in a position to answer the question: Where am I in the movement of my life?

We place ourselves between the experiences of our past and the possibilities of the future, and we do this in an active way. We do not construct a merely intellectual perspective of our life. We do not analyze our life as though we were an outsider to it. But we enter the inner movement of our whole life history and connect ourselves to it from within. In that way we extend our life in harmony with the inner principle that is trying to unfold through it. We are dancers joining the dance of our life as it is going on, and continuing it toward its fulfillment. We experience an inner perspective of our life as we work with the self-enlarging exercises of the Journal Feedback method.

The active inner perspective of our life which we build in the course of our first Journal Workshop enables us to position ourselves so that we know where we are at those times when we are at a crossroad or at a point of transition in our lives. The perspective of being positioned in this way is especially helpful in enabling us to make a well-considered decision. As we use it to place ourselves, the workshop becomes for us a mid-point in the movement of our lives, a moment in time that is midway between our past and our future. Insofar as the past is over and the future has not yet transpired, this mid-point is an open moment of possibility. Properly used, it becomes like the eye of a hurricane, a quiet place at the center of life, a free, unconditioned moment of opportunity.

For many persons the experience at a Journal Workshop is like entering a sanctuary, for it provides a protected situation safe from the outer pressures of the world in which an individual can quietly reappraise his relation to his life. The procedures that are followed through the workshop give him a methodology to use, and the compactness of the workshop program will enable him to cover the salient areas of his life experience within a limited time. The presence of others in the workshop, each exploring the individuality of his own life history, builds an atmosphere that supports and strengthens his inward work at the same time that the *Intensive Journal* workbook ensures his privacy. Being with many others while each is delving into the uniqueness of his own life has the effect of reinforcing our intuitive sense of the integrity and validity of each individual existence. A Journal Workshop thus serves as a retreat in the traditional spiritual sense of the term. It provides a protected pause in our life activities during which we can deepen and expand the perspectives of our existence.

The first purpose in attending a basic Life Experience Workshop is to establish an overarching perspective of our whole life history, and to begin the process of drawing ourselves into harmony with the inner movement of our lives. Toward this end, our second and very important goal at such a basic Journal Workshop is to become familiar enough with the sections of the *Intensive Journal* workbook and the procedures for using them so that we can work with the Journal by ourselves after the workshop is over. The Journal Feedback method gives us access to an open-ended instrument for balancing and directing our growth throughout the continuity of our lives. If, therefore, once we have had our basic introductory experience in the use of it, we

feel that its style of approach is personally congenial to us, our first
Journal Workshop will become the launching point for a continuous
program of inner discipline. We shall have taken the first step in the
ongoing use of a self-adjusting technique that will be available afterward for us to use according to our own rhythm and sense of need.

One context in which we can understand the relevance of the *Intensive Journal* process is the conception of *self-reliance* of which Ralph
Waldo Emerson spoke and which he described as the basis for human
growth and dignity. Emerson saw self-reliance as a principle of truth.
The *Intensive Journal* program takes that principle as its starting point,
and then provides a practical method by which each individual, at
whatever his present level and condition, can experience the active
power of self-reliance as a capacity available in the actuality of his life.

Emerson pointed out the easy temptation and the entrapment
into which we fall when we place our reliance upon external things—
on property, the chance of good fortune, and especially on our expec-
tations of what others will do for us. He showed us that the fallacy lies
in placing our center of balance outside of our own inherent abilities,
and not drawing upon the strengths that are inherent within us, more
important, not developing them further. The progressive strengthening of our inherent capacities gives us a resource that draws upon itself, and that is, therefore, self-sustaining and self-amplifying. Its energies and abilities arise increasingly from within itself. It is, in
Emerson's phrase, "that which relies because it works and is." It is self-
reliant because its capacities lie within itself and are progressively
being enlarged as they are used.

The *Intensive Journal* process and its procedure for personal work
provide an instrument and a method by which we can each develop interior capacities strong enough to be relied upon in meeting the trials
of our life. It gives us a means of private and personal discipline with
which to develop our inner muscles. When we rely upon these, we are
indeed self-reliant because these inner capacities *are* ourselves. Emerson says in his essay on self-reliance, "Nothing can bring you peace
but yourself." The *Intensive Journal* process is offered as an instrument
with a day-by-day method to make this realistically possible and progressively true for each of us.

2

Seeking the Elan of Life: The Dimensions of Private Journal Work

The shape of the *Intensive Journal* method became clear only gradually out of a series of provisional attempts. The criteria by which the sections of the Journal were marked off were provided largely by the data that had been gathered in the comparative study of creative lives at the Institute for Research in Depth Psychology of Drew University Graduate School. Once the categories were established, however, there was the essential step of establishing an interior structure for the workbook that would enable it to reflect and carry forward the process of growth as it was taking place uniquely in each individual. It required a dynamic of feedback in terms of the person's life experiences out of which new patterns of conduct would be formed.

A period of experimentation, of trying and testing and changing, was necessary in order to establish a process that allows individuals to promote their own growth. When that was done, however, the workbook emerged altogether transformed and given a wholly new shape. It was now the Structured Journal. A little later, when the next step was taken in devising the exercises and methods of using it, it was renamed the *Intensive Journal* workbook. This name emerged when we discovered how the journal in this format lends itself to being used intensively, within a short space of time, especially at a group workshop. Its

Events that seem to contradict one another all are part of the unity of process by which a life unfolds.

We require a broader
atmosphere of belief and
experience in which many
dimensions of reality can be
more fully known.

use as an intensive instrument enables a person to crystallize the present situation of his or her life in a telescoped perspective of the whole of his past and thus to place himself in a better position to move into his future.

When the structure of the *Intensive Journal* workbook was being established, it was clear that it should include much more than the act of keeping a diary. It needed to be an instrument that could reflect the inner movement of each life within its own terms. It should have ample room therefore for all the various aspects, fluctuations, and transformations contained in a human existence. It should provide the context and the mechanisms that would enable a person by working in it to identify, in the midst of the cycles and transitions of life, his underlying direction and potentiality.

To achieve this, the journal needed to be divided into sections, but the sections could not be merely compartments for a filing system. The divisions within the journal had to be of such a nature that they could be integrally connected with exercises and practices and disciplines of various kinds, so that the very process of working in the journal would have the effect of stimulating personal development. The *Intensive Journal* workbook had to provide a method for actively extending life experience.

As it happened, the structure of the *Intensive Journal* process moved directly into the development of an active method. This took place naturally, almost inadvertently, because the structure of the Journal was specifically modeled after the process of inner continuity and growth which I had identified in the comparative study of lives, especially in the lives of creative persons. In retrospect, the most important factor in making possible an active method was that it was not the contents of persons' lives that were taken as the model but the *essential process,* the fluidity of the inner movement.

The distinction involved in this is especially important because it is the Journal's capacity to carry the dynamic of the inner process that gives it its constructive results. It does this by compressing that process to its essence so that the active force in the person's life can be carried forward without being weighted down by the details of events and emotions. This was achieved by embodying the elements of the inner process in the structure of the Journal, but in such a way as to produce a mirroring and feedback effect.

At the beginning, I approached this by setting up the format of the Journal so that it would draw attention to the *interior relationship* to the contents. This emphasized the active, nonanalytical quality of the Journal work. It was clear that the effectiveness of this approach depended to a large extent upon the kinds of exercises that could be used with the individual Journal sections, and this, in turn, depended upon the way in which the sections themselves could be defined. What would they include, and from what point of view would we determine whether to deal with them in one division of the Journal rather than another?

During the early years of using the *Intensive Journal* method a great deal of experimentation was carried out in this regard. At the workshops I tried various conceptions of how the individual sections should be defined and what they should contain. Always the answer to these questions depended upon the kinds of exercises and journal usage that became possible when the sections were defined from a particular point of view. It depended further on the results that could be obtained from the exercises that accompanied particular conceptions of the Journal sections.

The trial-and-error testing of definitions and procedures was extensive and continuous over a period of several years. The essential methodology of Journal Feedback, however, is the result. In determining which procedures should be accepted into the permanent core of the method of Journal Feedback, one important criterion was the progressive building of the inner movement of energy drawing the life toward wholeness. Another criterion was that each technique should have more than one, and if possible several, constructive side-results or applications. Especially because the *Intensive Journal* method undertakes to have room for everything in an individual's life and to exclude nothing, it was essential to have an economy of techniques—enough to do the work but not so many as to be cumbersome. The protracted experimentation with the Journal in practice produced the refined core of Journal Feedback techniques that is currently in use, but it also led to some theoretical realizations that may have far-reaching significance.

One important observation that came from working with the *Intensive Journal* process during the transitional years of its development was that the Journal Feedback effect is cumulative. The reports of those using the method indicated that, as it generated energy and built a momentum, it accelerated their process of growth and deepened their life awareness. At first I did not understand why this should be so. The results were easily observed, but the reasons were difficult to identify. It seemed clear, however, that something of great importance for the larger process was involved in what was taking place.

Using a method that is now part of our regular Journal Feedback practice, I approached the problem of discovering why this accelerated life growth takes place by first reconstructing the sequence of previous events. The origin of the *Intensive Journal* process lay in my discerning the main aspects of growth in the lives of creative persons, and embodying these in the form of Journal sections. That was the first steppingstone in the development of the Journal. The next step was to devise working exercises that would make it possible to explore the contents of our lives by using the various sections of the Journal. As this was done, it became apparent that one entry led to another. What was written in one section of the Journal evoked old memories and new awarenesses and stimulated further entries in other sections.

By the second year of working with the *Intensive Journal* method it became apparent that the effect of using it consistently was to generate additional energy and movement in a person's life. At first I thought that the reason for this was simply that the original exercises were based upon a depth psychology that was active and evocative rather than analytical and diagnostic. But after a few years it became clear that the reason for the increased energy and growth in people did not lie in the depth psychological concepts with which I had begun. It was something other, something even more fundamental and of larger significance.

One of my original hypotheses, in fact, was the thought that, if the structure of the Journal could embody a composite and quintessence of creative development, it would be able to assist growth whatever the context of the individual life might be. Reflecting the fact that the lives of creative persons are strongly in motion and are full of change and energy, the sections of the Journal did not focus on the specific contents of their lives, but on the particular processes of their lives. Had the emphasis been on content, it would have led eventually to analysis, and the result would have been essentially static. The format that was chosen, however, had the effect of making each section a place where a mini-process in the unfolding of a total life was being expressed and was carried forward.

As the public use of the *Intensive Journal* method proceeded, the nature of these mini-processes and their relation to one another became increasingly visible. Through the Journal experience they defined themselves more specifically, especially as they demonstrated their active qualities, their capacity to unfold from within themselves, and to interrelate in an interior way, feeding back and forth to one another by means of the Journal exercises.

Outward activity propelled from within is the essence of the creative existence.

It became apparent that here was the source of the momentum of energy that was cumulatively generated by continuous work in the Journal. I began then to look more closely at these mini-processes as they were embodied in the individual sections. Reflecting as they did the unfolding of life in creative persons, it was clear that they were very close to the fundamental growth principle in human existence. In fact, they indicated one of the primary characteristics of creative persons, namely, that they experience their lives not in terms of static contents but in terms of the active unfolding of multiple mini-processes within them. They perceive the contents of their lives as being not the major realities but merely the raw materials of the process by which their artworks and other achievements are brought to fruition. *Outward activity propelled from within* is the essence of the creative existence. Thus one of the main indications of the strength of creativity in individuals is the degree to which they have brought themselves into connection with the multiple and interrelated movement of the mini-processes in their lives.

Developing the Intensive Journal Method

In this perspective, the next major task was clearly indicated. It was to develop a framework and techniques that would coordinate the various mini-processes so that they could feed into one another systematically and progressively. There would thus be a multiplication of energies activating one another, all feeding into a single integrative process of growth. It would be like many streams feeding into one river which draws their energies into itself and flows strongly out to sea as a unitary force. Something like this had been taking place in the first years of the Journal Workshops, but now it could be restructured on the basis of our experiences and observations.

Taking the lives of creative persons as the model for the *Intensive Journal* process led to a much larger principle and process. The dynamic factors were always implicit there, but it only became possible to see what they are and how they function when the *Intensive Journal* workbook gave them a place in which they could become tangible. Here they could disclose their form, and by means of the early procedures of the *Intensive Journal* process they could indicate the styles of movement and the rhythms that are natural to them. At this point it thus became possible to take a further step and to develop the specific techniques of the *Intensive Journal* method.

The feedback effects that occur in the use of the *Intensive Journal* method take place on several levels. One form of Journal Feedback is elementary and essentially mechanical, but it is important nonetheless. This is the feedback effect that is achieved simply by writing down nonjudgmental entries that record the inner and outer events of our lives. Following this, there is the feedback effect of reading these entries back to ourselves in our silence. Further there is the feedback effect of reading aloud the entries that we have written. We may read them aloud in private or in the presence of a group. Additionally, we may read our entries into a cassette recorder and then play them back to ourselves. Each of these provides an additional aspect of feedback and serves to carry the inner process a step further.

With the passage of time and the sustained use of the *Intensive Journal* method, a significant additional experience of feedback becomes possible. After we have accumulated enough of them, we can read back to ourselves the entries we have made in the various sections over a period of time. This experience of *continuity feedback* is a valuable means of maintaining a perspective of our lives in the midst of movement and change, and of readjusting our perspective to meet current situations.

All of these aspects of Journal Feedback are related directly to the elemental fact of writing and reading back to ourselves the entries we have made in our Journal. In this sense they are derived from the basic mechanics of journal keeping, and are classified under the heading of *operational feedback*.

There is, however, another, more subtle phase of Journal Feedback that is specifically connected to the movement of the miniprocesses. This is the feedback that becomes possible because the sections within the Journal provide a means by which our subjective experiences can become tangible to us and can express their energy in contact with other subjective aspects of our lives. Experiences that would otherwise be too intangible and therefore too elusive to grasp become accessible to us so that we can work with them. Indefinite bits of thought and emotion that would ordinarily be lost to us like water down the drain are transformed into specific Journal entries and feed back into other mini-processes and activate the energies of other subjective experiences.

The Journal makes tangible our subjective experiences.

We thus progressively build a cumulative movement that is fed into by the mini-processes of our inner life as they interact with each other and with other aspects of our interior life generating new energy as they go. The combination of these interactions via the interplay of Journal exercises brings about new constellations of subjective experience that have not only a greater energy but also a more clearly discernible content and meaning. They therefore often provide the base from which new directions and goals of life are formed, since what was intangible and inaccessible before now becomes a specific and active component of our inner life.

The composite of entries, exercises, and procedures by which this transformation of the elusive into the tangible is brought about is *experiential feedback.* It is that part of Journal Feedback by which the mini-processes of subjective experience are enabled to interrelate with and cross-fertilize one another within the context of each individual's life history.

The conception and formulation of experiential feedback on the basis of the first years of experience in using the *Intensive Journal* process was a major step toward drawing the Journal techniques into concise, effective form. It is, in fact, the principles underlying experiential feedback that have made it possible to expand and refine the program of Journal Feedback into a full method of individual development capable of being used in exceedingly diverse social situations.

The Log Sections and Feedback Sections

There are two additional points about Journal Feedback that are essential to be described as preparation for our Journal Workshop: firstly, the difference between the *Log* sections and the *Feedback* sections; and secondly, the general characteristics of the four dimensions of *experiential feedback.*

In the structure of the *Intensive Journal* workbook one basic distinction is that between the Log sections and the Feedback sections. The Log sections are those parts of the *Intensive Journal* workbook in which we gather the factual data of our lives. As the Journal Feedback procedures have evolved there are now six such sections: the *Period Log;* the *Daily Log;* the *Dream Log;* the *Twilight Imagery Log;* the *Life History Log;* and the *Meditation Log.* In each of these we record the facts of our inner experience from a particular vantage point, always without judging, censoring, embellishing, criticizing, justifying, or interpreting the facts.

In the Log sections we make our entries as objectively as we can, recording what occurred briefly and directly. Although a great deal of emotion may be involved in them, our entries in the Log sections are simply the *neutral observing* and recording of the inner and outer events of our lives. We may, for example, be filled with intense anxiety or great joy, or we may have a dream of terror or of exaltation. We simply describe these subjective states in as neutral and as objective a way as we can, without comment and without elaboration. That is the basic factual role of the Log sections. They are the collectors of the raw empirical data of our lives.

The Feedback sections, on the other hand, are the place where we carry out the active exercises that generate the energy and bring about the transformations of awareness in the Journal work. It is in the Feedback sections that the mini-processes are expressed and have their opportunity to unfold by means of the active feedback exercises.

The raw material for these active exercises is supplied by the Log sections. The neutral reporting of our experiences in our Log entries supplies the data that is fed into the Feedback sections. In the course of this Journal process of feeding in and feeding back, a significant transformation takes place in the nature of the material. When the entries are made in the Log sections, they are simply raw, empirical data. In that sense, they are information regarding the contents of our lives. When they are fed into the Feedback sections, however, they are immediately absorbed into the movement of the mini-processes that are embodied there. They are thus transformed. They are no longer static informational data regarding the contents of a life; they become active elements in the mini-processes by which the potentials of life are seeking to unfold.

This transformation has a major theoretical significance, but it also has tremendous practical effects. In it we can see the reason and the consequences of the fact that the Journal sections are not focused on the contents of lives but on the *inner movements of experience.* The Feedback sections carry the mini-processes of lives-in-motion. As a result, the Journal Feedback process does not get bogged down in intellectual or analytical interpreting. It is constantly in motion, absorbing the factual content of experience into the mini-processes within the life. This feeds into the larger process by which the contents of experience are consumed as logs in the fire of our individual existence, generating light and heat, awareness and emotion as they provide the energy that carries the life toward its meaningful unfolding.

The Four Dimensions of Inner Experience

In structuring the Journal so that the individual sections could serve as channels for the mini-processes, four natural divisions established themselves. The reason for this is that the Drew Institute studies of creative persons indicated four main types of inner movement taking place simultaneously. Each involves a particular aspect of life content, and unfolds within its own contexts, with its distinctive rhythms, tempo, and style of movement. Within them there are various mini-processes, and each of these is embodied in a particular Journal section. These clusters of mini-processes comprise the four *dimensions* of inner experience and provide the base for the experiential feedback procedures. Each of the dimensions is a major division of the Journal with its own set of individual sections.

At the time of designing the *Intensive Journal* workbook there were several indications, mainly operational, that it would be helpful to emphasize the distinctions among the four dimensions by using different colors for each. Thus the sections of the *Life/Time Dimension* are red; those of the *Depth Dimension* are blue; the *Dialogue Dimension* are orange and those of the *Meaning Dimension* are purple. There is no symbolic or esoteric significance to the particular colors used in this way. They are simply there as indicators of the different dimensions of experience and the style of mini-process carried by the individual sections. In practice, as our Journal Feedback exercises have stimulated movement back and forth within the Journal, the space within the Journal representing the inner space of our lives, these color distinctions have turned out to be very useful in expediting the active inner work.

The term *dimension of experience* has a very specific meaning as it is used within the context of the *Intensive Journal* workbook. By dimension is meant a composite of aspects of inner experience that not only comprise their own context in which a person's life reality is perceived but also carry their own modes of movement on the subjective level. The dimensions are self-contained realms of experience each with its characteristic contents and style of unfolding.

The *Life/Time Dimension,* for example, contains the mini-processes that reflect the inner continuity of a person's life history. It deals with the basic and obvious fact that our lives take place in objective or chronological time on the outer level of experience; and it deals also with the fact, which is central to our Journal work, that on the inner level our experiences take place in terms of subjective or *qualitative time.* The interior perception and experience of the movement of time is what we mean by Life/Time. The Life/Time Dimension includes all those phenomena or mini-processes that carry the progression of our experiences and cumulatively form our personal life history.

We perceive the events of the Life/Time Dimension in terms of the inner movement of time. Life/Time is time perceived and experienced qualitatively from within each individual's subjective perspective. Like a ray of light through a crystal, the movement of Life/Time breaks into many rays, or mini-processes, in each existence. The various mini-processes are reflected in the individual sections of the Life/Time Dimension. These are: *Steppingstones; Life History Log; Intersections: Roads Taken and Not Taken;* and *Time-Stretching: Backward and Forward.*

The *Dialogue Dimension* deals with the connective relationships within our personal life. It is the realm of interior communication, and it contains the mini-processes that have the effect either of drawing us together with harmonious relationships within ourselves, or of keeping us split and inwardly distracted. The Journal sections in which we work with the mini-processes of the Dialogue Dimension have the special function of opening the channels for interior communication, and of providing the techniques by which a vital inner contact can be maintained among the various parts of our lives.

Basic to the Dialogue Dimension is the realization that the main aspects of our existence unfold as persons in the universe. We shall see and experience the numerous implications of this as we proceed with the various procedures for using the *Intensive Journal* process. They all reflect the underlying process by which a unique person emerges in the course of each individual existence. A human being begins his life as a seed of possibility, and these possibilities are unfolded, frustrated, transformed in the midst of the varied circumstances of life. Out of the composite of our experiences and relationships in contact with our environment, we each build our unique life history. And at the center of this life history is the emerging person who is our self. It is this person within our life history who meets with the person in the life history of others and thus forms the dialogue relationships that are the basic units of experience of the Dialogue Dimension.

As we move more deeply into our lives, it becomes apparent that not only human beings but work that we do, institutions in which we believe, situations in which we become involved also have life histories. To that degree, human or not, they also are persons, and they can be related to as persons. It thus becomes possible to enter into dialogue relationships in all the meaningful aspects of our lives. This is the main content of the mini-processes of the Dialogue Dimension. The individual sections in this division of the Journal provide the place where we work actively on several levels with exercises that extend the range and possibility of our interior dialogue relationships. These sections are: *Dialogue with Persons; Dialogue with Works; Dialogue with the Body; Dialogue with Events, Situations, and Circumstances;* and *Dialogue with Society.*

The *Depth Dimension* is the realm of human reality in which the mini-processes move in terms of symbolic forms. It contains those aspects of experience that are primarily nonconscious in the moment when they transpire within us, but which are guided in their unfolding by a profound quality of consciousness that underlies their movement. This consciousness is more a directive principle than a literal piece of knowledge. It is a consciousness that discloses itself actively, but mainly in indirect forms as it guides the life process. In the beginning this consciousness is only implicit, invisible, and hidden in the depth, as a scientist is hidden in a child, as a tree is hidden in a seed, or as an inspiration is hidden in a person who has not yet had even the dream by which the new idea will be awakened.

To be transferred from the depths, where it is still unconscious and not yet visible, to the surface where it is expressed in life activities, consciousness requires a means of movement. The mini-processes of the Depth Dimension provide this interior locomotion as they are embodied in the individual Journal sections. There are five sections in this division of the *Intensive Journal* workbook: *Dream Log; Dream Enlargements; Twilight Imagery Log; Imagery Extensions;* and *Inner Wisdom Dialogue.*

The Depth Dimension deals with the nonconscious levels of the psyche from which consciousness comes. Its contents are sleep dreams, waking dreams, and the varieties of intuition by which we make our direct connections with the implicit wisdom of life. Of particular importance is the active style of intermediate depth experience, Twilight Imagery. This has a particularly important role in the Journal Feedback process because it gives us a nonanalytic way of evoking those potentials of our life that are veiled by the language of symbolism. Although the Depth Dimension is a realm of experience with many obscure symbolic contents, it is also the source of much of our creative and spiritual life. Its characteristic style of movement is allusive and metaphoric rather than direct and literal, and the mini-processes by which it unfolds therefore tend to be elusive.

The fourth dimension of the *Intensive Journal* process is the *Meaning Dimension.* It includes all the beliefs by which human beings find meaning in life, regardless of the objective truth of the belief. The Meaning Dimension includes all the varied experiences that give an integrated sense of life, especially those experiences of sustaining connection with factors of life that are larger than personal.

The Meaning Dimension was first called simply Process Meditation. It was not included in the first edition of the book that described the *Intensive Journal* method, mainly because I did not feel ready at that time to describe the subtle aspects of its role in the human being's life. It has since, however, found its place in the *Intensive Journal* method. It is represented by five sections in the purple segment of the workbook. These are: the *Meditation Logs; Connections; Peaks, Depths, and Explorations (PDE); Mantra/Crystals;* and *Testament.*

The Journal Feedback Method

All the dimensions of experience with which we work in the *Intensive Journal* workbook express the forms of energy movement taking place on the subjective level of our lives. In the individual sections of the four dimensions we work with the specific mini-processes that carry this movement. Primarily we use procedures in each of the dimensions that are in accord with its characteristic style of movement. For example, when we are working in the dream sections, we use procedures that follow the symbolic style of the Depth Dimension; when we are building the context of our individual life history, we use procedures that fit the characteristic style of the Life/Time Dimension. When we have progressed to an advanced level in the use of the Journal Feedback techniques, we learn how to combine the styles of movement of the various dimensions; thus we are able to evoke a broader range of inner experience. This is the later work of *Journal Interplay*.

At its essence, the method of Journal Feedback is a means of drawing upon the structure of the *Intensive Journal* process in order to generate energy, and to draw the movement of life forward. The feedback procedures become possible because of the active quality of the dimensions that are contained in the major divisions of the Journal, and because of the variety of life materials that are brought to the fore by the mini-processes of individual existence as we work with them in the special sections. With the full range of life contents as its raw material, the Journal Feedback method draws upon numerous sequences of exercises to reach into the life of the individual. The combination and interrelation of these procedures have the effect of drawing the energies and the potentials forward and fusing them into new integrative units.

The Journal Feedback method is based on Holistic Depth Psychology. It achieves its results by bringing about a multiplying effect within the psyche. Its impact is cumulative, and this generates a progressively stronger momentum. In time, as the force of this momentum increases, it attains an autonomous power, as though at that point it had become self-generating and self-directing. It then seems to be able by its independent capacity to carry the person forward to the next step of growth in his life. Often it is able to provide this accretion of energy despite the enervating effects of a person's anxieties and negative self-image. It is able to carry him forward despite himself, once the critical turning point in the work has been reached. This turning point can often be clearly discerned and marked off, for it is the moment when the balance shifts, as on a scale or a seesaw, and one side becomes definitely the heavier and the dominant one. In the context of our work with the *Intensive Journal* process, it is the point at which the cumulative buildup of energy by the process of Journal Feedback has become greater than the energy available to habitual consciousness and old styles of behavior.

This self-multiplying, cumulative effect of Journal Feedback makes it a great force for change. It generates a power which accumulates in the unconscious depths behind the mind in the very midst of conscious thinking and writing. And then it thrusts forward in the form of new experiences, new recognitions, new ideas and emotions. Thus the force of Journal Feedback breaks apart and breaks through the shells of our habits and those other psychological impediments which are the heavy baggage most of us carry from the past. It does this by building its energy invisibly, and then thrusting forward from behind the mind, drawing its new solutions out of the context of each person's unique existence and phrasing them in the terms of each person's life.

Since it does little good to approach our inner experience via our intellectual minds, we must learn to reach it from within. Underlying the irregularity of its rhythms, there is a consistent principle, and this we can learn to identify. As we perceive its movement, we are able to cultivate it from within and align our lives with it. To do this requires a capacity that is much like the *creative intuition* of which the philosopher Henri Bergson spoke. By means of it we can contact the *elan vital,* the vital force, in our lives.

From one point of view it can be said that the method of Journal Feedback provides a practical means of achieving the quality of being which Bergson envisioned and described. To achieve this requires a combination of intellectual understanding, intuition, and direct experience so that we can comprehend the operative principle that underlies Journal Feedback and document it with our life. As we fill our *Intensive Journal* workbook with our life, the cycles of unfolding that are reflected there generate a further movement. This is the elan vital of our inner self. It is being reawakened and reenergized, and given a personal frame of reference that will enable it to do its work and find its unique meaning for each of us in the context of our life history as we live it in the midst of the world.

3

The Atmosphere of
a Journal Workshop

A basic metaphor sets the tone and atmosphere of the Journal Work-shops. It is the image of a well connected to an underground stream.

    When we come together at a workshop with our *Intensive Journal* workbook, it is as though each of us is a well. We are each engaged in entering that well—which is the well of our life—and in reaching as deeply into its sources as we can. As we carry out the various proce-dures of our Journal work, we are taken progressively to ever more fundamental levels. This is our guiding principle of progressive deep-ening by which we use the *Intensive Journal* process as our instrument for making contact with and drawing upon the ultimate sources of life.

    We each go down individually into the well of our life. The well of each personal existence is separate and distinct from every other. Each of us must therefore go down our own well, and not the well of someone else's life. We find, however, that when, as individuals, we have gone very far down into the well of our life, we come to an under-ground stream that is the source of all the wells. Since the wells of our personal existence are each separate from every other, there are no separations here. There are no walls or dividers in the underground stream. We are all connected here in the unitary continuum of being.

    We each must go through our own personal existence, but when

We are engaged in entering the well of our life and in reaching as deeply into its sources as we can.

we have gone deeply enough we find that we have gone *through our personal life beyond our personal life.* This is the transpersonal connection which we experience in the underground stream. We each work toward it individually within the context of our own life history. When we reach it, however, we do not remain in the depths. Those waters have the effect of renewing our energies and giving us access to abundant resources for our life. We draw upon these sources and carry them back with us to the surface of the well where we incorporate them in living the next time-unit of our lives.

The symbol of the well and the underground stream thus carries us through a continuing cycle of experiences. While the outer events of our lives take place at the surface of the well, we go inward to the underground stream to reach our deep sources, and to have the revitalizing experience of reconnecting ourselves with the larger unity of life. Having broken through the walls of individuality to enter the deep source, we then return to live our personal existence in the world of external reality.

This cycle of experience, symbolically understood, provides the prototype of the way we proceed in working at a Journal Workshop. Each individual is engaged in entering the well of existence as deeply as possible so that he or she can draw new resources for his or her life from the underground stream. Another way to say this is that each existence is engaged in finding the way of life and of being that will be true to its own nature. It is seeking its own integrity, and in the course of this quest the inner person emerges and grows. It is this *inner person* that is the essence and the meaning of the life.

We may wonder, since the emphasis is so strongly placed on the experience of the individual in the depth of each person's privacy, why do we meet in a group? What is to be gained by bringing many people together in order to have each of them remain essentially private?

The heart of the matter was very succinctly stated by a participant in a Journal Workshop. As the weekend session was coming to a close, we were engaged in writing a meditative reflection in the closing exercise that is called, "Now: The Open Moment." That particular exercise is one that leads to many diverse forms of expression, but for one woman in the group the meditation became a short poem dealing with her group experience. In it were the lines

> This solitary work
> We cannot do alone.

She was expressing her realization that the work she had done in her Journal was at its essence a private work. In the course of the workshop she had dealt with the most intimate parts of her life, in most cases for the first time. She had opened those questions and had let herself explore them. They were exceedingly private; yet she had been able to write about them in the group with a depth and fullness that had not been possible when she was alone. She had written many intimate things and had even voluntarily read some of them to the group. But nothing of her privacy had been violated in the reading.

The task of coming into contact with the depth and fullness of our lives is a solitary work, for the essence of it is privacy. The paradox is that it is not a task that can be carried through successfully when an individual works at it altogether alone. It requires the assistance of others, and especially it requires the presence of others. It requires a situation and a method that enables the person to work *side by side* with others while doing the solitary work that reaches deeply into the private person within oneself.

The presence of others, each engaged in reaching into the past and the potentials of his own life, seems to have the effect of assisting the solitary work of everyone. One of the goals of a Journal Workshop is to provide such a situation, a place where people can come together to meet at a deep level, with full freedom of expression and with their privacy protected. Here we are shielded from the outer pressures of our life. In a sense we are withdrawing from those pressures, but not in order to escape from them. We are withdrawing into the protected depth of the group in order to be better able to work more actively at resolving the truly fundamental questions and issues of our lives.

In the meeting place of the Journal Workshop we are free from judgment by others and any artificial restraints upon either our conscious or our unconscious thoughts. It is not a negative freedom as in drawing away from something we do not like. It is a freedom with the purpose of enabling us to work with a specific method that will build a dynamic movement at the depth of ourselves. And especially it is a freedom that enables us to use that method with the benefit of the psychic support and validation of others, while we ourselves are giving the support of our sincere presence to the other participants in the group.

The active quality of many working together each in their own depths, each giving their silent and psychic support to those around them is a great source of psychic energy. In an intangible way it generates a power very much as prayer does. Working in one's *Intensive*

Journal workbook in a group is not just an introspective and psychological work. It is a systematic attempt to build a reintegrative effect in our lives by working deeply in our inner process using the *Intensive Journal* workbook as our instrument. We do this as a work carried out by each within the context of his own life. We do it alone, and we do it together.

For these reasons, the Journal Workshops are not group workshops in the ordinary sense of the term. We do not come together for the purpose primarily of being in a group situation. We come together rather for the specific purpose of being able to work more deeply and freely in *Intensive Journal* workbooks, making fuller use of the Journal Feedback method, drawing upon the psychic assistance that comes from doing an intense and dedicated work in the company of others who are similarly engaged. Once again, a group participant spontaneously offered an apt description of what the Journal Workshops are about. "These are not group workshops," she said. "These are working-in-the-Journal shops." And that is indeed their essence. We come together in order to work in the *Intensive Journal* process with a depth and extent that would not otherwise be possible.

Once we have defined them as working-in-the-Journal shops, we have a clear criterion to guide us in the methodology to be followed at a Journal Workshop. There are two main factors. The first is that we require specific techniques that will enable individuals to build a momentum that carries them to a greater depth as they work privately in the midst of the group. The second is that we require an atmosphere in the group that progressively forms from the moment the group convenes. At public workshops it is usually the case that most of the participants have never met before, but that does not impede the formation of a deep atmosphere. Just as in a cathedral the atmosphere does not depend on the prior acquaintance of those present, so it does not in a workshop. Since we come together to work in the cathedral of our lives, it does not matter whether we have met before. We have each come to the Journal Workshop to perform the equivalent act of private dedication. To the degree that we each focus on that act in our individuality, a deep atmosphere forms around us in the Workshop. We find then that the specific techniques that we use at a Journal Workshop contribute to the forming of the atmosphere; equally, the atmosphere deepens as the exercises proceed enabling us to carry out our private work at ever deeper levels. Thus the two aspects of workshop methodology, the exercises and the atmosphere, mutually support one another. The interplay between them sets the pace and rhythm at which the Journal work can proceed. The guidance of this interplay is a primary factor in conducting a Journal Workshop.

The atmosphere of the group makes it possible for each individual to work at a deep level; but the work that is done is different for each person since each is at a different point in the process of life. For each one, the purpose of Journal work is to pick up the process of growth wherever it is in the individual and to draw it forward to its next stage of unfolding in keeping with its own inner timing.

When we are working in a group situation, we must allow that as a person moves through the cycles of life, there is a change from moment to moment in the inner conditions that will best nurture growth. Multiplying this by each of the individuals participating in the workshop gives us a seemingly impossible number of special needs to harmonize in the group. But we find that we are able to harmonize the multiplicity of special personal requirements simply and naturally by enabling each person to go down to the *underflow* level of human experience in his own terms. Each goes through the well of his or her own life to the depth level that is beyond the well and beyond the person.

In this way the opposites of multiplicity and privacy are naturally reconciled. They complement one another, and they blend into one another to form a larger whole. The working etiquette of the group is essentially designed to establish a situation that will reinforce mutual respect for the delicate process by which the inner growth of a person takes place. We seek to protect the psychic space around the individual so that the seed of potentiality may grow in him, and so that the growth that begins in a workshop can continue to be cultivated afterward until it bears its fruit. In order to do this, we maintain our privacy and separateness at the same time that we are working together. We each work in our own well; by maintaining the integrity of focus, we assist the process in everyone.

In the course of a workshop, it sometimes happens that the Journal entry which a person reads expresses a difficulty or a painful problem in his life. He or she may become upset, distraught, or tearful while reading it. How shall we respond?

We may feel love and sympathy for the situation, but we do not rush in to help. We may feel that being neutral outsiders we see the solution to the person's problems and we wish to help by giving advice.

But if we do really wish to help we will maintain our good wishes in silence. We will preserve the space and freedom that will enable each person to find answers to problems in the rhythm that each life requires. If allowed to have the leeway in which to experience both the pain and the searching, he or she will eventually not only be able to solve the problem, but something much more meaningful will take place. He or she will be able to hear the larger message for life and consciousness that the problem is trying to disclose. In the course of discovering this, each of us will also be strengthening the inner muscles of our psyches. This is of the greatest importance, since it is this that enlarges a person's capacity for further growth.

Because we follow the principle of honoring the integrity of each person's inner process, we restrain ourselves from graciously giving our advice and guidance in a workshop. We keep our own counsel, and thus we give one another a far greater gift, the gift of freedom and time. We also give one another the silent support that comes from trusting the self-healing wisdom of life. There is a great power in this that cannot be put into words. By our silent restraint, we express not only our love for the other person, but also our respect for the integrity of the life process at work in each of us. This is a most basic rule to follow in participating in a Journal Workshop.

In a similar way, it sometimes happens that a person who is working in the Journal at a workshop is moved to tears, even to heavy sobbing. Then also we may feel an urge to rush over with our loving hugs and caresses, to tell that person that we care and that everything will be all right. But should we do that with our intentions so pure and full of love, we may actually be preventing the person we wish to help from fulfilling the needs that his sobs are expressing. We must hold firm to our fundamental awareness that the psyche knows what needs to be done, that it will eventually do it in its own authentic timing, and that we have the responsibility to protect its freedom to move through its necessary cycles.

A person who cries at a workshop may have been waiting for many years to gain the courage and strength that would enable him to release the long-stored pains of sadness in life. If we rush in with our embraces and assurances, we will close off the space in which he can express those old emotions. Our good intentions may then stifle the open expression that was just beginning to be strong enough to let itself be heard.

Often the tears and sobs are the mourning that was not allowed to take place when we suffered a death in the course of our life. It may have been the death of another beloved person, a person who was important or dear to us. Of even greater significance, and an even greater reason for mourning, it may have been the death of a part of our lives that was cut short before it could grow. Holding the perspective of the principle of inner continuity in the life of persons, we recognize that such spontaneous mourning is the internal ritual that is necessary before a person can be freed to take the next step in his life.

Spontaneous mourning is the internal ritual that is necessary before a person can be freed to take the next step in his life.

We wish to be especially careful not to close in on another person and limit the space and time in which he or she can live through the necessary mourning for the past sadnesses of life. Especially in those persons who have repressed their sorrow for many years, when they finally find a situation, as many do in the Journal Workshops, in which the open atmosphere gives them the inner freedom to let the crying happen, it is important that no one intrude. If we did intrude with our well-intentioned comforting, we would get into the other person's well. We would close it off at the point where it was freeing itself from the excess material so that it could regulate itself from within. We must give it more time so that it can eventually restore its own inner balance and reestablish contact with its deep sources.

Sometimes, when a person is experiencing this spontaneous ritual of mourning, the external manifestations may seem to be very extreme. Sobs may rack a person's body, and the wails of sadness may have an eerie sound. Many of us, having been conditioned by the prevailing belief in a psychology of pathology, will feel that we recognize a syndrome and feel that there is a diagnosis to be made. We will then rush to the quick judgment that the person is caught in a serious psychotic disturbance, and that something immediate and drastic has to be done.

In all our experience in the workshops, we have found that only one thing needs to be done, and to do it properly always balances the situation. What is necessary is that each person in the workshop remain quietly in his or her own well, reaching within toward the underground stream that sustains us all. Feeling that quietness and stability in the group, the mourning person finds that the waves of pain go past their crest. Passing their crest, they gradually subside. Soon he or she begins to feel quiet again with a sense of having been carried by something greater.

That person is indeed being carried by something from beneath, for the waters of the underground stream are buoyant. They sustain through the cycle of tears. When he emerges on the other side of the crying, the person has added to his life the experience of having passed through a full cycle in the process of the psyche. He now possesses a direct knowledge of what is involved in passing through "the valley of the shadow," reemerging, coming up the mountainside again. Having been left free to express inner pain, the person has begun to learn of a process and a power in the depth of his or her own life. Having endured a full cycle successfully, he or she now knows it directly. In the future, therefore, he or she may be able to rely upon it, and even trust in it.

Just as we are free in a workshop to express whatever is at the fore at that moment in the process of our life, so we are also free not to express it. In the course of the workshop we have an opportunity to write in the various sections of the Journal, and we are then invited to read. But no one is required to read. No one is required to speak. It is against the principles of the workshop to prod a shy person into speaking or reading from the Journal. We never go around the room so that we can all take turns at participating. We maintain the privacy and integrity of everyone so that the workshop situation can be a place where each person is free to honor and express the inner principle of his or her own being.

Just as we make no judgment about the content of what a person reads, so we make no judgment about the person who remains quiet in the workshop. We do not say: "What are you hiding? What are you afraid of?" We respect each person's silence with our own.

We let each person follow the integrity of inner promptings. We leave it to him or her to decide whether or not to read—now or later—and whether or not to speak in the workshop at all. We know that there may be experiences in a person's life that carry with them a great need to be spoken in the group, but that are not yet able to push their way through to the surface. The person does not yet feel strong enough to say them in public. The time when they can be spoken aloud has not yet come, and we must therefore respect this reticence. There may be something maturing in the depth of the person that we do not yet know of, since it has not been able to reveal itself. We therefore allow it the time that it requires.

There also are some things that cannot be spoken in a group, because in doing so we would intrude on the writer's or someone else's privacy. There are some experiences that are so delicate that they would break if they were spoken aloud. And there are some experiences that cannot be told without violating the integrity of a larger principle in one's life. For all of these reasons, we respect the validity of silence. They need not be spoken in the workshop, but these experiences can be written in the Journal and developed in the various exercises in the course of the workshop.

It has often happened in our experience that a person participates actively in a full weekend workshop without saying a word in public. This person may converse at mealtimes and talk freely with the other group members during coffee breaks, but not speak at all during the group meetings. Then at the close of the workshop the person comes to the group leader and indicates how important, even transforming an experience it has been. As partial verification, he or she points to the Journal and to the large amount of writing done in the workshop.

I recall a man in California during the early years of the Dialogue House program whose experience provides a good illustration of silent participation in Journal Workshops. Traveling to different locales, he attended three consecutive workshops within a period of two weeks, but he did not speak a word in public during any of them. As he phrased it to me afterward, however, he "wrote reams."

His reason for attending such a concentrated program was that he had reached a major crossroad in his life. He felt that if he could gain a perspective of where he was in the Now-moment of his life, he would be able to make a valid decision for his future.

Hearing me speak at a public lecture, he had grasped the conception of *repositioning* one's life through gaining a new time perspective by means of the *Intensive Journal* process. He felt that the concept spoke to his present condition, and he resolved to put the Journal method to a full test. He had, in addition, a particular problem which arose from the fact that his career had involved him with public figures in the entertainment industry, and he did not feel ethically free to reveal the nature of his relationship to them. Therefore, he could not speak openly in the group. But he had a great and immediate need to put his life in order and to be able to see his inner processes from a new vantage point.

When he had first come to the workshops, he thought that he, as an intellectual person, would receive from the *Intensive Journal* method with its structure and classifications an objective understanding of his subjective life. What did take place for him, however, was something of a different and more far-reaching nature than he had anticipated. It was not so much that he gained an intellectual perspective, as that his life was actively repositioned in the course of the workshop. He was placed in a new relationship to the inner movement of his experience. From being at a dead stop, his experience of working in the Journal at the workshop set him into motion upon a new path without his consciously or deliberately choosing it. He achieved this in silence, by working intently in all the exercises of the Journal during the workshops which he attended. Especially he achieved it by working in his Journal in his privacy during the days that intervened between his workshop experiences.

When the series of workshops was over, he said that even though he had not spoken in the group, the fact of his being part of a group situation at this critical time of transition made it possible for him to work intensively in his Journal. The presence of the other members of the group gave him strength, and the atmosphere of the group quieted his nerves. The fact, also, that other people were seriously involved in the same process, and that each in his own way was directing his attention inward to achieve a deeper relation to his own life, helped him stay on an even keel. Thus, he said, he was able to write in his Journal with a consistency and fluidity that would not have been possible had he been working with it at home alone. At least at that early point in his work with the Journal, he said that he could not have sustained his work in privacy without the supporting presence of the group.

When the three workshops were over and he had had time to survey the results, his judgment was that the intensity of his use of the Journal in the workshops had had the effect of crystallizing the multitude of his jumbled thoughts and feelings into a single perception of his life. What had seemed to be very complicated decisions had thus fallen naturally and simply into place. In the course of the sustained Journal exercises in the workshops, decisions he could not make by conscious thought had seemed to form by themselves. They were shaped beyond analytical consciousness through the working of the inner process. He added to me that he thought that an analytical therapy would not have made such a consolidated experience possible. It would have taken a great deal longer, if, indeed, it would have happened at all. The fact was, he told me, that the reason he had come to the workshop in the first place was that analytical therapy had held him at his impasse.

Reflecting further on what had taken place in him, he felt that even with the use of the *Intensive Journal* process he could not have worked through to the change by himself. His jangled nerves and anxieties would not have permitted him to concentrate and devote himself to the work for a sufficient length of time. But the atmosphere of the group enabled him to do this because it calmed him. The presence of the others, each working on his own, strengthened his resolve and enabled him to return to his central task whenever his attention wandered.

The group had a steadying and sustaining effect upon him. It was as though, he said, he were held up and carried by the group whenever he faltered. And he felt this as a great suffusion of love in the room. But there was no specific or overt relationship of love taking place between him and anyone else in the room. He was aware of that because no personal communication was occurring in the form of speech. But he felt that a tone of love in the room rose up around the persons present while they concentrated on their individual work and reached into the depth of themselves. This love he felt as a mode of communication that did not require him to speak. It left him free to explore the wide range of past and potential in his life. It gave him an energy and a capacity he would not otherwise have had; this enabled him to stimulate new inner experiences and awarenesses and to record his most private feelings.

That atmosphere in the group strengthened him in another way. It sustained him when the workshops were over, so that when he was by himself he was still able to continue his communication with himself in his Journal. At those times, he needed only to recall the situation of the group and place himself back in its atmosphere. Because of this, the days that intervened between the workshops which he attended were especially fruitful for him. He was able to enlarge explorations that had begun in the group. When the series of workshops was over, the momentum that had been generated enabled him to reenter his Journal and extend the process he had started there. By now the Journal had established itself in his consciousness as an instrument that was securely his to use. It carried with it the quality of feeling that had been present in the workshops, so that this atmosphere was now as much a part of the Journal as its pages and its sections. Thus, he felt free and

A major part of the meaning of life is contained in the very process of discovering it.

able to use it in the future on all occasions, whether he would be at a workshop or not.

The feeling of being free to use the Journal after the workshop is over is a very important part of the whole program. It is this that gives continuity to the discipline of personal growth. The Journal Workshop begins the work, but the work itself continues for the whole road of life. With this in mind, a primary goal in attending a workshop is that as you become familiar with the use of the Journal through carrying out the exercises, you will become increasingly comfortable in using its procedures. But whether you use this book to teach yourself the Journal process or attend a workshop, you will then be able to take the *Intensive Journal* workbook with you out into the midst of your life and continue using it in all circumstances.

At that point it will become much more than a book in which you write. It will become a companion, a portable alter ego, and an intimate friend who will respond and discuss with you in dialogue the decisions of your life. A person's relation to his *Intensive Journal* workbook becomes, with time, very similar to a musician's relationship with his instrument. It is a special kind of friend, a friend whose nature it is to be used. And in this type of relationship, the more one friend is used by the other, the greater are the possibilities of what the two can achieve in living relationship together.

Let us now begin. As you move into the next section of this book you will be giving yourself a Journal Workshop. Take the time to construct a workbook for yourself, if you have not already done so, using the sample pages from Appendix D in this book. Have that workbook next to you as you read the rest of this book, and when it is indicated, turn to your workbook and do the exercise as described. You will be laying the groundwork and learning the basic procedures for self-understanding and growth.

Part 2

FIRST STAGES OF YOUR
JOURNAL WORK

Positioning Yourself in the Present: The Period Log

Now is not limited to the instant but is elastic.

We clear a time and space and begin as though we are in a group, preparing for a work and experience that will be profoundly private for each of us. We shall be making our own Journal, following the model, which is in the Appendix. As we wait for the workshop to start we sit in stillness. We let our breathing become progressively slower and deeper. We regard the workshop as a pause in the active, outer movement of our lives. It is a time of sabbath, a time of quietness in which a new inner movement can begin. We take a few minutes now to sit in silence, our thoughts at rest, waiting to begin to work in the depth and magnitude of our lives.

Beginning With Now

Now that we are at a Journal Workshop, where shall we begin the work of drawing our life into focus? We begin with *Now.* But Now is not limited to the immediate instant. It is not just here and now, not just the spot on which we stand, nor this moment when we speak. Our Now moment is elastic. Therefore, we stretch the present moment back as far as it needs to go in order to include as much of the past as is still an active part of the present.

The Now of our life thus becomes more than a moment. It is a unit of time that is as long or as short as the situation of each life requires, and it includes the most recent part of the past that is a meaningful factor in the present. This forms the period that is the Now of our lives, our most recent relevant past as it moves into our present. This is the period to which we turn our attention in the Period Log section of the Journal at the start of a workshop, as we do now. (From this point onward, refer to the model in the Appendix each time reference to the workbook is made.)

For each person, this elastic Now has a different content and a different duration. We may now be in the midst of a great love, or between loves, or deprived of a feeling of love. We may now be in the midst of a meaningful work, or between meaningful works, or feeling ourselves to be without meaning in our work and seeking it. We may be in a time of exhilaration, or in a time of depression, a time of gathering fruits, or a time of planning, and planting, and preparation. Whatever it is, it is the Now for us, our own Now. It is the particular present moment in which we find ourselves.

This present moment of our lives may cover a short period or a longer period. Whatever its duration, whatever its content, whether pleasant or painful, this is the unit of time, the period when we begin our work in the *Intensive Journal* workbook. It is a unique period for each of us. The *Period Log* is the section of the Journal where we make the entries, succinct and objective as can be, to record this period as a whole. We describe the main outer and inner events that come to the fore of our minds when we reflect on the period and recall its primary aspects. Thus we begin our work, each with a different base, and in the context of a life-situation that is distinctive to ourselves.

For one person this present period in his life may reach back three years since he had a car accident and was hospitalized. Because of the changes it brought about, the period of time since that event is the Now. For another person this present period may be merely a few weeks since she met a new friend, moved to a different city, began a new job, or underwent some other significant change in her circumstances. Since that time her life has borne the imprint of that event, and it, therefore, is the definitive factor in this present period.

The period that is Now varies with each individual. It is our basic point of departure whenever we prepare to do any significant work in the *Intensive Journal* process. This is true whether we are coming together for a full workshop, or to work in privacy or in Journal Dyad. Our focus and starting point is always the present moment in time from which we can position ourselves in the time movement of our lives. We begin by placing ourselves between the past and the future in the particular situations that are at issue in our lives.

Let us begin by closing our eyes, relaxing, and quietly, inwardly, feeling the movement of our lives. We let ourselves feel the implications of the question, "Where am I now in my life?" We let the answer to this shape itself only in general terms behind our conscious minds. We do not direct ourselves into thinking about it deliberately, but we let ourselves *inwardly feel* the movement of our life as it has been taking shape in this present period.

As we do this, the boundaries and characteristics of this present period in our life take shape for us. We find that we are now able to give spontaneous answers to the question of what is this present period in my life? What events mark it off? How far back does it reach? What have been the main characteristics of this recent period?

Perhaps this recent period began when you had an idea for a new project. Or perhaps it began when you married, or had a child, or had a rift in your marriage relationship. Perhaps it has been a time of hard work, or a time of confusion, or a time of waiting.

We hold ourselves in a condition of openness in which no particular thoughts are dominating our minds. We are silent. Thoughts may come, but they are not any particular thoughts. They are not directed thoughts. They are not thoughts that we consciously seek. They are thoughts that simply come to us. We let them come, and we let them go. They will soon return to us, but in the form of images.

We sit in stillness paying no attention to any special thoughts, not thinking, but feeling the movement of our life. We sit in this quietness for some moments. We find that there comes to us a generalized awareness of what this recent period in our lives has been. An inward sensing of the tone of our life in this recent period. Now we let the quality of our experiences during this time of our life express themselves to us. Perhaps they will take the form of an image, a metaphor, a simile, or some spontaneous adjective that describes it in a word. If so, we will take notice of this inward awareness in whatever form it appears to us.

We are in silence, our eyes closed, feeling this recent period in the movement of our lives. While our eyes are closed, as we sit with no thoughts, in the quietness, images may take shape in our minds. We see them inwardly, and they carry a feeling of the movement of our lives. They reflect the quality of this recent period in our experience.

Images of the Present

Sitting this way, many different images and feelings can come to you, reflecting the quality of movement in your life. Whatever form it takes, let yourself perceive it. Do not reject or censor it. Neither should you affirm it; certainly you should not interpret it. Simply observe it and take note of the fact that this is what came to you when you closed your eyes and let yourself feel from within yourself the inner continuity and movement of your life. Take a few moments now to record it briefly in the Period Log of your *Intensive Journal* workbook.

We are especially vulnerable to the temptation of excessive writing in the Log sections when we are beginning our Journal work in private without the discipline and atmosphere of a Journal Workshop. Working by ourselves, we are not restricted by the limitations of time. One memory will then beget another, and our writing may then become exceedingly fluid and extensive. It is important to bear in mind then the reason for which at a Journal Workshop we deliberately set a time limit upon writing in the Period Log. We do this in order to establish a nonconscious process of selectivity that will draw into the foreground of a person's attention those factors that are truly of primary significance in the situation of his life. We wish to achieve this in the shortest possible time, and with as little interference as possible from our self-conscious thought processes. We want to leave as little time and temptation as possible for a person to rationalize his life, thereby obscuring and possibly falsifying the facts of experience. To encourage spontaneity, therefore, it is best for the entries in the Period Log to be brief and direct without amplification and without premeditation.

In doing this, many different kinds of experiences can come to people, different kinds of perceptions and images reflecting the present situation in their lives.

One person sees an image of dark smoke stuck in a chimney. "It can't get out," she says.

Another person, a student, sees a seed under the ground. It is softening and breaking apart. It is beginning to grow.

Another person sees an airplane flying a bumpy course through heavy clouds. Presently it comes into clear skies where the sun is shining.

Still another person sees nothing, but hears strains of music. This is not a visual image, but an auditory image. The tone and tempo of the music expresses his feeling of the movement of his life.

Another person neither sees nor hears an image, but feels a movement of emotions within herself. She experiences a welling up of joy, a suffusion of love. This is a feeling image. One person experiences the love in relation to a particular individual in her life. Another experiences it as a promise of deeper connection to life, as a love of God.

Still another person feels the movement of the recent period of his life and perceives a visual image of darkness, followed by a feeling image of heavy sadness, followed still further by a body image that becomes a knot forming in the pit of the stomach. All are expressions of the present situation of his life.

Whatever comes to us in this way, we record in our Journals; and we make no judgment about it. We do not say, "Oh good, I have an optimistic or encouraging image of this time in my life." And we do not reject the image because it was dark or doleful, or because it indicated that further difficulties may lie ahead.

We bear in mind, rather, that the significance of such images is that they express the quality of feeling that corresponds to this present moment in our life situation. Whatever it is at the moment, we accept as a fact that this is what it is, and that these are the images by which the inner situation of our lives is being reflected to us. We also know that whatever the images and our life situation are, they will inevitably change as they continue in their movement. If we perceive a plane flying in clouds, the cycle of the image will carry it through to clear light and sunshine. If it is an image of a seed in the ground, the organic movement of the image will carry it through to growth. If it is a flower blooming, it will wither; eventually it will become a seed again. Therefore we make no judgment in the midst of the movement of our imagery experiences. We simply observe the movement of our images, write them down, and continue with our experiences.

As we are feeling our way into this current period of our life, a simile or metaphor may come to us. "It has been like walking along a desert road and not seeing any trees." "It has been like eating at a banquet where each dish is more surprising than the last." This period in my life has been like a . . .

As we write down the comparison, some additional adjectives may come to us, describing this time in our life. Not words that we deliberately think about, just words that come spontaneously to us. When we allow words to come to us without thought in this way, they often say a great deal to us about our lives. And they say it in a very cogent form. They are verbal images.

The Next Step: Focusing on Specifics

Now, after preparing ourselves by working at the nonconscious level, we are ready to focus more specifically on the contents of this recent period of our life. We are ready now to write in our *Intensive Journal* workbook. When did this period start? Was there a particular event with which it began? Or, more likely, is there a particular event that stands out in our minds as we think back over it, an event that we identify with the beginning of this period?

Sometimes the period is marked off by very obvious and dramatic events, the death of a friend or a relative, finding a new job, or being fired, moving to a new city. Frequently we find that a lengthy and significant period in a person's life begins without anything specific happening. Basic situations often establish themselves in ways that are hardly observable. Gradually, without announcing themselves, they become a fact of our lives; and they may be there for a long time before we recognize what the situation has actually become. In such circumstances, there is often some particular memory with which the period is identified. It may not be a memory of the event that started the period, but the memory expresses the essence of the situation. Often this is embodied in the moment of realization, the time when we recognize the nature of the situation as it has developed. If there is such a memory, write it down, then add to it any other facts that define the period and mark off its boundaries.

When we began to work in the Period Log, first closing our eyes in order to look inward for images, and then letting the essence of the period express itself in a metaphor, we were not proceeding by conscious thought. We were relaxing our conscious controls and letting images and feelings come to us. Now we are ready to work consciously again. As our next step, we reconstruct the outlines of the period. We begin by recalling the salient and specific details of this now period in our life.

We let our minds go back over this time. What memories come to us? Were there special events that took place? Were arguments, angers, physical fights of any kind important in the period? Were there events of friendship, of loving, spiritual or physical loving that played a significant role? Were there family relationships, or work involvements, or social activities that we now recall? Were inner experiences important? Did you have any particularly striking experiences of a spiritual or artistic or extra-sensory type? If so, indicate them briefly here. At a later point in your Journal work you will be able to deal with them in the detail they require.

Do you recall any dreams from the period? There may be dreams that stand out in your mind because they were especially striking or dramatic. Or there may be dreams that continued to recur although they had first appeared in an earlier period of your life. Dreams that continue to return should be considered carefully, for they are like persistent callers who have a message that needs to be heard.

Do you recall any strange or uncanny events, coincidences or psychic events that seem to have a meaning for you? Were there strong religious experiences during this time? Were there inspirations, great new ideas? Were there times of great good luck or of misfortune? Were there physical illnesses?

Whatever comes to us as a memory relating to this period is to be written in our Journal in the Period Log section. As we do this we should bear in mind that the concept underlying the keeping of a log section is that its entries are to be brief. Working in our Period Log, we jot down as many of the relevant facts and memories as we can, simply getting them down on paper, not elaborating them. With brief entries we can, in a short while, recapitulate the period as a whole and place ourselves fully in the present moment.

Taking the Entries Further

There will be some entries in the Period Log which will lead us to feel, even as we are writing them, that they need immediately to be described in full detail. Others can first be recorded briefly and then elaborated at length later on. Many of the entries that we make in the Period Log suggest to us as we are recording them that they merit a great deal more of our attention. Such events and memories often have a great deal to say to us about our past and future. They are especially important in providing the starting point for the feedback exercises that we do in other sections of the Journal. In general, however, it is best to limit our Period Log entries to the essential factual description of our experiences. At a later point in the workshop or when we are using the active Journal Feedback exercises in our post-workshop private work, we can explore them more extensively and enable them to reveal their further message for our lives.

Working in the Period Log serves several very important functions in the use of the *Intensive Journal* process. Primarily it provides the point of focus at which we begin the process of positioning ourselves in the movement of our lives. The Period Log is the first section of the Journal to be used at each Journal Workshop. We begin with it in order to give ourselves a reference point in the present time unit of our lives.

It is important to bear this in mind if your first experience is using the *Intensive Journal* process by using this book as your guideline without actually participating in a Journal Workshop. In that case, you will find it best to begin with the Period Log, and to carry through the exercises as described until you have brought yourself up to date with respect to the current situation of your life.

Take care, however, not to write too much at this point. It is not beneficial for you to be exhaustive in the descriptions and statements that you write in your Period Log. Remember that it is a Log section, and that a primary quality of Log entries is that they be written briefly. Our experience has shown that brevity in the Log sections is especially helpful in the early stages of the work. We must ever bear in mind as we carry out our Journal work that the basic entries which we make in our Log sections are a *feeding-in* of our life material which the Journal Feedback process will progressively integrate in a dynamic way by means of its exercises and the varied procedures of Journal Interplay.

To make it possible for this reintegrative, life-focusing effect to occur at a later point in our work, it is essential that we overcome at the beginning the temptation to overwrite in the Period Log. Sometimes the excitement of a new discovery as the movement of our thoughts and memories accelerates makes us want to continue writing on and on. It is important to remember, however, that excessive writing at the beginning may weaken the larger dynamic of the Journal Feedback process as a whole. It will draw us off into the type of experience that characterizes ordinary journal or diary writing; then we will lose our access to the special reintegrative powers which the Journal Feedback process provides.

A Journal Checklist

There are two general approaches for us to follow in gathering data for our Period Log. The first is to recapitulate the occurrences of the period spontaneously as we have done, drawing upon the memories that come directly to mind when we turn our attention to this recent time in our lives. The second way is to review the events of the period briefly but systematically. The structure of the *Intensive Journal* workbook gives us a convenient means of doing this. We refresh our memory by using certain of the feedback sections as checkpoints recalling to our attention the relevant contents of this period in our life.

The basis of this checklist is its reference to the individual feedback sections. The nature of their contents and the way that we use them will be better understood later when we have had the experience of carrying out the specific Journal Feedback exercises. In the meanwhile, however, we can begin to refer to these checkpoints in a general way in order to assist our work in the Period Log.

Going back in your mind once again over the period that you have marked off, let yourself now recall the relationships with individuals that have been important during this time. They need not have been pleasant or satisfying relationships. Whether they were fulfilling or frustrating is beside the point. It is important that they were meaningful to you. Jot down in your Period Log now the names of the persons with whom significant experiences took place during this period of your life. Do not describe the occurrences in detail, but merely add some comments and brief descriptions after the name of the person. A few phrases followed by two or three explanatory sentences should be sufficient to express your memories and record your feelings and observations. Do this for each of the individuals who are significant for you during the period. These brief entries will then give you a starting point for additional exercises that you may carry out in the feedback sections later on.

Now we move to a further checkpoint. What work projects or outer activities were important to you during this period? It may be that you did not have a definite work involvement and that you were seeking one. Or it may be that there were frustrations and tensions in your life during this time because of the lack of a meaningful work. If so, that is an important fact to be entered in your Period Log.

If you were engaged in a project or work activity, it will be valuable for you to record briefly the various phases and changes through which it passed. What were the hopes and plans and difficulties that you encountered? What is the situation at the present moment with respect to your work? The cursory entries that you make in this regard now in your Period Log will also be the base for further experiences in the feedback exercises.

Let us now continue moving through the Journal checklist for additional brief entries to be made in the Period Log.

What events were important with respect to the physical aspect of your life during this time? Was health or illness a significant factor? Do any particular events now come to mind with respect to diet or athletics or love-making or drugs or the enjoyment of nature? If so, record them and add only whatever brief comment or explanation is necessary.

Have there been events during this period that involved you with social or political issues? Was it a time when your beliefs or group identifications were called into question? Was this a time when you had a particularly strong experience with respect to music or drama or any of the other artforms? Record these briefly now, making a mental note of the fact that you will elaborate them further at a later point in your Journal work.

Consider now whether any events have taken place during this period that were particularly striking or dramatic or meaningful in your life. Was there any single event that drastically changed the course of your life experience? Perhaps there was an accident of some kind or an event of unexpected good fortune. Perhaps there was a striking coincidence, an experience of extra-sensory perception that was particularly meaningful to you, or perhaps you had a strong experience of a religious quality, whether in a church or in direct closeness with nature. If such an event occurred during the period and now comes to your mind, record it briefly. Its significance will be expanded for you in your further experiences in the Journal.

When you have made the brief entries to record the contents and occurrences of this recent period that are recalled to your mind by using this checklist, your basic entry in the Period Log will be complete. Bear in mind that you are interested in recording memories and facts of experience without judgment and without censorship. Your Period Log is the place where you draw together an outline picture of this recent time in your life. It contains the specific contents of our experience, but not the details. It is our first step toward positioning ourselves in the larger movement of our lives and drawing our life experience into focus.

5

Twilight Imagery
and Life Correlation

Having completed our basic entry in the Period Log, we sit in stillness again. We now reapproach this present time in our life from another vantage point.

    While we were reviewing our recent experiences and describing them in our Period Log, our attention was directed toward the memory level of our minds. This was necessarily so because we were engaged in recalling specific events and situations. In order to do so, our attention was focused toward the surface of the psyche where conscious thoughts and memories take place. To that degree, it was turned away from the depth levels where our deeper-than-conscious intuitions occur. As we work, we wish to have access to the knowledge that comes not only from the conscious and rational side of the psyche but also the direct awareness, hunches, and inspirations that come from our nonrational depths. Having made our first entries from the vantage point of conscious memory, we now *shift our psychic position* and reapproach the present period of our life from a depth point of view. We do this by means of *Twilight Imagery.*

    The key to Twilight Imagery lies in the fact that it takes place in the twilight state between waking and sleeping. We find that by working actively in that intermediate state of consciousness, we are able to

Twilight Imaging, the intermediate state between waking and sleeping, enables us to reach the symbolic images contained in our depths.

reach depths of ourselves which are very difficult to contact by any other means. Once we have learned the Twilight Imagery procedures, however, we find that these experiences are relatively easy to achieve. As long as its essential guidelines are observed, authentic creative contact and spiritual awareness can be gained. It is necessary however to follow the basic principles of Twilight Imagery which require that it be carried through in a nonguided, nonconscious way, with the flow of imagery being neither manipulated nor directed.

We can understand what is involved in Twilight Imagery by referring back to our metaphor of progressively entering the well of inward experience until we are able to reach the underground stream. When we follow the symbolic discipline of moving into the well of our self, we find that we develop an increased capacity of inward perception. This capacity seems to be inherent in human beings and is a natural mode of awareness. Since it is inward, however, it tends to be little used in everyday situations where the individual's attention is constantly being preempted by the pressures of the outer environment. But when we establish an atmosphere that makes it possible for the attention to be turned inward in a quiet way, this capacity shows itself to be very actively and strongly present in persons who might have thought they did not possess it at all. At such times it often expresses itself in a way that catches the person unawares, but with an enlightening and even an inspirational power.

The term *Twilight Imagery* has the overtones of a visual experience. It implies specifically that the experience involves images that will be seen inwardly. This is misleading and is not actually the case. The primary quality of Twilight Imagery lies not in its visualness, but in its *twilightness,* the fact that it takes place, as though by itself, on the intermediary, or twilight, level of consciousness. The term *imagery* refers to the fact that its main expressions are not literal in the sense of being thoughts or ideas, but rather that they are representational or symbolic. They may indeed be visual, as they often are; but in many cases they are not visual at all. They may take the form of perceptions that come through any of the other, nonvisual senses. But they are *inward* perceptions, and thus, if they carry an aroma or come as sounds or body feelings, they are to be understood as being not actual and literal as physical perceptions, but as being symbolic and inward.

Of primary significance is the fact that we do not consciously or deliberately put these perceptions there. We ourselves do not determine what they shall be. Rather, being in a quiet and passive position, we *behold* them. We turn our attention inward as we wait in stillness, and let ourselves observe the various forms of imagery that present themselves. We let them come of themselves. We do not put the imagery there, just as we do not put our dreams there. They appear unbidden. With our attention turned inward, we observe them as though they were dreams. We follow the direction of their movement without directing or altering their contents. Then, at various convenient points in the process, we gather our observations and our beholdings together, and we record them in our *Twilight Imagery Log.*

We describe the contents of our Twilight Imagery experiences in the same neutral, noninterpretive, nonjudgmental way that we record our dreams. We describe them as we perceive them, with just enough elaboration so that a reader—primarily ourselves—will be able to recognize what took place in the experience. As we proceed in the movement of our lives working in the *Intensive Journal* process, we keep a record of these experiences consecutively in the section of the Journal called the Twilight Imagery Log. This log section becomes our empirical source of the facts of our inner experiences as we perceive them on the twilight level.

As part of our general, ongoing Journal work, we gather our Twilight Imagery experiences together over a period of time, so that at the right moment we can turn to this log section and draw upon them for a variety of Journal Feedback exercises. The exercises that begin with the data drawn from our Twilight Imagery Log often have a special power and productiveness. They draw upon the personal depths that are unique to each individual, but they reach into the transpersonal depths as well.

Twilight Imagery: The Technique

Now, however, we wish to work in the Twilight Imagery Log from a special point of view and with a particular purpose. We have made our basic entry in the Period Log describing our memories and adding brief observations and comments. We let that entry rest there without further elaboration in the Period Log section while we turn to the Twilight Imagery Log. Here, at the head of a sheet, we write the phrase, *Period Image,* and the date. (It is well to note at this point, and to emphasize and remind ourselves that we must remember to mark down the date at which we are writing each entry. At a later time, when we draw

Creative persons who reach out for the deeper mystery of reality in the midst of materialism are also expressing their seed nature.

together our cumulative entries and reenter them by the procedures of Journal Feedback, the dates at which they were written will be important facts contributing to our knowledge and adding to our further experience.)

The significance of the phrase, *Period Image,* is that it opens a subsection within the Twilight Imagery Log that enables us to reapproach this recent period of our lives from a symbolic point of view. Having described from the side of rational consciousness the unit of Life/Time that comprises our Now-moment, our experience of the Period Image will give us the perspective of the depth dimension. It opens to us the perspectives of both conscious and nonconscious awareness.

It is good to have our *Intensive Journal* workbook open to the Twilight Imagery Log with our pen handy while we sit in stillness. We breathe slowly, softly, letting thoughts drop away without our thinking them. We remain in quiet calmness.

Sitting in quietness, our eyes close. We let this take place gradually. It is as though the stillness and the softness of our breathing draw our eyelids together so that they seem to close of themselves. We realize that when our eyes close gradually and softly in this undeliberate way the darkness we enter is not unpleasant. It is, in fact, rather comfortable. It carries an atmosphere of calmness with it as we let ourselves quietly drift into the twilight level. Our attention has naturally readjusted itself and has turned by its own tempo to the inward dimension. Here we may perceive the realities of life, and especially the realities of our personal life, in the varied aspect of their symbolic forms. This *inward beholding* gives us the added vantage point of a depth perspective.

As we are doing this, we let ourselves *feel* the tone and quality of the period we have described. We do not think about it, we do not evaluate or make judgments about it. Having described in the Period Log the main factors that came to our mind, we now do nothing further on the conscious level. We merely sit in quietness, our eyes closed, our attention turned to the twilight level of experience. Here we let images come to us again, images of every kind. We do not specify what kind of images they shall be, whether we will see them, smell them, hear them, intuit them, feel them in our body. Whatever their form, they will be twilight images, coming to us out of the middle level of consciousness between waking and sleeping, and just presenting themselves to us so that we can observe them in a natural way and record them.

When we were making our first entry in the Period Log the imagery was not extended. It was sustained only long enough to take us to a deeper than cerebral level and to let our individual image or metaphor set the tone for the conscious remembering and recording that followed. But now that we have completed the conscious part of our exercise with the goal of positioning ourselves in the present of our lives via the Period Log, we are free to let our Twilight Imagery extend itself as fully as it wishes. We can let it range as far as it requires in order to reflect to us the other-than-conscious side of this present period in our lives.

Now our eyes are closed and we are sitting in stillness. Our attention is turned to this recent period in our lives which we have described and explored in the Period Log. We are not thinking of it but letting it present itself to us in the form of images, impressions, emotions, and especially through symbolic awarenesses that come to us in many sensory forms. We may see them, hear them, smell them, intuit them, but always by *inward perception* at the twilight level. It may come at first as stirrings in our body, as joyous surges or as stomach knots. By whatever form of perception they come to us, we observe them neutrally, without judgment, and we record them under the subsection which we have marked off in the Twilight Imagery Log with the heading of Period Image.

In the silence now we open ourselves to these Twilight Imagery awarenesses, and we record them as they come to us.

Discerning Life Correlations: Conscious and Nonconscious Symbolism

When this has been completed, we have one further question to pose to ourselves with respect to the entries we made in the Period Log and the experiences we have recorded in the Twilight Imagery Log as our Period Image. As we consider these two side by side—the actual outer events of our lives and the spontaneous imagery that comes from our inner depth—do we observe any perceivable relationship between them? Do they seem both to be saying the same thing, but in a different style of language? Or does the meaning of our imagery seem to be different from the message that comes to us when we recapitulate our life experiences with our memory? To say it another way, does the information that comes to us from our nonconscious depth confirm the opinions we have in our consciousness? Do they contradict one another? Do they balance and complement one another?

There is a great deal that we can learn about the inner movement of our lives when we set our conscious and our nonconscious perceptions side by side. It is essential, however, that we let ourselves truly feel and give full value to the perspective that is given to us from each side. We must not prejudge either one, but consider each one fully within its own terms, and then balance both together.

Considering and balancing these two types of experience which we have just had is not a thought process. It is not helpful to approach the question by thinking about it, nor by intellectually analyzing and interpreting the contents of our life and our images. What we wish to do, rather, is to establish an *inner correlation* between our life events and the imagery that reflects the movement of our experience and comments upon it in symbolic form. The best way to do this is simply to let the two fit themselves together out of their own natures, and to present their comment upon each other in their own terms.

To do this, it is best to sit in silence while setting side by side within ourselves the conscious experiences of our life and our twilight imagery. We let ourselves *feel* the quality and the tone of each of them. We do not analyze them; we merely feel them, we enter into them, and we let ourselves respond to them in an inward, undirected way. Thus they can balance themselves within us in relation to one another. Together they form a *whole message* which can speak to us without words from within ourselves.

To be able to hear the larger message which the two can give together, it is important that we refrain from making a judgment regarding any single experience taken by itself. This is particularly so when our imagery experiences seem to be saying the opposite of our recent life experiences. It may be, for example, that while we have been living through a period when our projects and relationships have been going well, we have a visual image in which we see a glass fall off a table and break. Or we may see an automobile driving along a thruway at high speed and suddenly come to a place where the traffic is at a standstill, or where there is an accident.

A similar experience may come to us from the opposite direction. The recent period of our lives may have been filled with pain and disappointments, but the image that comes to us may have an optimistic or encouraging tone. It may be of the sun rising out of darkness, or of a child being born, or a seed germinating in the earth. If it comes in a nonvisual form, it may be a choir of voices, or a symphony of joyous music; or, less definitely, it may be a feeling of strength or renewed energy welling up inside us.

In whichever direction the correlation experience moves, we should not rush to any premature conclusions. We should not jump too quickly to joyous celebration, nor should we let ourselves fall into a negativistic fatalism. What is important is that we learn to observe objectively the nature of our subjective perceptions. We *perceive inwardly* the wholeness of the situation of our lives as it is presented to us in the many aspects of its organic movement. By means of the interior perception of Twilight Imagery we see that each moment contains its opposites inherently within itself. Growth and decay, conflict and harmony, all the opposites, are part of the movement of time. One overarching truth that presents itself repeatedly to us as we observe the organic continuity of life is that whether they are pleasant or painful, all circumstances will eventually be transformed in their time in accordance with their inner nature. The indications of that change in their next immediate stage within the context of our lives are often shown to us ahead of time on the symbolic level by means of Twilight Imagery.

When we set the two together, the outer and inner perceptions combine to enable us to perceive the organic wholeness of time as it is moving in our lives. If we become alarmed when our imagery tells us that there is an element of difficulty around the corner of our present optimism, or if we begin to celebrate when an encouraging image indicates that a period of pain is coming to a close, we are cutting short the whole movement of time in our experience. There is an *organic inner continuity* in the movement of our lives, and it is expressed both inwardly and outwardly.

Perhaps, for example, it has been a time of rapid change in our life, one new situation coming in after another. In the turmoil we feel a mixture of emotions, confidence and fear, and the tension which the two produce. These are our conscious attitudes. In our Twilight Imagery we see a forest in full bloom, then in fall colors; we hear the chirping of birds, then silence; we see the trees barren in winter, then in spring growth again. Through it all we feel the process of change continuing in its permutations.

It is apparent that the many contents in this imagery reflect the active movement in the person's life. The two run parallel to one another, each reflecting the other. The inner experience of this Twilight Imagery, however, adds an additional dimension when it is set side by side with the outer movement of the life. It gives us an additional awareness, an *interior perspective* by which we can recognize the integrative principle that is present beneath the surface of our lives and is the connective thread of our existence.

To experience the inner continuity in the movement of our lives through the opposites of change is the purpose of our exercises in *life correlation*. From time to time as we work in the Journal Feedback process we shall come to phases of our life experience that are difficult and ambiguous, and at those times we shall find that the quiet work of life correlation is an especially valuable source of quiet guidance.

At this point in our work we let ourselves perceive the inner relationship between the movement of the outer events of this recent period and the imagery that has come to us on the twilight level. We record whatever recognitions or impressions or intuitions come to us in the Twilight Imagery Log in addition to the entries we made describing our Period Images. When we have written all the awarenesses that have come to us in this regard, we read them back to ourselves just to see whether there is anything that we wish to add to the entries we have made in the Period Log, additional memories that should be recorded and additional awarenesses that come to us from the Life Correlation with Twilight Imagery. We read the entries we have made in the Period Log back to ourselves to make sure that we have written all that is relevant there. When we have written all the awarenesses that have come to us, we return to quietness and get ready for the next phase of our Journal work.

6

The Daily Log

The work in the Period Log places us in contact with the continuity of our life experiences so that we form an inner perspective of our relationship to their movement. It begins the process of positioning ourselves in the movement of our lives, bringing us up to date with ourselves. Once that has been done, we require a means of maintaining the relationship that has been established. This is the primary function of the *Daily Log.*

In the Daily Log we make entries that enable us to keep on a current basis with the movement of our lives. We work day by day as much as possible to keep ourselves in an ongoing relationship with whatever is taking place inside ourselves.

The purpose of the Daily Log is to provide a continuing source of Journal Feedback material for use in the other sections of the Journal. This purpose sets the focus and style of the entries we make in it and also defines the differences between the Daily Log and the ordinary keeping of a diary. Diary writing usually involves the unstructured, chronological recording of the events of a person's life. We have to recognize though that the mere fact of continuously writing entries, as is done in the keeping of a diary, is not sufficient in itself to bring about deep changes in a person's life. To achieve a significant transformation

To achieve a significant trans-
formation in a personality,
strong forces of energy must be
generated.

in a personality, strong forces of energy must be generated. This is done by the feedback procedures as they draw upon the Log entries and build a momentum through the interplay of the various sections of the Journal.

In writing in the Daily Log, we especially wish to record the unpremeditated flow of the events of our inner experience. One first guideline for writing in the Daily Log is that the individual entries be succinct reflections of the mental, emotional, and imagery occurrences taking place within us. As much as possible, our writing should focus on the essence of the experience. Often a very few words are sufficient to indicate the quality of the experience that is taking place. The important thing is that we record it as close to the time of the actual occurrence as possible, and that we write enough to enable us to hold it in our memory and for future use. Afterward, when we have written sufficiently in the Journal so that we can draw together several entries and read them in continuity, we find that each entry fills in and recalls the context and details of the others. Thus, with relatively little being written at any one time, it becomes possible, even in the midst of a very busy life, to accumulate the data that will enable us to gain the long-range benefits of working in the Daily Log.

Entries should be brief, but brevity is by no means a fixed rule. It is merely that brief entries enable us to record the largest range of material, so that we can then have a greater flexibility in choosing the subjects and the directions in which we shall proceed in the active feedback exercises.

Sometimes, when we begin by making a brief entry in the Daily Log, we find that, without realizing it, we have launched ourselves upon a strong-flowing stream of inner experience. As the movement of it builds, the experience enlarges itself. At such times, a creative process is spontaneously taking place in us in the midst of writing in the Daily Log. We certainly do not wish to bring such entries to a short and arbitrary stop by our rule of brevity. On the contrary, we want to encourage them and evoke them further so that we can draw to full expression the possibilities and the implicit awareness which they contain. We have to take advantage of the strength and momentum of our writing while it is in motion. Later on, after these entries have extended themselves as far as they could, we can transfer them to another section of the Journal.

Transfers and cross-references play an important role in building the momentum of Journal Feedback. We try to make our entries in such a way that they will be available to us in the various feedback sections to which they may pertain as leads to possible future experiences. This increases as the facility in making Daily Log entries increases. Correspondingly we have found that those persons who have made daily entries in a diary can get very useful feedback leads for the future from reading back to themselves old entries in their diaries. Those old diaries can serve very much as old Daily Logs and they can contribute a great deal to the Journal Feedback process.

Two Ways of Working in the Daily Log

The two main ways of working in the Daily Log are *Recapitulation* and *Current Recording.*

In Recapitulation, we recall and re-create the events of a day, treating the day as a unit. We do this at the end of the day or as soon afterward as we can. Sometimes, unfortunately, several days must pass before we have the opportunity to make our entries. If this is the case, then the memory may begin to blur, and too many events may accumulate in our minds for any of them to be clear. Nonetheless, even though we may lose many of the details, there is a great value in trying to recapture in the Daily Log as much of the general movement of the days as we can.

The second way of working in the Daily Log, the way of Current Recording, has certain obvious advantages, but it is not always convenient or feasible. To the degree that it is possible, however, it enables us to gather the raw data of experience before it can be forgotten, and before our memories can falsify it.

In actual usage many more of the Daily Log entries are made by Current Recording, writing in the midst of the experience, than we might expect. The reason for this is that when a person makes it a practice to write a Recapitulation of the day as often as possible, the act of doing this connects him more and more closely to the inner movement of his life. As he writes recapitulations of events that have happened, new inner events are stimulated. He is thus led, while in the very act of recapitulating the day, to fresh experiences in the immediacy of the Journal work.

We prod ourselves to remember as many specific details as we can.

When you awakened in the morning, how did you feel physically? Did you awaken slowly, as though you were emerging from a dream? Or did you awaken quickly, full of energy and alertness? Are you aware of having had a dream during the night? Did you write it down during the night, or did you assume that you would remember it in the morning? Do you remember it now? All of it? Or some small part of it?

Now is the time to record as much of your dream as you can recall. Even if you remember only a small fragment of it, that small part is worth describing. While you are writing it down, additional segments of the dream may be recalled to your mind. To remember a small piece of a dream is like catching a fish by the tail. If we hold on to it, we can draw in the whole fish.

Remember though that the Daily Log is not the section of the Journal where we describe the *fullness* of the dream. The *Dream Log* is the section that is devoted to dreams. In the Daily Log it is sufficient if we make a brief entry recording the fact that we did have a dream and indicating briefly something of its general nature. In the Dream Log (which is in the Journal section dealing with *Depth Dimension*), we describe the dream as fully as we can, neither analyzing nor interpreting it, but simply recording the events and impressions of the dream in a neutral, nonjudgmental, reportorial style. We wish merely to have it on record so that at a later time, we will be able to accelerate the process of Journal Feedback by working with the continuity of our dreams.

We may give the dream a name there, indicating also the primary image in it. As we do this, the identifying image becomes the title of the dream and gives us an easy means of referring to it if we have occasion to work with material from that dream in other sections of the Journal. We indicate also the cross-reference to other sections of the Journal where we have worked with that dream, and especially to show that we have described it more fully in the Dream Log.

WRITING YOUR FIRST DAILY LOG ENTRY

Now, holding our minds back at the time of the beginning of the day for the recapitulation of the Daily Log, let us begin to reconstruct the events and feelings that drew the day into motion. Have your workbook ready. Remember to date your entry. As you read, pause to write as feelings and thoughts come to you.

We begin once again by being quiet. As our writing proceeds, we find that we are able to recall more and more of the thoughts and emotions that were present in that transitional time when we moved from sleep to waking consciousness.

What were the emotions and desires, the anxieties, the hopes, and the plans as you began your day? Was there a basic tone of emotional feeling, or of body feeling? Was it enthusiastic, or was it anxious? Was it light or heavy, as you were emerging into the waking state?

While you were not quite asleep and not quite awake, did visual images, or intuitions, or strong, clear feelings come to you? That time between sleep and waking is a twilight state in which important awarenesses often come to us, if we are able to perceive them. Did fantasies come to you at that time? Imaginings? Or sexual feelings? Without censoring and without judging, record whatever you can recall of that early part of the day in your Daily Log.

Now let us proceed to the further movement of the day. Let us bring back to our minds the sequences of events and emotions as the active part of the day began.

How did you begin doing the tasks of the day? What were the thoughts that came unbidden to your mind? While you were doing the things that were necessary, were you aware of feelings and fantasies moving through your mind without your wanting them to be there? Did you find yourself worrying about things that you did not want to be thinking of? Did you find hopes or wishes entering your mind without your consciously putting them there, or wanting them to be there?

What kind of relationships came about in the course of the day? Were there experiences of love and affection? Did you experience frustration and anger? Now let yourself feel again the emotions that arose in you and that were brought forth in others. Record them briefly and describe as well as you can the movement and the interrelationships of your emotional responses and those of the other persons involved with you during the day.

Do not judge the emotions, but simply report what took place. As you describe the movement of your emotions, you will find that the external movement of events will fit around them, and the pattern of the day will take shape for you. To follow the movement of our emotions enables us to retrace the formation of our lives from the inside. Thus you will begin to recognize how your day unfolded from within yourself.

Now, as you are retracing the inner movement of your day's

By remaining in silence, we recall more thoughts and emotions that came to us during the transition from sleep to waking.

Describing, without judging, the movement of our emotions enables us to recall the external movement of events.

experience, let yourself feel again the atmosphere of the various moods through which you passed. In particular, let yourself recall the variation in your feelings, as your mood of the morning continued or changed as you came to lunchtime, and then midday, and as different people entered the scene of your experience. Consider how it varied in the latter part of the afternoon, and in the evening. What was your mood and the tempo of your thoughts and feelings as you continued into the night, and as you prepared for bed? Are you aware of how your body and your emotions began to be fatigued, and how they prepared for sleep?

Now, as you view the day in retrospect, consider the rhythms of the day. More important than the rhythm of outer events is the rhythm of your inner experiences. We find these rhythms not on the surface of our actions but in the changes of feeling-tone and attitude that take place at levels deep below our consciousness. To reach these rhythms and to identify them, we let our minds go back over the movement of our inner experience as it took place in the course of a day. As much as possible, we reexperience the fluctuations that took place in our feelings so that, as though we were marking off an interior graph of our lives, we record the shifting phases of our moods. When you have finished writing the recapitulation of this period, or when you have written as much as feels sufficient and right for you at this time, let yourself become quiet again. Sit in stillness, breathing slowly, not thinking, but letting your whole being absorb the feelings that you have been describing.

What feelings do you find within yourself now that you have recorded these varied facts of your experience?

How did you feel while you were writing them?

As you consider this, record whatever additional feelings and thoughts and memories and observations come to you.

Once again, after making this additional entry in your Daily Log, return to quietness. Let your breath become slow and regular, and for at least a few minutes, let no further thoughts enter your mind. The exercise we have done of reentering the movement of our life is bound to stir up a variety of emotions and energies. We therefore wish to make sure that we give ourselves sufficient time to settle ourselves and become inwardly quiet. We do not rush ourselves when we work in the inner experiences of our lives. Having written a basic entry in the Daily Log, we sit in quietness. We do not analyze nor interpret, but we let ourselves absorb the movement of the day as an integral piece of our life. It is an atom of time in our existence.

Absorb the movement of the day. It is an atom of time in our existence.

Conclusion

The questions we have raised and the areas of experience that have been indicated are to serve as starting points and guidelines for the entries we make in the Daily Log. Even when our lives seem to be uneventful on the outside, the range of content and movement within us is very great. That is why we realize, when we have worked regularly in the *Intensive Journal* workbook for some time, that it is truly worth our while to record in our Daily Log without censorship and without judgment everything that we can perceive as it is taking place in the inner movement of our lives. Later, when we reapproach this material from the point of view of Journal Feedback, we are able to see how varied a resource we have been carrying in the depths of ourselves.

As you write these entries in the Daily Log, take care that you do not inadvertently censor or edit the material you are recording. It is all too easy to slant your reporting without even realizing that you are doing so. Do not exclude some things because you are ashamed of them. Do not emphasize other things because you are proud of them. It is important for us to maintain a strongly neutral position in the recording that we do in our Journal. This will not be difficult, however, if we bear in mind that what we are recording in our Daily Log is only for ourselves and for our own later use in the Journal Feedback procedures. We are engaged in gathering honest, empirical data for use in deepening our own inner process.

We find, also, that this goal of neutral fact gathering is best achieved if we write in the Daily Log primarily in the form of brief entries. It is also best if we write in the Daily Log as much as possible without premeditation, recording our entries spontaneously in the order in which they come to us. We should not be concerned at all if, upon rereading our entries, they seem to be haphazard and disorganized. We should remember, then, that when we write in our Journal, we are not composing an essay but only recording the unedited expressions of our inner experience. Therefore we should pay no attention at all to the style of our writing. The Daily Log is not an exercise in literature; it is an exercise in our lives. There is no need for us to be concerned about grammar, or literary style, or the use of polite language. It is important, rather, that we feel free to write in our everyday language, letting the flow of our words reach the paper with neither editing nor censorship.

Part 3

THE LIFE/TIME DIMENSION

Introduction to the Life/Time Dimension

An essential factor in developing the capacity of *Life Intuitions* in this Journal workshop is the work that we do in the Life/Time Dimension, especially the exercises of Time Stretching. These exercises have varied and wide-ranging applications in the practice of Journal Feedback because of their value in helping people navigate their lives through periods of transition.

Chapter 10 focuses on one of the key exercises in our work in the Life/Time Dimension: *Time-Stretching*. The concept and practice of Time-Stretching enables us to move back and forth through all the segments of time in our existence. It is based upon the fundamental distinction between *chronological time* and *qualitative time*. Chronological time refers to the objective sequence of events as they are perceived by an observer who is outside of them and who therefore sees them externally with no emotional involvement in their content. Qualitative time, on the other hand, refers to the subjective perception of objective events in terms of the meaning and value they have to the person who is experiencing them. Qualitative time is the movement of Life/Time perceived from within the process of a life.

In the Time-Stretching exercises, we use the Life/Time sections as the outer embodiment of the inner process of our lives, and we move flexibly in and out of these sections in a manner that corresponds to the inner movement of qualitative time. The nature of the entries that we make and the procedures for using them enable us to move in and out of the present and the past and the future, going back and forth among them, drawing forth their variations, their interrelationships, and especially, their implications and possibilities. Because of the nature of the inner movement of time that is involved in these exercises, we do not carry them out by working in one section of the Journal alone. Rather, in order to enlarge the range of the interplay in the movement of Life/Time, we work simultaneously in the three main sections of the Life/Time Dimension. We begin with a series of deepening exercises in the Steppingstones section to give ourselves a sense of the fluid and changing contexts of our life. We then reach into the various corners of our life by moving back and forth between the Life History Log and Intersections: Roads Taken and Not Taken, opening out the contents of our lives with an open curiosity that is non-judgmental. We are stretching our relationship to Life/Time so that our perception of it can include whatever is relevant or necessary for us in order to reposition ourselves in our lives. We use the Time-Stretching exercises to achieve this, and the Steppingstones section is the hub of them. It is here that we begin.

7

The Steppingstones

In Steppingstones, we draw out of the jumbled mass of our life experiences, the thin and elusive connective threads that carry our potentials toward a fuller unfolding.

When we speak of the *Steppingstones* of our life, we are referring to those events that come to our minds when we spontaneously reflect on the course that our life has taken from its beginning to the present moment. The Steppingstones are the significant points of movement along the road of an individual's life. They stand forth as indicators of the inner connectedness of each person's existence, a continuity of development that maintains itself despite the vicissitudes and the apparent shifting of directions that occur in the course of a life. The Steppingstones are indicators that enable us to recognize the deeper-than-conscious goals toward which the movement of our lives is trying to take us.

The special value of working with the exercises of the Steppingstones section is that they serve as vehicles by which the reconstruction of a life can take place concisely and effectively. They enable us to draw out of the jumbled mass of our life experiences the thin and elusive connective threads that carry our potentialities through their phases of development toward a fuller unfolding. The exercises enable us to mark these off and strengthen them, especially during those stages when we are weak and still unsure of ourselves. At certain points in our lives there may be more than one connective thread of growth moving as a line of continuity through our experiences. Sometimes the lines overlap, or they may disappear for long periods as though they have entered a dark underground cycle from which they eventually reappear. By working with the Steppingstones, we make contact with these elusive lines of continuity that are seeking to establish themselves as patterns of meaning in our lives. By discovering them and identifying them, we are able to affirm possibilities in ourselves that might otherwise be lost. (We shall see the details of this a little later in our Time-Stretching exercises.)

Working with our Steppingstones, we go back into the past of our lives, but not because of fascination with the past. We do not wish to lose ourselves in the field of memory. We go back into the past by means of the Steppingstones in order to reconnect ourselves with the movement of our personal Life/Time, and so that we can move more adequately into our future. In this respect, the work we do with Steppingstones is comparable to a running broad jump. We go back into our past in order to be better able to leap forward into our future. This is the essence of our work in the Life/Time Dimension.

WRITING OUR FIRST SET OF STEPPINGSTONES

To enter the atmosphere in which we can best work with our Steppingstones, we close our eyes and sit in silence. In this stillness, we let our breathing become slower, softer, more relaxed. As we are quieted, we let ourselves *feel* the movement of our lives. We do not think about any specific aspect of our life, but we let ourselves feel the movement of our life as a whole. In our silence we let the changing circumstances and situations of our life pass before the mind's eye. Now we may recognize the varied events in their movement, not judging them or even commenting on them, but merely observing them as they pass before us. We perceive them and feel them in their generalized movement without actually seeing the details of them.

As you do this, it may be that the events of your life will present themselves to you as a flowing and continuous movement, as a river moving through many changes and phases. Or it may be that your life will present itself to you as a kaleidoscope of disconnected events. Whatever the form in which the continuity of your life reflects itself to you now, respond to it, observe it, and let the flow continue. If images present themselves to you on the twilight level, images in any form

Passive receptivity is the best attitude to adopt. Let the cycles of your life present themselves.

whether visual or not, take note of them. As soon as you can, record them as part of your Steppingstones entry.

Sitting in quietness, breathing deeply at a slow and measured pace, let the continuity of your life as a whole move before you. Let yourself feel its movement as a total and unfolding process. Passive receptivity is the best attitude to adopt in doing this. As you sit in silence, let the cycles, the rhythms, the tempos of your life present themselves to you. Let them be free and undirected so that they can shape themselves into whatever form truly reflects their basic qualities; let yourself be free in your quietness to perceive them as they come to you without editing or falsifying them.

They may come as memories or visual images or inner sensations of various kinds. Especially they may state themselves in the form of similes or metaphors in addition to expressing the literal facts of past experience. Let your attitude be receptive enough that the continuity of your life as a whole can present itself to you both in symbolic forms and in literal factual statements. Whatever comes to you in this preparatory time of quietness should be entered in the Steppingstones section.

After sitting in silence and recording what comes to you, you are ready to make the first listing of your Steppingstones. Since they are the most significant points in the movement of your life, the list should be limited in number. Spontaneous selectivity is the essence of marking off our Steppingstones. No matter how old we are and how long our life, the best practice is to place eight or ten Steppingstones on our list, but in any case not more than a dozen.

While the essential tone with which we carry out the Steppingstone exercise is that of undirected spontaneity, the one conscious guideline that is necessary concerns the number of Steppingstones in each list.

The special point of the Steppingstones exercise and the main reason why it works dynamically to crystallize new perspectives for our lives lies in the fact that it reaches beyond chronological time. It gives us an awareness of the qualitative movement of our life events as these may be recognized from *within* our experience of them. To achieve this, we insert an element of deliberate tension into the spontaneity of the exercise. We set a limit to the number of Steppingstones that we place on our list. We do not record all the meaningful events of our past, but only those which we feel have been significant factors.

It is helpful, also, the first time we are listing our Steppingstones to begin by stating the first basic facts drawn from the vital statistics of our life. The first Steppingstone, for example, may be the event of your birth followed by such objective markers in your life as entering school, graduating, changes in your family and in the location of your residence, the death of close relatives, major financial changes in the family's fortunes. These external events have a certain objective factuality in that they have taken place in the outer chronological time of your life. They express the external movement of events. They thus provide the objective background against which we can perceive and reexperience the subjective realities of our lives.

While the external facts of our lives are recorded objectively in terms of chronological time, the events of our inner world take place in qualitative time. They lead to the inner experience of meaning in our existence, but their base and starting point lies in the external circumstances of our life. For this reason we often find that when we are having our first experience of working in our Steppingstones we obtain a truer reflection of the movement of our life if we begin by listing the basic objective events that have taken place in chronological time. By reflecting the outer movements of our lives, these provide a base from which we can proceed to our more intimate and more subjective experiences of meaning.

As we continue with the listing of our Steppingstones, we find that they tend progressively to take the form of events that express the uniqueness of our individual selves. The tendency is to move from basic chronological events, like place of birth and education, to qualitative events that carry the maturity and the private meaning of our lives. Thus the Steppingstones that describe the early years of life tend to be basic and biographical, while the Steppingstones of later years are more subjective and specialized in tone. Correspondingly, the first two or three lists that a person compiles when he begins to work with the Steppingstones exercise usually reflect the factual outline of his life, while subsequent experiences move ever more deeply into the personal, qualitative experience of Life/Time. It will be good to bear this perspective in mind when, at a later point in your Journal Feedback work, you review and reread the Steppingstone exercises that you have written.

It will become obvious to you as you begin to list your Steppingstones so that your life can be reconstructed from several different vantage points. How shall you decide on which approach you are to choose? Bear in mind that it is *not* for you to make any decision at all in this matter. This is the reason that we begin our exercise in quietness and adopt an attitude of passive receptivity. We wish to intrude as little as possible of our conscious choice into the listing of our Steppingstones.

To set the process into motion, begin by indicating some basic facts of early years in the first entry or two. Then return to your quietness letting the movement of your life present itself to you. Perhaps a memory of a particular event will come to you. In itself it may not be the most important event of that period of your life, but it is calling your attention to a particular unit of your Life/Time. Make note of it, for you will probably wish to make use of that memory at a later point in the Time-Stretching exercises. Its immediate value for you, however, is that it directs your thoughts to a period of your life that is one of your Steppingstones.

At this point it is sufficient for you to choose a descriptive phrase. Even a single key word will suffice. In making your basic listing of Steppingstones, it is not necessary to be elaborate. All that is required is a word or a brief phrase that will be indicative of the Steppingstone period. After all, no one but yourself will be reading that list, and the brief reference will be intimately clear to you. There is also, as we shall soon see, a special value in brevity of phrase for the basic listing of your Steppingstones. Afterward there will be ample opportunity to enlarge upon them in detail and to expand them in several directions.

With your eyes closed, there may be a memory that comes to you, an image that represents a particular time in your life, or an indication in any other form that calls your attention to the period of a Steppingstone in your life. Write it down as it comes to you.

It may be that as you are letting the Steppingstones of your life come to you spontaneously, you realize that they are not appearing in chronological order. Steppingstones from the latter half of your life may be coming to you before the earlier parts. Do not let that deter you. Record them as they come to you. When enough have been listed to cover the main movement of your life so that you feel satisfied that you have reflected your life to yourself in a fair and representative manner, it will simply be a matter of renumbering the Steppingstones you have listed so that they will correctly represent the continuity of your life.

Other than renumbering them, however, you should not alter or edit the Steppingstones you have listed. The spontaneity with which they have presented themselves to you is an integral part of the experience. Bear in mind that the Steppingstones are the significant points of movement along the continuity of your life. As we draw them together out of the depth of our lives in our quiet atmosphere, those that are called up to our minds are the ones that are meaningful to us in the context of the present moment of our lives. The spontaneity of the experience selects the Steppingstones for us from a place in ourselves that is beyond consciousness, and thus it enables us to see a thread of the inner continuity moving in our lives.

Each list of Steppingstones is such a thread of continuity drawn together from the vantage point of a particular present moment. It is called to the forefront of the mind by the circumstances of our life and our consciousness at that moment, and it has the qualities of that moment. After a while, when our work in the *Intensive Journal* process has given us occasions for drawing together several sets of Steppingstones, we are in a position to recognize the integrity of each list. Each represents a special thread of continuity in the movement of our life. When, after the passage of time, we reread a number of Steppingstone lists at a single setting, they come together as the threads that form the tapestry of our life. And we ourselves have woven it.

When you have completed your list, pause and let your mind return to a condition of quietness. In the silence you may contemplate the movement of the list that is outlined by your list of Steppingstones. Here are some additional questions to consider.

What feelings were stirring in you as you recorded this list? Write this as an addendum to your Steppingstones.

Reading Your Steppingstones

Now you may read your list of Steppingstones silently to yourself. What emotions or awarenesses arise in you as you do this?

If you are participating in an *Intensive Journal* workshop, the leader will ask those who would like to read their Steppingstones to do so. You may wish to read yours aloud to yourself if you are doing this work alone. Bear in mind that the reason for reading your Steppingstones in the group is not at all so that you can tell your life story to the other participants. Your purpose is not to communicate with the others, but to feed back into yourself the experiences of your own existence. That is part of the progressive deepening in the Journal Feedback process.

If you choose to read your Steppingstones aloud, it is best to read only the brief headings you have written for each. If you have written any elaborations or explanations, do not read them aloud at this point. Merely read the short phrase or single word that you have used to denote each Steppingstone. By maintaining this conciseness, you will be able to experience the essential continuity of movement in your life. The starkness of the outline of your life will heighten its impact on you. As you read it, let yourself hear it; also let yourself be free to feel whatever emotions are stirred in you as you recapitulate the course of your life.

You may wish also to read your Steppingstones aloud into a cassette recorder. Reading your list into the recorder will give you the benefit of the feedback experience of speaking the Steppingstones. You should take note of your feelings as you do this and add them as a further entry in your Steppingstones section. Of even greater feedback value will be your experience in hearing your Steppingstones spoken aloud. This places you in the position of being briefly an observer of yourself.

The reading of the Steppingstones measurably deepens the atmosphere of the group. We very often become aware that a profound presence has become part of the atmosphere of the workshop as people are reading their Steppingstones. As the readings take place, it is as though each individual is offering his or her most personal possession, life, but presented objectively, even transpersonally. He or she is not exalting it, not embellishing it, not defending it, only reading the markings of a life history in their honest actuality, without comment and without special requests, seeking neither praise nor sympathy. Each human existence is presented as a factual offering placed on an unseen altar before the group. Perhaps the atmosphere of depth and awe that enters the workshop is the cumulative effect of many human existences being set forth as offerings in this sincere, unprepossessing way, each primarily engaged in clarifying itself to itself. Again and again in the Journal Workshops we are shown evidence that the sincere examination of the individual human life is one of our fundamental religious acts.

Each set of Steppingstones is unique, for no two human beings have the same combination of life experiences. This individuality shows itself also in the diverse ways that people list their Steppingstones. The details of the material must remain private, in keeping with the underlying ethics of the *Intensive Journal* program, but we can see examples of this diversity of forms in the Steppingstone lists that are read at the workshops.

Even though the specifics are left out in the sets of Steppingstones that are made by listing indicative phrases or just a single word, such lists are extraordinarily effective in reflecting the movement of a person's life.

Consider the following stark, and yet poetically expressive list of Steppingstones that was read at a workshop: "I was born. I loved. I danced. I wept. I posed. I suffered. I was entranced. I was humiliated. I got lost. I am trying to find my way."

It is obvious that we, who are outsiders to the life that is described in that listing, cannot know the details of the experiences to which those cryptic sentences refer. Nonetheless we do feel the quality of the person and the tone of the life in which he is engaged. It is not for us but for the person whose life it is that the details of what is involved in those Steppingstones have meaning. He alone needs to know, and each person who makes such an outline of Steppingstones is well able to fill in the private details as he continues with the Time-Stretching exercises. To make such a listing of Steppingstones does, however, help us to identify the thread of continuity that has been moving through our life; most importantly, it enables us to wind that thread fine enough to draw it through the narrow eye of the needle formed by the circumstances or the crises of the present moment of our life.

Our sincere examination of the individual human life is one of our fundamental religious acts.

Ways to Use the Steppingstone Exercise

There are several ways in which we use the Steppingstones exercises as a means of fine-winding the elusive threads of continuity through the narrow crises of our lives. When we reach a time of transition in life, come to a crossroad of decision, or when one phase of life has ended and we must find the resources with which to begin a new unit of experience, it is of great value to be able to find and to grasp the inner thread of our lives by working with the Steppingstones.

Consider the situation, for example, of a woman who comes to a

Each individual can experience the wholeness of his life with a movement toward a future that is being formed in the present moment.

Journal Workshop at a point in her life where her child-rearing years are coming to an end. She is a housewife, living what she feels to be a regularized existence in the modern suburban manner, and wondering what her future holds for her. Working with her Steppingstones is the first step in positioning herself in the movement of her life so that she can discover her resources and her possibilities. The first listing of Steppingstones that she makes reflects primarily the external events of her life. "I was born. I went to school. I graduated from college. I held a job. I married. I bore three children. The children are growing up. Everything is fine but I am discontented. I don't know what to look forward to."

As we consider them, we realize that those last Steppingstones with their mixture of fear and a vague yearning for something not yet known are the link to her future. At the moment when she lists these Steppingstones, she has no indication of what they imply or where they may be moving. She only knows that she feels troubled as she writes her Steppingstones. When she is asked about them, she says that she feels her Steppingstones are boring and that they are of no interest to anyone. She also says that she felt very much like crying as she was reading the list in the presence of the group.

Her response and description of her feelings are direct expressions of the Journal Feedback process in motion. They are, in fact, continuing the process. The movement of her life was clearly in a low phase. In another situation when she expressed such unhappiness, there would undoubtedly be some helpful person present to give her sympathy, some sensible advice, and a reasonable interpretation of why she is feeling that way. At a Journal Workshop, however, we refrain from doing that. In order for our operational principles to bring about their changes, it is essential that we do not intervene with helpfulness but that we honor the integrity of the individual. We must leave ample room for the organic process of their life to continue through its valleys until it finds the means of restoring itself out of its own resources. It is essential that we do not intervene with ourselves as well.

Since the Steppingstones embody the inner continuity of a life, the act of listing them is in itself a step in carrying the life process forward. Writing them and considering them in a focused exercise has the effect of drawing that process one notch further at the nonconscious level.

That movement is often visible in the very first listing of Steppingstones that a person draws together. We could see that in the set of Steppingstones of the woman whom we quoted. She began by recapitulating her life in terms of her birth and the external facts of her early life. The first Steppingstones were general, being primarily objective in content. As she came closer to the present period, however, subjective feelings came more strongly to the fore. We could see then that in describing a Steppingstone of her life as a period of discontent, she was also moving the inner process onward. The urge to tears was part of this movement as well. An energy was stirring underneath and was in motion. Of necessity, the first forms of the movement expressed her frustration and boredom, since those were the inner conditions creating the need for change. The question that comes to mind, then, is how the change will be brought about. How will a new, more meaningful condition of life be established?

As a person begins to think about this rationally, a new sense of frustration and even a panic may be felt. The reason for this is that deliberate and rational thinking cannot direct us to a satisfying and meaningful experience in our life. That can only be brought about in the same way that inspiration comes to an artist, by *cultivated spontaneity* as he works persistently at the nonconscious levels of his inner experience. Working in the procedures of Journal Feedback is the equivalent of the creative process in the artist, not because it is directed toward a particular artwork, but because it systematically stimulates and draws forward the process at the depth of the person. Working with our Steppingstones and using them as the base points for our later Journal Feedback exercises fulfills this same function with respect to the organic process that is seeking to unfold in our lives.

In the case of the woman of whom we have been speaking, the movement of this inner process will be reflected in the next set of Steppingstones she lists. Especially if enough time has passed for her to have worked seriously in the *Intensive Journal* process, the vantage point from which she views her life will have moved to another position. Her perspective will be different. When she lists her next set of Steppingstones, it is likely that only the very first one, her birth, will be the same and will be in the same position. Instead of making a routine recording of her education, she will focus on a particular subject that interested her, an event or relationship that took place during her college years, or a decision she made at the time which had unforeseen consequences in later years. Instead of stating the cold statistical fact of how many children she bore, she may now place her attention on some particular experiences in relation to her childbearing and child rearing.

On the other hand, with her emphasis shifted toward the lifestyle that is emerging in her future, she may find that she does not even list her children at all in her next set of Steppingstones. This will not be because she is rejecting them, but because she is now evaluating the past events of her life in terms of their contribution to the next step in her development. She may recall now as a Steppingstone her emotions when she learned that her brother would go to medical school while her own schooling would be curtailed. Or she may now list as Steppingstones quite different events which she would not have considered to be important before. They may have been sources of frustration, or of stimulated imagination, or unfulfilled hopes, satisfactions, and detours. As the context of her life is enlarged by her newly opening perspectives, the contents of many experiences in her past become meaningful to her in new ways. Events that seemed insignificant before now take their place as Steppingstones as she sees a meaning and a potential in them pointing toward the future. In the course of this, what may be called a *transvaluation* of her life experiences will have taken place, and new goals, meanings, and hopes will have begun to emerge.

This transvaluation will express itself in changed attitudes and a new life perspective. At successive Journal Workshops or in her private experience after she has worked with the Journal Feedback exercises and Steppingstones, she will find that the events continue to change. As she compares the several lists when she rereads them in sequence after some time, she will recognize that hardly any of the Steppingstones that were on her original list appear on the later lists; those that do reappear will be in a different context, for the old events will now have a new meaning. Hearing itself read in sequence these successive sets of Steppingstones will reinforce for her a fact that she already knows, namely that her life has changed. She is now a new person with a different life history than she had before.

In this modern period of history when the life expectancy is much longer than it was in previous generations and when the resources offered by society are much greater, many people are able to live through two or three distinct cycles of life. In each of these, they are a different person with different values and lifestyles. To be able to look forward to such successive developments opens a large potential not only for the later years of one's life but for the fullness of meaning in a human existence as a whole. The main difficulty lies in the period of transition between two major units in a person's life. When the old period has ended and a new period has not yet been substantially established, the emotional burdens of anxiety and self-doubt may be heavy to bear. That is a time when it is especially important to have a progressive and organic method for enabling the perspectives of one's life to reshape themselves.

This is the situation of the person who has come to a crossroad of decision in life where he or she has to choose between two major pathways, or both of which are already parts of his experience. It may seem that such a person is suffering only from an excess of riches, but the tension can be very great indeed.

In such circumstances it is often helpful to draw up two or even more sets of Steppingstones within a very brief period, even within a single workshop. In that way, if there is more than one thread of continuity seeking to unfold in a person's life, each will have ample space in which to reveal the strength of its roots and the scope of its possibilities.

Sometimes it is not a question of decision or of conflict, but simply of a change in emphasis taking place in a person's life. Situations of this kind come to the fore especially when the time for retirement is approaching, or when other circumstances are bringing about a change in the main activity that has dominated an individual's attention.

I think in this regard of a man who came to an *Intensive Journal* workshop at a point in his life when he was preparing to retire as chief executive of a large corporation. He had already determined what was to be the new direction of his life. He wished to develop his spiritual capacities to the point where he could serve society effectively in an altruistic way during his later years. Toward this end, he had come to the workshop in order to set his life in perspective.

When he came to the Steppingstones exercise, however, he found that the Steppingstones of his life were not willing to come together in a single list. Following our procedures, he undertook to write them spontaneously with the assumption that they would place themselves in a single unified format. But his Steppingstones had their own point of view in the matter. Like people who will not speak to one another, they would not come together. It strongly suggested that there was a marked antithesis between the two sides of his life.

In that situation there was nothing to do but to let the Stepping-stones have their way and to let them record themselves simultaneously in two separate lists. As he did so, he discovered that each set of Steppingstones contained the chronology of a separate development that had been taking place within him over the years. The first list contained the Steppingstones of his rise to business success. It listed his birth, the poverty of his early years, his personal unsureness during his education, his chance meeting with a public figure who became his sponsor, the redirection of his education into the legal profession, and then the various events that led to his progressive rise up the corporate ladder.

Parallel to this, and altogether separate from it, was the list of Steppingstones that marked the continuity of his spiritual life. Among these were his memory of his grandfather as a figure who personified wisdom; various books on philosophy and religion which had come to his attention, but which he had failed to read; hearing a lecture on mystical subjects, rejecting it, but being haunted nevertheless by the speaker's thoughts; becoming acquainted at a later point with an author on spiritual subjects; then, a personal, inner experience that brought about his decision to bring one of his lives, his business life, to a close and to begin an altogether new style of experience.

Reading those two lists of Steppingstones to the group was a very moving experience for him. It was as if he had read the life histories of two separate individuals. It told him, among other things, that the new life he was beginning was not at all new to him. It had its own history, and had had its own continuity and growth, but that growth had taken place beneath the surface of his life. Now the rhythm and timing of that second person within him was coming to the fore and was ready to become the dominant person in his existence. The fact that the two persons insisted on chronicling their lives with two separate sets of Steppingstones dramatized for him the distinctness of their existence *at that particular time in his life.*

It was not something to be diagnosed as a psychiatric split, but rather an inherent aspect of the transition through which he was passing. While it was establishing its strength, the new self had to insist on its independence and separateness. It was in a position very similar to that of an adolescent establishing his identity and freedom from his parents and teachers. But such times of transition pass. At a later time, after the businessman had moved through his transition and had retired from the life of his old business self and had established a way of life for his new self, it was possible for him to experience all the events of his life as part of one larger unfolding unity. Therefore, on a subsequent occasion he could reconstruct his life in one single integrative set of Steppingstones, thereby giving full value in perspective to both the business side and his spiritual nature.

These examples may give some perspective of what is involved in listing the Steppingstones. Each time we do this exercise we are recapitulating our life from the special point of view provided by a particular moment in our life-history. But it is not merely a procedure that we carry out with respect to our past. The very act of listing our Steppingstones reshapes the context of our life, and thus draws us a step further into our future.

We see in this an important key to the dynamic effect of working with our Steppingstones. The purpose of the exercise is to move us forward in the Life/Time Dimension, constantly recrystallizing our perception of our life, and thereby drawing us onward. It is not at all intended to give us an intellectual understanding of our past. That is one reason why there is no such thing as listing the *correct* Steppingstones. They are inherently in flux. Therefore the key to working with the Steppingstones is to let the list be created spontaneously out of the fullness of the present circumstances of our life, whatever they may be. We should be open and receptive to these circumstances without being judgmental about them. Then, as we begin each exercise in quietness, listing our Steppingstones in an atmosphere of deep stillness as we are listening to the inner flow of our life, directions of experience of which we were not previously aware may be reflected to us. The Steppingstones thus provide us with essential, nonconscious life-information to feed into the interplay of exercises in the other sections of the Journal. This, in turn, will build the momentum of Journal Feedback, and will provide the inner guidance we require for the next step in our life.

8

The Steppingstone Periods in the Life History Log

The *Life History Log* is the section of the *Intensive Journal* workbook in which we gather as many of the facts as we can of the past of our lives. (Again, refer to Appendix D for the sample workbook.) It has two subsections: *Remembrances* and *Steppingstone Periods.* The first is for memories on any subject that come into our minds when we are involved in doing something else; the other is for memories that are being specifically cultivated in order to fill out the description of a particular Steppingstone Period. In both, the memories are recorded with neither commentary nor censorship and especially with no judgment being passed on the memory, neither praise nor blame.

Steppingstones are essentially markings which enable us to retrace the pathways of our experience. The fact that they are markings, however, implies that the area of our experience which they represent includes something more than the markings themselves. Each area includes the composite of events and experiences which took place both before and after the markings themselves occurred, and which comprise a full unit of Life/Time.

This is what we mean by a Steppingstone Period. It is a unit of Life/Time, a period in our life in which many varied experiences are contained. The period as a whole is symbolized to us subjectively by

the partic... which represents the primary and
governin... ...r life. In this sense, each Steppingstone th... ...mbolizes for us and evokes to our
memor... ...stone Period.

T... ...stones which we have made to reflect
the m... ...at, then, to have a further significance
and t... ...n our Journal Feedback work. More
than... ...taneous demarcation of the *qualitative*
units... ...ir existence has subjectively divided itself... ...when we are looking back at the move-
me... ...vantage point, the divisions will be dif-
fer... ...gstones will suggest themselves to us in
th... ...past, so will other Steppingstone Periods
b... ... which our lives will divide themselves
... ...in the future from a new, or different,

...nal Feedback, a *life period,* as we mark it off
...orking with the Steppingstone Periods, is a
...ime which an individual perceives as a gener-
...eriod is governed by a particular life theme, or
...see this expressed at Journal Workshops in the
...erize the present period in their lives when they
... They may say, for example:

...n I am learning how to live in America after emi-

...en I am getting used to being retired."

"It is a ... when I am taking care of my small children, and
wondering what I will do when they are grown."

"It is a time when nothing at all seems to be happening and my
life is at a standstill."

"It is a time when I have passed through many discouragements
finally ending in a new field of employment."

This type of statement summarizing the recent period in a person's life applies also to the Steppingstone Periods. While each of the
periods of the past includes a variety of factors that are operating and

unfolding at different levels and degrees, there is a generalized unity to each period. This unity is given by the underlying tone of events, goals, and circumstances during that particular period in the individual's life. It is expressed in the tonality of what was happening and what was trying to happen in the person's development.

"It was a time when . . ." That phrase serves as a doorway by which we can enter each of the Steppingstone Periods. We wish to recapture for our private experience the atmosphere of the period, the quality of feeling, the tone of energy and striving at that time, the difficulties, the hopes and the anxieties which comprised our inner world and our outer experience during that period.

We begin with our starting-phrase, "It was a time when . . ." As we move from this, the style of the observations that we record tends to be generalized and impressionistic at first. Especially at the beginning as we are reestablishing our contact with the period as a whole, our first Journal entries tend to deal with the underlying tenor and atmosphere of the time. As we continue, however, the reconnections of our memory become progressively stronger and more definite, and they enable us to enter more deeply into specific events. It is at this point that our work with the Steppingstone Periods feeds into the other Time-Stretching exercises and builds the cumulative effect of Feedback Interplay.

We now take our next step in these Time-Stretching exercises. We begin by returning our attention to the list of Steppingstones which we brought together. Each Steppingstone refers to an actual event in our lives, and it also is part of a larger, encompassing time-unit in which many other events are contained. The individual Steppingstone is an indicative marker of the time-unit as a whole. It expresses the tone of the Steppingstone Period as an encompassing qualitative unit of our Life/Time.

Eventually our goal is to enter and explore each Steppingstone period. Since that is a large task, we proceed toward it gradually, working in one Steppingstone period at a time. As we do this, we are learning a procedure that will enable us to work continuously in each of the Steppingstone periods on our present list as well as those that will emerge from future exercises.

Our first step is to choose the Steppingstone period with which to begin. While it might seem logical to start with the earliest period in our lives, we have found that Steppingstone work is more productive when we proceed qualitatively. We start therefore with a period which seems to us to have played an especially significant role in the movement of our life.

Selecting a Steppingstone Period

In our quietness now, we reread our list of Steppingstones to see whether there is any single Steppingstone Period which, because of its meaningfulness for the transitions of our life, stands out from the others. Whether it was a period in which we felt successful, or happy, or fulfilled is not relevant. It is important rather to choose as the first Steppingstone Period one in which the most formative events were taking place.

Choose a time when possibilities were opening for you, when alternatives were present in your experience, and when critical decisions were being made, or were being left unmade. If the consequences or implications of those decisions and the events deriving from them are still being felt in your life, that is a good indication of a Steppingstone Period worth your attention. You will find that it is especially valuable to choose a time-unit in which you have serious questions about your behavior and its attendant circumstances. It is good also to choose a period that held fertile possibilities that seem not to have been adequately fulfilled. Bear in mind, however, as you reopen the past periods of your life, that this work is not to be done judgmentally. We are to give ourselves neither praise nor criticism, but we are to make neutral observations of our life, being as objective as we possibly can about the subjective experiences of our life.

It may be that as you are going over your Steppingstone list you will feel that there is more than one Steppingstone Period that would be fruitful for you to explore more fully. Take note of them and set up a format for working with them at a later time. One good and helpful practice we have found is to set up a fresh page within the Life History Log for each of the periods that suggest themselves to us from our Steppingstone list as being valuable for our future work. That way we concentrate our attention on the Steppingstone Period which we have chosen as being of primary importance; but it also leaves us free to jot down on those sheets whatever thoughts and memories come to us spontaneously while we are working in the Time-Stretching exercises.

Later we can return to those pages and complete our exploration of all the Steppingstone Periods that call for our attention.

Exploring the Steppingstone Period

Having decided upon the Steppingstone Period, our next step is to place ourselves in the atmosphere of that time in our lives, with our workbook open to the Life History Log. We begin by reexperiencing the events of that time in their general aspect, gradually enabling our perceptions of the past to become more specific and definite.

We sit in stillness and close our eyes. Our breathing becomes slower and softer. We become quiet inside ourselves, letting our minds move back to the time of the Steppingstone Period. We do not deliberately try to recall any specific event, but we let ourselves *feel* into the atmosphere of that time in our lives. Gradually the atmosphere of that past time becomes present to us, and we feel the tone and quality and the circumstances of that period in our experience. Now we can begin to record and describe the general aspects of what was taking place in our life at that time.

"It was a time when . . ." Since that phrase is the doorway through which we re-enter the Steppingstone Period, we place ourselves there, and then begin to write, filling in, bit by bit, the relevant pieces of information. With concise statements, we indicate the type of events that were taking place at that time in our life. In general terms we say what was happening, give the tone and the quality of the circumstances, of our inner life and of our environment. "It was a time when . . ."

What are some adjectives that come immediately to your mind to describe the period as a whole? What are some brief phrases? Write these down. If the movement of events was reflected in markedly different phases within the period, indicate this with the various adjectives that you use corresponding to each sub-unit of time. The nature of the changes that took place is an important aspect of the period and should be reflected in your entry.

Perhaps a metaphor or a simile comes to your mind to describe the content and the movement of the period. "It was a time that was like . . ." Record whatever you now feel it to have been like. Permit yourself to be free and impressionistic in the metaphors that come to you regarding that time in your life. The freer you are, the more fully they will reflect your nonconscious perceptions of that period.

As your eyes are closed, as you reenter the period and feel its atmosphere, you may find yourself moving to the twilight depth of the psyche. At that level, images may present themselves to you, visual or nonvisual images in various sensory forms, that will reflect the tone of your experiences during that period. Hold yourself open to these twilight imagery perceptions and record them directly as they come to you. Do not edit or interpret them, but simply describe them as you perceive them. Here, in the Steppingstone section of the Life History Log, when at a later time you read back to yourself these instances of Twilight Memory you will find the memories that come in this way tend to have a sensory reality that helps place us in the atmosphere of the Steppingstone Period that we are seeking to reenter.

What you have written up to this point about the Steppingstone Period is of a generalized nature. Now you can begin to become specific. What do you recall of the feelings you had about yourself at that time? Briefly describe the kind of person you were then. If there were ambiguities, or uncertainties, or variations in the kind of person you were, describe them. If they changed from time to time in varying circumstances, indicate the nature of the changes and how they took place.

What was your attitude toward life at that time? Did you have any particular beliefs about your personal destiny, favorable or unfavorable, fortunate or unfortunate? Did you have any intimations about what life might hold in store for you? Did you have any special hopes or plans for your personal development? Did you have any strong religious beliefs or commitment to any social group or teaching? Did you have a philosophy of life? Was there a particular attitude you had at that time that guided you or set the tone for your actions?

These attitudes and images of life are fundamental to our experience, but it may not be easy for us to recall them and describe them when we are beginning to re-create a Steppingstone Period. Many of us will find that it is easier for us to remember the specific contents and events of an earlier time in our life when we are asked about them directly. Then, as a by-product of many cumulative memories, the feeling-tone of our underlying attitudes will come together and the composite picture of our life will reestablish itself.

With this in mind, our next step is to follow the checklist of the

Journal sections as we did in the Period Log so as to stimulate our memories with respect to the specific contents of the period. When we have done that, we may wish to return to these general and yet basic questions regarding the subjective attitudes we had in the past. At that point, also, having reconnected ourselves with our past by reactivating our memory of specific events, we will find that we have a much fuller awareness of our earlier attitudes. After we have worked in the detailed contents of the period, therefore, we will be stimulated to return and enlarge our original descriptions of the Steppingstone Period.

Journal Checklist

We turn now to our checklist of Journal sections, which serves as our basic guideline for recapitulating and exploring the time-units of our life. We follow the same procedure in using it as we did when we worked in our Period Log. At this point, we may work with the Journal checklist more closely and in greater detail, using it also as preparation for the dialogue exercises. It will, as a matter of fact, be very helpful for us to return to this phase of the Time-Stretching exercises after we have carried through the sequence of dialogue feedback exercises as they are described in later chapters. At that point, having more experience in the use of Journal Feedback techniques, we shall be able to work in greater detail and to expand the range of our work in the Steppingstone Periods. But it is good to begin and set the base for our later work by following the outline of the Journal checklist with respect to the particular Steppingstones Period we have chosen as our present focus. We may answer the following questions briefly at first and progressively expand them. Later we may cross-reference them in the Journal section for which they are relevant. (Note that we are working in the Life History Log and that the questions in the Journal Checklist given below are to be read in the context of reconstructing a period in our life.)

1. *Dialogue with Persons.* During this Steppingstone Period were there significant events or relationships with persons who have an inner importance to us in the unfolding of our life? It is easy to recall in this regard the dramatic encounters of love or anger or abrupt changes that took place, but we should not over-

look the more prosaic, everyday relationships that continued through the period.

2. *Dialogue with Works.* Were there any outer activities that became a focus for our energies in a way that held an inner meaning for us? These artworks may be of many kinds, and may include works that were carried through to completion during the period, works that were begun and were left incomplete, and also works that were conceived and planned but were not actually started or given an external form.

3. *Dialogue with the Body.* Were there occurrences or situations during this period that were especially concerned with your relation to the physical aspect of your life? This may include illness, health programs, sensory pleasures, contact with nature, sexuality, athletics, drugs, indulgences, and addictions of any kind.

4. *Dialogue with Society.* Was this a period in your life when you were deepening or changing your relation to groups or institutions that have a fundamental connection to your existence? Were you reconsidering old allegiances to country or religion or political party? Were you redefining your identification with your race or your family or social group? Was it a time when events took place in history that involved you in serious questions of personal commitment? Did you find yourself during this time deeply involved in literary or artistic works of past or present time, the artworks of others that brought you into profound consideration of the nature of human existence?

5. *Dialogue with Events.* Was this a time when unexpected, and often unexplained, events took place in your life? Were there situations in which it seemed that life was testing you either with pain, as with physical accidents, or with pleasure, as with unusual good fortune? Were there especially difficult or challenging circumstances during this period, outer and inner pressures that forced you to come to closer grips with the riddles of human existence?

6. *Dream Log.* Do you remember having dreams during this period that stood forth with special force and had striking

impact on you? The strength of these might be great enough to cause you to remember them even if you did not record them at the time. On the other hand, many people have kept an unstructured diary at various points in their life in which their dreams are recorded. If you kept such a diary, it may be valuable to consult it now when you are working on your Steppingstone Periods, especially with respect to your dreams.

7. *Twilight Imagery Log.* During this period do you recall having waking visions or other experiences at the twilight level of consciousness? Were there any that had a major impact upon you and influenced your decisions or other actions at the time? As you consider these experiences in the retrospect of the events that have taken place in your life since that time, do any of them seem to have had a prophetic quality, or a symbolic meaning for your life which now suggests itself to you? Consider their inner correlation to the movement of your life.

8. *Inner Wisdom Dialogue.* What experiences do you recall in which you recognized a profound truth of human existence that was new to you at that time? Perhaps you did not reach an ultimate answer then, but the question has continued to stir inside of you. Who were the persons who played the largest role in stimulating and deepening your thoughts and feelings at that time? Were they individuals with whom you had direct contact in your life? Were they persons from history whose books you read or whose lifeworks you studied? Or were they persons whose reality lies beyond history in the symbolism and teachings of a great religion or philosophy?

9. *Intersections: Roads Taken and Not Taken.* During this period of your life did you come to crossroads of decision that affected the course of future events in a fundamental way? Perhaps it was an intersection in your life path that depended upon an act of decision which you yourself made. Or perhaps it was an action which you failed to take, which was to that degree a decision made by omission. Perhaps it was an intersection in your life in which the decisive factor was not left within your discretion but was forced upon you. In either case it was a crossroad in your life and the fact that one road was actually taken for whatever reason meant that another road was not taken. Has

that untaken road remained a possibility of life that has not been lived?

As you consider these situations of intersection in your life, it is especially important that you perceive them and describe them without judgment. Do not record either criticism or praise for the actions you took or for the circumstances that were forced upon you. There is a special value, however, in recognizing them and in describing as objectively as possible the ambiguities of life that were contained in them. To be able to reenter the intersections of past periods of our lives gives us access to the unlived possibilities of our existence which the future may still give us an opportunity to fulfill, albeit in a different form. When we are writing these basic statements of the contents of a Steppingstone Period, it is best that we describe the Intersections briefly at first, but that we call upon as much quiet awareness as we can muster to enable us to recognize their existence in our life. We wish simply to perceive and to list as many crossroad situations in the Steppingstone Period as we can, but we do not amplify them here. We leave that to the next phase of the Time-Stretching exercise for which they provide a main starting point.

When you have made the entries in the Life History Log that were triggered by this checklist, you will have covered the main factors in the period. Do not at this point review or edit what you have written. Let yourself, rather, sit in quietness and continue to feel with increasing depth the atmosphere of the period, as we prepare to continue our work with the Life/Time Dimension of our experiences.

Remembrances

Often, when we are working in the feedback exercises, we find that memories are stimulated that call our attention to areas of our life which had lain buried and hidden within us. Memories which people have felt to be blocked and beyond recall are quite frequently activated by the interior movement that is generated by our active Journal work. They are spontaneously remembered while we are in the midst of a Journal Feedback exercise that deals with some other aspect of our life.

At such times we do not wish to be sidetracked and drawn away from the work in which we are engaged, but we also wish to retain the memory that we have inadvertently unearthed. The Life History Log serves as the section where we record the memory briefly, while we remain free to continue with the exercise in which we were working. At a later time, we can return to it and enlarge our experience of that past experience, reentering it and expanding it in further feedback exercises.

We have found that the more a person uses the *Intensive Journal* workbook, the more he or she will activate memories that were thought to be blocked and covered by psychological amnesia. The fact that the memories were not deliberately sought seems to increase the remembering. We use the Life History Log as a place where we record these memories while we continue with whatever Journal exercise we were engaged in. We hold the memory there until the time comes that it is convenient for us to reenter it and move it further.

The second subsection in the Life History Log has another function of memory. It is the place where we describe each of the Steppingstone Periods. Very often remembrances that come to us out of the blue, and are recorded in the first subsection as a casual memory, eventually serve to help us recall the contents of the Steppingstone Periods that we have forgotten. But a memory that comes to us when we are engaged in something else may be just the right Feedback Lead that we require to call our attention to a particular Steppingstone Period that we would otherwise have overlooked. In this subsection for Steppingstone Periods there may eventually be a number of smaller subsections for each of the periods on our Steppingstone lists. As we work in our Journal over time, we find that we are easily able to reenter Steppingstone Periods that we did not think we remembered and that we are able to record memories and awarenesses of things we did not think we knew.

Before Moving On

Having begun the detailed exploration of our Steppingstones, we can now take a further step in our Time-Stretching work. The entries we have made in the Steppingstone sections become a center point from which we move in two directions of Life/Time. In the Life History Log we move back into our past, recalling and recapitulating the experiences that comprise the Steppingstone Periods of our lives. We draw on all the sources of memory that are available to us in our effort to feed the data of our lives into our journals. As our life data come together to form the collages of our Steppingstone Periods, they gradually give us a perspective of our lives. At the same time that we recapitulate our past, we explore the possibilities of our still unlived future. We find that the key to our future lies in the Journal section for Intersections: Roads Taken and Not Taken. These two sections, the Life History Log and Intersections, are the heart of the Time-Stretching work that we do in the Journal. The list of Steppingstones serves as a hinge for us, a life-hinge by which we can swing back and forth between our past and our future, expanding our relation to our Life/ Time as we do so. We shall now first describe the qualities and contents of the two Journal sections, the Life History Log and Intersections, and then proceed to the steps by which we use them in the Time-Stretching exercises.

9

Intersections: Roads Taken and Not Taken

Our life is like a road that passes through many environments. As conditions change, it varies its style of movement. But it remains the one road of our life.

The work we do in this section of the Journal takes us into the very midst of the movement of our lives. With it, we place ourselves back in those experiences that brought us to a point of transition, to an intersection in our lives, where a change of some kind became inevitable.

Some of these changes took place because of decisions which we ourselves made. Others took place because of decisions that were made by others, or that were forced upon us by the impersonal circumstances of life. However they occurred, they were particular experiences which determined the direction and shaped the contents of our lives from that point onward. Their effects were felt throughout that unit of Life/Time, the period which began at that crossroad and continued at least until we came to a further point of intersection. Now we reenter those moments of crossroad, not to judge them by hindsight but to reconnect ourselves with the inner movement of our lives and thus to give ourselves access to the possibilities which they contain for our future.

Roads Taken and Not Taken

Basic to the exercises of this section is the image of the road. Our individual life is like a road that passes through many environments. As conditions change, it varies its style of movement. It takes detours. When necessary, it moves very slowly and cautiously on a broken roadbed. It shifts its direction or moves in circular paths in order to avoid mountains and other obstacles. Through all its changes, however, the road remains itself; so does our life maintain its identity by sustaining the inner continuity of its movement despite all the variations and cycles through which it must pass.

Working in the dimension of Life/Time, especially as we use the Steppingstones, we place ourselves back on the road of our life so that we can develop an inner perspective of its movement. Retracing our Steppingstones has the effect of marking off the lines of continuity in our development. We can see where we are, and we can follow the succession of events by which we came to the present situation of our life. We also recognize the points along the road of our life where we came to intersections, and where we had to choose which road to follow. Very often, at those moments of choice the signposts were unclear. The information available to us was very limited, and we had no way of knowing what sort of terrain lay farther along the road we would choose. Very often, also, we had to make our decisions in the midst of the pressures of events, while traveling at full speed and without an opportunity to stop and study the alternate possibilities. Of necessity then, we have all made many blind choices at the intersections of our life.

As we pause now to consider our life in retrospect, we recognize that the choices we made at those intersections left many potentialities untouched and unexplored. We discern that there are, in general, two kinds of roads in our life: the roads we have actually traveled and the roads we did not take. What we found on the roads that we traveled is now known to us, for it is this that has comprised the contents of our life. What was to be found on the roads that we did not take, however, is not known to us. Those untaken roads contain the experiences of our life that have remained unlived. In one sense they are now beyond us, like river water that has flown out to sea. But in a deeper sense they still contain many possibilities of life that are still present and available to us; it is these that we now have the responsibility to explore.

These unlived possibilities of life have never been given their chance; yet many of them have been carried silently in the depth of us year after year waiting for a new opportunity. They are capacities of life that were bypassed because of the pressures of our existence, but

Our unlived possibilities of life (Roads not Taken) have never been given their chance but are often carried silently within us waiting for their opportunity.

many of them retain the strength of life and await the *appropriate moment* for being given form and expression. Any new life they are to have, however, is dependent upon our remembering them and finding them in the depth of ourselves, so that they can be reactivated now in a new context. The primary purpose of working in Intersections is to give us the means of doing this.

We begin by making an open-ended list of all the Intersections, all the Roads Taken and Not Taken, that we can think of in our life as a whole. We can follow the list of Steppingstones in reminding us of Intersections at various points in our life. We do not restrict this list to the particular Steppingstone Period that we have chosen to elaborate, but we draw for the list from the whole of our life. That being the case, we can assume that we will not recall all of the relevant Intersections at once. That is why we keep our list open-ended. We will likely remember additional Intersections at another time, and we can then add them to our open-ended list. Take some time now to turn to your Journal Workbook and begin to list your Intersections. Be sure to date your entry.

Our Life Potential

Considering the unlived potentials of our life is reminiscent of an event that took place in the nineteenth century when an ancient Egyptian tomb was opened. In that tomb a portion of a tree was found, and imbedded in the wood was a seed. The scientists involved in the expedition planted the seed out of curiosity, merely to see if anything would happen. Behold, after three thousands years the seed grew! It had missed its chance to grow in ancient Egypt, but its strength of life had remained intact, dormant and waiting for its next opportunity.

The parallel is clear between the Egyptian seed and those capacities that have remained unlived on the roads not taken in our lives. Because time has passed them by, we assume that the choices we rejected or waived are now dead, and that there is no longer any potential in them. We have, on the other hand, many indications that projects which we planned but could not carry through at an early point in our life became ripe for fulfillment at a later time. As the author of *The Cloud of Unknowing* states it, "We grow by delays," and for this reason the later expressions of our plans are often more productive and meaningful than they could possibly have been at the earlier time.

It is a question of the appropriate moment. There are often painful feelings of frustration associated with letting a potentiality of life remain behind us on a road not taken. But that potentiality is not necessarily lost to us forever. It retains its energy and its capacity for expression, waiting for the right time and the right circumstances. Often, however, because of the painful feelings of frustration, we try to erase the memory of them. By doing that we permanently deprive ourselves of the energies and the possibilities they held for us.

The natural wisdom of the depth dimension has its own way of reminding us of the unfilled potentials we have left behind. One of these is by our dreaming.

The natural wisdom of the depth dimension has its own way of reminding us of our unfulfilled potentials. One of these is by our dreaming. It is not uncommon to have a dream that takes us back to a time and to circumstances in our life which now seem to be altogether irrelevant to us. Very often a dream focuses on a person who no longer holds any interest for us and about whom we have not thought for a long time. We may assume that such dreams have no significance, that they are only the pointless replay of old memories, and we may ignore them. But dreams of this kind call our attention to an earlier period of our life, to make us aware of some significance that we are overlooking. The dream is expressing the nonconscious awareness in our depth that intuitively knows that something of great importance for our present situation is hidden in those forgotten events.

It usually turns out to be very fruitful to follow the lead of the dream—to return to that time in the past and explore the possibilities and the implications of past events. When we place ourselves back in the period to which the dream is recalling us, we often find that a decision was made at that time, knowingly or not, in which we chose one path and left another untaken. If it does this in an ambiguous way that is easily misunderstood, that is only because the dreaming process has no other means of speaking than by indirect and symbolic allusions. Though we may not be able to recognize immediately what dreams are trying to say to us, we can at least follow in the direction that they are pointing. This is facilitated by the interplay exercises of Journal Feedback, as we shall see at a later point in our Journal work.

The principle that underlies the Intersections section of the Journal is the stimulation of the time-guidance which our dreams and Twilight Imagery seek to give us as expressions of our own deep psychic nature. We are stimulating the movement of these depth processes and providing exercises by which an equivalent intuitive cognition can become available to us through our Journal work whether or not we remember our dreams. Just as dreams and Twilight Imagery take us back down the time track of our life history, so also do the time-stretching exercises. They make it possible for us to explore afresh the decisions and choices we made in the past.

We use the section Intersections: Roads Taken and Not Taken as a vehicle to go back over the road of our life looking for unlived possibilities. We can retravel that road in our Journal work because we gain access to it through the varied exercises we do in the Steppingstones section and in the Life History Log. As we retravel it, we mark off each of the crossroad situations that we are able to recognize.

It may be that, at the time when the actual events took place, we were not aware that we were making a choice, for we did not see the alternatives that were hidden just around the corner. We went to this school, entered that career, took this job, married that person, not being aware of the variety of additional options that were also, though implicitly, available to us. Now we can reenter those situations of the past and explore the possibilities of the roads not taken. We do not let ourselves become entangled in idly thinking about what might have been, but we place ourselves actively upon the road of our life and we reapproach each crossroad situation.

Those potentialities of our life for which we couldn't find an avenue of expression earlier may be at a further stage of development now. When we first felt them as a possibility and had to reject them, they may have been premature intimations of capacities or talents which, though present, needed more time to mature. Or perhaps the external situation was not favorable at that time.

Being rejected, those roads that were not taken may have gone underground. They may have remained out of view, not dead but inactive, resting in a time of latency, fogotten and unobserved, incubating beneath the surface of events. It may be that we have developed as persons so that we are more knowledgeable now, and more capable. It may be that the potentiality we felt in ourselves has matured and is now more viable. It may be that external circumstances have changed so that the moment is now more opportune.

We can reexamine these avenues again now, by exploring equally without judgment and without self-recrimination decisions made by ourselves and made for us by others, choices made and left unmade, roads taken and not taken. By going back to the various intersections of our life and treating them as new starting points, especially by following the roads not taken so that they can indicate the destinations that are possible for us, we draw from our life history those seeds that have not grown in our past but can grow very meaningfully in our future.

10

Time-Stretching:
Backward and Forward

Now that we have an understanding of these two sections, the Life History Log and Intersections, we can proceed with the Time-Stretching exercises. At this point the physical structure of the *Intensive Journal* workbook plays a very helpful role because it embodies in a tangible way the inner space of our lives. It enables us to move about within ourselves not only exploring but changing things. Moving around in the sections of the Journal corresponds to our traveling back and forth through the inner time and space of our life. This capacity and freedom for inner movement is the essence of our Time-Stretching work.

Beginning Time-Stretching

We begin by sitting with our Journal open to the Steppingstone entries. This section is at the center between the other two that are important in the Time-Stretching work because it serves as the hinge for our inner movement. When we turn back to the section preceding it, we come to the Life History Log where we recall the experiences of our past. When we move forward to the section that follows Steppingstones, we come to Intersections where we consider not only the roads we have taken in our past but the roads that we have not yet taken and that may still hold possibilities for our future. The descriptions we made of the Steppingstone Period provide the base point from which we move back and forth.

This is the sense in which it can be said that we are stretching time like a rubber band that is being pulled at each end. We pull it back to encompass the past, and forward to reach into the future. The rubber band itself is the unit of Life/Time that is our Now Moment. It is an atom of time, a unit of Now, whether it is a period of the present taken from our Period Log, or whether it is a period of the past taken from our Steppingstones. As we draw the rubber band back into the time preceding the period, as we draw it forward to reach into the time that lies ahead of it, we are stretching the unit of Life/Time that is our focus, and we are including past and future in the atom of Now. Thus we help ourselves reach by degrees a unitary inner experience of the movement of time in our lives.

With our Journal open to the Steppingstone section, we see our checklist descriptions of the Steppingstone Period. We reread what we have written. As we review our entries, more of the circumstances of that period of our life are brought to our mind. Soon we are able to recall additional details of specific situations. Our strength of memory grows, and increasingly these occurrences of the past become clear to us. They are not only becoming clearer to us in terms of memory, but our emotions are becoming more flexible and freer to write of the past without judgment.

As we reread the checklist entries that we made for the Steppingstone Period, we encourage ourselves to recall the details of any events that took place at that time. As one comes to mind we turn back to the Life History Log, the section where we record the events of the past. There we describe the event as we remember it. It may be a memory of a house where we lived as a child, or an incident that took place there. It may be a quarrel, or an act of love, or a situation that gradually developed during the Steppingstone Period.

As you recall it, let yourself slide back into the atmosphere of the actual occurrence. As much as possible, feel yourself to be there. For the purpose of describing it in your Journal, let that past become your present, although only momentarily. We wish to re-create for ourselves the quality of life of our past so that we can be there for the moment and capture it in the Life History Log. We feel again the smells and the sights, the pains and the joys that were part of those experiences in all their variety. We recall the feeling and the sensations, and we record them without judgment. Take a few moments now to do this using your workbook.

Increasing Awareness

One of the main purposes behind our Time-Stretching work is to give ourselves a very large awareness of what was contained and what was implicit in each of the units of our Life/Time. Thus we begin by turning our attention to the Steppingstone Period, steeping ourselves in its feelings and atmosphere until a memory is recalled to us. Then we turn to the Life History Log to describe our recollection.

When we have completed our entry, we return to the Steppingstone section to reread what we have written there, reentering its atmosphere until another memory comes to us from that period. Again we turn to the Life History Log to make our entry. We do this several times, each time opening up another vault of memory and describing as much as we can.

Sometimes the entries we make in this way are brief recollections. Others are lengthy descriptions and may require many pages before we are satisfied that we have dealt with them adequately. The criterion lies within ourselves. We write enough to permit ourselves to remember and describe all that is relevant to the event. We must satisfy ourselves to know that we have not left something hidden, and that there is nothing that we have censored or falsified. Once again, since the *Intensive Journal* workbook is for ourselves alone and the entries are for our own scrutiny, we are the only judge of whether any particular entry we have made in the Life History Log is complete and truthful.

We can assume that, since our entries in the Life History Log involve a calling back of memories from the past, we will not necessarily remember everything at once. Very often we find that after we have completed an entry and have gone on to another section of the Journal, an additional memory will come to us. We should have no hesitancy about adding that to the original entry. We want to collect as much of the raw material of memory as we can in our Life History Log. Whenever a memory is recalled to us, whatever we are doing at the time or whatever section of the Journal we are writing in, we make a note of it in the Life History Log. This reopening of memory is an important part of drawing ourselves into the continuity and inner atmosphere of our life. For this reason it is good to use the exercises described above as an occasional stimulus to our inner experience.

These spontaneous rememberings can also decide at that time whether it is a memory that will be appropriate to use as a base for a feedback exercise in another section of the Journal. From whichever Steppingstone Period we draw them, we consider all the entries that we make in the Life History Log as potential starting points for further feedback exercises that will enable us to deepen or extend our experience of our lives. In this sense, the Life History Log is a gathering place where we collect as much of the raw data of our lives as our memory can provide, so that we can draw upon it as a factual source for our active feedback experiences as we continue our Journal work.

In the Time-Stretching exercise in which we are now engaged, our attention is focused on the one Steppingstone Period that we have chosen. Up to this point, we have described that period in general, and we have filled in many of the details of our description by following the Journal checklist. We have thus already recorded considerable material regarding that period in our lives. This data now becomes the base for us from which we call up memories of events and situations that occurred during the Steppingstone Period. These rememberings often serve to reopen parts of our life that have been closed off to us.

At the same time that we are doing this, we also wish to open up our past experiences from another point of view. As we are involved in thinking about this period and as we are recalling the meaningful incidents that took place in it, we seek also to become aware of any turning points or crossroads of decision that took place during that time. It is, in fact, not always easy to recognize these intersections in our lives because we are often not aware of their being intersections when they occur. We merely take them for granted and we proceed with the events of our life without considering that alternate paths of experience may also be available to us. It is only in retrospect that we can realize that we were actually at a crossroad of decision.

One of the goals of the Time-Stretching exercises is to open out our past experiences so that we can see the latent possibilities contained in them. Toward this purpose it is very helpful to include the type of recollection in our Life History Log that will have the effect of drawing us back into the total atmosphere of that time in our life. To place ourselves *there* so that we can feel it again, even in a sensory way, tends to facilitate the movement of memories. It becomes easier for us then to reexperience the events that occurred in that earlier time and to recognize the intersections and alternate possibilities that were present but hidden in the midst of the pressures of our life.

For example, suppose that the Steppingstone Period that we are exploring is the time in our childhood when we moved to a new neighborhood. The specific Steppingstone is probably our memory of the actual move that our family made. The Steppingstone Period refers to the surrounding period as a whole, including some of the years preceding it and the time after it. The memories which we record in the Life History Log for this period will thus cover a variety of activities.

It is good to begin the process of recollection with a memory that draws us back into the atmosphere of that time, perhaps by recalling where we lived or a definite event that places us there. We may begin, for example, by describing the old house or the neighborhood from which we moved, and then by describing the new one. We may place ourselves back into the moment of moving to reexperience the feelings we had as we left our old place and friends; we may relive the emotions and events that happened when we began life in the new place.

When we make entries like these in the Life History Log, it is helpful to let our minds and our pen move freely, recording whatever comes to us without our censoring what is unpleasant and without being self-judgmental. This free, unhindered movement has the effect of drawing us into crannies of experience that would otherwise be inaccessible. We find that events that were hidden from memory in small corners of our life now recall themselves to us. There is a cumulative movement in this. One memory begets another. Each entry that we record further loosens the nonconscious levels of our psyche, and thus we increase the fluidity of our memory.

As we do this, continuing in terms of our illustration, we make varied entries in the Life History Log in the course of exploring the Steppingstone event of our having moved to a new area. We will describe memories of places and events and emotions as they occurred just before and just after the actual move. As we write these, our descriptions transport us back into that Steppingstone Period as a whole. While we are doing this, we also let a special kind of memory come to us, the memory of a crossroad in our life experience when we took one path and left the other untaken.

Exploring Intersections

Many different types of such Intersection memories may now be recalled to us out of that Steppingstone period. Some will seem to be of minor significance in themselves, and yet, in retrospect, may speak to us with great significance for subsequent periods of our life. For example, we may have neglected to say good-bye to an old man who was a friend of ours in the neighborhood. That was a small oversight in itself, that road not taken. But in the perspective of our life as a whole it may speak to us of a type of oversight that has recurred in our life from time to time. Now that we recall it, we realize that this *road not taken* has left a painful void within us. It needs to be remedied, but how can we do so now that time has passed? Having recorded it in Intersections: Roads Taken and Not Taken, we now contain it in our Journal and will be able to work with it actively later on. We will be able to carry it to another level of awareness by means of subsequent Journal Feedback exercises.

Other crossroad experiences that may be recalled to us from that Steppingstone Period may have had much greater and more obvious consequences on the practical level of our lives. It may be, for example, that we needed to find new friends and that we formed our friendships with very little information to guide us. We had to choose this individual and not that one, this group and not that one. Whichever we chose, we did so without knowing the consequences in advance. Now, in retrospect, we can see the multiplicity of events and subsequent developments in our life that began at that crossroad.

Perhaps the individual or the group with whom we allied ourselves at that time turned out to be hard working and to have special interests that added to our knowledge. Perhaps it was because of that friendship that we were stimulated to move into the career we eventually chose. Perhaps they were socially very congenial to us and knowing them led to our meeting the person we later married. The consequences may be exceedingly varied, as wide-ranging in their ultimate consequences as they were unpredictable at the time. Now, as we draw ourselves back into the atmosphere of that time in our lives, we turn our attention anew to the road we took at that time. We reconsider it as deeply and as fully as we can. We describe it, and open ourselves to its varied consequences and implications, which the perspective of time now enables us to recognize.

Reflecting upon it, we find numerous overtones and levels of meaning implicit in the decisions we made at the points of intersection in our life. We recognize the results of having chosen the path that we followed; we also consider the unlived experiences that may have lain in store for us upon the road that we did not take. There are Journal Feedback exercises for us to use later in our work if we wish to explore the possibilities of the roads not taken.

Suppose that the group we chose as our friends was one that led us along destructive or frivolous paths. In league with them, we may have neglected our studies, or developed an addiction, gone afoul of the law, and perhaps dropped out of school prematurely. Now, in the context of our life as a whole, we place ourselves back at that crossroad. We recall and describe as much as we can of what transpired then. We know what we found on the road that was actually taken; now we explore the road that was not taken.

Even though we cannot know how the courses of our life would have unfolded had we taken the road-not-taken, there are in most situations a limited number of alternatives that can reasonably be considered to be among the possibilities. We can explore these possibilities and describe them with a degree of objectivity. For example, we can consider the developments that would have followed if, when we were at the crossroad, we had pursued a particular course of study, or if we had entered a particular field of business, or if we had chosen to spend our social time with one group instead of another. Up to a point, the range of the possible consequences of our following each of those paths is foreseeable by us. Barring chance factors, we can project what they might be and describe them objectively in our Journal as the possibilities of our life that lay along the roads not taken.

Chance factors are, however, inherent in our lives, and that is ultimately why it is impossible for us to know what would actually have happened if we had taken those other paths. A large part of each individual's destiny is brought about by factors that are of a chance, or at least an unpredictable, nature. Often it is the combination, or synchronicity, of events that are unrelated that determines the special quality of an individual's fortune. These cannot be known objectively, but they can be explored, even if only in subjective ways and on non-conscious levels.

Using Twilight Imagery To Travel Roads Not Taken

Twilight Imagery gives us a means of traveling along the roads we have not taken. But in using Twilight Imagery to explore the Roads Taken and Not Taken in our lives, it is important not to use it too early in our Time-Stretching exercises. Sufficient groundwork should be done first so that the context of a life perspective will have been established. When you are working with an Intersection in a Steppingstone Period, the best way to begin is to delineate the circumstances of the situation as you experienced them at the crossroads. Set all the facts down as simply and as nonjudgmentally as you can as indicated earlier in this chapter.

When you have done that, describe the path that you actually took with emphasis upon its beginnings and the early stages of its development. At this point, we want to keep our emphasis and focus close to the time when we were at the crossroad.

Having described our decision at the crossroads and its early consequences, we may proceed to the roads not taken. This is inherently a subjective exercise since we are speaking of events that in reality have not transpired. We are dealing with possibilities and especially with our desires and inclinations. There is a significant truth in the saying "that the wish is father to the act." But, when we speak of roads not taken, we are often dealing with wishes that did not lead to an action. At least they have not led to one yet. One of the reasons we are interested in exploring our roads not taken is that they may involve wishes that are valid but whose time had not yet come. Their moment of actuality may be in our future. We are therefore dealing with possibilities that are real to the degree that they reflect wishes or inclinations that have an organic root in the depth of our being. Those seedlings of potentiality may eventually come to full growth if we nurture them patiently and with a sensitivity to the rhythms of our inner development.

We begin by calling to our mind the various roads not taken that we can reasonably believe were feasible at the time. These are the roads not taken that may still be taken in some new form in new circumstances. We list and describe these possibilities briefly. These are all based on our conscious knowledge and our intellectual appraisal of the circumstances at the time. Now we take a further step beyond what we cerebrally know to have been possible. We project intuitively and imaginatively the varieties of possibilities, even those that went beyond our immediate vision of practicality. Perhaps they were not actually available to us in the reality of our life, but our imagination projects us onto that road. Perhaps it was not a possibility at the time; perhaps in being a road not taken it was a road that could not possibly have been taken at all at that time. But it speaks to us now as a deep desire, perhaps as a symbol of some other possibility of life that we might follow. Therefore we let ourselves explore it.

Exploring the Road Not Taken

We close our eyes in quietness and place ourselves out on the road of our life, specifically on each of the roads not taken. We project ourselves forward on each of the roads into the type of situations in which those pathways of experience would likely place us. We let the imagery form and present itself to us on the twilight level. We do not guide or deliberately direct the movement of this imagery. We merely place ourselves in the atmosphere of a road not taken as that now suggests itself to us. And we let the process of Twilight Imagery take it from there, shaping its script with its symbolism of person and action out of itself without our conscious guidance.

By Twilight Imagery we can move along the road of our life through and beyond the intersections. It becomes a vehicle by which we can go in more than one direction at once, exploring the possibilities both of the roads taken and of the roads not taken. We can use it to reopen crossroads that occurred in the past, and it can also guide us in making decisions in the midst of conflict or crisis at the present moment of our lives. While our conscious minds often balk at making decisions and acting upon them no matter how clearly indicated they may be, we possess a deeper-than-conscious resource that strengthens not only our understanding but our will to action. Twilight Imagery places us in contact with this resource, allowing us to experience it directly and draw upon it as a support of our actions and as a source of energy and will power.

Using Twilight Imagery in Decision-Making

In the context of our Journal work, many situations arise in which Twilight Imagery facilitates a difficult decision at an intersection. Using it in conjunction with the Period Log and the Dialogue sections of the Journal, it can be very helpful in adding its dimension of knowledge of facilitating the decision-making process. A simple example concerns a young woman on the verge of dropping out of high school. She was at a crossroad with two clearly marked roads from which to choose, to continue or not to continue with her education.

On the conscious level she knew the negative consequences of dropping out of school, but for various emotional reasons she seemed determined to do so nonetheless. She was a person who was very much in protest against the advice that others gave her, even when she agreed with it. As is often the case with young people who are in a conflict of transition, she was especially in protest against the guidance of older people. The more her conscious mind perceived the reasonableness of what was being suggested to her, the more rigidly her will became set against it. It was necessary, therefore, to have a means of reaching beyond her conscious mind so that her life decisions would not be based merely on her negative reaction to friendly advisors. She needed to reach the deeper-than-conscious levels of her self, not only in such a way as to give her information and insight, but so as to engender an energy and a conviction within her that would carry through her decision by its own power. In the context of her Journal work, Twilight Imagery provided such a vehicle.

Sitting in quietness she closed her eyes, looked inward to the twilight level, and placed herself on the road of her life. Presently she came to an intersection. One road went to the left, the other to the right. They were the alternate roads of dropping out of school or staying in.

"Go down one of the roads to see where it leads and observe what you find along the way. Then you can come back to the intersection and go up the other road. When you have seen what is on both roads, you will be able to make your decision. See if you can do this." Those were her instructions.

The young woman first took the road to the left. This was the road she preferred, the road on which she would be freed from having to go to school. She saw herself walking along that road, laughing and at ease, having fun. She continued up the road when suddenly the scene changed. It became a street in a deteriorated part of town, and there were slum buildings on it. She saw herself in one of the apartments of these buildings. It was a dingy apartment. Apparently she had several children, small ones. She was trying to feed them, but they were noisy, crying, disobeying her, not eating, but pulling down the wet laundry she had hung out to dry in the kitchen. The scene was bedlam for she had become a young harassed mother. She hated it.

Now she left the apartment and returned down the street. It became once again the road on which she had been walking, and it took her back to the intersection. This time she took the other road. It also became a city street, but now it was Park Avenue in New York City. She had apparently continued in school and had eventually become an interior decorator. Her office was in a fashionable store on Park Avenue. Now she herself was emerging in the image. She saw herself opening the door of her store. Elegantly dressed, she was coming out of her store.

Where was she going? "Oh yes," she said, "parked at the curb there was a limousine." She saw her chauffeur holding the door of it open for her so that she could enter and be driven to her next appointment.

With imagery like that coming spontaneously from within herself, there was no need for interpretation, nor for any discussion to help her make a decision. But the imagery did more than give her guidance. Coming from the depth of herself, it carried an *inner knowing* that was self-generated from its own private, integral source. It did not come from others but from within herself. For that reason, it could not be reacted against in the style of her old pattern of behavior. It could only be affirmed. The affirmation, we should note, was not only of a particular decision, but it was an affirmation of her existence as a person in whom decisions could naturally form themselves. The energy and resolution with which to carry it out was inherent in the decision itself. Since it came from within her depths, it was organic for her to follow through with it.

The drawing up of energy from the organic depths of our life is one of the major capacities of the Twilight Imagery process. Coming from the nonconscious levels, it is not inhibited by self-consciousness, nor by our previous attitudes. It merely presents itself, speaking out of its own nature. It uses symbolic forms much as dreams do, but these eventually become self-disclosing. They explain themselves to us without analytical interpretation but simply by their intimate correlation with the actuality of our lives. When we are working in the depth and the continuity of our life history in the Journal process, the symbolic message which the imagery carries for our life becomes self-evident. That is why, when the young lady saw the chauffeur holding the door open to her limousine, she did not take it literally. She did not assume it was an imagery-guarantee that promised her success and affluence if she stayed in school. She understood the message of her imagery rather as a metaphoric way of being told by the depths of her psyche that life will go better for her if she takes one path than if she takes another.

In this unprepossessing way, the Twilight Imagery process gives us guidance with a conviction that enables us to do what our inner nature tells us. It is moving organically from our depths, and therefore we feel no reason not to pay heed to it. The movement of imagery is especially reflective of the potentials of our life and the possibilities of our future. It enables us to see how the future is trying to unfold. For this reason Twilight Imagery is a method that is especially helpful to us in exploring the roads not taken in our lives.

Now we may each individually use the method of Twilight Imagery. We begin by choosing a road not taken that at the present time still involves a decision that is difficult for us to make. In the silence, we place ourselves on that road to explore it and to experience the possibilities that it may hold. We allow ourselves to move along that road, observing all that is at the side of it, and how the atmosphere on it changes. Now we have a key to our decision in the new nature of the atmosphere. If it feels right to us, the answer is Yes; if it feels wrong to us, the answer is No.

We may use Twilight Imagery in this way in the present moment of our life if we are at a crossroad or a crisis where a difficult decision has to be made, and especially when we require the energy and inner resolution with which to follow through in action. In this part of our Journal experience, working with the Life History Log, Steppingstones, and Intersections, the use of Twilight Imagery provides a bridge between the Depth and the Life/Time Dimensions of Journal Feedback. It expands the range of possibilities available to our life. By stretching our contact with the past and future in a fluid and symbolic way, it draws us into an intensive experience of the unity of the Now moment in which all of our life history, what is past and what is still to come, has its immediate focus.

Reconstructing Our Autobiography Over Time

As we work in the Life/Time sections, we progressively reconstruct our life histories. We do not do this all at once, but a segment at a time. We begin with the generalized outline of our life movement when we list our Steppingstones. Then we fill in the details of the past, but always with an active methodology that treats the past as part of the present and opens it toward the future.

We begin the work of Time-Stretching by drawing ourselves into an atmosphere of stillness. Our eyes closed, we let ourselves inwardly feel the movement of our life. We try to keep our judgments and our opinions out of the way. Without commentary, we simply let the movement of our life present itself to us in whatever forms and divisions it wishes. That is how we get the basic listing of Steppingstones that gives us our framework and starting point.

With the Steppingstones as our frame of reference, we begin the work of drawing ourselves deeper into the specific contents of our existence. We sit in stillness with our Journal open to the entries we have made in the Steppingstone section. With our attention directed to a particular Steppingstone Period, we let memories come to us. These will be recollections of our past experiences, and they will also be recognitions of intersections in our life. We become progressively more aware of those earlier circumstances in which, whether by our own decisions or the pressure of events, the course of our life was drawn in one direction rather than another.

We describe these memories and awarenesses as they come to us, writing about them as fully as we can. We than return to the center, to the hinge of our experience in the Steppingstone section, and we sit in quietness again. Always we return to stillness so that our Steppingstones can provide a fresh point of departure from which we can move both back and forward in our Journal, back into the Life History Log to record a memory, and forward into Intersections to describe an experience that we recognize as a time when we were at a crossroad in our life. Thus the contents and potentials of our life become increasingly accessible to us.

The procedures of Journal Feedback begin to operate after we have worked in all the sections of the *Intensive Journal* workbook. We have then completed one full cycle in using it and have adapted the sections and their accompanying procedures to the specific context of our individual lives. The work of active inner interrelationship among the contents of our life as carried by the Journal sections can then begin. Once we have become accustomed to its procedures, we find that the work of Journal Feedback is cumulative and that it has a multiple, cross-fertilizing effect.

The exercises that we carry out in one section of the Journal serve as a starting point and stimulant for exercises that we carry out elsewhere. In this way we find that we are progressively opening out more and more of our life history, and at the same time we are reconstructing our autobiography.

It is a self-enlarging process drawing more and more into itself as it proceeds. When, for example, we are working in the various sections of the Dialogue Dimension, we shall be dealing with the details of our relations with other persons, our work activities, and the contents of physical and spiritual experiences. As we are describing these and are deepening our relationship to them, we shall also be reactivating many memories that are adjacent to them in our minds. When we move one box on the shelf of memory, we cannot help but jar the box next to it. And what is more as we do that we also jar our curiosity so that we cannot help but look into that box as well. Consequently, as we proceed with the various Journal Feedback procedures throughout our Journal work, we find that a side-effect of what we are doing plays a major role in accelerating the total work. But that is inherent in the indirect method of our process. Journal work that we do in one aspect of our life has multiple reverberating effects in other sections of the Journal and therefore in other areas of our life. Specifically, the active exercises which we shall soon begin in the Dialogue and Depth dimension of the Journal, will feed back to the Life/Time sections additional memories and awarenesses. These will become a continuous source of new factual information to be fed into the Journal Feedback process to further expand the inner perspective of our lives.

Whatever the source of this additional life data, we enter it in the Life History Log as it comes to us. We record the entries briefly and without judgment or interpretation, especially since we do not wish to interrupt the feedback exercise in which we are engaged at the time.

We make a concise entry at the moment that the memory is recalled to us. Afterward, when we have sufficient time and opportunity we describe it as fully as it requires. We pursue its further feedback implications. In this way, working indirectly and cumulatively, we gradually draw together, while working in the various feedback exercises of the Journal, the memory data that will fill in our Steppingstone Period and provide the necessary basic information for our biographies.

The process by which we reconstruct our life histories moves in two directions. On the one hand we gather in our Life History Log the facts of memory that are recalled to us while we are working in the feedback sections. We later expand these as life-recollections and increase their contents. We use them to provide the details of each of the Steppingstone Periods and to make us aware of intersections in our lives when we followed certain paths and left other roads not taken. This is the way we fill in the sections of the Life/Time Dimension, thus recapitulating the movement of our lives.

On the other hand, as we gather the data of the Life/Time sections we are also providing ourselves with materials that will serve as starting points for the active exercises we carry out in the feedback sections. This, in fact, is a fundamental aspect of the structure of the Journal Feedback method. All the facts of memory and experience that we collect in the Log sections of the Journal, and especially the data that we draw together by our entries in the Life/Time sections, serve as raw material which we extend and explore in our active Journal work. Having begun the process of recording this data, and bearing in mind that we shall continue to gather it all through our active Journal Feedback work with additional entries that are by-products of that work, we are ready now to begin working with the feedback procedures themselves.

Part 4

THE DIALOGUE

DIMENSION

Introduction to the Dialogue Dimension

We are now at the point in our workshop when we turn our attention to the Dialogue Dimension of the *Intensive Journal* process. Having begun by recording and exploring many of the contents of our life history, we can now take the step of deepening our relation to them and letting them speak to us. Taking as our base the factual data of our past as we have assembled it so far in the Life/Time sections of the Journal, we move toward a dialogue relationship with the meaningful aspects of our life. We shall find that it is not necessary to force any of the contents of our life to speak to us. As we work in our life history and learn the dialogue procedures, we build a context in which dialogue relationships can establish themselves as they become ready.

The work we do in the Dialogue sections of the Journal combines the specific dialogue procedures with all the additional techniques that are available to us from the other dimensions of Experiential Feedback, that part of Journal Feedback by which the mini-processes of subjective experience can cross-fertilize one another within the context of each person's life. Together they have a cumulative effect, activating potentials and crystallizing decisions at a deep level that bypasses psychological analysis. The momentum and continuity of the Journal Feedback process evokes an awareness of inner direction that is deeper than consciousness, and this is articulated in the dialogue scripts.

When we reread our dialogue scripts, it is not uncommon to find that information that is significantly new to us has been stated in them or to recognize that attitudes of long standing have been transformed in them—and in our own handwriting. These cumulative results do not arise of themselves, however, but are the outcome of a definite sequence of procedures in our use of the various dialogue sections. It is important that we follow these carefully and that we prepare for our dialogue work by establishing a deep enough base in each of the areas where we use it. Then we can reap the benefit of the cumulative feedback effect.

As part of this preparation we should recognize that the term *dialogue* has several levels of meaning in the context of the *Intensive Journal* process. Its most obvious reference is to the specific technique of the *dialogue script* in which we write a dialogue in our Journal; or, more accurately stated, we make it possible for a dialogue to be written. Underlying these written dialogues, however, is the more fundamental sense of dialogue not as a technique but as a *way of relationship.* The dialogue relationship is a mutual meeting of persons, each accepting, speaking out, and most important, listening to the other. This is the I-Thou relationship of which Martin Buber spoke. It is the deeper, more satisfying aspect of relationship between persons in society.

Beyond such outer dialogue, there is the further step of inner dialogue within a person's life. This involves the inner relationship between the separate aspects of an individual's life. Often the various aspects of a person's life proceed as though they were out of contact with one another. In the familiar phrase, it is as though the left hand does not know what the right hand is doing. One of the important functions of the *Intensive Journal* process as an integrative instrument is that it provides a unifying field and numerous techniques by which the diverse aspects of a person's life can be brought into relation to one another. This is the condition of wholeness, the integral relation of the parts to the whole of the life. It is a quality of *inner relationship* that enables the varied facets of an individual existence to change and move and develop in relation to each other. It is, in fact, a multiple dialogue taking place within the unfoldment of a life.

This is the broadest sense in which the term *dialogue* may be used. As a major goal of our work, it refers to the encompassing dialogue

The dialogue relationship is a mutual meeting of persons, each speaking to the listening to the other. This is the I-Thou relationship of which Martin Buber spoke.

which we seek to establish between our inner self and the whole unfolding movement of our life. This is an ongoing dialogue which we seek to maintain through all our daily experiences. As we become attuned to it, it enables us to deal with our immediate and pressing problems in a large and open-ended context. It becomes an intimate inner communication carried on continuously in a variety of forms between our conscious self and the nonconscious mini-processes of our individual unfoldment.

As we turn now to work in the dialogue sections of the Journal, we are beginning the large process of establishing an inner relationship with all the significant areas of our lives. We shall do this a step at a time, first drawing upon the facts of our life history as we have described them in our entries in the Life/Time sections, and then proceeding with the additional entries we make on a current basis as we continue with our daily use of the Journal. We draw upon our past experiences and upon our unfolding present for the life material that we feed into our dialogue process. We take the facts of our life experience as our starting point, and by means of the exercises of our Journal work, we reenter those experiences so that from various vantage points they can speak to us and guide us with respect to the future conduct of our life. Section by Journal section we shall establish a working relationship with each of the aspects of our life as we carry out the basic dialogue exercises and as we learn the procedures for continuing them.

11

Dialogue with Persons

We begin the active work of Journal Feedback by turning to the section *Dialogue with Persons.* (As always, refer to the sample workbook in the Appendix.)

This is the aspect of our Journal work in which we focus our attention upon our relationships with other people. We do not do this in order to analyze our interpersonal relationships, but to open them and to draw forth the potential in them. We are already familiar with the external aspect of our relationships, but our dialogue exercises enable us to reenter them from an interior point of view. This places us on the inside of our life situations so that we can open them from within, as a bud unfolds. Thus we establish an inner relationship to the people who are significant in our life as we work in Dialogue with Persons.

As we proceed in our Journal work, the persons with whom it is meaningful and necessary for us to carry out dialogue exercises will be indicated to us by the events and circumstances that arise in our life. As we start our dialogue work, however, it may be difficult for us to decide who should be given priority. Who would it be most beneficial for us to meet in dialogue? Who should come first? The primary criterion as to the persons whom we choose for our dialogue exercises is that they be individuals whose existence, as well as actions, has an impor-

Death ends a life, but it does not end a relationship.
ROBERT ANDERSON

tant bearing on our life *as we experience it from an interior point of view.* Our relation to them may be one in which we are actively engaged in the present, or one that took place in the past. It may have been a relationship that was difficult and brought problems into our life, or one that was pleasant and fulfilling.

We know by the strength of our feelings, by our intuitive and emotional perceptions, whether our relation to a particular individual has an inner importance for our life. Especially we know by the magnetic way that we are drawn into the relationship, and by the degree to which we find ourselves thinking about the other person, either with pleasure or anxiety, when we want our mind to be on other things.

Whatever our opinion of that person, whether we love them or like them or merely respect them or do not like or respect them at all, our nonconscious feelings make it clear that their existence matters to us, inwardly if not outwardly. Our emotions give us criterion enough to judge their inner importance for our life.

What do we mean when we say that a person has an inner importance for our lives? It may or may not include actual time that we have spent or will spend with them on the external level of life. But it does mean that we feel that that person has an internal significance for us with respect to aspects of our lives that are still seeking to unfold. That person whom we meet externally represents to us something that is still to come to fruition within ourselves. Therefore, he or she awakens intimations of greater meaning in our lives and we are drawn to the person.

Relationships that are based on direct and intuitive attractions may easily be analyzed away in terms of *projection,* or *transference,* or some other interpretive category. Those analyses are correct as far as they go; but it is important for us to recognize that when a person is drawn to another by a strong attractive force, the seed of the person is reaching out to a new avenue of experience. Beyond the analytical factors which are obviously there, the relationship contains possibilities which his or her growth requires him or her to explore. The felt attraction expresses an intimation of the fact that the person to whom he or she is drawn embodies an aspect of his or her life experience which future growth requires in some form.

Whether it is to be a harmonious relationship or one that will eventually be painful, we feel drawn to add this further experience to our existence. There is an inner urge in this that reaches beyond pleasure or pain, and beyond prudence or folly. It is the direct sensing that this new experience is in some to-be-discovered way an integral part of our unfolding life. We know that we shall have to live it regardless of consequences. Using the exercises of Dialogue with Persons, however, we can enter into such relationships within the context of the Journal so that, without analyzing them away, we can explore their possibilities and at least prepare ourselves for what life has in store while determining whether we actually wish to take the plunge.

Probably the largest proportion of relationships that have an inner importance for an individual's life are those between persons who are in close and constant contact, especially where the relationship has an objective as well as an emotional content. This is the case between parent and child, between siblings, or between relatives within a larger family unit as uncles and cousins. It is also true for persons who have had a close friendship over a long period of time, especially where the roots of the friendship reach back into the adolescent period of development. In such extended relationships between persons, the closeness of the repeated contact—the frictions as well as the harmonies—give the relationship an inherent and unavoidable importance in the individual's life. It becomes an integral part of the house of one's existence, like the walls and the windows. They may not be large in relation to the whole, but if they are allowed to fall into disrepair, rainwater will leak into the whole building.

We thus find that the personal relationships which call themselves forth to be explored and extended in the section Dialogue with Persons are often relationships that reach back into our past, and are not in the forefront of the current involvements of which we are aware. The persons who become the subjects of the most fruitful exercises in this section are often individuals whom we have not seen in many years. Quite often, also, they are persons who are deceased, and that fact places no limitation on the importance and the vitality of our inner relation to them.

Persons who have been an integral part of our inner life retain that importance whether or not we were fully aware of their meaning to us at the time of our close contact with them. Often we find that such relationships have opened a possibility within us, but that their promise has not been fulfilled in the course of our lives. Consequently we all carry around within ourselves the traces of relationships that have unfulfilled potentialities.

In the motion picture, *I Never Sang for My Father,* there is a line that expresses the essence of the work that is done in Dialogue with Persons. At the point in the story where his father dies, the main character says, "Death ends a life, but it does not end a relationship." The implication of this, which we experience as a fact in our Journal Feedback work, is that relationships have lives of their own. They carry potentialities which press us from within until, either inwardly or outwardly, they are resolved or fulfilled or completed. The fact of relationship is its own reality.

Beginning the Dialogue: Listing the Persons

We begin our work in this section by drawing together a list of those individuals with whom we feel our relationship, past, present, or future, warrants further exploration. There are two primary criteria for those whose names we place on this list. They are, in the first place, persons with whom we feel a connection of inner importance in our lives. And, in the second place, they are persons with whom we feel our relationship has some further step of development or clarification that needs to be taken. Our Journal exercises make it possible to take that next step and to explore the future possibilities and implications of the relationship.

Relationships of inner importance to an individual's life are often elusive and difficult to define, but we feel their emotional pull and their meaning to us in a way that is more than casual. Such relationships should have an opportunity to move forward and to unfold their possibilities in our lives. That is what our dialogue exercises make possible. Since we are primarily interested in the potentialities for meaning that lie in a relationship, the question of whether it has been pleasant and satisfying, or has been tense and difficult, is beside the point. Whatever it has been, there is something else that it can become. Our primary criterion in choosing the persons for the dialogue exercise is our feeling that there is something potential in our relationship greater than what the relationship has so far produced. Of even greater consequence is the possibility that whatever has been inadequate or conflicted in the relationship in the past will be resolved and drawn toward its next step when we work with it on the dialogue dimension.

We now compile our list of persons with whom we feel it will be meaningful to carry out the dialogue exercises. At Journal Workshops we make it a practice to draw together a full list of such individuals. At the workshop itself we usually carry out the dialogue exercises only with respect to one or two of them, but we extend the list to six or eight or ten persons. By listing them, we have their names before us for future reference so that we can carry out the dialogue exercises with them at a later time when we are working with the Journal.

It is helpful while we are drawing up this list of persons to refresh our minds by going back over the entries we have already made in the Journal. When we were working with our Steppingstones, we were already laying the foundation for this feedback exercise. As we elaborated the Steppingstone Periods of our past, we made special note of those individuals who played a meaningful role in our lives at that time, and now we can draw upon those entries in preparation for our Dialogue with Persons. For the persons who have an inner importance in our life at the present time, we draw upon the entries we have made in the Period Log and Daily Log. For the persons from the past, living and not living, who hold the potentials of an inner relationship with us that may now be carried to a further point of development, we draw upon the entries we have made in the various Steppingstone Periods.

With these resources from our earlier work in the Journal to draw upon, we sit in quietness to prepare for our dialogue experience. We shall have three categories on this list, present relationships, past relationships, and persons who are not now living. This list may be as long or as short as we wish it to be. It need not be exhaustive. We can always add to it. In fact, as we continue to work in the Journal Feedback process, our life experiences will themselves add persons to our list of dialogue relationships.

Now we are working in our silence and in our privacy. When our list is ready, we shall choose for our first exercise a person from the list either from the past or the present, either living or not living. Eventually, as we continue in our Journal experience, we shall enter into dialogue with several of the persons on our list, but let us choose as our first subject a person whom we spontaneously feel to be of current significance in our lives.

DESCRIBING THE RELATIONSHIP

When we have decided upon the person with whom we will conduct our dialogue, we begin by sitting in stillness. We are nurturing a quiet readiness for the inward speech of the dialogue experience. We write the name of the person we have chosen at the head of a fresh page. Now we are concentrating on that person and our attention is focused on the relationship between us as we perceive it. We let ourselves consider the situation in a general way, not thinking of the details, but feeling its tone and quality. Now we write a brief and direct statement describing the essence of the whole relationship. We want to make this a forthright and spontaneous statement that sets forth without embellishment just where things are, how the situation is at its core, between the other person and ourselves.

This statement should be direct and written with a minimum of conscious deliberation. It should reflect our thoughts but also, and more important, our feelings. It should be brief, perhaps two or three or four paragraphs, but it should contain the heart of the matter. It should indicate, though without the details, what is affirmative and negative in the relationship, what is satisfying and frustrating, what has been freely expressed and hidden. If possible, it should also indicate the movement of the relationship. The various phases through which the relationship has passed should be mentioned to show how it has arrived at the present situation. We should freely state where things are now between us, even including some hopes and possibilities as well as anxieties and misgivings.

We describe the relationship *where it is now* even if the person in question is someone whom we have not seen in many years, or if it is a person who has died. Our statement places the situation where it is now. We are presenting the factuality of the present moment as objectively as we can, including in that statement our own subjective feelings and the subjective feelings of the other person as far as we know them. We state it all briefly and in a neutral way, making no judgment. Here it is. This is how the situation and the relationship between us reflects itself when I hold a mirror up to it. Our statement will be such a mirror if we write it spontaneously. It will reflect the essence of just what is seen through our eyes at the moment when we write it. Then it can serve as a base and starting point from which our dialogue can proceed.

Write your statement now, briefly and directly. Remember that it is not to be an exhaustive essay, and it is not to be interpretive. It is to state the heart of the matter concisely. Literary flourishes are not necessary. In fact, it is usually better to avoid them since they may divert you from your primary purpose. (Remember to mark down the date on which you are writing your statement. That can become a very important piece of information, as it may be very meaningful to you at a later time.)

When you have finished writing your statement, read it to yourself. As you do so, you may feel that you wish to make some changes in it. That is good to do, but do not make the changes by editing what you have written. Let the original stand, but make your changes as additions to what you have written. In that way you will preserve the record of your spontaneous feelings and perceptions, and you will also give yourself a valuable reference point for further feedback experiences.

Writing the statement of *where it is* in the relationship and reading it back to ourselves begins to carry us into the atmosphere where the dialogue can take place. This preliminary feedback enables us to make any additions that we feel to be necessary in order to give a truer picture of the situation. More important, it enables us to make whatever adjustments we find to be necessary within ourselves. To make these inner adjustments is an essential part of the preparation for the dialogue exercises. We have to recognize the fact, however, that when we write a spontaneous and uncensored description of our subjective feelings, we are taking ourselves into an area of our inner self that may be strange country to us in which we may feel both unfamiliar and uncomfortable.

When we write our statement of the situation as objectively as possible, we have given tangible embodiment to subjective feelings that may be very delicate. We may be very sensitive about them, much more sensitive than we have realized. It may be that we have been guarding them privately for a long time, even hiding them from ourselves. When for the first time we let ourselves give written expression to emotions which we have been concealing both from ourselves and from others, why should we not expect to feel deeply moved, perhaps shaken, unsettled and even disturbed to some degree?

These emotions are an integral part of the process in which we are working, the process of loosening the soil of our inner lives. Having stirred them, we must now recognize them, give them space and time to be felt, and then record them as part of our Journal Feedback work. As we read the statement back to ourselves we take note of whatever feelings now arise in us. It may be that we were quiet and objective when we wrote our description, but that strong emotions stir in us as we read it. Or it may be that our emotions were churning as we wrote it, and that we are calm now as we read it back to ourselves. Many combinations are possible. Whatever our experience, we accept it. We leave room for it to move through its full cycle. We observe our subjective responses, and we record them as objectively as we can. In this way, we *feed into* the Journal the raw, empirical data of our inner experience, cumulatively gathering it so that it can feed itself back to us at progressive levels of reintegration as we proceed with the Journal Feedback process.

Opening to Possibilities

We come now to a very important step in our dialogue work. Our goal is to establish a deep dialogue so that we can open out the full possibilities and implications of our relationship. To do that, we cannot let ourselves fall back into the old patterns of communication—or non-communication—that have characterized the relationship in the past. We wish to reach a level that we have not reached before, not the superficiality of old conversations that have skirted the issues, and not the repetitious arguments that carry so many relationships in angry circles. We want to get beyond the outer mask to the inner person so that we can speak from an authentic depth in ourselves to the deep core of being in the other. To paraphrase the words of the Prophet, when depth speaks to depth between persons, that is dialogue. The questions is, how can we make it possible for dialogue *truly* to take place in the actuality of our experience?

Our first step is to reach through beyond the accustomed patterns of our relationship to the essence of the other person as he or she is living life. We do this by placing ourselves inside the actuality of his or her life as though we were participating in it from within. Once we feel the other person's life from the inside, we can be aware of what it is secretly seeking to become. Then we can enter into deep dialogue with that person.

To achieve an inner perspective of our own personhood in an earlier exercise, we listed the Steppingstones of our life. Now, to reach a comparable interior view of the person with whom we wish to establish a dialogue relationship, we shall list that person's Steppingstones as we did our own.

To do this, we begin by sitting in quietness and letting ourselves feel the movement of their life as much as we know of it. We may not be familiar with all the details of the other person's life, but it is the outline of the main direction that is of primary importance to us. We place ourselves within their life and we reconstruct the movement of their life just as we did our own. As we did for ourselves, we record their Steppingstones in the first person. The first Steppingstone for them, as for us, begins with the phrase, "I was born." And then. And then . . .

We let the list form itself, and we record it under the statement of the situation that we have written in preparing for the dialogue.

Just as we did for ourselves, we list about a dozen Steppingstones for the other person. When we listed the Steppingstones for our own life, the most important factors were the subjectivity of our intimate memories. The spontaneity with which we drew the list together, and especially our inner knowledge of the events by which our life has un-folded so far. It is probably not possible for one person to have a full intimate knowledge of the contents of another person's life, no matter how closely related they have been. But it is possible for us to feel an empathy for the hopes and the frustrations, the successes and the emo-tions, the times of wondering and fearing and summoning up cour-age. To do this we let ourselves sit in stillness and gradually feel our-selves to be present within that other person's life. We are walking with their feet over the road their life has taken. Thus we write on their be-half, "I was born." And then we recapitulate the next important event in their life that we know of, and the next, and the next until we come to the present time.

You will probably find that in reconstructing another person's life it is more difficult to limit the number of Steppingstones to a dozen because the factors of selectivity and spontaneity are less effective here. Do not let this become an obstacle to you. If you find yourself listing a large number of events or marking points in the other person's life, as many as twenty or thirty, do not restrict yourself. List as many as sug-gest themselves to you, and as are helpful in drawing you into the movement of that other life. List them briefly and simply. A word or a phrase will suffice, just as when you drew up the list of your own Step-pingstones. It is the thread of continuity in the movement of the life that is important here, not the details. At a later time, if you wish, you can describe the details of those Steppingstone periods in the other person's life with which you are familiar. That will be a further step in building your dialogue relationship.

When we have completed our list of the Steppingstones of the other person's life, we settle back into quietness. We close our eyes. We breathe slowly, softly, maintaining a gentle and regular rhythm. Our eyes are closed, and we are looking inward. Our consciousness is directed toward the person of whom we have written. Now we are letting images come to us. These may be images that we see on the screen before our mind's eye; they may be sounds or words that we hear spoken; they may be memories that are brought back to us, body feelings, emotions, or intuitions, that come to us when our eyes are closed in stillness and when our awareness is turned inward and moving around this particular person.

For some minutes we give ourselves over to this spontaneous movement of Twilight Imagery, letting the images take their own form and carry themselves by their own momentum. The immediate focus of the images is the person and the relationship of our exercise, but we do not suggest the content of the images or guide their movement. We let them direct their own movement and take themselves where they will. As we observe them proceeding within us, whether visually, by sound, or in whatever sensory form, we perceive them inwardly. We behold and record them. We then add our perception of the movement of Twilight Imagery to the listing of the other person's Steppingstones and to the statement that we have written describing *where it is* in our relationship. We began with a statement describing our conscious attitude; we then brought together facts of which we are aware in a more general way; and now we have added perceptions that have come to us from the nonconscious depths of ourselves.

We write these imagery perceptions in the Journal, but we do not let ourselves leave the twilight atmosphere in which they came to us. We remain in that deep and quiet place. We feel the movement of the images in their twilight atmosphere. We feel the soft quality of the inner space in which they, and we, are present.

Now, within that atmosphere and with that quality of feeling, we let ourselves feel the presence of the other person. We may see the image of him or her before our eyes. We may feel the person as being present, though not seen. In whatever form it takes, we focus our attention toward the person, and we become quiet with him or her. The two of us are alone in our inward place.

As we are together now in our silence, we feel the movement of our life; and especially we feel the movement of the other person's life. In the twilight atmosphere of our imagery we feel the wholeness of life, and the fullness of time in its ongoingness. We place ourselves again within the other person's Steppingstones as we listed them, and we experience the inner continuity of the life history, what his or her life has been seeking, what it has found, and what it has not been able to find. And we feel again the inner movement of our own life history. We feel the flow of Life/Time as it moves in all of us. Specifically, we feel it moving through the other person, and we feel it moving through ourselves. It carries the person within the process of our lives. It carries the inner person of each of us.

We perceive that inner person and we feel its presence in the soft quietness of the twilight level. We feel that inner person carried on the flow of Life/Time. We feel it in the past and moving toward the future. And especially we are with it in the *place between,* in the Now moment between the past and the future. This *place between* is an open moment in time. It is where the process of a life is fluidly moving, moving out of the conditioning of its past and into a future that is not yet formed. This open moment in our lives is the free space for our inner process. It is the space where the *person within the process* of our lives has its opportunity to give a new shape to our existence. This is therefore the place and the open moment where we can meet with the person within the process of the other's life. In this open moment, the person within them and the person within us can meet and speak with one another without the burdens and without the restrictions either of the past or the future. We meet as we are in our naked being, as we are at the depth of the unfolding process of our lives. There we speak to one another in a totally unconditioned way.

Starting the Dialogue: Speaking and Listening

We are in our silence now, feeling the presence of the other person, and letting the dialogue get under way. We speak to them. We greet them. Perhaps we refer to something that was in the statement we have already written. Perhaps we open an altogether new line of discussion. However it happens, without conscious or deliberate thought, we say what comes to us to be said; whatever that is, we write it in our Journal.

As we write, our inner attention is directed to the other person. We feel their presence, and thus they speak to us. Perhaps we inwardly hear their voice in the silence, perhaps they speak to us via our pen.

However it takes place, we let it all be written, whatever is spoken by each of us. We speak and we listen. The other speaks, and we record it as it comes to us. A *dialogue script* is forming itself.

As we proceed with it, we find that the dialogue writes itself. We may begin by thinking about what is being written, but increasingly we realize that the dialogue is merely using our pen as its vehicle. We freely allow it to do that. We let our pen become the means by which speech takes place between the person within ourselves and the person within the other. We do not guide it. We do not create the dialogue script. We do not think about it and deliberately write it. We let it come forth of itself. And we let it continue to move along its own path wherever it wishes to go. Even when it says things that do not seem to be rational, things with which our conscious mind does not agree, we let it continue. We trust the dialogue script to find its own way and to bring us unpredictable awarenesses.

That is the general approach we follow in enabling the dialogue scripts to be written. With practice they will come more fluidly and will take us more quickly to deep levels of experience. As we work in other dialogue sections of the Journal and become more accustomed to the Journal Feedback process as a whole, many nuances of dialogue will become apparent to us and it will become an increasingly effective technique for us. But the basic steps in the exercise as they have been outlined here are sufficient if we follow them and practice them. Let us at this point, therefore, pause in our reading, go back over the steps of preparing for dialogue. Create your dialogue script now with the person you have chosen.

Concluding the Dialogue Exercise

After we have written our dialogue script we return to stillness. We let ourselves become aware of the emotions we felt while the dialogue was being written. Whatever these were, we record them now as an addition to the dialogue. We make no judgment and no interpretation of them, but we describe as objectively as we can the subjective feelings that accompanied our dialogue exercise from the time that we began it by choosing the person for the dialogue and writing our statement of the situation through our writing of the dialogue script itself. To record this interior movement is an important part of our work.

When we have rested from this, we begin to read the dialogue script back to ourselves. We do this in silence, taking note of the emotions that arise in us as we read it. Are they different from the emotions we felt when it was being written? We record our observations.

Having experienced the feedback effect of reading the dialogue in silence, we may now wish to take the further step of reading it aloud, and especially of hearing ourselves read it. You have two or three paths open to you. If you are at a Journal Workshop or working with a group, you may read it aloud. Or if you wish to keep it private you may read the dialogue aloud to yourself when you are alone. Or you can read it into a cassette recorder, and then play it back to yourself. The latter method has the double advantage of enabling you both to read it aloud and to hear it read, and these are valuable aspects of Journal Feedback. Whether you use the cassette or not, it is important to observe the emotions that arise in you as you are reading the dialogue and hearing it read. All this should be added to the continuity of your Journal entry.

When enough time has passed after the workshop to give you distance from the dialogue script, it is good to read it again. You may see it in another perspective now. As you reread the script, the atmosphere in which you wrote it will reestablish itself. You may find yourself back in the dialogue, feeling the other person to be present as at the workshop. Now the dialogue script can pick up where it left off before. It may continue the line of discussion that was followed in the original dialogue, or it may proceed in another direction and open a new subject matter. In either case, let the dialogue script be free to move as it wishes, extending itself out of its own atmosphere and momentum without your censorship or conscious direction. Let it continue in this way as much as it wishes, and then be free to stop. You can always pick it up again and let it continue when it is ready to move further out of itself. Make sure, however, that you remember to record the date of each of these entries and dialogues so that you can reconstruct the continuity of your experiences when you read them back at a later time.

If we maintain separate subsections within the Dialogue with Persons section, we soon find that a full picture of a relationship-in-motion has begun to take shape. This is particularly true if the individual is one with whom we are currently in contact. Then, in addition to the basic steps of preparation for the dialogue script and the recurrent additions to the script, we make a number of other types of entries, all of which are gathered together in the subsection. We make the entries regarding current meetings, conversations, and events involving that other person. We record also the stream of our thoughts and feelings and the variations in our emotions with respect to them. Sometimes, when we let our thoughts go free as we record them it does not take the form of a dialogue but is more of a Journal soliloquy. Such monologues often carry the movement of our thoughts in a very effective way, and thus the work we do with them within the Journal helps us deepen the level of the relationship.

All of these entries, exercises, inner experiences, and outer events which we record in the subsections of Dialogue with Persons contribute to the dialogue relationship as a whole. It is this that we are seeking to develop with our work in the dialogue sections of the Journal. It is not merely the dialogue scripts that are important, but all the forms of our contact with the other person, inner and outer. As we record these in all their variety, and as we work with them by means of the various Journal exercises, our inner connection to the other individual deepens and strengthens. This is the dialogue relationship. We fill it in with the flesh and blood of daily reality as we work with it in the continuity of our Journal entries and exercises. Working progressively in the interior dimension of our actual life, we may establish deep dialogue relationships not only with those persons who are actively present in our current life, but also those who belong to our past but who are kept alive by our inner experience of them. In Dialogue with Persons and its subsections we work in manifold, ongoing ways to deepen our dialogue relationships with those persons who play or have played a meaningful role in our life.

12

Dialogue with Works

As our work in the Journal proceeds, a pattern of back-and-forth movement becomes apparent. Sometimes we begin at the surface of our life, starting with external events and taking them inward to explore and enlarge them. At other times we begin with our interior experiences which are indefinite and elusive as images and ideas, and we carry them outward in order to give them form and expression. We are constantly engaged in an inner-outer movement, working in the actualities of our lives and then moving to the depth levels for imagination and inner awareness. We go from one opposite to the other. Thus we gradually bring our lives into balance, filling in the empty spaces of potentiality.

This dialectical movement expresses an underlying principle in human development, and it is especially important for the person who is actively involved in creativity. Our growth as persons is an inner process. It proceeds from within us as the seed-potentials of our life unfold and seek to realize themselves; but it can barely proceed at all if it does not possess a specific and tangible task, an artwork, to serve as its external point of focus. The movement of energies, both physical and psychic, comes from within. An outer work, however, is necessary in order to activate it, to stimulate it, to draw it forth, and give it direction.

In this respect, the life of the artist provides a prototype by which we can recognize the necessary movement of energies in an individual's life. The artist is a person who directs energies toward an outer work with the goal of carrying that work to a significant level of fulfillment. The interesting fact is that, as long as the artist is able to work well in relation to the outer object of the work, he or she feels harmonious with it and continues to grow inwardly. When this relation to the artwork breaks down, however, interior life falls into disorder. That is why there is a profound significance in Otto Rank's description of the neurotic person as an artist who has been blocked and frustrated in carrying through his artwork. Our ultimate artwork is our life itself, but it helps a great deal if we have a good relationship with the specific works in which we are engaged. A major goal of the exercises we carry through in the *Dialogue with Works* section is to enable us to maintain a strong inner relationship with the varied outer works that are meaningful to us in the context of our lives as a whole. In this way we may hope to become, in the largest sense of the term, artists-in-life.

Dialogue with Works is the section of the workbook in which we apply the Journal Feedback procedures to those activities in our lives in which our energies are directed outward toward specific projects and goals.

The conception of *works* has a special meaning in the context of the *Intensive Journal* process. It does not refer merely to a job that you have to do, or to a task that is placed as a burden upon you. Having a *work* implies a strong and warm caring, a special interest and concern. It means to be engaged in an activity which you value as something meaningful and valuable in your life, and which you are seeking to enlarge and to strengthen.

A work is a specific project that emerges as an outer activity drawn from an inner source in a person's life. It takes a definite external form, but its meaning and direction come from within the person. It also draws its main energy and inspiration from inner personal sources while serving in a balancing way as the continuing outer focus for the person's activities. In this sense, a work begins in the depth of a human being. It begins as an idea, a hunch, and especially as an urge to bring something new into existence. The basis for a work is always a deep desire, not in the sense of an egoistic or sensual desire, but in the sense of a desire to create something and to bring it to fruition. To have a work is firstly, to have a feeling or a vision of possibilities that may be brought to fulfillment; secondly, to devote oneself to bringing those possibilities into actuality in a way that is as authentic for the work and as satisfying for oneself as may be possible.

The process of growth in a human being, the process out of which a *person* emerges, is essentially an inward process. It involves an inner balancing, an integration, a strengthening of inward capacities, and an unfolding of the self. As we observe the process of unfolding in a person, however, we recognize that it is not altogether inward. It begins within the person, as the growth of a tree begins in its seed, but then it moves outward. The inward process of growth moves in an external direction in order to fulfill itself. It does this because it needs to be embodied in a tangible content in order to fulfill itself in the actuality of life.

We perceive in this also that the process of growth in a human being proceeds by a multiplicity of effects. In order to grow within, an individual needs to conceive and carry out works outside of the self. These outer works thus derive their power from a source that is within the person; but the person draws the strength for his or her future growth from the very process by which he completes his work in a satisfying way. The work and the person, the artwork and the artist, in every field of activity, are thus in a mutually creative relation to each other. Each requires the other. Each has something to give to the other. Each has something to communicate to the other. The relation between a person and his work is a living expression of dialogue.

The format and exercises of the Journal section, Dialogue with Works, are specifically designed to assist the mutuality of dialogue that is inherent in this relationship. Our goal is to enable each individual to focus more clearly on the works that are possible, and to give tangible means of fulfilling them in a way that will extend the inner process of his or her growth as a person.

As we follow the inner relationship between a person and work, we observe two main phases of energy movement. The first is an inward movement of energy that activates the image within the person on which the work will be based. This provides the inner vision that sees the possibility and sets the goal. The second phase of movement is outward, and it extends over a longer period of time. This is the continuing process of focused activity by which the seed of possibility that is present at the outset of the work is nurtured through the cycles of its growth, and is progressively brought to fruition in the form that is most appropriate for it.

In this second phase, the phase of *doing the work,* there is an implicit criterion guiding the work, drawing it onward, and setting the standards for its goal. This criterion is the original image, and it calls for fulfilling the inner possibility of the work, to make the work as effective, as esthetic, as satisfying, and especially, as *whole unto its inherent nature,* as can be.

Beginning the Dialogue: Listing the Works

A good first step to take in preparing for the feedback exercises in the Dialogue with Works section is to draw together a listing of the varied works that have been meaningful to us in the course of our life. A convenient way to gather these is to turn ahead in our Journal to the Steppingstone section and reread the descriptions we have written for each of the Steppingstone periods. For each period we ask ourselves the question: During the length of time covered by this period, what were the projects and activities that were especially meaningful to me and that had an inner importance for my life?

As we ask ourselves this question, we must bear in mind that the works which we are seeking to identify are activities and goals to which we feel an emotional commitment. We *care* about them as we invest our energies in them. Therefore we are not carefree nor haphazard when we are engaged in these works. We do them as well as we are able up to the limit of our emotional commitment and our capacities. To the degree that we care about them in this way and that we seek to fulfill them as well as we can up to their highest possibilities, we are treating these works as artworks, regardless of whether their content is in the fine arts or in the more prosaic aspects of our lives.

As we go back over the Steppingstones to remind ourselves of works that were meaningful to us in the past, we find that our list becomes exceedingly varied. During the childhood periods of our life, the works we undertook were multiple and we quickly lost interest in them. Some, however, left a stronger imprint upon our minds, either because we remained with them for a long time, or because we felt drawn to them and were prevented by the circumstances of our childhood environment from pursuing them further. These works that have made the stronger imprint on our minds are the ones that we should place on our list so that we can explore the possibilities they open for us, lived and unlived.

It is helpful to include on our list projects and goals from earlier years that now have passed altogether out of our range of interest. We merely jot them down, briefly adding a phrase to describe them. When we have drawn our list together, covering the various Steppingstone periods, we find that reading the list as a whole opens a larger perspective for us of the interests and commitments we have had in the course of our life.

As we draw our list together, we should bear in mind the definition of works that we are using. By works we mean the outer activities in which we place our energies as goals or commitments that have an inner meaning for our life. Studying music as a child may be such a work, and stopping it, by necessity or desire, may also be a significant entry in the Journal. So also are our plans of being an athletic star, including the commitment of time and effort, and the success or failure that came with it. Sometimes hobbies that we pursue casually in our earlier years become meaningful work commitments which we treat as artworks. Photography and the childhood experimentations in science are examples of this. Farming and gardening and the care of animals are instances of meaningful works in early years.

In some cases your work will cover an entire field of study or interest, a profession or career as a whole; at other times, it will be limited to a specific task or artwork. It may be farming or horse-racing as a whole; or it may be taking care of a particular stallion. It may be the fields of writing or art as a whole; or simply a particular story or painting. In each case it will depend on how we subjectively perceive our own relation to the work. If you find that the field of work as a whole is of great meaning to you and that a particular artwork within that field is also important, there is no need to make a choice. Record them both on your list. As you proceed with the feedback exercises, they will draw your entries into balance and indicate the best way to proceed with them.

As you go over your list of Steppingstone Periods, many works may come to your attention. Choose those that seem to be the most meaningful in terms of the possibilities of your future. In this regard, your emotions and intuitions can be a valuable guide to the areas of work that have significance for your life. It is good, therefore, to look closely at those work activities of the past that awaken a twinge of sentiment in you when you recall them. Sometimes this sentiment is only wistfulness, but that, in itself, may be an important sign for you. It may be calling your attention to possibilities that are still present in activities which you began in your earlier years, but which you did not carry to completion. The energy of emotion that is attached to these old, unfinished works indicates that they still are alive and relevant. Works of the past which we have neglected or discarded often have very valuable suggestions to make to us with respect to our current work activities.

Stimulating Other Feedback

We often find that when we go back over our Steppingstone Periods to recall the meaningful works of our past, we make ourselves aware of roads not taken in our life that now have come to a new point beyond their earlier detour. We now have new possibilities because, as we have traveled the road of our life we have arrived at a new intersection. We thus often find that we are opening a productive new situation as we recall and reactivate memories of our earlier work activities. New circumstances now provide a new context, and they open potentialities of experience that were not present before. It often is exceedingly fruitful to explore the possibilities of these new developments of old projects by using exercises that involve the other feedback dimensions of the Journal, especially when we work in the Intersections section and use the techniques of Twilight Imagery.

The interplay among the Journal sections based upon past works stimulates the Journal Feedback process and often opens unexpected possibilities for the future. We find that roads that were not taken in the past now become available to us in a fresh context. We were not capable of meeting their requirements at that earlier time, but now, as we have the benefit of our additional life experiences, we can approach them anew. This is one reason why the basic exercise of recalling and listing in our Journals the outer activities that have had an inner meaning to us in the past often leads to valuable new projects. What was old and rejected becomes the seed of future works. The cumulative movement of the exercises of Feedback Interplay enables us to draw them to fruitful, and often to very unexpected, results.

When we have drawn together our listing of meaningful works, we sit in quietness. It is good to read the list through as a unit so that we can have a feeling and a recognition of the range and variation of the works that have been important to us in the course of our life. As we read, we may be reminded of additional works which we briefly began, or toward which we have a strong impulse and which we always wanted to do. We may add these also to our list.

Now, for a second time, we read the list through to ourselves, this time amplifying it. We add brief comments, a word, a phrase, expressing an emotion that is aroused in us or a memory. As we reread our list, we will be taking ourselves back into the circumstances of our lives at the time when we were engaged in each of our various works. Our minds will be stimulated to remember the events and the feelings of those times, and we may now wish to add some further comments and descriptions regarding them.

As memories, thoughts, and additional realizations are stimulated in us, it is advisable to make the entry immediately in the appropriate section. We write our description and our comments in the Life History Log, in Intersections, or whichever is the relevant section. As we do this, it is also good to make a cross-reference in Dialogue with Works so that we will have a record for ourselves of the way that our thought processes were stimulated to move in interplay through the various aspects of our life experience.

These derivative entries may be lengthy in contrast to the brevity of the entries which we make at this point in the Dialogue with Works section. Now we are merely listing the works that have been and are still meaningful to us. We are recalling them to our minds, describing them succinctly, and adding brief comments or specific remembrances of them. Later, we shall choose from our list of works the few that are most significant to us, and we shall direct our attention to these in a full and active way.

Describing the Work

We begin by choosing one of the works on our list as the subject of our first dialogue script. Eventually, as we continue to use the Journal, we will find ourselves drawn by the interplay and the momentum of the feedback method to carry out our dialogue experiences also with a number of the other works on our list. But now, to begin, we choose a work, whether past or present, or a work that we are contemplating for the future, a work which we feel has something further to say to us and a work with which we wish to speak.

Our primary criterion in choosing the work on which we shall focus our attention in establishing a dialogue relationship is not that it contains problems that we wish to resolve. We choose it, rather, because it is a work that seems to contain meanings and potentialities greater than those that we have so far recognized and understood. We choose a work that has a further possibility of development. It will then in all probability also be a work that has something to teach us. When we choose the work for our first dialogue exercise, we bear in mind that this is only the first of a series of exercises by which we shall establish contact with the various works that are meaningful in our life.

Whichever work we choose, whether it is a work from the present, the past, or the future, we begin by making a statement of the situation in which we find ourselves with respect to that work. If it is a piano that we have not touched in twenty years, if it is an ambition that we have repressed since adolescence, that is the fact of the situation which we begin by saying in our statement. If, on the other hand, it is a difficult set of circumstances in our business or at our job, we express that also in our basic opening statement. Our purpose at this point in establishing our relationship with the work is to place ourselves in an honest and realistic position with respect to the facts as we perceive them at the present moment. Whatever the particular work may be, this brief statement draws our thoughts into focus with respect to the present relationship between ourselves and the work.

THE STEPPINGSTONES OF OUR WORK

Having made our statement of the situation as it is at the present with respect to the work that we have chosen, we now go back over the steps by which the work has developed. We are interested in all the important aspects of the work and our relation to it. Thus we recapitulate the Steppingstones that have formed the life history of the work. We list them briefly. Just a word or a phrase with a minimum of embellishment is sufficient. Our purpose at this point is to establish contact with the inner continuity by which the work has been trying to unfold and fulfill the potential of its own unique existence. We are seeking to identify and to meet the person within the process of the life of the work. We therefore begin by listing its Steppingstones as we listed the Steppingstones of our own life, and of the lives of the other persons with whom we conduct our dialogues.

In doing this, however, we do not restrict ourselves to any specific number of Steppingstones. This list need not be a short one. It should be long enough to reflect the full chronological development of the work, and for this purpose it is usually better to include more material rather than less. In this regard, we follow a slightly different procedure in drawing together the Steppingstones of a work than in listing the Steppingstones of our own life where the factor of selective subjectivity is important. For the purposes of reaching the person within the process of the work, we recall all the information we can to mark off the various stages and phases in its development.

We ask ourselves, for example, when did it begin? And we record our answer as a Steppingstone. We write the Steppingstones in the first person on behalf of the work so that we can list the Steppingstones of its life history as the unfolding of the process in the person within the work. There are a number of relevant questions for us to ask. What led to the idea or inspiration that brought the work into being? Was some other person instrumental in bringing it about? Did it come from a dream or some other interior experience of ours? Once the idea was formed, what were the events that enabled it to continue? What difficulties did it encounter? How did it manage to continue? What variations and compromises did it make? Were there long pauses when the work was at a standstill? What was taking place during those seemingly silent times? What feelings have you had about the work and your relationship to it? How has it proceeded in the recent period? What is the situation now?

These questions may serve as your general guide in reconstructing the life history of the work. We must take care, however, not to list the answers to these questions merely as an intellectual exercise. It is important that when we list the Steppingstones we do so not as outsiders to the work, but from a position that is *inside* its life.

To make this interior connection, it is good to stop the movement of our conscious thoughts. We sit in stillness and close our eyes. We let our breathing become slower, softer. We relax our body and let our concerns drop away. Breathing slow, our minds emptied in the stillness, we let our attention turn to the life of the work. We recall its beginnings, its sources, its possibilities, its phases of development, its difficulties. As these present themselves to us, we record them. Thus we gather events and situations that comprise the Steppingstones of the life of the work. They may not come to us at first in their correct chronological order, but we record them as we recall them. Later, as we read them back, we can renumber the individual Steppingstones so that the list will reflect the inner unity of movement in the development of the work.

Having drawn together the Steppingstones of the work, we perceive the continuity of its life history, thus we can recognize the reality of the person unfolding within it. It is this person with whom we wish to communicate in dialogue. We set the atmosphere for this dialogue by loosening our conscious thoughts and going to the twilight level of imagery. We sit in stillness with our eyes closed, feeling the presence of the work as a person. We do not think about it, but we let ourselves feel the work and our relation to it. Now we let images come. We do not direct these images. We do not make suggestions to them. We simply let them come of themselves, totally unguided, and we observe the symbolic forms which they take.

Our Twilight Imagery may take many varied symbolic forms. It may come to us in the image of an individual with qualities that represent the work; or it may come to us as a series of changing Twilight Images that reflect the movement in the life of the work, its past and its future. Whatever these images may be, we take note of them and we record them as part of the continuity of our entries here in the Dialogue with Works section.

We record these Twilight Images reflecting the life of the work, but we do not leave the state of stillness. When the images are recorded, we close our eyes again and sit in quietness. We feel the presence of the work. We feel the images that have come to us. We feel the quality of the work. We feel the quality of the continuity of its life, and especially we feel the inner existence of the work, its goals and its life history. We feel the work as a person.

Speaking and Listening

We remain within this atmosphere of quietness, letting it deepen around us. Since we now perceive and feel the work as a person, there can be a relationship of equals between us. We can actually dialogue with the work. Sitting in stillness and feeling the presence of the work as a person, we speak to it. We address it, greet it, and speak to it with whatever words come to us. Very probably we shall soon find ourselves speaking to it of the things we have written in our basic statement. This is the essential subject matter. But the relationship between ourselves and the work is person to person. It comes out of the quietness, and it proceeds out of itself, reflecting its own nature and its own needs.

We speak to the work and it speaks to us. We record the words as they come to us, as we say them and as we hear them. We do not think about them nor contrive them, but we let them come of themselves and write themselves through our pen. We speak and the work speaks, and we record what is said as the words come to us. It is thus that the dialogue script builds its momentum and continues itself. Once it has begun and has established its movement in this way, we serve merely as the vehicle for the dialogue. We hold the pen by which it writes itself. The person in the work speaks and we speak, and the dialogue carries itself onward. We enable it to be written until it has said all that wishes to be said at this time.

Concluding the Dialogue

When the dialogue script has gone as far as feels right to us, we return to our stillness. We take note of the feelings we had while the dialogue was being written, and the feelings that come to us as we sit in silence now that the dialogue is completed. We record these in the Journal as objective reportings following the dialogue script.

When we have added these entries, we may go back over the dialogue and read it silently to ourselves. We do not edit or change what has been written, we merely read it to ourselves. If further thoughts or feelings come to us, or if we wish to add a comment, we do not insert it within the dialogue script. Rather we add it as an afterword. We also describe the feelings that led us to make this additional entry. Having recorded the series of our thoughts and feelings in this way, it will be clear to us when we reread the series of entries at a later time what the actual movement of our experience has been.

When we have read the dialogue back to ourselves, there may be some substantial comment, thought, or feeling that comes to us. Perhaps it will be a further awareness about what is involved in our relationship with the work. Perhaps we are making a new resolution as to a course of action that we wish to take in the future. Whatever it is, we add that as a further entry.

As we make these additional entries, it becomes evident that the dialogue relationship between ourselves and the work is not limited to the actual spoken and written dialogue. The dialogue relationship involves much more than the dialogue script itself. It includes all the events and feelings, thoughts, hunches, and decisions that form the active continuity of our relationship. It includes also the intensity and the intimacy of the involvement between two equal persons. That makes it a dialogue. The dialogue script is part of this larger dialogue, together with the recording of the outer events and the inner thoughts and feelings that continue to occur in the relationship. All of these entries in the Journal are part of the enlargement of the total dialogue relationship.

After reading the dialogue script to yourself, and having entered your further comments in the Journal, you may find that the dialogue with the work now wants to extend itself. By all means enable it to do so. We very often find that the first segments of a dialogue script serve primarily as an introductory warm-up exercise. Their halting and uncertain movement clears the way so that freer and fuller dialogue experiences can follow. When we find ourselves impelled, after rereading our dialogue script, to make additions to it and to extend it, it is good to follow that impulse. Those extensions which we add to the basic entry are very often the most valuable parts of the dialogue script because they carry the fruitage of the whole experience.

A certain part of what has been described of the above exercise and experiences can be carried out at a Journal Workshop or in your own private Journal experience. (The atmosphere of the group is of great help in deepening the level at which the dialogue script can be written.) But to draw out and clarify our relationship to our meaningful works may be a very large task. It will require more time for writing, reflection, and inner experiencing, more time than the duration of a workshop or a one-time experience permits. In addition, since the works in which we are currently engaged involve us in an ongoing activity, they constantly require new Journal entries and exercises. The writing that we do at a Journal Workshop serves, therefore, to lay the foundation for the further entries and exercises that we carry through as our experience continues. Especially in this section, the Journal work that we do after the workshop is of the greatest importance. For many people the Dialogue with Works section provides the ongoing laboratory in which the contents of their productive activities can be progressively formed, tested, and reshaped.

When a workshop is over—whether a group or your own private time—the momentum that has been generated often continues into the days that immediately follow it. That is a good time to make the additional entries in the exercises which we began but left incomplete at the workshop. For the most part these entries involve further background material, descriptions, and elaborations of the life history of our works.

With respect to the dialogue script, however, it is good to allow a lapse of time before you reapproach it and seek to continue the dialogue. Let a few days or a week pass before you reread the dialogue script. Then, if sufficient time has passed to give you some distance and a fresh vantage point, it may be productive to reenter the relationship and let the dialogue carry itself further if it wishes to do so.

13

Dialogue with the Body

In Dialogue with the Body, we seek to deepen our relationship with the physical world in all its aspects.

Having established a dialogue relationship in our Journal with the persons who are significant in our life and with the work activities that are meaningful to us, we turn our attention now to the physical side of our existence. In the *Dialogue with the Body* section of the Journal (see the Appendix) we seek to deepen our relationship with the physical world in all its aspects, especially those relationships to life that come to us by means of our body.

While the meaningful contents of our lives are *expressed* in our emotions, our aspirations, and our deep inner experiences, they are all *carried* by our body. To that degree, our personal existence is dependent on our body. In a further sense, we make our contact with the world of nature, with music, the physical arts of dance and sports, sexuality and the realm of the senses all by means of our body. The body of a human being is the primary instrument of connection between his personal life and the fullness of the physical universe. It is with our bodies in this large sense as open-ended instruments of connection with the world that we seek to establish a deep relationship in this section of our Journal work.

We may be familiar with the phrase, "The wisdom of the body." Many of us have had the opportunity to experience the presence of that wisdom in our lives in a variety of situations, as when our body has given us warning signals, or when it has spontaneously healed itself. Animals possess this wisdom as their instinctual heritage, and they rely on it. It serves as a self-regulating mechanism for them, telling them when they have eaten enough and copulated enough, when they need to be active, and when they need to rest. It guides their basic biological functions. The complications of living in modern civilization, however, tend to blur this natural wisdom so that not only modern people but even their domesticated pets lose their contact with this primordial source of guidance. One of our goals in building a dialogue relationship with our body is to reestablish our access to its natural wisdom, and to provide the means for this wisdom to articulate itself in forms that can be directly applied in our lives.

One goal in building a dialogue relationship with our body is to reestablish our access to its natural wisdom, and to articulate that wisdom.

The body of a human being functions by principles that are universal in the species, but each individual body is unique. Each begins with a different seed-nature unfolding in its own time in its own particular environment. Each body builds through the years its own life history with its unique combination of growth and illness and activity. Each physical body has its past, lives in a present moment, and moves toward a future of its own. The combination of these for each is unique. Each body has its special continuity of life, just as a person does. And this is the key to our dialogue relationship with the body. The essence of the life history of a body is an *inner person,* a person at the core of the process of the body's ongoing life. This person within the body carries the wisdom of the organic depths, and also carries the direction of the needs of each body's development. When, therefore, we are able to establish a dialogue at a deep level between the person in ourselves and the person in the process of the body, the result may have very profound effects in integrating our life experience.

As we consider the unfolding of our individual existence, we realize that our body is the physical counterpart of our whole life history. Our inner life, our creative and spiritual growth, our problems and our pleasures, all are accompanied by the life of our body. Our experiences of exaltation as well as of pain come to us through our body, and that is one main reason why we are accustomed to think of our body as supremely private. Our body is the instrument for our most intimate relationships and our most meaningful participation in the life process as a whole.

The life of our body parallels the movement of our personal life.

To a degree each of these is distinct in the sense that each has its own principle of unfolding, the physical and the psychological. But they share one another's experience, so that the successes or frustrations of one are reflected in the strengths or illnesses of the other. The life history of our inner, personal existence and the life history of our body are mirrors of one another, but they each have their own style of speech and their own perspective.

To establish a dialogue relationship with our body, we have to make contact with the inner continuity of its life history. In that way we shall meet the person within the process of our physical life.

Recreating the Life History of the Body

Our first step is to recreate as much as we can of the life history of our body. Another way to say this is that we are now going to list the Steppingstones of our physical life in as full and far-ranging a way as we can.

Listing the Steppingstones of our body is a very similar exercise to the listing we made of the Steppingstones of our life. But it has certain differences. This listing is not limited to a small number as in the case of our Life-Steppingstones. In drawing together the Steppingstones of the body our purpose is to give ourselves as broad a view as possible of the continuity and unfolding of our physical life in all its many-sidedness. We are not interested here in pin-pointing the main markers that outline the movement of our life, but in calling to our awareness the richness and variety of experiences, pleasant and painful, that comprise the whole life of our body.

To do this, we let ourselves go back into memory and recall spontaneously past experiences that relate to any aspect of our physical life. We let these recollections come to us of themselves. We sit in stillness, opening the doors of memory, and letting earlier experiences of our physical life return to our mind. As they come to us, we record them briefly. A single word or a phrase is sufficient at this point if it will indicate to us the contents of the memory. Later we can set them in order by numbering them so that we can reread them in continuity. But now we merely record them as they come to us.

These Steppingstone memories of the body may be of many kinds. It may be a memory of standing in a crib crying. Or being tossed in the air by a playful father or a visiting uncle. Perhaps a memory of looking up at a tall adult and thinking how small we are. Or being ill as a child with a high fever. The feeling of thinking you would die of illness. The memory of running in the snow, playing games, breaking a leg, seeing a sunset, being frightened by thunder, discovering your sexual difference, dancing, sweating, swimming, fighting, making love, being in a car accident, seeing a dead person, climbing a mountain. All the varieties of physical experience may be among these memories, and we draw them together from all the years of our life, from early childhood through adolescence and maturity to the present.

In drawing up the Steppingstone memories of the life history of the body, we often find it is helpful to hear other participants in the workshop speaking out their memories, especially when they are similar to events in our own life that we are reminded of. To find them in the life of another person often has the effect of relaxing the restraints that we felt. We are free then to dig deep into ourselves to draw up experiences that may have been tightly packed and hidden beneath layers of inhibition and repression. As others speak, we also are reinforced in accepting the experiences that we have had as being the normal contents of a human existence. Thus we can be assured that we will not be judged or diagnosed for those experiences of which we may have been ashamed. We are free then to draw up memories of the life of our body without any self-imposed reservations, without censorship or self-reproach. (If you are not in a group workshop, give yourself permission to have but not to judge your memories.)

By listing the Steppingstones of our physical life, we recreate the life history of our body.

THE STEPPINGSTONES OF THE BODY

We now sit in quietness and turn our attention back into memory to draw up key recollections of our physical life. We speak our recollections out into the air as they come to us, and we record them on our list in the Dialogue with the Body section. The following are some Steppingstones of the body that were spoken by participants at a Journal Workshop.

I remember being fat as a kid.

Running fingers through the muddy sand at the beach.

We played Doctor, and my grandfather caught us. I felt foolish.

Playing football in high school. Sometimes I was afraid but I loved the contact.

I started to menstruate.

Driving a car fast when I first learned to drive.

Blisters on my feet but I kept on dancing.

The dentist drilling.

Locked in a dark closet. My father yelling.

Seeing the autumn leaves and feeling connected to their colors.

Making love for the first time. Confused.

Turning cartwheels.

Having headaches day after day.

Enjoying sex after many years. A great discovery.

Realizing I was getting old. Walking slower.

Necking in a car.

Jumping on a hayloft.

Being massaged.

Sitting quietly in the park. The sun is very warm.

Smoking a good cigar. I enjoy it. But it makes me nauseous sometimes.

Childbirth. Some I forget; some I remember and feel again.

Fasting. It's unpleasant but it feels good to be doing it.

A hangover.

Being at one with the waves of the ocean.

Cuddling a baby.

Awaking from anesthesia.

Those are some of the Steppingstones of our physical life that we might hear spoken around us at the workshop. We hear them only with our outer ear, for our inner ear is attuned to our own experiences. We continue listing these until we have about fifteen or twenty, sufficient to give us a sense of the phases and changes through which the life of our body has passed. The entries we make are brief. It is important to keep the Steppingstones of the body in the form of a list so that we can have the feedback experience of reading our entries back to ourselves in continuity at the proper time.

Now we continue in silence recording our body memories until our list is long enough. Before we stop we should check to make sure that we have at least one or two entries from each of the major time periods in our life, childhood, adolescence, maturity, including the present. As much as possible but without straining, it is best if our list of body Steppingstones is representative of the movement of our life as a whole. We draw it together and sit in silence.

In a little while, allowing enough time so that we can feel some distance from our list, we read the memories back to ourselves in continuity. It is good if the list is in chronological order, but that is not essential. The composite effect is sufficient. As we read the list to ourselves, perhaps rereading it two or three times, we let ourselves feel the fullness, the variety, and the ongoingness of the life of our body. Especially in our rereading of the list, we experience the inner connections among the various entries. In all their diversity, the events of our physical life come together as the varying phases of a single line of development. A process of unfolding has been taking place within the life history of our body. As we reread our list, we perceive this process to be a single continuity of life. It is as though a specific person is present, unfolding the continuity of his experience through the life history of our body. This person within the process of our body's life is the one whom we shall now meet in dialogue.

Writing a Focusing Statement

In the course of carrying out this exercise up to this point, as we are rereading our list and as we are feeling the presence of the person within the continuity of the life of our body, we are necessarily recapitulating the relationship between ourselves and our body as it has been taking place over the years. As a next step in establishing a dialogue relationship with our physical life, we now write a summary statement of this relationship. What is the situation as it has been and as it is now between ourselves and our body? We write a brief, objective, nonjudgmental statement describing our attitudes and actions in relation to our physical life as they have been and as they are now.

A few sentences will be sufficient. Depending on what the circumstances of our physical life have been, however, several paragraphs will not be too much for this basic statement. It should be as short or as long as is necessary to enable us to draw into focus the essentials of our relationship to our body and to the physical world as a whole in whatever aspects we have experienced it. We write the focus statement now for our relation to the person in the life of our body.

DEVELOPING THE DIALOGUE

When that statement has been written, we can take a further step toward our dialogue relationship. We sit in quietness and close our eyes. We turn the focus of our attention inward and we feel the inner continuity of the life of our body. We feel its presence as a person, the person within the process of the life of our body. Feeling this with our eyes closed, Twilight Images may come to us. If they do, we take note of them. We observe them, and we record them in the continuity of our entry.

We remain in quietness with our eyes closed, now progressively feeling the presence of a person, a being who personifies the inner continuity of the life of our body. We feel the presence of the person within the process of our physical life, and we speak to it. We greet it as a person. We address it, saying what comes to us to be spoken. Whatever we say, we write in the Journal.

The *person within the body* responds, and we record this also. Then we speak and the person speaks, and thus our dialogue script is under way. Perhaps we begin by discussing the subject matter of the basic statement that we wrote. Perhaps something altogether different, altogether unexpected becomes the subject of discussion. We do not direct it. We let the dialogue script compose itself as it moves. It writes itself through our pen. We speak and the person in the body speaks.

The dialogue takes shape by itself out of its own nature. We let the inner speaking proceed now in the silence.

When the dialogue script has gone as far as it wishes, we let it rest. Many persons have found that when they let a dialogue come to a stop without trying to prod it forward, that stoppage becomes merely a natural pause. Soon it resumes by itself. For this reason it is good to remain in silence for some time after a dialogue script seems to be finished. It may merely be resting before it moves ahead to further statements.

We sit in silence for a while. When we are satisfied that the dialogue is finished for the present, we go back and read it to ourselves. At that point, also, it may be restimulated and resume its movement. If it does, we give it an opportunity to continue. If not, we take the further step of recording the reactions that were stirred in us as we read it back to ourselves.

Were we moved by it, or surprised, or disturbed, or interested to explore it further? Does the content of the dialogue script suggest to us another line of approach that we can follow elsewhere in the Journal? If so, we should make note of these dialogue leads that may be given us. They provide the kind of inner guidance that eventually produces very valuable Journal Feedback experiences.

At a Journal Workshop some of the participants will read aloud their Dialogue with the Body. These scripts have the greatest variety, and often take unexpected turns. Sometimes they seem to be facetious, but their humor is mainly unpremeditated and is an unanswerable means of responding to some of the dilemmas of human existence. One college student, for example, turned his dialogue script into a poetic exaltation of the grandeurs of the human mind. He waxed poetic about the marvels of philosophy and science which the human mind has achieved. In contrast, he told his body that it plays only an insignificant role in his life. Thereupon the body responded in the dialogue script and said, "That's all very well. Your mind is high and mighty. But try going to the toilet without me!"

And the young man added as he read it at the workshop, "I don't know how that got to be written. It wasn't what I was thinking at all."

Or again there are the several occasions when priests and monks at workshops have understood the Dialogue with the Body in the context of the tradition of St. Francis who addressed his body as "Brother Ass," and engaged in friendly dialogue with it. The two approaches fit together naturally, all the more because St. Francis' conception of the body parallels the definition that we follow in these exercises, namely, that the body is each individual's instrument of connection to the whole of the physical world. It is not at all surprising, then, that sisters and priests as well as monks have found this to be a congenial way of working with intimate personal problems in a modern framework.

We often find that when persons with a religious background take the "Brother Ass" approach to the Dialogue with the Body, as has been done spontaneously on a number of occasions, the dialogue scripts tend to begin with a tone that is gentle and often humorous. When they are read at the workshop, they may evoke strong laughter at the beginning. As these dialogues proceed, however, and especially as the person's dialogues with "Brother Ass" continue in the active context of Journal Feedback, they display a marked capacity for tough-mindedness. Beginning with gentle humor, they move progressively into realistic confrontation with the difficult issues of physical life that are inherent in the experience of persons who are living under religious vows.

This pattern of Journal experience is characteristic of the progressive development that takes place when the Dialogue with the Body exercises are used by diverse types of persons. At the outset the experiences tend to be light and somewhat self-conscious, possibly because it seems strange to be speaking with our body as with a separate person. After a while, however, as we become more accustomed to the dialogue relationship, it feels natural to us and we are able to reach deeply into the physical realities of our life. Thus, when a business man or professional man of middle years carries through his first dialogue with his body, it may take the form of a self-conscious recital of guilt confessing all the sweets he eats, the alcohol he drinks, and the tobacco he smokes. In the dialogue he will very likely apologize to his body for abusing it and promise to treat it better in the future. That promise, of course, is as valid as a New Year's resolution, and it usually lasts just as long.

If he continues to work in the dialogue relationship with his body, however, an integrating development soon takes place. As the Journal Feedback process continues to build, the dialogue scripts move beyond the surface level of concern with food and drink and good behavior, and they turn to the more fundamental questions of a person's way of life. At that point the business man finds himself considering how much longer he can expect his body to continue functioning well for him. He finds himself discussing with his body the prospect of death, and with that comes the question of the meaning of his life. Soon the conduct of his whole existence has become the subject of his dialogue with the body. Not infrequently, in situations of this kind, the body becomes the spokesman for a profound wisdom and guidance that relates not only to the physical, but to the whole conduct of a person's life. At such times, also, the dialogue opens issues that can very profitably be explored in other sections of the Journal. These dialogue leads can be very valuable and should not be overlooked.

The movement of the continuity of the dialogues over a period of time is a major factor in bringing about change through the Journal Feedback process. The first dialogues with the body of a person who is physically handicapped may be mainly expressions of anger and the resentment of an unjust fate that placed this difficulty in the life of a person who had done nothing to deserve it. When these things have been said and responded to in the dialogue, it begins to be possible for the relationship to move to a deeper level. After a person has articulated his resentments it is common to feel emotional fatigue; that becomes a time when he falls silent and therefore can listen.

At that point the body can speak more fully. Specifically, that is the point at which the illness can speak for itself, can describe its genesis, its purpose, place, and meaning in the individual's life. Questions can be asked and dialogue can proceed at deep levels, moving toward transpersonal understanding of the ultimate conditions of life and its suffering. I think in this regard of the blind woman at our Journal Workshops who struggled long with the unfairness of her blindness until it described to her the kinds of inner vision that her lack of outer vision made possible. She had not been asked whether she wished to pay the price, but having paid it anyway and having her blindness explain it to her from its own depth, the angry waves could become calm in her and she could begin to see from within.

Sometimes it is not a dramatic illness or physical incapacity that carries the dialogue to a deepening awareness, but the universal fact of aging from which none of us is immune. I recall the West Indian lady at one of our workshops who began her Dialogue with the Body in a laughing, teasing way. "It used to be," she told her body, "that any old rag I had would look beautiful on you. But now I can hardly find a dress big enough to fit you."

As we might guess, the body of such a lady was not daunted by her chiding remarks, but it spoke up for itself. It called her attention to her eating habits, and as the dialogue proceeded it made some other criticisms as well. At a certain point, however, the tone of the discussion changed. The fact was, they both agreed, that the two of them were getting older together. Their children were grown, the midpoint of life was past, and all the manifestations of their life were changing. "If you still want to be beautiful," her body told her, "you can't count on me. You'll have to find some other way to be beautiful." And with that wisdom to guide her, laughing and serious, she could say *yes* to the transitions of her age.

Wherever we are in our life, the deepening of the quality of consciousness within us is our most important attainment. Whatever contributes to this inner atmosphere is of value to us, especially if it enlarges our awareness in relation to the actualities of our life. This is the goal of our Journal Feedback exercises, and our experience up to this point has indicated that it involves a continuous and cumulative process. No single dialogue script, however exciting and revealing it may seem to us at the moment when we write it, carries the entire process. In principle it cannot, for the very definition of *process* implies a *series in motion,* with variations and changes and developments as part of its continuity. We therefore expect that all the experiences of our life will move through a continuity of changes, and our Journal procedures are designed as vehicles to carry these movements and variations.

When we write our dialogue script with the body, we recognize that it is one step in a process. The process as a whole is the ongoing dialogue relationship which we are establishing with the various aspects of our physical life. We have noticed that the writing of the Dialogue with the Body itself moves through a process of variation. It begins at the surface where its style is often self-conscious and its subject matter very generalized. As the dialogues proceed, however, the process of the work seems to take over so that the dialogue scripts write themselves spontaneously at deeper than conscious levels. That is the point at which the wisdom of the body enters the dialogues, often showing itself to be a large wisdom of life. It also shifts the subject of discussion to the specific problems and situations that require our attention.

We try in our dialogue exercises, whether we are at a Journal Workshop or in private, to allow the dialogue script to move as far as it wishes and then come to a natural stop. The important next step in extending our dialogue relationship is what we do when the script itself is no longer in motion. We read it back to ourselves and we record the feedback experiences that come to us. By that time, the dialogue process will have become specific, and it will be directing our attention to our body's particular interests and requirements.

Often, the body becomes the spokesman for a profound wisdom and guidance that relates to the whole conduct of a person's life.

Deepening and Continuing the Dialogue

How do we proceed in the Dialogue with the Body section after the basic dialogue script has been written? Our goal is to extend our dialogue relationship to the body in such a way as to position ourselves for solving whatever problems arise. One of the results of our dialogue script is that it enables us to draw into sharper focus those aspects of our physical life that require our attention. Very often these are issues that we have bypassed and tried to ignore, but the dialogue articulates them so that we have to give them recognition.

Perhaps there is an illness with which we must deal, or the danger of one to protect against. There may be a decision we have to make as to the approach to treatment we shall follow and the doctor we shall choose. We may be considering a new type of diet or a new physical regimen that will give us a constructive approach to health. Our dialogue with the body may have called our attention to the need of altering our style of life, perhaps changing our habits of personal conduct. It may involve our attitudes toward drugs or alcohol or other tendencies to addiction to which we are vulnerable. Perhaps we have raised several questions about our attitudes toward sexuality, or we have brought new light to them, so that there are new approaches to our social behavior for us to consider. It may be also that our relationship to sports is changing both as participant and observer, or that we find ourselves developing a new approach to the world of nature.

In subsections within the Dialogue with the Body section we contine to work with whatever issues have been brought to the fore by our dialogue script. We work with them on a current and ongoing basis and thus draw them toward new resolutions and awarenesses.

It may be, for example, that your dialogue script raised questions about your physical treatment of yourself in some particular area, perhaps food or drink, work habits or sexuality. One way of approach is

Dialogue with the Body   165

to keep a particularized Daily Log within the Dialogue with the Body section. Brief daily entries should be sufficient to enable you to form a perspective of what is actually taking place. Bear in mind, however, that you cannot gain a new perspective without working for a *continuity of time*. One insightful entry is not enough. A series, brief though the individual entries may be, but extended over a sufficient length of time will enable a perspective to form naturally out of itself. When you are groping your way toward new decisions, there is a valuable protection in taking sufficient time to accumulate a number of entries. The series enables a self-balancing principle to operate, and thus your entries can self-adjust themselves if you are being led off-over-enthusiastically in an unwarranted direction.

As you are making your daily entries in your Dialogue with the Body subsection, you may find that your mind is stimulated to move strongly in exploring a particular line of thought. Let it be free to do that. Let its stream of thought and associations range as far as it feels impelled to go. Only make sure that you record the flow of it in this section without censoring or judging it. Let it move fully and freely, and record it as it comes to you.

14

Dialogue with Events, Situations, and Circumstances

We come now to the section of the Journal where we establish dialogue relationships with the specific events and situations of our life. (Refer to your sample workbook in Appendix D.) As we learn to work with the exercises that become available to us here, we find that the circumstances in which we live no longer exert a cold, hard force upon us. They are no longer fixed and opaque, but they become accessible to us as persons with whom we can communicate. Thus they can speak to us and indicate what their requirements are, and potentials of life can be opened to us by means of them. Aspects of our life to which we had resigned ourselves with feelings of futility may then be renewed with hope. Situations we had thought to be inflexible may even be softened until they give us a message that guides us to next steps in new directions.

The events of our lives take many forms; we tend to respond to them in the immediacy of the moment in terms of pain or pleasure. Some we rejoice in, some we treat as disasters, others we merely endure. Beyond the outer form in which we experience them, however, there is an inner principle of movement in the events of our life. This interior factor is the key to the dynamic that forms our individual destiny, and the exercises in this section of the Journal give us a means of establishing contact with it.

When we speak of *events* in the context of Journal Feedback, the term has two levels of meaning. One is broad and generalized, referring to the underlying factors of change in our life. Its other usage is more limited, referring to the specific occurrences that take place within each individual existence. It is, in fact, the interplay between these two levels of meaning that enables us to discover what the varied events of our lives are trying to say to us. One sequence of events is taking place on the surface of life and another is happening at hidden levels. If we are attentive we can discern the relationship between the two within the context of our individual lives. There are large implications, both of universal and personal import, in the fact that the point at which the underlying flow of events coincides with and becomes an individual event is the point where human destiny is shaped. One of the purposes of the Journal Feedback approach as a whole is to provide practical methods of enabling individuals to relate their personal lives to the larger flow of events.

The *Dialogue with Events* section of the Journal plays a particularly sensitive role in reaching that goal, and it does so in several ways. One is that it is the section where we work with those aspects of our life whose meaning is elusive and ambiguous. These are events in which we feel, not knowing why, that the hand of fate or destiny, good or bad, is touching us. At certain points we become engaged therefore in unraveling the mysteries of our personal existence.

Secondly, the exercises in this section of the Journal serve to complement and augment the dialogue relationships that we have begun to establish in other areas of our life. When we come to blockages in our life experience, or when we have difficulties in working in other dialogue sections of the Journal, the procedures we use here give us an additional vantage point that enables us to break through the impasse.

Further, these procedures serve to stimulate the interplay among the other Journal sections so as to give us access to advanced levels of techniques and experience. At this time, however, we shall work with the fundamental exercises of the Dialogue with Events section as they feed into the basic integrative experience of a Journal Workshop.

Events

When we use the term *events* in its larger, encompassing sense, it refers to all the varieties of occurrences that emerge out of the flux and flow of human experience. Every event that occurs in an individual's life is an outcropping of an ongoing process that is moving at the depth of his or her existence. It is an interior process, and the events that take place on the surface of experience at any moment are its external manifestations. They are embodiments of the fundamental principle by which growth and change take place in our lives. This underlying and encompassing process carries the inner dynamic of experience. It creates the specific contexts of life, the situations in which our life experiences can move forward, and then it breaks these situations apart by bringing forth additional events which establish ever new sets of circumstance. It is with this inner process of perpetual life transformation that we seek to establish our contact through our dialogues and other exercises in this section of the Journal. We wish to build a continuing inner relationship with the process of movement and the goals that are unfolding through the multitude of events that shape our individual lives.

This is the general sense in which we speak of events as including all the experiences that feed our interior process. But there is another, more specific meaning of events in the context of the Journal Feedback process.

For the specific purpose of our feedback exercises, we define events as the particular occurrences that take place with meaningful impact on the movement of our lives. Events of this kind call attention to themselves by their dramatic quality, by the questions they raise about the mysterious movement of human existence, and especially by the effect they have on other aspects of our experience. Sometimes they are specific happenings that mark themselves off by the sharpness of their impact, their unexpectedness, their irony, or their pathos. At other times, they are less dramatic and take the form of *situations* that have established themselves over a period of time without our realizing they were happening, and they now are present as facts of our lives. They may also take the form of *sets of circumstances* brought about by factors external to us but which provide the context for important parts of our life experience. In these varied forms they comprise the content of our *Dialogue with Events, Situations, and Circumstances*.

A main criterion of the events that we choose as the focus for our exercises is that they are experiences that have had a strong emotional impact upon us, whether in the past or in the present. This is an indication that they have an inner importance for the movement of our lives and that our entering them in the feedback exercises will be valuable for additional areas of our experience. They are outer events that have an inner importance.

They may be events that have occurred unexpectedly or dramatically and have substantially altered the conditions of our lives. For example, a well-to-do man experiences a major reversal in his business, altering his financial situation with the result that all the members of his family undergo a change in their style of life. It is an event that will speak to each of them in a different way, each in the context of his life. Outwardly it will be the same event, but inwardly it will be a different event for each of them.

In general, regardless of their specific content, what we are dealing with here are events that life has presented to us. They come unbidden, unexpected, and mostly undesired by us. Often they carry a paradox of life, express an irony of existence, and present us with a dilemma. It may be, for example, that all has been going well in our lives when suddenly we are brought low by an illness. Or by a car accident. Or our career is progressing well when unexpectedly the company that employs us loses its contracts and we are left without a job. Or we have been careless and committed an error in judgment that has resulted in a sharp interruption of our career. Many people in the modern world have experienced rude breaks in their lives because of political events or natural catastrophes over which they have had no control. Other people experience the impact of events in more personal terms, through a change in the composition of their family or divorce or remarriage or the birth or death of a member of the household. For each it is an event that sharply affects the situation and circumstances of life. Some may react to such events with anger or frustration. The question, however, is whether these occurrences have a larger meaning for us, whether we can find their message and learn from it.

We require a perspective that reaches beyond the particularity of events and encompasses our life as a whole. Since all the events that we experience are part of the moving process of our life, they reflect something of our past and they also carry the possibilities of our future. Those events that we perceive as adversities may be experienced as painful, and we may wish that they had been avoided; but they may also be the vehicles by which an expanded awareness of the meaning of our life is being opened to us. There are mysterious questions of personal destiny that are difficult to answer, and we know that they often reveal themselves to us in circumstances which we initially regard as catastrophes.

The choice we have before us whenever a striking event takes place in our life is whether we shall react directly to the event itself, or whether we shall place it in the context of the movement of our life and let it speak to us. In general, it is more usual for setbacks or other painful occurrences to serve as the events that have a message for us. These are very often the events that have the most to say to us when we engage them in dialogue, but the same may be true for any event that has a strong impact upon us.

Successes may be as meaningful as failures. Favorable events may have as much to say to us as disasters. It is especially important that we speak with them in order that we may discover what lies behind them. Whether an event comes to us in a form that is pleasant or painful, it is important that we place it in the context of the moving cycles of our ongoing experience. Whatever it is, it is subject to change in terms of the larger process that is unfolding in our existence. Behind each event some effective element in our life process is at work. It is with this that we wish to establish an *inner relationship* by means of dialogue. The primary criterion is whether its subjective impact upon us leads us to feel that it has an inner importance for the further development of our lives.

The expressions of this may be exceedingly variable. Sometimes it is simply that an event occurs without apparent meaning or reason, and yet it has a strong effect upon us. We feel, then, that there must be something behind it that we need to explore. To open it, we enter into dialogue. Sometimes an event leads us to a conundrum about our life, an inexplicable situation about which we can make no decision. Such life riddles suggest to us that the events which brought them about contain a hidden message for us.

Sometimes, also, events that are meaningful for our lives occur as coincidences, or as synchronistic events with no apparent cause. These coincidences often seem to have an uncanny quality so that it is common for people to feel that there is a more-than-human agency directing them. They therefore treat such occurrences as signs and often base far-reaching decisions upon them. The emotional impact that accompanies these events indicates that they do indeed have a message for us. Whether that message is demonic or providential, or whether its source is the inner wisdom of our organic depths, it will be valuable for us to establish a dialogue relationship with it. We can then extend our contact with it and discover what the nature of its guidance is, whether it is valid for us to follow it, or whether its message for us is what we had earlier assumed its meaning to be.

Not all the events that have an inner importance for our lives take place with striking and dramatic impact. Some do not occur visibly and are not brought about by a definite set of actions. They do not come into existence at any single moment but only gradually establish themselves. Suddenly we realize that a particular set of circumstances has become a fact of our lives without our realizing it. Although it has been a long time in taking shape, the moment when we recognize it is like the discovery of something new that has just arrived upon the scene.

The circumstances that have gradually established themselves in particular areas of our lives are events with which we can enter into dialogue. Often these provide not only the background, but the key to the personal relationships that are most important in our lives, in our friendships, our families, our work relationships. The situations that develop as the contexts in which we live may very well have more to say to us about a relationship than the relationship itself. Where there is a problem, for example, within a marriage, it is very important to establish a dialogue relationship with the marriage itself, as well as with the other person involved in it. The Dialogue with Persons section is the place where the relationship between the two individuals can be worked with directly; but we work with the situation itself in Dialogue with Events.

Background for Our Dialogue with Events

When we consider the inner quality of such personal situations as a marriage, a friendship, or a close business relationship, we realize that each one has its own life history. Each situation, with the set of circumstances that lies behind it, has its own past, its inherent seed of potentials, and its own characteristic movement through the present toward its goals. Recognizing this life history enables us to perceive the presence of a *person* as the essence of the situation. The marriage, the friendship, each relationship, and each set of circumstances, has its own life as a human being does. When we reach this *person within the process* of the situation or the event, and when we establish an inner relationship of dialogue with it, we make it possible for the movement of our life to speak to us with openness and with fluidity. We often find that when we apply this procedure in the Dialogue with Events section we open a channel for deeper contact with the contents of our lives than would be possible with any of the other dialogue sections alone.

This supplementary function of the Dialogue with Events exercises gives them a very important role in building the dynamic of Journal Feedback. Whenever the exercises in other sections of the Journal lead us to an impasse, the procedures we have available here give us a means of breaking through and opening new ground. This is particularly true of the three dialogue sections—Persons, Works, and Body—in which we have just carried out our exercises.

As has been pointed out, a common example of this is a marriage that is in difficulty. For one reason or another, marked disagreements have developed between husband and wife and whenever they attempt to discuss things amicably, it ends in the same type of argument as in previous attempts. Each seems to be saying the same thing again and again. The usual situation is that these areas of discord have been reinforced by so many previous encounters and have broken down so often into anger or acrimony or a sullen stoppage of communication that patterns of habit have been formed. Whenever a new attempt at discussion is made, it quickly falls into the same old circular grooves. The result is the usual impasse and additional frustration.

In the context of Journal Feedback, the place where we take such a situation is to the Dialogue with Persons section. Since we are aware of the pitfalls inherent in such troubled relationships, we undertake to set an atmosphere that will draw the dialogue to a level deeper than its accustomed conflicts. We do this by moving away from the externals of the immediate situation and invoking a sense of the whole, unfolding life of each of the persons in the relationship. Very often at this deeper level of dialogue it becomes possible for a new quality of understanding to be achieved.

In many situations, however, the dialogue with the other person is only a partial first step. It serves to push the door ajar, but it is not sufficient by itself to overcome the repeated angers and frustrations that have accumulated over the years. Very often, dialogues of this kind move a short distance, make a little progress, and then become bogged down in the same, circular misunderstandings of one another that had devastated their actual relationship. Repeated attempts at renewing the dialogue between persons can gradually improve the situation until eventually a breakthrough is achieved. But there is a better way. To re-approach the situation from a different point of view, from a second vantage point, often has the effect of taking the relationship to another level. We achieve this in the context of Dialogue with Events.

After we have carried the Dialogue with Persons as far as it can go, we shift to this other section of the Journal. In the first dialogue, the husband, for example, undertook to speak with his wife and, after a sympathetic beginning, found that he could not move beyond the self-righteousness and the antagonisms that had developed in the relation-ship. Now he resumes his attempt at dialogue, but this time it is not with his wife. It is with the marriage itself; or, if he prefers, he con-ducts the dialogue with the relationship as a whole.

To begin this dialogue he goes back over the series of events by which the relationship has grown. He lists the Steppingstones of its life history. He lists the events of its beginning, the first meeting, the later friendship and growth of intimacy, the marriage and the acts done together, homes furnished, children born and reared, experi-ences of love and anger, warmth as well as antagonism. With all of these he reconstructs the outlines of the life of the marriage, and from it a person emerges. This person is not himself, and it is not his wife. It is the person within the process of the life history of the marriage. It is this third person with whom he conducts his dialogue. This is a neutral person, but one who is intimately involved in the situation. The com-bination of the two dialogues, coming as they do from different but complementary perspectives, often throws the light of a new aware-ness on the relationship.

The same procedure of combining the Dialogue with Persons and the Dialogue with Events can be used effectively in the relationship between a parent and a child. Especially when the child is no longer young and the circular patterns of noncommunication have been re-peated over many years it can be very difficult to establish dialogue. I have been present on many occasions when a person tried to dialogue with an elderly or deceased mother or father only to find that their bit-terness and blame cut the dialogue short. Often such dialogues open of themselves after sufficient time has passed and repeated new begin-nings have been made. To add to that dialogue, however, a dialogue with the event of that relationship, and to converse with the person within the process of the ongoing situation between them, often breaks directly through the circular repetitions of resentment. Many times it has made possible a reconnection by love at the deep level of one another's lives.

In a similar way the Dialogue with Events exercises may be combined with Dialogue with Works to gain an additional perspective. Suppose, for example, that you are in a job situation where you feel yourself being enclosed and cut off from future opportunities. When you dialogue with the job, it tells you that it is limited, that it has nowhere to go, and that it holds no stimulation for you. You feel frustrated and at a dead end. At that point it would be productive to dialogue with other areas of work so as to open other possibilities. The difficulty is that, when people are in a frustrating work situation, the probability is that their energy level is low and that their emotions and imagination are also in a depressed state. Whatever additional Dialogues with Work they may attempt at that time therefore tends to have a minimal effect.

That is when there is a special value in turning to Dialogue with Events in order to enlarge the perspective and to stimulate additional energies. Each person will approach it in his or her own way but, however it is phrased, the focus will be placed on the event of being in a dead-ended job, the larger situation that it involves, and the circumstances of life that are its background. With this as the focus of the exercises, we are progressively drawn into a number of areas of our life experience that open additional avenues of approach to our work situation. Also, while we are taking the steps in the exercises to establish our dialogue relationships with the event of our work situation, many feedback leads to other sections of the Journal will suggest themselves to us. As we follow these, we shall thus be generating additional energy by building the momentum of the Journal Feedback process.

An indicative example of what is involved in the full cycle of this process is found in the Old Testament. We are familiar with the story of Joseph, the event of his brothers selling him into slavery, his career in Egypt, his imprisonment, his prophetic interpretation of dreams for Pharaoh, his being placed in a position of administrative power, and his finally being the person who could allocate food for his brothers in a time of famine.

We can imagine the thoughts, the inner dialogue, that Joseph had when he saw his brothers and they knew who he was. If we follow the parallel of the depth process as it moves through the *Intensive Journal* workbook, we can project the equivalent of the Dialogue with Persons that Joseph carried out with his brothers in the secrecy of his heart. That dialogue could not have been without anger and bitterness at the painful experiences he had been forced to endure. But there was another important step that Joseph took. Just as we do in the Journal Feedback process, he established a dialogue relationship with the event of his captivity. In principle, he recapitulated the life history of the event, its past and its future. It then became much more than an episode of a brother betrayed. It included then a long series of events, some of them reaching back before Joseph was born. It included the hard life of the older brothers, the father's favoritism for a younger son, the understandable jealousy of the brothers, the bitter act of selling him into slavery, and then the further unpredictable series of events that gave him a saving role in the social crisis of his time.

The life history of the event of captivity reached far beyond the particular happening itself. In fact, the simple act of his being sold into slavery became a small and necessary event in the larger scenario. Its ultimate meaning was shown to be much different from the personal meaning it had in the moment when it transpired. Reconstructing the whole sequence, it seemed indeed that the event had its own life history as a person unfolding a unique and meaningful destiny. Establishing his dialogue relationship with the person within the process of that whole continuity of events, Joseph could see them in a much larger-than-personal context. When his brothers recognized him and begged his forgiveness, he was therefore able to speak from the full perspective of the situation and say in the language of his day, "You intended it for evil but God intended it for good."

A major role of the exercises in Dialogue with Events is to enable us to experience the movement of life in so broad a vista that we are not enclosed by the emotions of the moment. We perceive the ambiguity that is inherent in events. They may have not one or two but several levels of meaning, and these disclose themselves not at the time of the happening but only at later points in the course of our experience. It becomes essential, then, that we keep ourselves free from fixed conclusions and have a means of holding ourselves open for the further recognitions of meaning that will come to us with the passage of time. The Dialogue with Events becomes a means of positioning ourselves so that we shall be free and able to see the next steps that will become possible for us in the future. In this regard it serves as an active supplement to much of the dialogue work that we do in other sections of the Journal and progressively expands the range of the Journal Feedback process.

Beginning a Dialogue with Events

With this as our background, let us now prepare to take the steps that will establish open-ended dialogue relationships with the meaningful events, the situations and circumstances of our lives.

We begin by opening our Journals to the Dialogue with Events section. Our first step will be to draw together a flexible listing of the varieties of events and situations which we feel have something more to say to us with respect to the larger movement of our lives. These may be from any area of our experience and from any time-unit, past or present. One criterion of the events that we list here is that they had a striking impact upon us at the time they happened. Another criterion is that we feel there is a further step to be taken in our relationship with them. Especially it may be that we are still contained within the emotions of anger or resentment that accompanied the original occurrence, and we sense that it may be possible for us to reapproach that event now in a larger perspective.

To assist ourselves in recalling events of this kind, it may be helpful to turn to the section where we recorded the Steppingstones of our life. We may not have mentioned such events there specifically, but as our memory moves back over the outline of our life we may be reminded of them. It may also be helpful to check back over the entries that we have made in the Life History Log. In the course of describing some of the past situations of our life, we may also have alluded to events that had a striking impact upon us. A place where it is particularly important for us to look is in the section, Intersections: Roads Taken and Not Taken.

Let us recall instances of events that had a striking impact upon our lives and place them on our list. For example:

The experience of returning from a trip and finding that our father had taken his belongings and left.

An automobile accident that left us with a severe injury. Or perhaps an illness that has had lasting effects.

Receiving a scholarship that opened up opportunities for development that we had not anticipated having available to us.

Being tricked or misled in a business venture. Or in a personal relationship. Feeling that we were betrayed by a friend.

Having an intense religious or conversion experience happen to you, an experience that changed your attitude toward life, and comes as though carried by an external force, like "a bolt from the blue." Such experiences may not be limited to religion, but may extend to political life or to ideologies in general.

Being physically molested or attacked, as by rape. Alternately, the surprising and moving pleasure of an unexpected physical or sexual experience.

These are a few instances of events of striking impact in our lives, events that were significant and also ambiguous in their meaning for us. There is, of course, a virtual infinity of all the types of such events that we may have encountered in our lives. We wish also to add to our list, however, those situations and circumstances that may hold a message that is larger than what we have so far been able to perceive, for example, the social circumstances of our birth, our being born into poverty or affluence, a persecuted minority, or a dominant majority. Correspondingly, the social circumstances in which we are presently living: a situation in which we find ourselves; a triangled love affair; a crime or error of our youth being discovered or returning to embarrass us; a commitment or promise we have made that no longer feels valid to us.

We may find ourselves in a situation or relationship that seems to have come into existence by itself. We did not plan or deliberately call it into being, but now, without having chosen it, we find ourselves living in the midst of it. Many questions of the ambiguity of our life open here as we become more aware of the circumstances in which we have inadvertently placed ourselves.

When you feel that your list contains the main items that are meaningful to you, that it is full enough for your present use, draw it to a close, but also leave it open so that you can add further entries to it as they come to your mind. It is good practice to leave lists of this kind open ended in the Journal so that there will always be room for more to be added. To ensure this, we begin the next phase of our exercise in this section on a new sheet.

Developing the Dialogue

Now, with our list before us, we sit in silence. We consider the entries we have made and the implications they may hold for the past and future movement of our life. Several of them may be meaningful for us to explore in detail, but we shall choose one as the focus of our Dialogue with Events exercise at this Journal Workshop. We bear in mind as we are making our choice that this is not by any means an absolute decision. We are not eliminating any of the others. We are merely choosing one as our immediate point of focus, holding open our option to work with any or all of the others at another time.

We begin by writing a brief description of the event or situation that we have chosen. In placing it on our list, we described it only very briefly. We wrote only a few phrases, just enough so that we ourselves would know which experiences in our life we were thinking of. Now, however, we write a full statement of what is involved in it. In writing this, we want to mention all of the main factors that are relevant, but without losing ourselves in detail. We want to write a focusing statement of the event or situation.

Having made this basic statement to crystallize our awareness of it, we are ready now to reconstruct the life history of the event. What are the Steppingstones of its life? We may go far back in time in recapitulating these Steppingstones, back beyond our own birth. A young man who was dropped from law school, for example, may go back to the fact that his grandfather was a lawyer. He may then list his family's expectation of him to continue a tradition, and his own expectation of himself. Added to that would be other relevant facts and events, like his study habits, his intrest in the law, his interest in other fields of study and work, the role of other persons in his life, professors and friends, all as they have contributed to the striking event that finally came to pass.

Now let us sit in silence. Our eyes are closed. Our breathing is slower and slower. In the quietness our attention is turned inward. We are feeling the inner movement of our life, and especially we are feeling the particular events and circumstances that we are considering now. We feel that situation inwardly. We perceive it in its wholeness, all sides of it, all perceived by us now without judgment.

In the silence, our eyes closed as we are looking inward, we let images come to us at the twilight level. Whatever they may be, we make note of them. But mainly in the silence we are letting ourselves go back down the track of time that is the life history of our event or situation. We let ourselves be carried inwardly back down to its very beginnings, and as these memories present themselves to us, we record them. Now in the silence we are listing and describing the Steppingstones of the life history of the event or situation that we have chosen.

We allow as much time as we need to satisfy ourselves that we have described these Steppingstones adequately. When we have finished, we remain in silence. Again we close our eyes and let our breathing become slow. In the stillness we let ourselves drift inwardly down to the level of Twilight Imagery. This time, having completed the writing of the Steppingstones, we let ourselves remain there longer, letting images present themselves to us in whatever form they wish. We record them as they come to us without judgment and without interpretation. They have come to us as part of our listing of the Steppingstones and later we shall read them together, in correlation with one another.

As we are sitting in silence, we read back to ourselves the top line of each of the Steppingstones. It is as though we are reading the given name of each. As we read them in sequence, the consecutive life history of the event forms itself for us and we feel the process that has been moving within, moving in the past, through the present, and into the future. We feel that continuity of the inner movement of life as it has come together and has crystallized in this event. Now we feel that process of life as it has moved into this event, as it moves through it, and as it moves beyond it. We feel the inner process of the event as it moves through all the phases of time, as it has moved through the Steppingstones of its life. This is the person within the process of its life. We feel the presence of this person.

Writing the Dialogue Script

Now we are ready to write our dialogue script. In the silence, our eyes closed, our breathing slow, we let ourselves feel the presence of this inner person, the person within the process of the unfolding life history of the event. We feel the inner continuity of its life, its past, and its movement into the future. We feel the presence of the person within the process. And we speak to that person. We greet it and speak whatever comes to us to be said. And we write what we say as the start of our dialogue script.

We speak out of our deep silence, and it speaks to us. It speaks out of the deep place where its process has been moving, and its words reflect that movement. We write all that is spoken. We record it as it comes, without editing, without directing it, without censoring it. We let it come, and we let it flow directly into and through our pen. The person within the process speaks out of the deep movement of life, out of the deep movement of our life. It speaks, and we speak. So it continues. It speaks through our pen. It speaks and we speak together in deep, undirected dialogue. It continues on by itself, out of itself. It continues until all that needs to be spoken has been spoken. And has been written. We let it be written, in the silence, in the silence.

When the dialogue script has finished writing itself, we remain in silence. Let the breathing become slow again, for it may have become agitated during the writing. Presently we return to the dialogue script and read it back to ourselves. We take note of how it feels to us as we read it now, and we compare this with the feelings we had while it was being written. As we read it back to ourselves, the dialogue may wish to resume its movement. If so, we let it do as it wishes. When it has finished, we also shall have earned our rest. We set it to one side. Later, some days or a week later, we shall take it up again and read it to ourselves anew.

Then we shall see what new feedback leads it gives us, to which other sections in the Journal it directs us. We shall then let it show us what next step it desires in deepening its dialogue relationship with our life.

15

Dialogue with Society

More-than-personal aspects of our life are of profound importance for our growth and it is of great value to be in a dialogue relationship with them.

The exercises with which we have worked so far to build our dialogue relationships have been concerned primarily with the personal aspects of our life. They have dealt mainly with what is subjective to our individual existence, the persons with whom we are intimately involved, our work activities, the condition of our body, and the impact of particular events upon our lives. As we have proceeded with these Journal Feedback sections, it has become increasingly clear that our personal lives have a background that is more than personal. Each of us, in our own way, draws upon history, traditions, the world of nature, the realm of the spirit, the arts, and other transpersonal resources for the experiences and potentials of our lives. Sometimes these sources present a problem to us, confusing us and filling us with personal conflict where matters of faith and belief are concerned. At other times, they become a source of inspiration and enlarged awarenesses for us. In either case, it is clear that these more-than-personal aspects of our life are of profound importance for our growth in wholeness and that it is of great value for us to have a dialogue relationship with them. This is the work that we do in the *Dialogue with Society* section. It is the section of the Journal in which we work out our relationship to those who have been in the world before us.

In the context of this section of the Journal, the term *society* refers to all those aspects of our experience in which we draw upon our cultural and historical rather than our individual sources for the conduct of our life.

In Dialogue with Society we explore the less direct but larger significances of our relationship to our family. Here we deal not so much with the relationships within the family as with the more general contexts of society into which our family has placed us by reason of our birth or the circumstances of our life.

It may be that we have been born into a family with a long lineage and distinguished social position; on the other hand, our family may have only a moderate or a meager social status, or we may have no family at all, or we may have been adopted into a family. Each of these is an authentic fact and circumstance of our life. Whatever our particular situation may be, it is meaningful for us to establish our relationship to it. At various points in our life, it becomes important that we deepen our relation to our cultural background, including the time, place, and group situation into which we were born. This may be a national group, Italian or English or Japanese. It may involve not only biological connections but the geographic ties of living in a particular area, being mountaineers or farmers or city workers, living in the South or West or East of a particular country.

In earlier generations, the units of social identification were often based primarily on biological or on geographical connections among people, but recent times have brought a substantial change in that respect. With the mobility and development of individuals, the sense of group belonging tends to be based increasingly on subjective interests as well as on the more primal factors of blood ties or territorial affinities. We now feel our cultural connection to be not only with people who are related to us physically or who live near us but, even more, those who share the interests of our life involvement. This extends our group identification into a broad variety of areas. We share with others and perceive ourselves to be members of a single social group on the basis of being artists, musicians, scientists, sports enthusiasts, rebellious youth, the retired aging, or whatever other bond serves as a means of self-identification and belonging.

Questions of Race and National Origin

One of the major subjects that is included in Dialogue with Society is the question of our race or our national origin. Especially in countries like the United States where the population is a mixture of peoples, it is important for individuals to have a means of clarifying and maintaining a continuing relationship with their racial or national background. That is particularly true of those groups that are in a minority, or are placed in the position of being socially weaker or less highly regarded than other groups. Where a particular group is regarded as being weaker on the social scale, the individuals in that group often ascribe that stereotype of inferiority to themselves personally, and the integrity of their individual development is thereby undermined.

With this in mind, we work here to establish a dialogue relationship with the larger group units into which we are born. Here we can explore our identification with Black nationalism, or Zionism, or Irish independence, or whatever nation or race is relevant to us. Of special importance is the fact that the dialogue exercises make it possible for these identifications to speak to us and to articulate out of our nonconscious depths the meaning they hold for our life. Beyond this, what holds possibly the greatest value of all for us is that, as we continue to work in the *Intensive Journal* process over a period of time, these relationships have an opportunity to grow and change and deepen themselves. Our social identifications are not necessarily fixed, therefore, by a decision or commitment that we make at any particular point in our lives. As our inner experience deepens, our social identifications can be correspondingly deepened and enlarged in their meaning and in the quality of action which they suggest to us.

An important aspect of the Dialogue with Society is that it enables us to draw ourselves into relationship with the historical sources of our life. The contents of this are more specific and also more subjective than our relation to the movements of political or social history in general; they are also more personal than our relation to the history of the particular people or nation from which we are descended. It is here that we work with whatever connection we subjectively feel between ourselves and any of our personal sources, or resources that lie in the past.

It may be, for example, that in the generations preceding us there lived an individual who made a particular contribution to the world, or who expressed a special wisdom, or sensitivity, or commitment in life. That person may have been related to us in a direct line of family descendance, or may have been more loosely related to us by having been a member of the same nation or race, or perhaps only having lived in the same area. Whatever the actual physical connection, if that person's life has a stimulating or inspirational meaning for us which we feel in an intimate and personal way, it may be exceedingly valuable to explore the possibilities of an inner relationship with him or her by means of the dialogue exercises. It is a means of establishing a working connection to the past in such a way as to make it accessible to us in the immediacy of our present situation.

There may be a particularly strong emotional factor involved when the individual is someone who lived directly in our line of ancestry. A personal charismatic element is present then and a great energy may be felt, as when the person is a known relative, as a grandfather, or a great aunt or uncle, or a kinsman, a member of the same clan or tribe or guild. Sometimes it is a person who is removed from us in time by more than a few generations so that blood ancestry cannot actually be traced. Or, where blood relationship is not involved, we may feel our kinship by virtue of being part of the same cultural tradition. Sometimes it reaches beyond the reality of a known person and is a cultural hero of the distant past, a person whose life is meaningful not only to us but to many others as well. Such a person is of great inner importance to us, even though the actuality of his or her physical existence may be in doubt. His or her spiritual existence is nonetheless a fact for us, a fact that is essential for us to recognize and to work with in our Journal. Such individuals constitute a great inner resource for those who can understand the nature of their presence and can allow it to express itself without being falsified. They provide a personal connection for us to the traditions and the wisdom of the past, insofar as we have a means of contacting them via the depth of our selves.

Our Relationship to Political Events

Our Dialogue with Society can serve not only to give us a means to deepen the connection to sources of the past in personal terms, but it can also enable us to maintain a continuing relationship with the political events of our time. We may be in dialogue with our country, with its leaders, and with the general issues that are at the fore of discussion. During periods of social tranquillity, these political issues may be only of moderate interest, except for those individuals who are involved in politics as their special area of lifework. During periods of social ferment or political crisis, however, these issues become the focus of intense personal involvement. At times of political turbulence, it becomes especially important to have an instrument like the *Intensive Journal* workbook available to us as a means of clarifying our personal role in the events taking place around us, so that we can each determine individually where our social commitment lies, and so that we can act both creatively and responsibly. This section of the *Intensive Journal* workbook is one private place to which individuals can go in making political decisions and commitments that will feel valid to them both personally and as members of their community.

Another subject of importance in our dialogue relationship with society is our relation to the institutions and organizations with which we have an affiliation whether by belief or membership. As the pace of social change quickens in the modern era, the question arises for many persons of what they still require and desire from their old institutional affiliations. And the question arises equally from the other side of what these institutions require of them. Many important dialogues take place in this context, carrying the seeds of new social developments.

This is the section of the Journal where you can work out your relation to the institutional aspect of religion, to your labor union or business organization, or to the cultural institutions in which you participate. It has been a very instructive experience for many persons in these dialogue exercises to discover that social institutions do indeed have a life of their own, that they may be understood as persons who have a seed-nature, a life history, and purposes that carry them into the future where they may change, grow, or outlive their reason for existence.

Our Relationship to Art

An exceedingly fruitful, although less obvious, phase of our Dialogue with Society occurs in our relationship with the artworks that other people have created. The making of works of art, in literature, drama, music, or any of the other artforms, is inherently a social process. Some artforms, like the movies and the ballet, require the cooperation of a large number of persons, and thus they are obviously a product of society. However, even those fields of art such as poetry and music, where much of the creative work is carried through in lonely isolation, depend upon the social continuity of humankind. The artist in every field stands upon the shoulders of those who have gone before; to the degree that his or her work is valuable, it provides a base and an inspiration for those who are to follow. The artist is therefore always an intermediary of history. A question that is raised in one generation is inwardly experienced, responded to, transformed, and carried further, as the artwork gives the old issue a new aspect and suggests new possibilities for its further development. There is thus a social process of continuity that is inherent in the ongoing history of the arts, and this is the lifeline that supports and supplies the individual artworks of the future.

Ordinarily this social process is participated in and carried further only by those who are actively engaged in the creative process of art. For the most part, the exercises that these persons would carry through in building their dialogue relationship with the arts would be in the Dialogue with Works section. Here, in the Dialogue with Society section, however, we have a place and procedures that enable each of us to participate in the continuity of the arts and to contribute our psychic energies to their unfoldment. Whenever we read a book, see a painting, hear a symphony, or experience any other work of art that is deeply moving or significant to us, this is where we may record the feelings, perceptions, and other responses that have been awakened in us. We may then proceed to explore and expand them by means of the procedures that are used in this section of the Journal. As we deepen our own inner involvement in the artwork, we add our experience of it to the cumulative psychic process and social atmosphere by which the history of the creative arts moves forward.

Beginning Our Dialogue With Society

With this as our background, we can now begin the basic exercises with which we work in the Dialogue with Society section.

Our first step is to draw together a list of those areas of interest or concern that will be meaningful for us to work on in this part of the Journal. Out of this list we shall choose one for our dialogue script exercise at the Journal Workshop.

It may be that as we have been describing them, a subject for dialogue has already come to the forefront of your mind and you have decided upon it. Often, as we continue our Journal work, we find that the leads into Dialogue with Society come from the exercises that we do in other sections of the Journal and especially our current experiences in the Daily Log. It is good, nonetheless, to have a reserve listing of the areas of social interest and involvement that are personally significant to us. To have them available in the Journal places them where we can see them and be reminded of them again. It may then be that one day after you've made this listing, they will come to mind again and stimulate you to establish a dialogue relationship with them. We make a list in order to prod ourselves to dig deeper inward and to loosen the soil of our lives.

In making this list, we have one major point of reference: our life. The place to look, therefore, to find our meaningful social interests is among our Steppingstones. Let us turn to that section now to review the Steppingstone Periods that we listed earlier in the workshop. Each of these periods covered a significant unit of time in our life and contained many different interests and beliefs and concerns. Now we reenter those periods of our life in order to refresh our memories with respect to the social factors that have had an impact on our lives. These may be in various forms.

They may be the recollection of specific events, as marching in a parade, voting for the Presidency, entering the Army, being tormented for being a minority person. It may be also a more general remembering of attitudes or continued experiences or group affiliations that persisted for a long period of time and then changed, like being a Socialist or a Ku Klux Klanner, or an environmentalist.

To begin, we direct our attention back to the Steppingstone Periods as we listed and described them earlier. We reenter those earlier times in our life and draw out the memory-events that relate to this area of our inner and outer experience. At the workshops we have found it to be helpful if we speak these recollections aloud as they return to us. We do not elaborate them or explain them. We merely speak them out into the air of the workshop. As we say them aloud with no comment, we record them in our Journal. In this way we compile our list of memory-events related to the social aspects of our lives. Let us now do this together, as at a Journal Workshop.

I was born in a working class Irish family. Friday night we expected our father to be drunk. I hid my books when he came home, and I resolved that knowledge would change my way of life. Later I discovered the history of Irish culture, and now I want to dialogue with the two sides of it.

I am a black girl in the South. I know I had better not be on the sidewalk. I will dialogue with my blackness.

Hearing Franklin Roosevelt give his Inauguration speech. My parents believed in him, and he became my idol. I wonder what he would say now.

Being taught you had to use your fork a certain way, and dress and talk a certain way. I thought the whole world was like that. Then I found out that only a certain class was that way, and I didn't have to be the same if I didn't want to.

Being in Parochial school. I believed in God, but I couldn't accept the way His representatives were treating us. I didn't know what to do about it, but I was going into revolt. I'll talk to the institution.

When I came to America, I was shocked to see how different it is to be a woman here than in Egypt. It's so completely different. I'm not used to it yet, and I wonder what it means to have two such different ways of life.

In college I believed in a social revolution. Then I gave it up and became a business man. I would like to dialogue with both systems.

I listen to Bach and I think of when he wrote his music. I think he is deeper than civilization. Maybe he will tell me.

I am an Arab in this country. I think a great deal about the history of my people, its glory in the past, and I wonder if it will return. I also wonder if it is relevant, considering the problems of modern civilization. I will dialogue with the Arab world.

I am a woman and I never thought of myself that way before. It exhilarates and frightens me. I have to find out what to do with this new feeling of being a liberated person.

I think of the evolution of the human species. I feel identified with mankind.

I am an engineer and I have always taken science and technology for granted. I have always thought, if it works, it is good. Now I think I had better talk to both of them.

I remember my mother covering her eyes when she lit the candles on the Sabbath eve. Now that is irrelevant to me. Or I think it is. I could never do that myself. But there was something good and beautiful in it. Where has that world gone? I will dialogue with the Jewish world of the past.

Pacifism. I believe in it. Several times in my life I have taken a stand for it. But I think the problems are more subtle than I have admitted. I'll talk to it."

The Labor Unions. I have always supported them. And the working man, I have believed in him or the working class. Maybe they are not all the same, and I should talk to all of them.

I went into the Army during the war. I will dialogue with both the army and the war.

Sexual freedom. I found it. Now I'll talk to it.

The earth. I love the earth and we depend on it, but we are spoiling it. I'll dialogue with the earth. Then maybe I'll dialogue with the people who spoil it.

The ghetto streets. They used to be the only world I knew. I remember those feelings. I have very different feelings now.

I am an American and I am a Puerto Rican. I have studied here and I am part of Western civilization. But I also belong to the Puerto Rican people, and they need to be free. I will dialogue with them; then I will dialogue with America.

The listing that we make is open ended. As many items as we place on it now, we will always have room for others. When we are working in other sections of the Journal, additional realizations will come to us with respect to social factors in our lives that are or have been important to us. We shall always keep room on our list for these to be added. In that way we give them a place of recognition so that later, whenever the appropriate moment comes, we can establish a dialogue relationship with them. In order to keep our list open ended, it is a good idea also to leave a few pages blank before we begin the next phase of our exercise. Then we can maintain each as a separate subsection.

When we feel that we have made sufficient entries on our list, we sit in quietness. Now our eyes are closed, and in the silence we contemplate the experiences we have mentioned. Taken together, they combine the movement of the social aspect of our life. Now we choose one of them to enter with us into a dialogue relationship.

BUILDING OUR DIALOGUE RELATIONSHIP

When we have made our decision, we begin by writing a brief statement to draw into focus the essence of our experiences and our attitudes. This is simply to indicate the nature of our subject and the general direction in which we are going with it. It should not be a detailed statement, since the details of it are not necessary at this point. They will unfold of themselves as we proceed with our dialogue exercise. All we wish to do now is write a brief focusing statement. In fact, most of the examples of memory-experiences that were spoken aloud in the workshop a little earlier when we were each forming our basic list would be quite adequate for this purpose. Some of them could use a sentence or two for further clarification, but in general they would serve very well just as they are as focusing statements.

When we have written our statement, our next step is to begin establishing a personal relationship with our subject. We need to identify, and then to come into contact with, the *person within the process* of its life. To do this, we draw together the Steppingstones that mark the continuity of its development. As much as possible, we try to list the Steppingstones in chronological order, but that is not always necessary just as it is not always feasible. The best guideline to follow is to bear in mind that out of this listing a life history is to emerge.

We should list the Steppingstones in such a way as to help establish this life history. As much as possible, therefore, we try to place the

Steppingstones in consecutive order; but we recognize that there is a great deal of overlap from time-unit to time-unit in this area of our experience.

When we list the Steppingstones here in the Dialogue with Society section, the criteria are very subjective. If we consider, for example, the young woman who was preparing to establish a dialogue relationship with her blackness, we recognize that she has a number of alternatives open to her when she goes to list the relevant Steppingstones. Since they are subjective, only she can choose among them.

One possibility is that she reconstruct those personal experiences in her life that relate to her being Black. This may include the circumstances of her birth and early childhood, perhaps her playing with white children and only later realizing that society had marked off a difference between them. Her Steppingstones could then include other instances of discrimination and separateness, and other events that led her to identify her blackness as a fact of her life.

Another line of approach would have a non-personal emphasis. This might be in terms of the Black people and Black civilization. She might list some of the main Steppingstones of Black history in Africa, in the slavery period of the United States, and recent worldwide developments. Her dialogue would then be with the *person within the process* of Black civilization as a whole, and her personal situation of blackness would be an individual part of it.

In a similar way, the man who had been a social revolutionary in his earlier years and had then become a respectable businessman would also have a number of alternatives before him. He could list the Steppingstones of the particular revolutionary movement with which he had been involved, and he could then dialogue with it. He could list the Steppingstones of the business ideology as a whole and dialogue with the business enterprise system. He could take a more personal approach and list the Steppingstones of his life as a businessman and make his contact through that channel. Or he could work out some combination of these that would express the movement seeking to unfold in his life.

It must be clear to us at this point in our workshop that there is no single correct way to draw the material of our life together. But we follow the guidelines of a basic, general format, and we improvise experimentally with the contents of our life until we find the combinations that speak to us most clearly in the dialogue relationship. We never assume that the Steppingstone list or the first dialogue script is just the absolute and final one. Rather we try it this way and see how it goes; then we come back from another direction and try it again.

Now, considering the various possibilities before us in listing these Steppingstones, let us return to quietness. We sit in stillness, our eyes closed, our breathing slow. In the silence we let the life of our subject present itself to us. Our mind is aware of the possibilities, but we do not make decisions on it at the mental level. We let it present itself to us in its own way and in its own format. We are open and receptive in the silence as the Steppingstones of its life take shape for us.

Presently the Steppingstones become clear to us, and as they do, we record them one by one. We write them briefly, only a sentence or two to describe them. At a later time we may elaborate some of them in great detail, but now we only describe them briefly. We continue listing the Steppingstones until they have taken us to the present moment in time. We read them back to ourselves in silence. Do we feel the continuity of a life movement expressed in them? Are there any significant points where something important has been omitted? If so, can we fill it in with honesty by inserting another Steppingstone? We check the list, add to it whatever is necessary in order to make it feel right to us, and then we return to our quietness.

WRITING THE DIALOGUE SCRIPT

We sit in stillness for our dialogue script. Our eyes are closed, and we are breathing softly, slowly. Thoughts are present but we are not using them, so they drop away.

We are sitting in silence, letting the self become still.

We are sitting in silence, letting the breath become slow—and slower.

We are sitting in silence, letting our thoughts come to rest.

Presently in the stillness we begin to feel ready to approach the dialogue script.

We read the Steppingstones again softly to ourselves. We let ourselves be especially sensitive to the inner continuity of its movement.

We let ourselves feel the process of its life moving within it. We become aware of the person within the process of its life. As that person becomes present to us, we acknowledge it. We speak to it. And it speaks to us. We speak, and it speaks. And we record in the Journal everything that is said. Thus the dialogue script begins and moves of itself. It continues through and beyond us. We allow it to go as it wishes to go, and we enable it to proceed as long as it wishes to continue. We are participating in the dialogue script, and we are also its instrument.

Concluding the Dialogue

When our speaking and listening and recording have gone as far as we wish, we return to our stillness. There may have been strong and significant emotions stirring in us while the dialogue script was being written. We take note and add them to the entry. Presently we may feel quiet enough to read the dialogue script back to ourselves. As we do that, we take note once again of the feelings that arise in us as we read it. Record them, comparing them to the earlier feelings that arose in us while the dialogue script was being written.

It may be that when we read the dialogue script to ourselves a further dialogue is immediately stimulated. If so, let it resume and extend itself as much as it wishes and as much as feels right to you. When that is finished, let it come to rest, and let the dialogue have its own silence for awhile. After some days have passed, perhaps a week, you may wish to read it to yourself again. At that time it may resume once more. Then you will know that you have established an ongoing dialogue relationship with this aspect of your life in society.

Part 5

THE DEPTH DIMENSION

Introduction to
the Depth Dimension

The personal aspects of our lives lead beyond themselves with implications for the transpersonal.

Working with the Dialogue exercises for Persons, Works, Body, Events, and Society leads us to explore the circumstances of our lives as they are on the surface. This work also draws us to the deeper-than-conscious levels underneath. While the dialogue exercises are working with the details of the situations and events that are at the forefront of our consciousness, they are also calling our attention to possibilities and implications of which we were not aware. That is one reason why we often find when we reread our dialogue scripts that we discover insights we did not know we had. It is a knowledge that is apparently carried at nonconscious levels and the Dialogue exercises serve as vehicles for drawing this knowledge to the surface without our realizing it. The dialogues thus point toward a second level, a deeper level of consciousness, with the implication that as we touch this further depth of ourselves, we are enlarging the capacities of our awareness.

As we work with the Dialogue Dimension we are drawn toward the Depth Dimension. (See the Appendix to look at this section of the workbook.) The personal aspects of our lives lead beyond themselves and have implications for the transpersonal meaning of our existence as a whole. We begin by directing our attention to the surface of our lives where our immediate problems and circumstances are visible. Progressively we discover that there are levels of experience beneath the surface, beneath our consciousness, and we realize that these may hold the key both to the problems and the potentialities of our life. We thus turn our attention from the surface to levels deeper than consciousness. We have a specific goal. We wish to move from a purely personal to the deeper-than-personal level of our experience.

In the Depth Dimension of the *Intensive Journal* workbook we have five sections—two for Dreams, two for Twilight Imagery, and a fifth, the Inner Wisdom Dialogue, used to clarify all the other dimensions, especially the Meaning Dimension. (Its use is not at all limited to the Depth Dimension in which it finds itself.)

In this section we begin our work with dreams and Twilight Imagery. The main difference between the two is that the dreams occur during sleep while Twilight Imagery occurs during the waking state. Both of them are, however, expressions of the Depth Dimension in the sense that they carry the potential of life in the form of images that are symbolic. Both dreams and Twilight Imagery are unconscious reflections that express all the various levels of the individual psyche as it is in movement. They express the outward circumstances of a person's life, current problems and fears, as well as the hopes and goals toward which he or she is consciously planning. Often the imagery that occurs at a depth level is symbolic of processes that are unfolding, or about to unfold, on the surface of the life. To that degree, the symbols that come out of the Depth Dimension are ahead-of-time, and the images that come in dreams and Twilight Imagery are often harbingers of things to come.

In working with the symbolic content of the Depth Dimension we shall direct our attention to finding where the symbols are going and what they are seeking to become. Our emphasis shall be upon the practical question of what the images are seeking to unfold to rather than on what they mean intellectually. We can see this in the way that we work with the Journal sections of the Depth Dimension. The Dream Log and the Twilight Imagery Log are, respectively, the primary collectors of the sleep dreams and the waking experiences of symbolic forms. The sections of Dream Enlargements and Imagery Extensions are the sections in which we extend the images by means of the various techniques of Twilight Dreaming. The fifth Journal section in the Depth Dimension, the Inner Wisdom Dialogue, is the means by which we communicate with and develop further the sources of guidance which are in the depths of us. The Depth Dimension is a primary means by which we can discover what our life is trying to become.

The Dream Log: Beginning to Work with Our Dreams

How shall we begin working with our dreams?

In the *Intensive Journal* workbook we have two separate sections that we use for developing our dreams: the *Dream Log* and *Dream Enlargements*. The first is the section in which we gather the basic factual data regarding our dreams. The second is the section in which we use the Journal Feedback procedures to work actively and nonanalytically with the dream material so as to see where the dreams are trying to go and what their message may be.

The Dream Log

In the Dream Log, without interpretation or analysis, and with a neutrality as objective as is possible, we write down all the dreams that we can recall. You may feel that this is a lot to expect you to do in a single session and it is indeed too much to require if you have been having dreams that you remember over a long period of time. In that case allow as much time as is needed for you to record your significant dreams. You may take the time over a period of days following a workshop, but make an effort to remember as many dreams as you can and record them. And remember to date your entries as best you can.

It is enough to record small fragments of dreams when that is all that we remember. Often we find that when we record only a small portion of a dream, perhaps the tail of one since that was the only part of it that remained with us when we awakened. The act of writing whatever we remember, as little as it may be, serves to draw the rest of the dream back to our consciousness. We catch the dream by its tail, and thus we recover it for our consciousness. Many people who believe that they do not remember their dreams would find that a large proportion of their dreams would return to them if they made a practice of writing down whatever small bits of the dream they retained upon awakening. It requires a regular practice, and a definite place in which the writing may be done. This is one important purpose of the Dream Log.

No interpretation of the dream is done in the Dream Log. As a Log section, it is merely a place for a succinct recording of basic facts. In the case of dreams, we describe whatever is relevant, not for understanding the dream since that is a more complicated matter, but we write all that will be necessary to enable us to remember what took place in the dream when we read it at a later date. We are gathering our dream data. Later, because of the entries in our Dream Log, we shall be able to retrace the movement of the various processes within our minds by means of the continuity of our dreams. Because of what we have recorded in our Dream Log, we shall be able to put ourselves back into the flow of our dream life and be able to reconnect ourselves with our dreams so that we can go where they are trying to take us.

To make this possible, it is essential that we make a practice to allow for a sufficient period of time for recording our dreams in the Dream Log. We should record them simply as we observe them and as we experience them. If we make any judgments about them as we are recording them, and especially if we undertake to save time by eliminating what seem to be the unimportant dreams, we shall probably lose the dreams that turn out later to have the greatest significance to us. It is important simply to be reporters in recording the elements of our dreams in our Dream Log.

The reason we keep a Dream Log distinct from the more general Daily Log is to enable us to build a continuous record of our dreams in the integrity of their own movement. In the Daily Log where we are recording the inner events of our life, it is valuable also to report on our dreams. But it is sufficient there if we make only a brief entry regarding a dream, just enough to identify it, and then we cross-reference it to the Dream Log where we record the dream in detail.

In the Dream Log we have nothing but dreams. We record the approximate date when the dream occurred, whatever background material is necessary, and then we describe the details of the dream as we experienced it. We record nothing but the dream in our Dream Log, no interpretations, no analysis, no feelings or thoughts about the dream that followed after it. We record only the dream itself.

By keeping our Dream Log free of everything but the actual dream material, we gradually accumulate a moving picture of the continuity of our dream life. When we read it back to ourselves there are no intrusions of theory or interpretation or reaction to the dreams. There are only the dreams themselves, as much of them as we could retain and as much as were recalled to us after we began to record them. Reading these back to ourselves after a period of time has passed enables us to feel the unity of movement of the dream process working within us. We can then perceive the *seriality* of our dreams, the inner continuity that is establishing itself at the core of their movement. Thus we see the direction, not only of our individual dreams, but of the unfolding process of our dreaming as a whole.

At the point where we read back to ourselves the continuity of dreams that we have collected in our Dream Log, a further step that extends our experience becomes possible. Our purpose in *feeding back* these dreams to ourselves in their consecutive movement is not to enable us to interpret their movement, nor to understand them (in the conventional sense), nor to analyze their pattern. Our purpose rather is to place ourselves back into the movement of our dream process as a whole so that the process can now freely extend itself. Having come this far, where else do our dreams wish to go? What else are they reaching for? What else do they wish to say to us? In the *Dream Enlargements* section (covered in Chapter 17) we make it possible for our dreams to indicate their messages to us.

RECORDING YOUR DREAMS

To begin your dream work in the *Intensive Journal* workbook it is good to catch up as best you can with the major dreams you have had in the past. If you have never recorded your dreams before, it is good to begin by describing in your Dream Log the earliest dreams that you remember. Perhaps there are some dreams from childhood years that have remained in your mind. They may be pleasant dreams, or painful dreams that you experienced as nightmares; or, as is often the case, they may be dreams that you remember because they were connected with a dramatic or traumatic event in your life, as the death of a beloved person or the end of a close relationship. Sometimes dreams of this kind are clairvoyant or telepathic in content, but they are part of our dream process and should be recorded in the Dream Log. They, like all the dreams that we record in the Dream Log, are to be described as objectively as possible.

When we have recorded the dreams of our early past, we come to a middle period between that past and our present during which many dreams may have occurred relating to the changing phase of our life. Give yourself leeway in recalling these dreams. They may not return to your mind all at once, but a dream at a time, or even a piece of a dream at a time. It is good, then, to leave room in your Dream Log so that you can insert these dreams of your past from time to time, as they recall themselves to you. You will very likely find that once you have turned your attention to your dreams, several of them will rush back to your memory. After that, however, as you are trying to remember more of them, the fact that you are trying will impede you. Therefore, after your initial recall of your dreams, let yourself relax, not deliberately seeking to recall them any longer. Go about your other activities, but with the silent resolution that whenever a dream of your past recalls itself to you, you will write it down and enter it in your Dream Log.

There are many of us who have recorded our dreams sporadically in the past in various contexts and situations. It may have been in the course of keeping a personal diary or writing about our inner experiences during a period of emotional difficulty. It may have been as part of a treatment in psychotherapy by one of several analytical techniques. Whatever the occasion for it, if you possess such a record of your dreams from any earlier period in your life, this is a good time to draw the old notebooks out of your files and read those dreams again. You can then transcribe them into the Dream Log of your *Intensive Journal* workbook. If you have recorded a great many dreams in the past, you may prefer now to choose only those that have a special impact and significance as you read them in the present. If you copy into

I became convinced that the various Freudian styles of psychology could eventually lead only to a dead end and great disappointment.

your Dream Log only a selective few of your earlier dreams, that will be the equivalent of recording your past dreams now without reference to an earlier journal, but only relying on your memory. For memory is in many ways a spontaneous selective factor with respect to our personal past, and it can have a great value in that regard.

After you have recorded the main dreams of your early life and also the general range of the past years, turn your attention to your recent dreams. Perhaps there is a dream of recent weeks or months that comes strongly to your mind. Record it in your Dream Log. While you are describing the dreams that return easily to your mind, others that were partially forgotten may also be recalled to you. Record them as they return to your mind, even if it is only a small piece of a dream. While you are writing it, more will be recalled to you. When you find it difficult to remember the contents of a dream, it is often helpful to direct your attention to the elements of movement in the dream. What changes of scene and of action took place in the dream? What shifts in the scenario or plot? Did the themes change, and what variations were there among the participants in the dream? Were there changes in the atmosphere or tone of the dream? Even if you do not remember the specific contents of the dream, questioning yourself about the elements of movement within it will very often serve to reconnect you with the general trend of the dream. That will put you in touch with what is important in the dream, for its interior movement is the essence of the dreaming process.

Let yourself now think of your most recent dreams, dreams of the last few nights, dreams of last night. Describe these in the Dream Log as fully as you can. Now you will have brought your record of your dreaming up to date so that you can work with your dreams actively by the Journal Feedback process.

WORKING WITH YOUR DREAMS

The first step that we take in working with our dreams is a negative one. It is what we do not do. We deliberately refrain from analyzing them. We refrain from interpreting their symbolic content no matter how profound are the insights into them that we feel we possess. We make no interpretations from the point of view of any special theory, not from Freud's, nor Jung's, nor Adler's, nor any other, nor any eclectic mixture. We do nothing which would in any way make the dream or its symbolism stand to reason. To do that would, in the first place, have the effect of rationalizing the symbolic material and thus violating the fact that its nature is inherently nonrational.

Of much more serious consequence, however, is the fact that to intellectualize dream material by interpreting it has the effect of lifting it out of the depth flow of the psyche which is its natural habitat. It thus is removed from the environment in which it was formed and on which its continued development depends. To interpret a dream in analytical terms has the effect of neutralizing its power, because it deprives the dream of its ability to continue its movement and to unfold its symbolism within its own terms. For this reason, the first step that we take is to refrain from interpreting our dreams. We allow them to remain on the depth level where they can be continued from within themselves and thus can expand their life.

Our second step, after having recorded our dreams in our Dream Log, is to return to the place in our experience where our dreaming occurred so that we can reenter our dreams and enable them to continue themselves. All our dreams are part of the moving flow of imagery that is continuously present at the depth level of the psyche. Each dream is an excerpt of that large and ongoing movement. It is a bucket of water sent up to us from the underground stream of imagery within us. In order to extend the movement of our dreams, therefore, it is not necessary for us to return to the condition of sleep in which the dreams occurred, but only to place ourselves back in the flow of imagery that is moving within us beneath our conscious minds. This is the flow from which our dreams were drawn.

For this next step in our work, we begin by sitting in quietness. Our Journal is open in front of us, the pages turned to the Dream Log. We close our eyes. In the silence we send our minds back over the movement of our dreams. We do this in a spontaneous and unguided way, not specifying in advance which of our dreams are to be called back to our attention. Rather, we let our minds go back over our dreaming as a whole. We wish to see which of our dreams will recall themselves to us when we place no restraints upon ourselves but merely let our minds roam over the generality of our dreaming.

It may be a dream or dreams from our earlier years that we now find ourselves recalling. Or it may be dreams from the recent past, or a current dream. From whichever period the dreams come, we turn our attention to them and we let ourselves *feel* them again. We do not interpret them, nor do we think now about what their meaning was. But we feel them again. We open ourselves to experience the quality and tone of the dreams, but without restricting ourselves as to the kind of feelings that will now come to us. We do not limit ourselves to the feelings that we had when the dream originally occurred.

In this freedom of emotion, we let the atmosphere of the dreams establish itself again. As it does, we deliberately hold ourselves in openness so that we can see without our predetermining it, which dream atmosphere draws us most strongly. We do not hold back but we follow the inner magnet of the dream that draws us to it. In this way we protect ourselves against letting our own preconceptions and opinions get in the way of the depth process that is seeking to unfold in us.

We hold ourselves in quietness, letting a spontaneously chosen group of dreams pass before our mind. We let our feelings move freely with respect to these dreams. We feel the atmosphere of the dreams, and we open ourselves to them so that we can be drawn into whichever dream-atmosphere has the greatest magnetic pull for us at that particular moment. Thus we bypass whatever analytical or intellectual preconception we may have had about which of our dreams is most important for us. We do not let our own opinions interfere, but we leave it to the dream process itself as it is working within us to draw us to the dreams that are important for us now.

When we feel ourselves drawn into the atmosphere of a particular dream, from whichever period of our life it may come, we open our eyes and return to our Dream Log. If we have already recorded that dream, we now go back and read to ourselves the few dreams that immediately preceded the dream. We reread the dream itself, and we continue reading back to ourselves the next few dreams that follow it in the Dream Log. Our purpose in doing this is to enable ourselves to experience the context of the *series* of dreams, the central one being the dream whose atmosphere drew us to it. The seriality of dreams is the key factor with which we build the momentum that enables us to draw the dream process forward.

If the dream that drew us into its atmosphere is not one that we have already recorded in our Dream Log, we should describe it now. The fact that it has called itself to our attention is a sign that it has something meaningful to contribute to our lives and that it will be worth our while to spend some time with it. As we record that dream, we should also try to recall any additional dreams of that period, dreams that preceded and also dreams that immediately followed the dream in question. In that way we can place the dream directly in a series. Whether or not there are additional dreams that we can recall with it, it is good to insert the dream that we are newly recording at the proper chronological point in our Dream Log. Thus we maintain the continuity of our dream movement, and we are able to work with the seriality of our dreams.

CONTINUING OUR DREAM WORK

Now we are ready to continue with our dream work. Sitting in stillness, we turn in our Dream Log to the dream that drew us back into its atmosphere. We go back a few dreams before it and we begin by reading the record of our dreams. We read them not in order to understand them, but in order to gain entry to them. We wish to get inside the movement of our dreams, as we would wish to be inside a train that is going in the direction we want to go. The train will carry us with it and take us to the next place we are to be in our lives, and so will the movement of our dreams.

There is one important difference that arises in comparing the movement of our dreams and the vehicle of a train. We may know in advance where a train is headed, and we are able to make the decision in advance as to whether that is where we also want to go. But the process of our dreaming has no destination printed on a sign at the front of it, and our dreams have no conductor to announce in advance the next station we are reaching.

We never know where our dreams are going. Many of them take us to places that are exceedingly unpleasant and very frightening. When those nightmare dreams come to us, we may wish that we were not traveling on the dream train at all. But that is the time when it becomes most important to remember the comparison between a train and our dream process. The nightmare dream that disturbs us is one of the points along the track. It is a tunnel through which we need to pass along the way, but it is not necessary that we remain there. That is why, when difficult or painful dreams come to us, it is important that we record them in our Dream Log. We thereby add them to the continuity of our dreaming, and we enable our dream process to move beyond them by going *through* them. Thus we can discover the destination of our dreams, and can recognize that the destination often contains the goal and meaning of the unfolding of our life as a whole.

In that lies the great experiment and the great wonder of working with our dreams. We do not know in advance where they are taking us, just as we do not know in advance the ultimate outcome of our lives. It is always, therefore, a process of discovery. What we do know is that our dream process is moving out of the seed-potential of our life, and that the direction in which it is heading is already contained in that seed, as the fruit is present in the seed of the tree.

The process of our dreams is moving toward the fulfillment of these potentials. That is its general direction. But the form in which it will arrive there, the specific place where the goals will be located, if indeed they are to be found at a specific place, and the difficulties that will be encountered along the way cannot be known by us in advance. Ultimately to discover what that goal of our life is, is the great experiment of each individual existence. To find it is the adventure of our lives. This is the adventure, or journey, that is depicted in the legends, and fairy tales, and myths of the hero in many forms. We each experience it, and live it, in our own way, supplied and carried by the symbolic process that moves at the depth of us, a main carrier of which is our dreaming.

The movement and unfolding of this symbolic process is the essential principle we follow in working with our dreams. Especially when we experience the nightmare dreams of anxiety and inner disturbance, we bear in mind that they are part of the ongoing process that underlies our dreaming. The central factor is the continuity of our dreams, and we must avoid breaking that continuity. That is one reason why we do not become involved in the analytical interpretation of our dreams. To analyze stops the movement of the process, and places us in the position of being outsiders who are observing an activity rather than being participants in the midst of it.

When we stop the movement of our dream process by analytic interpretation, we draw it off the track and away from its goal. We thereby prevent ourselves from discovering where the train of our dreams is heading. It is essential that we maintain that movement, regardless of the valleys and the difficult detours through which it passes. It is important also that the movement express each person's own integral dream process, without the insertion of the theories or suggestions of others intended to help the process along.

For these reasons as we work in our Dream Log we begin by reading a series of dreams. A single dream by itself may be very interesting and dramatic, but it is also very susceptible to having external meanings and interpretations read into it. A series of dreams, on the other hand, is a large enough segment of a moving process to carry some of the inner momentum of that process. Thus we read to ourselves a series of dreams, focusing on the one that drew us into its atmosphere as we sat in quietness.

We read the series of dreams now, feeling their inner movement. We become aware of the contents of the dreams as we read them to ourselves, but we do not think about them. We do not interpret the content, or seek to find meaning in them. We simply read the series of dreams and let ourselves become part of their movement. We feel ourselves to be within them. We are inside the dreams, and they are inside us, just as we experienced them when they originally took place. We let ourselves be drawn into their atmosphere. We are contained by the atmosphere of the movement of the dreams in the series. Gradually the movement of the series as a whole takes over and the separateness of the individual dreams becomes blurred. We read the dreams to ourselves a second and a third time. One technique that we can use at this point to help in the feedback aspect of the work is to read the series of dreams into a cassette recorder. We then play them back as a means of drawing ourselves into the atmosphere of the flow of the dreams.

Twilight Dreaming

Now, working alone, we read the series of dreams until we feel ourselves to be within their movement. It is a stream that carries us along with it. Our eyes are closed. We are not asleep, but we are not fully awake either. We are in the state of *Twilight Dreaming*.

Now, on the screen of our mind's eye, the dreams continue themselves. Some of the scenes from the dreams may reappear, but not necessarily the scenes nor their contents as they originally took place. It is not our specific dreams that we are continuing, but the inner process of our dreaming as a whole. We are letting it move freely out of its own context so that it can reach and reflect the full range of its possibilities.

Images and feelings and actions continue for us now, just as would be the case in our sleep dreaming. We let the inner movement of our Twilight Dreaming move on by itself. We do not guide it. We do not direct it. We do not restrict it. We encourage it to move on its own and in its own way wherever it wishes to go. Inwardly we follow it. With our emotions and our inner participation, we freely go with it. We let our Twilight Dreaming proceed as fully and as long as it wishes. We behold it, accompany it, and let it carry us as a vehicle driven by its own inner guidance.

In the next chapter we will work with our Twilight Dreaming.

17

Twilight Dreaming: Using Dream Enlargements and Imagery Extensions

As our Twilight Dreaming continues, it is often helpful for us to speak out the experiences that come to us. Even if we are alone, conducting our Twilight Dreaming in privacy, it is good to speak our experiences aloud. Although no one is present to hear them, to articulate them so that they can be heard seems to make them more tangible for us so that we do not lose them in their wispiness but can take hold of them and record them. Once we have described them, we are better able to work with them with additional Journal Feedback procedures. Speaking aloud our experiences of Twilight Dreaming seems to help us individually to carry our inner process further. Each experience that is spoken seems also to contribute to the atmosphere of the group, strengthening and reinforcing in everyone the contact with the dream level.

Recording Our Twilight Dreaming

We record the experiences that have come to us through Twilight Dreaming in the Dream Enlargements section of the workbook. While the experience is in process we record it in bits and pieces, just as it comes to us. The Journal entries that we make while we are in the midst of a twilight exercise are brief reportings of the inner events as they are taking place. We learn to write in our Journal with our eyes three quarters closed. Sometimes the atmosphere of our twilight experience is so strong that it holds us for a considerable period before we can break away at all to make even a hazy recording. At those times we have to carry a great deal in our memory while further experiences are coming to us. At other times we make a number of brief, half-legible entries, recording each new perception as it comes to us, and returning quickly to the twilight level. Because Twilight Dreaming is altogether spontaneous and unguided, it occurs in a different form each time we experience it. The practice of it teaches us to be free and flexible in relation to the depth of ourselves.

When our experience on the twilight level has subsided and we have recorded it in the Dream Enlargements section, we can proceed to work further with the material that has come to us. As a unit now, we read back to ourselves the continuation of our dreaming as it took place on the twilight level. As we reread it, we become aware of the feelings and emotions that arose in us as those experiences were taking place. We find that we have additional reactions now as we read them. We add to the continuity of our dream work now by recording all these inner responses in the Dream Enlargements section.

In making these entries, there are some key questions that can help us focus our inner process so that we can recognize and record what is happening within us. While these experiences were taking place, what feelings were present within us? What was the atmosphere and the tone that accompanied them? And now, as you read them back to yourself in a single continuity, what emotions and awarenesses are stirred in you? As you read the Twilight Dreaming, do you perceive a movement or direction within it? Do you feel in its symbolism a particular theme or thread suggesting that it has a message to communicate to you? Did you feel that direction or message to be present in the Twilight Dreaming while it was taking place? Or do you only perceive these hints and indicators now, after you have recorded it and are reading it back as a unit from your present position in consciousness?

Whatever additional thoughts or feelings, reflections or perceptions of any kind come to you now should be added to your Dream Enlargements section. When we go down, as we just have done, to the twilight level to extend the process of dreaming, we find that many inner awarenesses about our life, our past, and the possibilities of our future, are actively stimulated. Things that we knew, or half-knew, but did not realize we knew, now come to the fore of our mind. While they were vague or inaccessible to us before, once we have recorded them in the Journal, we can think about them lucidly. Now ideas that were merely intimations or hunches before can be considered critically and constructively.

We recognize in this a most significant paradox that is a fact of our deep Journal experience. By working with our dreams and their extensions on the twilight level where the contents are mainly non-conscious, nonrational, and symbolic rather than literal, we experience an unexpected reversal in the quality of our awareness. As we emerge from working within the realm of the unconscious at the deeper-than-personal levels, we find that our consciousness now possesses a greater acuity. After having opened our psyches to the symbolic material in the twilight depths, our perceptions of the outer world become sharper and clearer, and our thinking processes move more quickly and more relevantly than they did before. Many new thoughts, insights, intuitions, and recognitions of all kinds related to our life in general and to specific projects now come to our mind. Sometimes they come to consciousness in great volume, flooding us with ideas and awarenesses. At such times we have to learn to regulate their flow so that we can retain and record them. Above all, this bounty of new thoughts that come to consciousness in the wake of our twilight experiences should not be lost, but retained in the Journal for our future use.

A significant paradox of working with dreams is that we experience an unexpected reversal in the quality of our awareness.

Let us make sure now that we record in the Dream Enlargements section all the thoughts and feelings, everything that has come to our consciousness after the extended experience of Twilight Dreaming. The content of many of these will relate to other sections of the Journal. It is not necessary, however, for us to be concerned with the question of where in the Journal these entries belong and where we shall work with them. The important task of the moment is to record this new source of material while its momentum is strong and it is still flowing spontaneously. We therefore write it in the Dream Enlargements section regardless of its subject matter, recording it as fully as it comes to us. Later on, when the movement of this material has quieted within us, we can cross-reference its various aspects to other sections of the Journal and there, each in its valid context, explore and extend them with the appropriate Journal Feedback exercises.

The Guidance of Our Dreams

One of the most valuable contributions of our dreams lies in the clues and guidance they give us as to which areas of our life we should reexamine. Since they reflect without censorship what is taking place inside of us, our dreams direct us to those sections of the Journal where there is work that needs to be done. These *dream leads* can be especially valuable, and will greatly expedite our Journal work if we learn to follow them. The dream leads do not in themselves supply the answer to our problems. In fact, it is important to refrain from reading into our dreams some particular meaning that we infer is giving us specific directions for the conduct of our life. On most occasions when we interpret a dream in such a concrete way that we then say, "My dream told me to do such and such," we find eventually that we imputed to the dream a meaning that it did not necessarily have. It was not necessarily saying what we thought it was saying.

All too often we impute meanings to our dreams either because that is what we wished for or because that is what we were afraid of. Dreams are especially vulnerable to our reading meanings into them which they themselves had no intention of conveying. Dreams are defenseless against our misinterpreting them because their symbolic style is inherently ambiguous, and people have a tendency to see in them either what they are looking for or what they are afraid of finding. Depending on their temperament, many people use their dreams either to diagnose themselves or to encourage themselves by adapting the dreams to reinforce beliefs they already have. Beyond that, as a result of the psychological era in which we have been living, it is difficult for people to become educated in the terms of modern thought without absorbing the concepts of the famous psychoanalysts Freud or Adler or Jung or their numerous derivatives. Without realizing that they are doing so, they inadvertently read their dreams by the light of those particular theories and thus find meanings that may have been valid for Freud's life or Jung's life but not necessarily for their life.

It was Jung himself who remarked that every system of analytical psychological theory is a "subjective confession," including his own, as he was honest enough to say. He also made the very important point—which his particular theory (of the archetypes) frequently prevented him from following in practice—that it is always the context of the individual life as expressed through a series of dreams that holds the key to what the dreams are trying to say. To follow any particular analytical line of interpretation has the effect of entering the dream, and the life, from the outside with a preconceived theory. To that degree it violates the integrity of the individual life.

It is specifically to protect the integrity of each person's inner process that in the Journal Feedback method we avoid the interpretation of dreams. Instead of analyzing our dreams, we encourage them to further unfold by recording them fully and by extending their serial movement through the procedures of Twilight Dreaming. We then draw, both from the dreams themselves and from the dream enlargements, clues and directions as to where in our lives, as reflected in the various sections of the Journal, there is further exploration to be done. These dream leads then provide the starting points for further active exercises of Journal Feedback which we pursue in the appropriate Journal sections.

It is important to understand the principle that is the basis for this non-analytical way of working with dreams. In the first place we recognize that more fundamental than the dreams themselves and more fundamental than the Twilight Imagery is the process that is moving toward life integration at the depth of each person. The dreams are one of the forms by which this process expresses itself, and by which it indicates where it is trying to go, its problems and blockages, and its requirements. It is in order that we may get these messages of inner guidance from the depth of ourselves that we pay attention to our dreams.

The Limitations of Dreams

Dreams are subject to certain limitations, however. The first of these is the fact that many people do not remember their dreams. The way it often is phrased is, "But, Doctor, I don't dream!" We know, of course, that everyone does dream, since the process of dreaming is an inherent part of the psychic organism. It is true, however, that only a small proportion of our sleep dreaming is recalled in the waking state by anyone. It is further true that a large number of people remember hardly any of their dreams at all, unless the pressure of particular circum-

Instead of analyzing dreams, allow them to unfold by extending their serial movement.

stances makes them sensitive to certain big dreams of special impact, or unless they practice the discipline of recording their dreams in the middle of the night at the moment when they happen. Most of our sleep dreaming is lost to us, which is the reason that many people believe that they do not dream. This is a serious limitation, particularly if we are relying on dreams as the only or major road, the "royal road" as Freud called it, to the contents of our unconscious levels.

The second, and probably more consequential limitation of dreams is the fact that the language of dreams is exceedingly ambiguous. Dreams do not speak literally in the manner of our rational consciousness. They use a symbolic style, dramatizing their points and making veiled, indirect, allusive references. This is the reason why over the centuries it has been thought to be necessary to analyze and interpret dreams in order to find out what they are trying to say. The language of dreams is not rational and it has therefore been necessary to have some means of making the dreams stand to reason if we are to have access to their message for our conscious use in our lives. To find what is rational in the apparent irrationality of the dream's language is the goal that underlies all attempts at dream interpretation, whether it is by God-inspiration as for Joseph in the Old Testament, or whether it is by the analytical concepts of Freud or Jung. The problem is that the analysis of dreams is very susceptible to our subjective reading-in of our wishes, fears, or other preconceptions.

These two limitations of dreams should not be allowed, however, to obscure the more fundamental principle, and goal, of dreaming as an essential fact of our inner lives. There is apparently a primary life process moving in our depths carrying a direct intuitive knowing of the integral needs of each individual existence. When this process expresses itself in dreams, the symbolic language of the nonrational depths which it uses is ambiguous and is vulnerable to misinterpretation; but there are many indications that this fundamental life process is in fact trying to make itself accessible to consciousness and available to our rational understanding. It is stymied by the fact of its symbolism, which is ambiguous not only in dreams but also in Twilight Imagery. It is at this point that our use of dream leads provides valuable assistance to the depth process that is expressed in dreaming. It frees that process from the ambiguities of symbolism by enabling it to move through its dreams and imagery to the specific areas of life experience where its messages are needed.

Our Dream Leads

To see how we find and follow a dream lead, let us consider this example. Suppose you have a dream about a person whom you have not seen in many years and who has not been in your conscious thought. You may speculate intellectually about what or who he represents to you, but you run the risk then of making an artificial analysis that will falsify your dream by reading something into it. You will also be stopping the movement of the dream process by cutting it apart with analytical concepts. Instead, we stay directly with the dream contents, but we give them a place and an opportunity to continue to unfold out of themselves.

In the example we are using, a number of options would be available to us as our first step, depending on the feelings that come to us as we reread the dream. In general, it is best to proceed as concretely as possible, staying close to the actual content of the dream. We begin by recalling memories of our relationship with that person, places where we were together, situations, events, emotions that we associate with him. As these memories come to us, we record them in the Life History Log. As we are writing, our descriptions will open outward and enlarge themselves. One memory will beget another.

As we continue with this, we find that additional awarenesses are stimulated in us. We realize, for example, that this person who appeared in our dream was closely identified with a decision we made at an earlier time in our life, a decision that led us to follow one path of action and to reject others. We had not thought of him or her in that connection before, but the association is now clear to us. Following our dream lead, we now turn to the Journal section, Intersections: Roads Taken and Not Taken. We describe the circumstances at that crossroad of our life. As we unfold our memories and as we reenter the situation of that earlier time, many additional emotions and awarenesses are reactivated. We record these also.

As we make these additional entries, we ask ourselves to which other sections of the Journal are we now being led. Are any new indicators being suggested to us as we proceed? It may be that, as we are describing that earlier intersection in our lives, we are reminded of the choice we made and the various roads not taken while we were under the influence of that friendship. Perhaps it was a choice of a field of study, or a business opportunity, or a change of location that was involved. Following the direction of our Journal work, we might then turn to the Dialogue with Works section to explore the present significance of the avenue of work that was not pursued at that earlier time in our life. We might also turn to the Dialogue with Persons section to reenter our relationship with the person who was in our dream, and perhaps with others who have been called to our attention as we have been following our dream leads.

At this point it is clear that, taking the dream as our starting point, a momentum of exploration and new experience has been generated. We are now being carried in a direction that discloses its next turn to us with each new exercise we carry out. One step leads to the next one. In this sense it can truly be said that the inner movement of our depth process which was reflected in our dream has been enabled to extend itself in an open-ended way. It is unfolding and finding its direction in its own terms within the context of our individual life history.

It is significant to note also that while the dream originally presented us with ambiguous symbolism, the progression of our exercises in the Journal makes its message for us increasingly clear in the context of our everyday experience. Following our dream leads through the interweaving exercises of Journal Feedback enables the organic depth process of our lives to move beyond the symbolic obscurity of dreams toward a greater clarity in communicating its inner messages to us in terms of the actualities of our outer lives.

FINDING OUR DREAM LEADS

With this as our perspective, let us now reread our entries to find the dream leads that will be fruitful for us to follow in other Journal Feedback exercises. We go back over the dreams we have described in the Dream Log. Recent dreams are especially valuable in this regard. Now that we are familiar with this procedure, we can look at our new dreams as they come to us to see what leads they give us for further exploration in our lives via the Journal sections. Always we ask the question: Where else in the Journal do these dreams suggest that I work? Thus we find our dream leads. It is good to keep on as current a basis as possible with our new dreams. The sooner we let them lead us to the appropriate sections of the Journal, the sooner they will be able to communicate their inner messages to us, and the greater the momentum of movement in new directions we shall enable them to build in our lives.

While it is important to work with our most current dreams, we should not ignore our old dreams. They may be holding leads that are very valuable for us to follow but which we have overlooked in the past. In fact, even when we are working with our dream leads on a current basis, it is good to go back over our dreams from time to time, browsing through our Dream Log, looking for dream leads that we did not recognize before.

After we have reread our Dream Log, we continue through our entries in the Dream Enlargement section looking for further dream leads. Our experiences in Twilight Dreaming are often particularly fertile in this regard, possibly because they are a step closer to our conscious awareness than the dreams that come in sleep. The same is true of all of our Twilight Imagery experiences. We can find very valuable dream leads not only in the dream sections, but in the Twilight Imagery Log and in its follow-up section, Imagery Extensions. Drawing our leads from all of these sections and extending them with feedback exercises in other parts of the Journal enables us to channel our deep inner experiences into the activities of outer life. Conversely, it means that the active and available source of our conscious awareness will be in our depth.

Working with dream leads both from the sleep and twilight levels gives us a large resource for discovering and developing the potentials of our life. It is obviously not a type of exercise that is brief and simple. Rather it is open ended and ever expansive. We can work with it as little or as much as we choose, but the more proficient we become in finding our dream leads and following them in other Journal exercises, the greater will be our access to the larger sources of our individual lives.

We have been working with the inward level of reality as it moves on the depth dimension of our experience. Our dreams come from hidden parts of us often in strange symbolic forms, and the extension of our dreaming on the twilight level also proceeds beyond our rational control. We now come to the question of what correlation there may be between the experiences we have had in our inward depths and the experiences that have been taking place on the surface of our lives.

This is an important question, but we should not try to answer it by thinking about it. We can go to it indirectly and let it give us the awareness we desire regarding the inner movement of our lives.

The energy of our dreams and the rhythms of their movement express the emotional tone which is more important than any other detail.

Once again we sit in quietness. We close our eyes and let our breathing become slow. We are letting ourselves slide into the stillness. No thoughts. The slowness of our breathing and the emptiness of our mind enables us to feel the process of our lives as it moves within us. We do not think of what that is. We do not determine it with our minds. We let it present itself to us. We let it show itself and declare itself in its own timing.

As the stillness settles within us with our eyes closed, we draw ourselves back to the original series of dreams with which we began our dream work. As much as we can, we return to them. We see those dreams again and we feel the emotional tone that they carried. More important than the details of the dreams, we feel their movement, and especially the rhythms of their movement. We feel, for example, the energy of flowers growing in our dream, blossoming and then withering. And we feel the movement of the seed breaking in the ground and coming to the surface as new shoots of green. We feel the movement of prolonged submergence in our dream, of angry struggle, chase, escaping, recovery, of tearing down and building up. Whatever it presents to us, we feel the phases of change in the tone and the rhythms of movement in our dreams. We feel that in the silence.

And now we add to the dreams our experiences of the Twilight Dreaming. We draw the two together and feel them as a single continuity moving within us. We feel their unfolding and the ongoingness of their movement as a whole.

When the experience of this is full within us, we hold it. We stop the movement. We hold it where it is, as though we are holding it in our hand. We are holding our inner experience of the depth dimension as a base while we draw together the equivalent movement that has taken place on the outer level of our life as a whole.

With our eyes closed, now, we go back over the sequences of our life. We recapitulate in our minds the outline of events that we listed as our Steppingstones. We feel the rhythms of change and a variation among them, and especially we reexperience the flow and combination of circumstances that carried us into the recent period of our life. In quietness within ourselves, with our eyes closed, we are feeling the entire ongoing movement of our lives up to the present moment of time. Included in this are the external events and the inner events.

Mainly we wish to perceive and experience within ourselves the larger outlines of movement in our lives. But we let ourselves feel it all, the plans we have had and the obstacles to fulfilling them, the detours and disappointments, the renewed hopes and fears, the resolutions made, the decisions that we have held off and those that lie ahead.

We draw together the whole movement of our life as it has unfolded up to the present. A great many aspects of our life have opened to us and have been called to our attention in new ways in the course of our working in the various sections of the Journal. We include all of these as they return to our minds now, letting this moment become an experience of total reunification with respect to the movement of our life. As we do this, it is important to allow sufficient time to enable the process of inward integration to proceed and settle itself in its own timing.

Feeling the Oneness of Life

You are sitting in quietness. Your eyes are closed. The atmosphere is one of meditation, even of silence, unarticulated prayer. You are reexperiencing the essential movement of your life, allowing it to integrate itself into a new form as it proceeds.

In a little while as this is happening within you, you will be ready to take the next important step in the process of *life correlation*. Sitting in this stillness with the ongoing flux of your life taking shape within you, let yourself feel the moving unity of it. Maintain your perception of it, feeling the wholeness of it inwardly. You are feeling the reality of your life as a whole. It is taking form. It is tangible enough to touch, definite enough for you to hold it in your hand.

On the symbolic level of imagery, let yourself do that now. Whatever form your life is taking as it presents itself to you, hold it in your hand. Hold it in your left hand. Symbolically this is as though you are placing your life on the left side of your mind. It is your unconscious awareness of your life, as your life has been unfolding on the outward level of experience.

Now, still on the twilight level, take in your right hand the combined movements of your sleep dreams and your twilight dreaming as you have already drawn them together. Symbolically within yourself you are holding in your right hand the unified movement of your inner conscious life, and you are holding in your left hand the essential continuity of your outer conscious life. Balance one against the other. Balance each in relation to the other. It is as though there is a scale within your mind. Let the two sides equalize themselves so that the interior scale adjusts and places itself in harmonious balance.

When they come into balance, you can ask yourself the question of what the two sides of your life have to say to each other, and what they say to you when you draw them together and set them side by side. As this interior balancing is taking place, let yourself be especially open to any additional images, feelings, thoughts, insights, recognitions, ideas, perceptions, emotions, and especially new inspirations and plans that take shape in you. This is not a time for deliberate thinking but for being especially receptive to the awarenesses of every kind that arise spontaneously within you. The process of life correlation that allows the opposites of human experience, the outer and the inner, the conscious and the nonconscious, to establish their relation to one another is especially productive of new understanding. It is a process of inner life-balancing, of nonanalytic self-integration. As it sets the opposites side by side in a neutral, noninterpretive way, new integrative syntheses come forth, as though by themselves.

It is important, therefore, to be receptive and observant as you practice the life correlation of the inner and the outer. Take note of all the new experiences that now present themselves to you, and report them in your Dream Enlargements section. Record and describe them as fully as you feel impelled to do. But do not judge or interpret them in the moment that they come to you. Their significance for your life may not be apparent at that time. But describe them in the Journal, and then expand upon them at a later time, recording all the additional considerations they evoke in you. You will very often find as you do this that these experiences provide exceedingly valuable feedback leads for you to follow in opening out additional areas of your life in other sections of the Journal.

We can see from the varied procedures that are available to us for working with our dreams that the process of Dream Enlargement has numerous aspects and successive levels of depth to which it can be carried. Working with the seriality of dreams gives us a basic protection against our inadvertently inserting misleading analytical interpretations, and it also preserves the quality of flow that is inherent in the dream process. The procedures of Twilight Dreaming enable us to re-enter the dream process, drawing from the depths of sleep the seeds of fresh experiences that can readily be remembered, recorded, and extended. The process of life correlation permits us to move between the opposites of our outer and inner lives so that, as the two meet in a self-sustaining balance, new integrative syntheses are brought forth. Most important of all, however, are the dream leads which we draw from the enlargement of our dreaming, and which feed into the unfolding totality of our life as a whole. These enable us to resupply the Journal Feedback process continuously from the very depths of our being as we carry forward progressive integrations of our outer and inner lives.

Part 6

THE MEANING
DIMENSION

Introduction to
the Meaning Dimension

In the original presentation of the *Intensive Journal* process, the Meaning Dimension was referred to as Process Meditation. At that time we were seeking to evoke the experience of Process Meditation by describing the exercises that lead us to contact with the sources of creativity. We know from past experience that a person can be led to new and extended spiritual experiences by drawing upon the inherently integrative aspects of the Meaning Dimension. We do that by Process Meditation exercises that draw together the experiences of the three other dimensions, setting the present in the context of traditions of the past and forming new orientations for the future.

In the *Intensive Journal* process the start of this was the entries we made in the Life/Time Dimension. At that point we were seeking to experience the continuity of our life as we subjectively perceived it. Once this had been fulfilled we drew on these entries for our work in the Dialogue Dimension to extend the contents that showed themselves to be of primary significance in our lives. In the quiet atmosphere of our workshops we began to extend our dreams and our Twilight Imagery and thus we began to create new experiences of meaning.

Beginning in the Life/Time Dimension and extending our experience via the Dialogue Dimension we were drawn eventually to the symbolic forms of the Depth Dimension. The symbolism was

Only an experience of a meaningful life can make man whole.

enlarged in the terms of the Depth Dimension by means of the exercises of Twilight Dreaming and Imagery Extension. It brought us to the Meaning Dimension where we are now. Here we can see where the dream or Twilight Image is going. When this has been determined the intention of the dream is clear to us. We can return to desymbolize the dream and we can go, at least in our Journals, to where the dream was trying to take us. Now, being in the Meaning Dimension, we take the symbols drawn from our life and for a moment we absolutize the relative. We take personal symbols and we enlarge their transpersonal aspects in the Meaning Dimension.

By the use of Twilight Dreaming and Imagery Extension we draw the symbolism of the contents of the life: the material is carried from the personal level to the transpersonal level. The content of the life is experienced in archetypal terms, and the experience of meaning can begin. This leads us to the experience of meaning in the context of the life as a whole. The movement from the personal aspect of the object to the transpersonal level takes the contents of our life to another archetypal level where we can experience it in its transpersonal terms. A great deal is occurring while the movement of the transpersonal aspect is taking place. It is part of the reaching toward meaning that eventually establishes the Meaning Dimension.

We have here one of the keys to the Meaning Dimension. While the work in the self leads inherently outward and is limited by the number of experiences, their possibilities and the numerous forms in which they can appear, these forms being multiple enlarge as they are worked with. Larger concepts than were present at the beginning become part of the core of things and are integrated into the ultimate sense of meaning. We soon discover that it is at particular points in a person's life that the experience of meaning becomes important. Finding this experience of meaning, valuing it, and realizing the importance of the belief and the way we have been led to it becomes central in our life. The Meaning Dimension covers the aspect of life that we experience in terms of beliefs about the meaning of life. It deals with beliefs about fundamentals.

To carry out this role in the *Intensive Journal* process, the Meaning Dimension has five sections: The Meditation Log; Connections; Peaks, Depths, and Explorations (PDE); Mantra/Crystals; and Testament. Some of the sections have subsections, and all are necessary to enable us to work out the evolution of meaning in our lives.

18

Meditation Log I: Entrance Meditations

The Meditation Log is divided into three subsections, each of which plays an important role in stimulating a person's capacity for an active interior life. The premise underlying the Meditation Log is that human beings become more sensitive to the contents of their inner lives when they have a special method of working with them. What had been previously vague and elusive to them becomes tangible and a range of reality then becomes accessible to them.

The first part of the Meditation Log is the subsection that we use at workshops to help establish a deep atmosphere. It is a subsection with which we begin each major section of an *Intensive Journal* experience. We call it *Entrance Meditation* because it provides a neutral means by which we enter the deep and quiet place where our work is conducted. It is a means by which each person in their own rhythm enters their own psyche and proceeds inward until they come to a place that seems to them to have a quiet depth. Each person who participates in a workshop is necessarily engaged in a process of drawing his or her life together and is seeking to position the present situation of his life in a perspective of life as a whole. (Please see Appendix A.)

What we call Entrance Meditation is actually a form of Process

People become sensitive to the elusive threads of their inner lives when they have a definite method of working with them.

225

Meditation in which the person brings him or herself into an atmosphere of deep quiet and centeredness. This is one reason that Entrance Meditation is important in leading to the Meaning Dimension. In the conduct of workshops we undertake to establish a deep and quiet atmosphere by reading from one of the three series of Entrance Meditations printed by Dialogue House Library. The basic symbols in these, *The Well and the Cathedral, The White Robed Monk,* and *The Star/Cross* are essentially neutral in the sense that they are not connected with any special doctrine, and yet they have a spiritual focus. They seem to have a quieting effect when they are read aloud or when they are heard. At the workshops we read any one section leading to the repeated phrase, "In the silence, in the silence," which is a cue for all the participants to enter into the depths of their own psyche. The Meditation Log is different from the other Log sections in a very important regard. Where they are collectors and gatherers of the data of personal life, the Meditation Log not only gathers the data that pertains to the Meditation Dimension of our life experience but also carries it forward in an active way. Bearing in mind our broad definition and understanding of meditation as all the forms and methods by which we reach toward meaning in our lives and by which we seek the depth beyond the doctrines in religion and philosophy, we can see that there is large range of entries to be made in the Meditation Log.

We have already seen from our definition and perspective of it that meditation is not limited to any single type of religious practice. It is a generic human activity, for the reaching toward meaning is inherent in our lives. The experiences of meditation are taking place to some degree whenever human beings stop the mindless movement of their individual life experience in order to reflect on its significance, refocusing their relationship to its contents and its movement. Meditation includes all the forms by which we may turn our attention inward, first to consider our personal life within its own terms, and then to place it in the larger context of the universe. We are engaged in a form of meditation whenever we participate in a practice or an observance or a discipline that seeks either to explore a truth or to develop our capacity for greater awareness in any context, whether it be religious, philosophical, or our personal sensitivity to spiritual issues in everyday life.

We find that we can discern a variety of forms in which our inner experience presents itself as we proceed in the process of our meditation. Sometimes we experience our meditation in a dualistic form, sometimes in a unitary form, sometimes in an integral or holistic form that seems to draw the two together. Sometimes meditative experience comes to us in the midst of the activity and the turmoils of our life. Sometimes it comes in times of rest or in times of emptiness when nothing seems to be present and operating in our lives.

The movement of meditative experience has a paradoxical and often misleading appearance when looked at from the outside. One observation, however, that helps give perspective is our taking note of the fact that, like phenomena in the rest of the cosmos, the processes of our inner quest also move in cycles. In the course of our experience we touch highs and we touch lows, and we move back and forth through the gradations of expectation and disappointment. Understanding this adds a resiliency to the philosophy with which we can approach our life. Since neither the high nor the low is permanent, neither is necessarily to be preferred to the other.

The process of our inner quest moves in cycles of high and low. Understanding this adds resiliency to our way of approaching life.

The integral movement of the whole process of our inner life requires both of the opposites. Just as the sun cannot remain fixed at noon but has to set before it can rise again, so we must expect and prepare ourselves for a continuity of opposites to pass through our inner lives. We know in advance that we shall experience it with a sharp diversity of intensities, of fulfillments and frustrations. To meet it we require a method that will enable us to move through the continuity of inner change in a way that is harmoniously related to it even when the momentary message that it carries to us is so unpleasant that we wish to reject it.

One way to express it now is that the deep process of meditation requires us to accept all that transpires in our lives. But the word *accept* is too strong here and is not really correct. It is rather that we must learn to *acknowledge* whatever occurs in our lives, whether at outer or inner levels, so that it can move without being prejudged through the cycles of our life experience and eventually find its proper place and meaning in the continuity of our life as a whole.

In this context, a primary function of the sections in our *Intensive Journal* workbook is that they provide us with a tangible, flexibly structured place in which we can record and describe the outer and inner events of our lives. Once these are recorded and thereby acknowledged we can proceed to work with all the variations of our subjective life in an objective way. Then we can relate to them and see how the continuous movement of the cycles of life wishes to unfold within us.

From that we can discern the message that our life holds for us, and we can form our response to it in the course of our meditation.

In this way our individual destiny is shaped progressively as a deep dialogue with the messages that life gives us as we acknowledge and relate to the many levels of reality in our existence. To carry this through is for each of us a large, probably illimitable, enterprise. But it is an enterprise that is fulfilled by degrees. Thus we can know that if we work at it we shall find some measure of fulfillment as we proceed, even if it is never complete.

For such an interior undertaking, it is necessary that we be willing to work from a position in which we are freed from our personal and habitual opinions. That is the requirement that Socrates set in his day as he used his method of questioning (Maieutics) as his technique for achieving it. There can be little question of the fact that Socrates defined his goal correctly and that his method was a valid as well as a noble one. My experience in working with modern persons, however, has led me to conclude that it is too much to ask of human beings that they overcome their opinions to such a degree that they can actually be freed of them. There is simply not time enough in our finite existence. And yet it is necessary that our false and partial opinions be overcome.

The alternative is to move *with* our opinions in order to move through them to a place beyond them. In this way we avoid the difficult task of subduing our opinions. We let them be, but we place them in the position of serving our larger knowledge. Beyond their truth or error we let them be the vehicles that carry us to our next level of awareness, whatever that turns out to be as we continue our movement through the opposites of our life experience. In this context the whole of the *Intensive Journal* process may be understood as an instrument for meeting the goal that Socrates set. And our use of the Meditation Log to collect and acknowledge the unfolding facts of our inner reality is the step with which we launch the process of our work.

Using Entrance Meditation

We begin our work in the Meaning Dimension of the *Intensive Journal* process by establishing an atmosphere of quietness and depth. We do this whether it is a private workshop experience with ourselves alone or whether it is a workshop that we are participating in with many others. We begin by establishing a quiet atmosphere whether we expect to be engaged in our meditation for a short or a long period, whether we are setting aside a whole day or two days, or whether we are allotting it only a half hour at a time.

The units of our work may be thought of as atoms of time. They are holistic units—as Jan Christian Smuts used the phrase—each entire unto itself with its own nature. The needs and the potentials of such a unit are inherent within it, and they must be honored equally regardless of the length or the duration of the unit of experience. Each is whole unto itself, an atom of time. Thus even when we are allotting only a brief unit of meditation time, we must take care not to skip the step of establishing a meditative atmosphere. That first step is essential, and without it any unit of meditation, whether brief or extended, will begin by being off balance. And it will then be difficult for things to come into harmony.

One lesson that our varied experience with Process Meditation has taught is that the essence of meditation is not to be found in its content, nor in its doctrines or concepts or teachings. Its essence lies rather in the quality, the spirit of its experience.

The quality of meditation establishes an atmosphere that has a clear and discernible effect with respect to both the energies and the tone of the awarenesses that are brought forth. The atmosphere is like the space around a person, but not a physical space. It might better be described as a space that is within the person. It is important for our Process Meditation work that we place our experience within that space as an atmosphere that will nurture and sustain the inner process of our meditation.

What do we look for in an entrance meditation? One of its essential qualities is that the reading of it serves to quiet and center us. But it does this in a neutral way, postulating no particular doctrine of belief. The entrance meditation may describe a specific inner experience even to the extent of drawing us into that experience, but it does so only in order to take us inward. It uses the experience only as a means of securing for us a path of entry into the realm of meditation. It takes us through the entrance, and then it lets us go. It does not seek to mold us or predispose us toward any particular content of experience or commitment. It does not seek to suggest to us or implant in us any doctrine or concept, nor to have us follow any particular path of symbolism or imagery. It only seeks to take us through the entrance into the inner

Wholes are basic to the character of the universe. Holism as the operative factor in the evolution of wholes, is the ultimate principle of the universe.

Entrance meditations take us to a progressively deeper place in quietness and, once there we are able to perceive a larger realm of reality.

realm so that the atmosphere we find there will assist the process of our meditation and enable it to proceed unfettered. Unencumbered by external concepts, it will have the freedom to find and form its own profundities.

In Appendix A you will find passages of entrance meditations excerpted from the sequences that we use in the workshops. Each is a unit of experience, and they are given here so that you will have a convenient means of moving into a quiet atmosphere. Read them through briefly, and decide on the one that you wish to use as the starting point for your first experience. There is no great commitment involved in making this decision. Whichever one you choose is merely a temporary vehicle for you, and it will in each case be a thoroughly neutral vehicle. You are merely choosing a short unit of entrance meditation to help give you passage inward. Choose whichever one feels congenial to you now, and then we will proceed.

IN A QUIET ATMOSPHERE

When you have chosen a unit of entrance meditation to set the atmosphere, we are ready to begin. You will have your *Intensive Journal* workbook before you, open to the Meditation Log section. By way of preparation for the exercise write at the top of a fresh page the phrase "Entrance Meditation." And write beside it the date.

Take a moment to sit in stillness, doing nothing, letting your breathing become slower . . . and slower. When you feel ready, begin to read the passage of entrance meditation that you have chosen. Read it in whatever way feels most comfortable to you. Read it aloud or silently, repeating lines you need to repeat, phrasing it as fits your feeling. Presently you will come to the cue words, the phrase, "In the Silence . . . In the Silence." That is the point where we each go into our own silence. We have been carried by the reading through the entry way, and now we move further by ourselves in the open, inward spaces of our silent being.

As we go into the silence our eyes are closed. Our thoughts are quiet and our energies are not moving outward but inward. External phenomena do not distract us now, for our attention is directed to the events of our inner space. We perceive by sight, by sound, by each of our senses. All the senses by which we are accustomed to perceive things outwardly are available to us for our inward perception. Observations are presented to us, and understanding of an inner, intuitive kind comes to us as well when our eyes are closed and our energies are turned inward. We do not seek to control or direct what takes place in this interior space. We let it unfold out of its own nature. And especially we pay attention to what transpires. We observe it, and we record it.

This is the first use we make of our Meditation Log. As we move inward by means of our entrance meditation, we observe whatever comes within the span of our inner attention.

Perceptions of many kinds may be presented to us when our eyes are closed and we have turned our attention inward in the silence. Some are literal perceptions of things we know about from our past experience. Some are thoughts that now flow more freely than our ordinary thinking does. Some give new knowledge, but only indirectly by means of symbols. And some, being symbolic, seem to be intimations of things to come. Whatever form they take and whatever their message seems to be, we observe them as they come; and we take note of them without judgment, and especially without censorship.

To recapitulate: in order to establish a meditative atmosphere and to enter the twilight range of experience, we begin by choosing a segment of an entrance meditation. Reading that to ourselves, we allow it to carry us into its atmosphere, eyes closed in the silence. We let ourselves feel the inner atmosphere of the twilight level as we observe the varied types of inner happenings that come to pass, being formed as though by themselves.

Sometimes the field of inner experience is very active, sometimes it is simply a quietness. In either case we record impartially all that we observe as our attention is focused steadily and inwardly in the silence. We should bear in mind that at this point in our work our task is not so much to stimulate new experiences as to establish an atmosphere of quietness at the twilight level. We are therefore interested less in an active imaging experience—although we record whatever takes place—than we are in perceiving the depth and fullness of inner space and of experiencing ourselves as being there. Relaxing our conscious control, we let ourselves be absorbed into the stillness. That is the atmosphere in which we wish to enter the process of our meditation.

When we have recorded our entrance meditation experience, we remain in quietness.

19

Meditation Log II: Spiritual Positioning

To set the stage for the Spiritual Positioning exercise, take a fresh page in the Meditation Log section and write the phrase "Spiritual Positioning" at the head of it. And we write the date beside it. We are thus setting up a second subsection in the Meditation Log for our present and our future use.

We are sitting in stillness. Now we are sitting with eyes closed again, encouraging the further inner movement of our thoughts, our feelings and images. We are allowing them to move freely so that they can reflect any of the aspects of our life. We ask ourselves: How is it with me now on the spiritual level of my life? On the creative level of my life? On the believing level?

Spontaneously as it comes to us without considering intellectually or analytically, we write a few quick sentences to record and briefly describe the situation of our inner life at this time. Two or three sentences—four at the most—is all that we want to write now. Just a brief entry to record what we find when we look at our inner situation at this time. No censorship, no judgment, no interpretation. As spontaneously as we can, we record what we find when we look within to see and to describe our inner condition during this recent period of our life.

For example:

This has been a time when I have been wondering about many things. Things I used to take for granted are doubtful to me now. Perhaps it is because I don't see Mary any more that I don't go to church now. I seem to be spiritually in between things.

Or, the present spiritual position may be:

I find myself alone a lot and wondering. Reading many things is good and interesting, but it seems to increase my unsureness. I start to meditate, but I don't keep it up. I wish I could pray, but I don't think I know how.

Or it may be:

The experience I had with Rev. — in April has brought sunlight into my life. I understand now why they talk about being born again. That is exactly how it feels. But it does not answer all my questions and it has not solved all my problems. I still live where I live, in the same place with the same family and with the same job. I feel I am at a plateau of my life, but I feel that there is a lot more for me to do, and there is a lot more for me to know. And I don't yet know what it is.

Or it may be:

My political beliefs are my spiritual life. At least they have been. My ideals and my ethics have been there and I know that my commitment to political action has had a religious quality. But right now I am hanging loose. I miss the need for action, but it gives me a chance to look at things.

Or it may be:

I feel much more centered and less edgy since I am with Swami—. Maybe that is because I can be off drugs with him. I think he has more to teach me and I hope I will be able to learn.

Or it may be:

I remain true to the religious commitment that I made when I was in my teens. I know that truth is there and God is there. But quite often I cannot pray the way I should, or even the way I used to pray. And lately I have not felt the steadfastness in love that I should, or even that I used to have.

The entries can refer to any content or emotion. Whatever presents itself to us as the facts of our inner life is what we should record here. If we find that we are judging ourselves, that is a fact; so we record it. Often we are unduly harsh in our judgments of ourselves when we say what we should be feeling or what we should be able to do; and by the same token we may be over-quick in our self-praise or in our rejoicing at experiences that have come to us. But the fact is that we are feeling those self-judgments, invalid or premature though they may be; therefore we record the fact that we feel them. That is how we take the first step in establishing our spiritual position.

Sometimes in making this brief entry of spiritual positioning a metaphor or simile will come to us. Quite often these are especially valuable since they provide an expressive, nonliteral way of stating our inner condition. In the course of this work, because of the elusive quality of spiritual experience, we often have reason to remember that one symbol may be worth a thousand words. A symbol from a dream or an image that comes to you in the course of twilight imagery, or perhaps one that presents itself during the entrance meditation may convey a great deal in a few words.

When Leo Tolstoy, for example, was drawing together the spiritual journal that he called *My Confession,* he recalled a dream in which a fledgling bird fell from its nest. He felt that this expressed his inner condition at the time when he lost his faith. If Tolstoy were attending an *Intensive Journal* workshop at that time in his life, an appropriate entry under the heading of "Spiritual Positioning" would have been: "I feel like a fledgling bird that has fallen from its nest and cannot fly." With just another sentence or two to indicate the details of the circumstances, Tolstoy would then have placed himself in the spiritual movement of his life. That is what we mean by Spiritual Positioning.

Bearing this in mind, we let ourselves rest in the stillness that was established in our entrance meditation. Our eyes closed, we let ourselves feel and consider the present situation of our inner life. What is the atmosphere, the sense of meaning, the tone of our inner life at this time? What are its main contents? What are the messages we have had about it from our dreams or other spontaneous experiences that have come to us? What are the beliefs that are holding strong within us? And what are the doubts, the wonderings, the explorations? What are our involvements in outer activities? What are our concerns about social or political issues? And what are our concerns about the ultimates of truth in human existence? What are the commitments of our life? And what are our hesitations?

Describe the contents and the conditions that you find there when you look inside yourself, experiencing your feelings and awarenesses but recording them as an impartial observer of your inner life. Simply record what you perceive there, briefly, objectively, nonjudgmentally. Describe it just as it presents itself to you before you give yourself a chance to reflect upon it or to think of a comment about it or an interpretation to place on it. Put it on paper quickly, spontaneously, concisely—even if you write it ungrammatically, even if it is misspelled. We do not have to write the whole thing now, but just a few sentences. Just enough to give ourselves a starting point for the next steps that are to follow in our meditative work. Now write the brief statement of your spiritual position, in the silence.

✍

Writing this short, spontaneous summary of our present spiritual position has the effect of recalling many awarenesses and memories to our minds. But we do not let them intrude into our statement. We wish it to be brief and succinct, expressing the primary elements in our present inner situation. We find that, if we can hold the details to one side, the essentials are drawn into sharper focus, and this gives us the kind of starting point we require for our further work. That is why just three or four sentences written directly and unselfconsciously is the best way to proceed.

Although we do not include them in it, the thoughts and memories that come to us while we are writing our statement of spiritual position can be of great value to us. We certainly do not wish to bypass them and lose contact with them now that they have been recalled to us. They may contribute to our understanding of how we arrived at our present position and the issues that are involved in the contents of our beliefs. More than that, those memories and awarenesses may contain energy and ideas that will be drawn upon in a later phase of our inner experience. In the background of all our practices in Process Meditation is our awareness that we are cumulatively gathering data that will serve as an inner resource for us in the continuity of our work.

PLACING OURSELVES IN OUR PRESENT INNER LIFE

With this in mind, we now take a step to incorporate in our Meditation Log the various pieces of information that were recalled to us but that we did not include in our basic statement. At this point it is worthwhile for us to give them as much space and range of expression as is needed to record all that they suggest to us. We take a fresh page for this, so that the descriptions we write here will be separate from our statement of Spiritual Positioning. We want to let that remain by itself so that we can return to it in a little while, read it back to ourselves, and perhaps add some further thoughts and comments from another perspective.

We now begin to write what may become a flowing and open-ended description of the recent development and contents of our inner life. How did we arrive at our present beliefs and opinions? What questions were we asking that called those issues to our attention? What questions are we still asking? Who were the persons who influenced us and played a role in our inner experiences? What was the chain of circumstances, what were the outer events and pressures of life, the book we happened to find, the speakers we happened to hear, that led to our present state of belief?

We wish to recapitulate here and describe as fully as we can whatever has taken place in the recent period of our experience. We are retracing the presence, and also the times of absence, of a sense of meaning in our life, personal and more-than-personal. We want to recall and record as much as we can of the changing phases of our beliefs, our doubts and intuitions, our certitudes and confusion, our intellectual ideas, our symbolic understandings, our participation in rituals, our agreement with others, and our arguments on doctrines and beliefs. We want to reconstruct it all so that we can see our inner picture as a whole, and reexperience it in the depth of ourselves.

We focus our attention on the present condition of our inner life, however full or empty it may currently seem to be. We let the controls of our intellectual mind drop to a relaxed state at the twilight level so that memories and thoughts can move within us as a free-flowing stream. Whatever comes to our mind, we record. Just brief entries are sufficient here. Just a few words. Just a phrase or two. It does not need to be a complete sentence or a grammatical construction. Just enough to convey the thought or feeling or memory or idea that has come to us. And the memories need not be complete. Do not postpone writing it down until you can remember the whole thing. If you remember only a small bit, start with that. As you are describing it, more will come to your mind. It is a self-stimulating process, but it has to have a starting point in order for the evocative effort to be set in motion. As you put your pen to paper you will find that the act of recording one item, however insignificant it may seem, tends to stimulate the thought of something else.

As you recall events or experiences, describe all that comes to you. Write down more than you need to. Describe more than you feel is necessarily relevant. It is easy to eliminate or pay no further attention to things you recorded if, later on, when you read them back, they do not seem to be important. But if you do not write them down, you will not be able to make that evaluation. And perhaps they will become important in a later context. Furthermore, the act of describing them on paper will often elicit additional awarenesses you had not thought of before.

In describing the contents of this spiritual period in your life, it is good to open up as many issues as come to your mind. Do not restrict yourself to particular themes. You are not writing a school composition that has a beginning, a middle, and an end. Describing this time in your inner life is an open-ended work. You want to stimulate and mention as many different facets of your inner life as you can. In that way you can bring them to your own attention and you can come back to explore them further at a later time. Here we are engaged in progressively loosening the soil of our inner life.

Many of us, having been brought up in a materialist culture or, alternatively, in a rigidly traditionalist culture, may find that thoughts and feelings of a spiritual nature are packed hard and tight within us because we have not given ourselves the freedom to experience them. As a result we do not have easy access to them. Some of us may even be led to think that they are not there, that we personally do not have such awarenesses and desires. Little by little, however, by loosening the soil of our inner lives, we will each find that an inner reaching toward meaning in life and toward a larger-than-personal connection is present in all of us, although in each of us it takes a different form. If we have thought that it is not present in us and if we are not accustomed to working with it, its presence may not easily become apparent to us. But entry by entry, in the delineation we make now or as it will be stimulated in us, and gradually build as we proceed through the exercises that follow, we shall touch and find what is spiritually present in each of us at the depth of our being.

It is most important that we get the process started, and we do this by describing any significant aspect of the present phase in our inner life. Once our description has begun, recollections, observations, even specific rememberings will come through to us in increasing abundance. It is a self-sustaining process once it is set in motion. We do, however, have a number of checkpoints to which we can refer in order to help get the process moving and to build its momentum. We may stimulate our capacity of recall, for example, by asking ourselves questions like the following:

What have been my primary beliefs during this recent period with respect to the fundamental issues in my life? For example, in religion, or personal ethics, my political philosophy, my involvement in social causes.

What doubts do I have about beliefs that I have had in the past? Do I still believe in the things I was taught as a child? Is it changing? Or deepening? What wonderings and searchings, what deep thinking is taking place in me?

Have I had any strong inner experiences during this period? In dreams or at religious services or in meetings of any kind, with drugs or meditation or in the midst of discussions?

Have I had any special awareness at times when I have been alone?

Have I had any important prayer experiences either in privacy or in a group? Have I had any striking experiences that were not exactly prayers but might be considered the equivalent of prayers?

Have I had experiences that led me to feel that they had to be expressed in some form of art, as a poem or a painting or a song?

Have I had any moments of changes in my consciousness, a sense of deepening or heightening? Have there been any moments when I felt that I was able to know something important and that I knew it in a special way?

Were there any times of really intense prayer, of spontaneously asking out of great need? Times of prayers being answered? Of waiting? Of being anxious and disbelieving during the time of waiting?

Considering these various factors and states of interior life, and many, many more that will rise to our consciousness as we are recalling and describing these, we go back over the path of our inner experience during this recent time and recall what has taken place within us. What were we seeking? What were we convinced of? Or wondering about? With whom were we sharing our concerns? Our acts of faith? Our acts of anxiety? Agreeing or disagreeing? Believing and disbelieving? These experiences that we did not expect, or those that we heard about and wondered at, that speech we heard, that book we read, that dream, that image, that idea?

We go back in our minds over what there has been in our inner lives that has led us to where we are now, no matter where it is that we are now. These recent months, these recent years, the events on the inner road, the road that we have traveled with all its turnings, its changes, with its unknowings, that led us here to where we are now.

Sitting in quietness, we record as much as we can recall, describing it in the Spiritual Positioning subsection of our Meditation Log. We write it as it comes to us, without judgmental selecting or censoring. We reject nothing that comes to our mind but we describe it as objectively as we can, whether as the brief mention of specific facts or as the flowing recollection of contexts of circumstance. This is our delineation of the present period in our spiritual life. We write it in the silence.

✍

When we finish this piece of writing, we know that it is not ended, but that our reconstruction can extend itself at another time when the material is ready. We therefore come to a pause. Not pressing but relaxed, we return to an atmosphere of stillness.

Very often people find that by the time they have carried through

To find the present period in our spiritual life, we go back over our inner lives that have led us to where we are now.

the exercise of recalling the recent period and have described some of its main contents, their perception of the situation as a whole has been changed. They realize that the meaning and implications of this time in their life are quite different from what they had originally thought them to be, and thus their evaluation and emotional response to it are different as well.

For this reason, when you have finished writing as much of the recapitulation as you feel is appropriate for you at this sitting, turn back to the page where you wrote your original brief statement of spiritual position. Read it back to yourself now, observing what further thoughts and emotions stir in you as you read it. What changes would you make in it? Perhaps there are some enlargements or modifications that you feel should be added to your original statement. Or perhaps you now feel that your entire statement of position should be refocused and presented from another point of view in the light of the perspective that has evolved in the course of your writing.

Read it back to yourself again slowly, thoughtfully, giving it full consideration. And now write your second statement, taking note of any additional thoughts or feelings or awareness that have formed in you in the course of the *Intensive Journal* work you have done so far. This second statement need not be brief. Let it be as full and as encompassing as feels appropriate and satisfying to you. Or, if you prefer, let it be another short statement, but with some further comments relating to your original statement.

Whatever its length, or its content, let it be a statement that expresses the beliefs and the issues that you most profoundly care about, as far as you are presently aware. Bear in mind that this is a statement of spiritual position intended for no one's eyes but your own. Once you have written it, it will be your base point, the point from which you will set your active experience of Process Meditation into motion.

Let us be in silence, therefore, reading back our original statement and, as we are ready, adding our second statement to it. Together they begin to form a tangible record of the inner process working in our lives.

20

Meditation Log III: Inner Process Entries

When we have finished writing our second statement dealing with the present spiritual condition of our lives, we are ready to take the step that enables us to use the Meditation Log section continuously as an active instrument in our work. We noted earlier that the general role of the Log sections in the structure of the *Intensive Journal* system is to gather the factual data of our lives. This is true of the other five Log sections in our workbook, and it is true of the exercises we have carried through in the Meditation Log so far. But now we come to the point where the Meditation Log section takes on an active role. There are increasingly creative effects that arise from the way that we work with the third subsection of the Meditation Log, the *Inner Process Entries*.

We begin by taking a fresh page and writing the name of this subsection at the head of it. And we write today's date. The phrase, Inner Process Entries, has considerable significance for the principles that underlie the *Intensive Journal* work. It is the inner process of subjective experiences that draws a person's life together so that it can find its direction and eventually reach its meaning. That is why the subsection of Inner Process Entries is especially important for the Intensive Journal process. It is here that we gather the data of our inner process in a way

The inner process of subjective experiences draws a person's life together.

that gradually forms and shows us the personal and transpersonal meaning of our lives.

As we pause to consider what we have done so far, we must realize that even at this early stage we have already taken several steps that have set an inner process into motion. By means of an entrance meditation we quieted ourselves so that we could enter the twilight range of experience. In that twilight atmosphere we wrote our first statement regarding our present spiritual position. Then we proceeded to recapitulate the inner and outer events in the recent period of our life as these have set the background for our present inner situation. This description could be relatively brief and cursory, or it could be a very full delineation. The degree of detail in which we found ourselves exploring and describing the interior development of this time in our lives may in itself be a significant piece of information for us. And the effects of that exploration may have been expressed when we wrote our second statement.

Each of these steps as we carried them out in our exercise is an interior event in itself. Viewed in sequence, they comprise an inner process. And we are now beginning to give tangible form to this inner process here in the Meditation Log.

Our next step is to record and briefly describe the inner experiences through which we have passed in our *Intensive Journal* work up to this point. The details are already contained in the sections where we recorded the actual experiences, but here we want to build an overview of the continuity of our experience as a whole. With this goal in mind we go back over each of the steps that we have taken, listing them, describing them briefly if that is necessary, and summarizing what took place. It is especially relevant in this recapitulation of our inner process to describe what was taking place within us as we have proceeded from exercise to exercise. This is the place to take note of difficulties that arose and enthusiasms that we felt as we came to particular issues in our life.

What was the quality of our consciousness and the changes in it while we were engaged in the entrance meditation? What kinds of twilight imagery came to us? Writing now in retrospect, what observations can we make about the nature of the memories and the emotions that have arisen in us in the course of our experiences? We take note not only of the thoughts that came to us in the course of our experiences but the *lines of thinking* that were set in motion. Are we aware of new ideas and realizations that came to us now for the first time, interspersed with our emotions and our memories and our images? And are we aware of old ideas that we have thought of before and that we have pushed aside but that are now returning to us for reconsideration in new forms?

As we recapitulate our experiences, adding our observations and comments, we let the process of our inner perceptions continue and grow. We let ourselves extend the lines of thinking that bring old and new thoughts to us. We let them move of themselves so that we can eventually see where they are trying to go. We find that these lines of thinking and awareness tend to build while we are engaged in describing the inner experiences in which we have been engaged. That is why here in Inner Process Entries we recapitulate our experiences, describing our emotions and observations, and encouraging new lines of perception to be set into motion.

To prepare for this exercise, let us now return to our quietness. Sitting in stillness, we go over in our minds the sequence of interior events since we began our work, including our entrance meditation, our first statement of spiritual position, our delineation of the period, and writing our second statement of spiritual position. We go back over our experiences of each of these, recapitulating and describing them briefly, letting our perceptions move and flow as they come to us. In the Silence.

✍

Each person's experiences are unique. For this reason no Journal entry can be taken as a model for someone else. Some examples, however, may help us see the issues and the possibilities that are involved. Consider, for example, this Inner Process Entry by S.J.

> The silence of the entrance meditation was helpful, but it was not deep enough. I realize that I have to practice more at quieting myself. Not only for physical reasons, but spiritually.
>
> Reading back my statements of spiritual position, it occurs to me that they could have been written from another point of view. The facts are the same but I realize that I can look at those facts from two different angles. And they will both be true, at least in a sense.
>
> I mean, I have been following my conscience in political action, and that is one important part of my spiritual life. And I have also been working out my religious philosophy, and sometimes this fits with my politics, and sometimes it doesn't.

And I have also been working out what my personal and sexual life should be; and sometimes this fits with my religion and philosophy, and sometimes it doesn't.

I realize as I am writing this that in this past year my different interests and different activities have all been trying to achieve a single integration. I have been trying to work out a single point of view with which to live my life. But it is complicated. It has so many aspects. That must be why I find myself thinking of it in more than one way. But I want to be just one. I want it to be unified because I seek unity and consistency in my life. But perhaps that is not possible. Perhaps it is a wrong idea. It may already have caused trouble for me in my life. I have to find out more about this before I make further decisions.

In the entry just quoted we see a person placing himself in the midst of the movement of his life simply by stating the inner facts of that life. And we can see how his awareness is opening and expanding in the very act of the writing.

It would be correct to describe this as an example of working in your life, especially as we take note of the fact that the work is clearly not self-analysis and not self-interpretation. The journalist is writing a continuous statement that is conscious but is not self-conscious. It is an active consideration of the multiple contents of the life made in the midst of being engaged in the decisions of living. What we see here is not self-reflective thinking *about* one's life but, much more, the conscious act of living one's life by thinking through its issues. The journalist in this entry was carrying forward the qualitative contents of his life not by thinking about them to analyze them, but by intensely thinking them through as the forward thrust of his life commitment. It can be said that he was *thinking his life* forward with the continuous recording of his Inner Process Entries serving as the vehicle for his movement.

We find that when there is difficulty or confusion in a life, the best way to proceed in making Inner Process Entries is simply by stating the facts of our experience. Do it as naturally and as unselfconsciously as you can, and the process will begin to work for you. We see an instance of this in the following entry by R. N.

My first feelings when I went to describe my present spiritual position were confusion. I drew a blank, and I thought that must mean that I don't have a spiritual position. Other people do, but I don't. Then I decided to write about beliefs I don't have any more. In the present moment they are conspicuous by their absence. They are beliefs I used to have. I didn't think that I still had them on my mind, but when I went to write about them I became very teary. It was nostalgia, I guess. The tears took me by surprise. Otherwise I would have stopped them before they came. I realize that I have a lot of emotion tied up in those old beliefs even if I think I don't believe them any more. I think there's a lot of love blocked up in there too. It's love that I've been missing. I have opened something that I had hidden in a box. It scares me right now, but I feel warm where I felt cold before. I'll wait and see what happens.

In an entry like this, it is apparent that a process is beginning to move beyond the consciousness of the person. Something that had been dormant, perhaps lightly sleeping, has now been awakened and is becoming active again. We might have the thought that it would be better not to arouse it, but that possibility has another disturbing aspect. Following that approach, we might easily let a large part of the potentials of our lives remain asleep. In one frame of mind, when a person is in an atmosphere of anxiety and is fearful of whatever is not controlled, the impulse may well be to let sleeping beliefs and emotions lie dormant. As one begins to move into a more sanguine mood, however, as we see in R.N.'s entry, there comes the realization that those sleeping emotions have strong energies of life within them. The warmth of love is felt stirring in those emotions, and with it there is the intimation that something of wisdom lies latent there as well. It may well be worth working to draw them forth, as R.N. seems to feel. And it may be a great waste of potential if we let them sleep untouched.

Each of the subsections in the Meditation Log has a specific purpose and use. The segment for entrance meditation is the place where we go in order to quiet ourselves so that we can reach inward to the depth dimension. We go to this subsection whenever we are beginning a unit of *Intensive Journal* work, for it is here that we can establish the inward atmosphere that we require.

Spiritual Positioning is the subsection where we can place ourselves with respect to the movement of inner time. It also is the segment of our workbook where we go when we are beginning a unit of *Intensive Journal* work. Just as entrance meditation gives us entry to the depth dimension of our experience, Spiritual Positioning places us in the Life/Time Dimension. Thus these two subsections set a base at the beginning on which the continuity of *Intensive Journal* work can be built.

The subsection of Inner Process Entries, in contrast to these, is used throughout our practice of *Intensive Journal* work. It is the primary vehicle by which new data and experiences can constantly be added and assimilated. While the other two subsections are used occasionally, especially at the beginning of a unit of *Intensive Journal* practice, Inner Process Entries is used all the time.

In practice, because of its active and continuing use, Inner Process Entries is the main operational segment of the Meditation Log. As we proceed in our work, we shall see how this becomes a matter of accustomed *Intensive Journal* usage, especially where we use this subsection to accompany our other exercises. At those points, when we say that it is now time to make our entry in the Meditation Log, it will actually be the Inner Process Entries to which we are referring. If it is Entrance Meditation or Spiritual Positioning that we mean, we call it by its name. But when we are to make an Inner Process Entry in the course of the later exercises of our inner work, we find that we often refer simply to the Meditation Log.

We cannot yet see the culminating and integrative messages that the Meditation Log may be carrying and building for us. But they will appear in their time. In the meanwhile we shall be adding our entries there as we proceed in our work following each of the appropriate exercises in the other sections of our workbook.

21

Connections I: The Cycles of Connective Experience

A good way to approach the concept that underlies the work we do in the *Connections* section of the *Intensive Journal* workbook is to think in terms of its opposite. The opposite of connection is separation, and *alienation* is the special term that has come to be used in describing the experience of being separated from life in modern society. Alienated persons are those who do not feel a personal link to a group or to a tradition or to any established system of beliefs or behavior. They feel separated from the social and spiritual structures that ordinarily support individuals in the conduct of their lives.

Alienated persons feel separated from social and spiritual structures that support them in the conduct of their lives.

Persons living in modern times are particularly vulnerable to alienation because our period of history is one in which old traditions have lost much of their acceptance while new values have not yet been securely established. Individuals are therefore left very much on their own with no clear standards to guide them. They are subject to the pull of conflicting urges and desires but, not belonging to a culture that provides a solid frame of reference, they have no criterion for decision when circumstances call upon them to make an act of choice or an act of will. They are left in the disconnected world of alienation, vulnerable to the disorientation that results from living with unstable values. They are subject also to the symptoms of emotional disturbance that inevitably accompany feelings of unresolved conflict.

In the state of alienation, the modern individual is the drop of water that has been separated from the sea.

Over the years I have thought of the problem of alienation in terms of a Tibetan teaching that remains in my mind from the period in my life when I was first exploring the world's religions. It said, as I recalled it, that a drop of water will instantly evaporate if it is left by itself, but that it will last forever if it is united to an ocean.

In the state of alienation, the modern individual is the drop of water that has become separated from the sea. Because of aloneness the individual is in a very precarious situation, and in that state feels the angst that is the general condition of modern neurosis. The question is whether we can have a viable means of countering this angst. Given the many factors that tend toward alienation in modern society, is it possible to have a method of strengthening in individuals their inherent sense of belonging to larger contexts of life in order to extend their capacity for living? Can we help the drop of water maintain its connection to its ocean?

Human beings naturally reach for larger contexts of belonging and belief. The history of culture as well as that of religion bears witness to this, especially in those periods of intense social transition when broadly accepted beliefs have lost their hold on a population. History discloses that when the experience of connection does not take place, it leads to an emptiness of feeling and a disorientation in life. This is a social and cultural phenomenon but the experience of it is personal. Individuals feel its pain privately and with such intensity that they often seek to overcome it at all costs. In fact, one point of view from which we can understand the religious ferment in the second half of the twentieth century, especially among the younger generations, is that it expresses the spontaneous, and sometimes desperate, attempt to leap over the alienation of modern society in order to establish a personally meaningful connection to life.

Our *Intensive Journal* work seeks to provide a means of establishing strong inner connections while avoiding the dangers that come from leaping and jumping in the desperate quest for meaning. The life of the spirit is too important to be approached haphazardly, and the large energies contained within it make it too dangerous to be dealt with carelessly. That is why we proceed step by step and follow a systematic methodology in reaching toward the larger meaning of our individual lives. We begin with the contents of our life, including experiences of every kind, from suffering to exaltation. And we are especially alert for the small intimations that come to us from time to time giving us clues to the larger-than-personal meanings of human existence. We gather these intimations and describe them as fully as we can. We try to draw them into such a form that we can work with them as the raw material for new experiences and for larger realizations that will come to us, each within the context of our individual life considered as a whole. To collect the data of inner experience that will enable us to work toward the meaning of our lives is the main function of the *Connections* section.

An individual human being can be strengthened and sustained by being connected to a larger entity that may be of many different sizes or types. The connection may be to a larger political unit as a nation, to a local group in a neighborhood, or by blood ties to a tribe or to an expanded family of kinfolk. The connection may also be by less tangible markers than blood or land. It may come through subjective feelings of connection like shared beliefs and loyalties. It may come by being part of a religious tradition, holding a philosophy of life, being identified with a social ideology or movement, even appreciating or participating in the arts in a particular way. The forms in which connection to larger units of life may be experienced are exceedingly varied, especially in modern culture, where the pluralism of subjective values is constantly being increased.

In making these subjective identifications that will extend their connection to life, human beings are like drops of water seeking to be connected to a river or an ocean. They intuitively know that when a person is connected to a larger whole, the individual life is strengthened and sustained and extended. We must take note, however, of a special factor that is at work where human beings are concerned. Our human nature is such that we cannot be connected to larger entities merely by a simple physical joining. We are not like stones that become part of a pile simply by being added to it, nor like flowers that become part of a field just by being planted there, nor like raindrops that become part of a lake as they fall into it. Human beings become connected to a larger whole only through their subjective feelings.

The Connective Experience

Human connection has a physical aspect, but that is only the raw material. Even the blood connections of race and nation require the subjective feelings of identification and loyalty. Without them, such physical

When our life is perceived as having an inner meaning, it produces a great energy that can have tremendous effects.

facts as birth and color have no relevance. The critical element in human connection is the *inner* experience of the physical facts. If they have no emotional meaning to the person, they have no power. But when they are perceived as having an inner meaning, either emotionally or intellectually, they produce a great energy that can have tremendous effects. It can build the pressures that bring about radical social changes in history. And it can set the context in which individuals can deepen their perception of reality, enlarging their spiritual awareness. In broad terms, *connective experiences* are the means of *meaningful inner linkage* between a person's consciousness and the outer realities of the world. They thus have great importance not only personally, but socially and spiritually as well. The exercises that derive from our connective experiences become an increasingly valuable resource as we proceed in our ongoing use of the Journal process.

The need for connection leads to religious-type experiences and beliefs but is not necessarily limited to what we think of as institutionalized religion. The individual needs to be linked to the various social and philosophical frameworks in which persons can recognize the meaning of their life.

During the early years of life it is usually more accurate to describe the contents of connective experiences as being learned behavior. Beliefs tend to be taught or absorbed from the culture, and there is relatively little that takes the form of spontaneous individual experiences. During childhood the doctrines of religion are taught together with the various codes of prescribed behavior, rituals, social manners, ethics, and the like. While these teachings are being inculcated by the authority figures of the culture, the young person is absorbing them, acquiring beliefs that are being imposed from outside the self.

Soon, however, what has been absorbed from the authorities of the culture returns in new forms as the spontaneous awarenesses of the individual. These are the first bona fide connective experiences in a person's life. They are the occasions in which individuals discover in the context of their own life, and by means of their own capacities of cognition, the experiential reality of perceptions of truth which they had known before only as doctrines to be memorized.

Once connective experiences have begun to happen spontaneously and individually within the young person, the development of consciousness has moved to a new level. From that point onward, the process of learning has two main ingredients. In one aspect it is based primarily on information and beliefs that are drawn from sources outside the individual. In its other aspect it involves new recognitions and understandings that come by direct experience from within. The interrelationship, indeed the tension, between these two modes of life consciousness plays a major role in shaping the tone and style of the individual's growth.

The years of adolescence are replete with such mixed experiences of learning. There is much objective information to be absorbed. There is also a great deal that can only be learned when its basis has been subjectively accepted: for example, the groups to which one belongs, the acceptable activities for one's station in life, beliefs about the gods, and other ultimates of existence. In those societies where a single set of traditions dominates the culture, the process of adolescent learning is much simplified. There is a unilinear process, since the culture does not have competing doctrines and traditions that are being simultaneously taught from different points of view.

Even these simpler societies, however, do not consider it to be sufficient for a person simply to be taught the doctrines of the tribe. They must also have their own experience of it, at least in principle or symbolically, so that they will be connected to the religion of the tribe or to the secrets of the craft not simply by words that have been memorized, but by direct, inner experience. That is the significance of the type of initiation ritual that requires a young person to be alone for three days in the woods and to fast until a revelatory experience presents itself.

In modern culture the need for connective experience is at least as great as in earlier periods of history, but the circumstances are much more intricate. The complexity comes primarily from the fact that modern society is not limited to a single tradition into which every young person is to be initiated. In our pluralistic, secular culture there are many traditions from which to choose. Furthermore, in modern times the choice of the belief or the version of truth into which the person is to seek initiation is not determined by the society or the authorities of the society. It is left open for the individual to decide.

This freedom is exactly as it should be, but, ironically, it compounds the difficulty. Many persons, being young, are not prepared to choose. They are not yet in a position to specify to which philosophy they wish to be initiated, or to which religion, or social or political

The tremendous waste of human resources occurs because the values of life in the modern industrial culture are too narrow.

Since initiation has lost cultural support, individuals can reach a connection to life only through their own resources.

ideology, or to which way of life they wish to commit themselves, whether to the arts, or to athletics, or business enterprise, or pleasure seeking, or scientific research, or whatever other ways of life the modern world may make available. In modern culture the age of adolescence is much too early to be making a lasting life decision.

The central fact is that, since the experience of initiation has lost so much of its cultural support in modern times, the individual can reach an experience of connection to life only through his or her own resources. And the one basic resource we each have is our own life with our inner perception of its contents. It is now the individual life and not the culture that provides the framework and the content for initiation experiences.

The connective experience no longer comes at a specific, culturally-set time. It is no longer induced and protected by a ritual situation. Now it comes at the time, or times, when the vicissitudes of the individual's life, its pressures, its circumstances, and the self-directed seeking by the person, bring about experiences so intense that they are connective to the larger scope of life. Initiation to meaning now takes place in the midst of the individual existence, forced by the pressures of its evolving life context. That is one important reason why our *Intensive Journal* work begins by providing a vehicle for drawing our whole life history into view. It is by this means that we get access to the raw materials of our life and establish a life context for the various connective experiences that take us toward our own recognition of meaning.

The complexity of individual spiritual experience in modern times presents certain disadvantages but it also opens many new possibilities for us. For one thing, if modern persons are not able to have their full connective experience at the time of adolescence, they may nonetheless have a series of connective initiatory experiences in the course of the ensuing years. And since we have a much longer life expectancy now than in earlier centuries, there is the possibility that many modern persons may have connective experiences of their own in their later years that will be of significantly greater profundity than the ritual initiation they might have passed through in their youth. In some lives we can discern a definite inner process by which successive connective experiences, occurring from time to time in the course of a long life span, bring a cumulative deepening of spiritual knowledge.

The Cycles of Connective Experience

There is also a process that operates within our connective experiences. It is a cyclical process with highs and lows that can be deceptive to us when we are caught up in the emotional intensity of our personal experiences. It is very helpful to have a perspective of the movement of the cycle as a whole. With it we can sense where we are and can understand which transient pressures are working upon us when we find ourselves in the midst of the fluctuations of a cycle of connective experience.

The cycle of connective experience begins with its opposite, with separation from meaning, with the consciousness of alienation. Painful emotions accompany this phase of the cycle, the negativity of feeling that there is no meaning to be found, the anxiety that it will never be achieved, that one is not capable of ever finding it. And there is the depressive lack of energy, a phenomenon that is seemingly physical but is mainly an indication of the absence of connective experience.

During this low phase of the cycle there will also be a variety of experiences that take place in the twilight range of cognition. Some may be visionary, some may have the quality of nightmare dreams, some may activate intense emotions, and others may carry an intuitive foreknowledge. The experiences that come during this phase tend often to have a dark, unpleasant quality, and for that reason they are often bypassed, repressed, or ignored. It is important, however, to realize that, pleasant or not, these are integral parts of the whole process, and therefore that they must be acknowledged in neutral terms. We make no judgment of them but we take note of their presence as we proceed.

In the latter part of this time of darkness there begins to be a more affirmative opening. Possibilities become more apparent and we are made aware of them at the twilight level.

Gradually there is an increase in the energy level and a more active seeking for new understanding. Presently we feel that a new discovery has been made, that a new awareness has been given to us. In varying degrees a new connective experience takes place at this point and it often has the quality of a conversion to a newfound truth. At first the atmosphere may be one of uncertainty as we are unsure of our new belief. Once the doubts have passed, however, we may find our emotions taking us to the opposite extreme. Soon we find ourselves feeling the unrestrained enthusiasm that is common in new converts to anything. We experience the enthusiasm of new discovery and express it, for all of this is part of the *entry* or conversion phase of a new connective experience.

Once the entry phase is over and we are within the new belief or attitude, our emotions can settle into a more stable condition. Now it is as though we are in a new country with a great deal of exploring to do. We may also feel that we are on a plateau of awareness where the light looks different because we are up on a height. Subjectively we feel ourselves to be on a high and this affects our perception of reality. During this time a variety of experiences may come to us in the twilight range, often visionary and symbolic, tending to confirm our new beliefs. At least, while we are in this atmosphere of convinced believing, we tend to interpret our symbolic experiences as confirming our new understanding. It is a time of confidence and self-congratulation.

After a while this feeling of being on a plateau begins to diminish. The situation as a whole starts to follow a cyclic rhythm as it moves into another phase. The dreams and other twilight perceptions that come to us now raise questions we had not thought of before. Our initial enthusiasm is beginning to wane. We have absorbed so much of our new experience that we are now wondering, with some new anxiety, about what comes next. We are on the other side of the hill and so we now see things from a different angle of vision.

We began by moving through the entry phase of our new connective experience, but now doubts and questions give us another perspective. We are moving toward the *exit* phase of the experience. It may be that events have taken place that have the effect of disillusioning us in our beliefs. It may be that our new knowledge has led us to still further knowledge so that we are now considering other doctrines or ideas side by side with our present beliefs. We may not have come to the end and we may not yet be moving through the exit, but the atmosphere is now markedly different from the enthusiasm with which we began. We no longer have the certitude with which we moved up to the plateau.

As it comes to its closing phase, the connective experience may merely be changing its form. It may not be an ending. The time of exit from a connective experience can have many variations. Sometimes the end is abrupt and final. At other times it is gradual. Often the person does not make a specific decision to alter or drop the belief, but reaches a point of realizing simply that it is not believed in anymore. That becomes a statement of fact. From that point on, whatever one professes, the fact is that one has already moved through the exit gate of that belief.

Because changes in belief often move gradually, there may be no single perceptible point at which belief ends. It may not actually end at all, but simply neutralize itself and move into an incubation period during which nothing shows on the surface. When the incubation period, which may also serve as a time of reassessment, comes to an end, the old belief may reemerge. Whether it has been only slightly changed or totally transformed, we often find that the core of an old belief returns in a new form at a later period of a person's life. It seems, indeed, that beliefs have a life of their own, and that they move through their own life cycle across the decades of an individual's existence, disappearing and then reasserting themselves in new forms.

Sometimes the old belief is immediately replaced by a new one so that there is no period of emptiness intervening. At other times there is nothing to replace it and we are left with a void when our connective experience has dwindled away. That is when we feel we are in a valley once more, or lost in the wilderness, alone in the desert. It is a dark night of the soul, a time of waiting and not knowing.

At such times we are brought back to where we were before we made our entry into our connective experience. The experience has gone full cycle. We are returned to the emptiness and the unsureness once again. But it is not the same as it was. Something has been added in the interim. It is we ourselves who are different now. We have passed through a full cycle of connective experience, and that means that an additional number of *interior events* have taken place within us. They have left their mark. The quality and the capacities of our inner being are different now in some aspect and in some degree because of them.

What are these interior events? They are the many small units of experience that take place within us as we move through the cycles of experience by which we reach for, find, lose, and find again in new forms a contact with the larger contexts of life. These interior events are the doubts, the fears, the hopes, the awakenings, the new awarenesses, the faith that arises during times of strengthening and growth, and the confusions that come during times of weakening and decline. They are the many subjective perceptions and activities by which successive inner transformations take place in our lives.

Each time a person passes through a full cycle of connective experience it is as though a cycle of life has been lived.

These small units of interior events are the steps and phases that comprise the full cycles of connective experience. Often they do not seem to be of great significance in themselves, whether they are inner events of emotional intensity or intellectual events bringing new insight and awareness. As a whole, however, the context of the encompassing cycle of experience may be of great importance.

Each time a person passes through a full cycle of connective experience it is as though a cycle of life has been lived, although in miniature and on the interior level. Something of the past, some qualitative belief, has been lost or has been given up, has been allowed to die. And something new has been found. Something new has been brought to life and given form for as long as it can maintain itself. Until it too dies, or is transformed in some other way.

In the course of the interior events that comprise these cycles, many tensions and pains are felt, many hopes and plans, disappointments and renewed efforts. Because they are experienced with an inward pressure, individuals are forced each time to reach more deeply within themselves to draw on previously untouched inner resources. Moving through each cycle of inner experience, therefore, serves as a challenge to us. It exercises our inner being, creating a pressure that stretches us from within.

Since it is an unpleasant feeling, most people try to avoid such times of tension as when an old cycle of connective experience is coming to an end, or when a new one is trying to be born in the midst of anxiety and confusion. Times of spiritual transition are painful to bear, personally and psychologically. The fact is, however, that the process of continuous inner growth requires that we pass through cycle after cycle of experience, learning to absorb the pressures so that they may be transformed into unitary understanding. We require a sense of inner timing as we move through successive cycles of connective experience in our lives. And we require also a means of reentering those cycles so that we can draw from them the seeds of our next experiences and our further awareness. To acquire the techniques for both of these, for developing an inner perspective and the ability to use our personal history as a profound spiritual resource, is the purpose of our next exercises.

22

Connections II: Gatherings

We come now to the practical step of assembling our spiritual history in the Connections section.

We begin by setting up a subsection in our workbook, *Gatherings,* which will serve as the collection point for the individual events that have an inner importance in our lives. This is the place for gathering our spiritual data, the raw material for our developing work.

To start, write the title of the subsection, Gatherings, at the head of a page. And write the date beside the heading. We should make it a point as we continue our *Intensive Journal* work that we record the date each time that we make an additional entry. In that way we can track the changes in our perceptions of our life when we read our entries back to ourselves at a later time. In the case of the Gatherings subsection there are two dates to be recorded. There is the date on which we are making our Journal entry, and also the date when the event that we are describing actually occurred, as best we can recall it.

The purpose of the Gatherings subsection is to draw together into one place our awareness of all manner of events that may have an inner significance to us and thus play a role in our spiritual history. These events may be of many contrasting kinds. They may be interior events that transpired altogether within our subjective lives. Or they may be exterior events that took place in outer time and space. In either case, whether they are outer or inner events, the important question is whether they have an inner meaning to us either now or at the time they occurred.

How shall we recognize an inner meaning? We spoke earlier of the sequence of interior events that form the cycles of our connective experiences. These events may take place in the external world, or they may take place altogether within us. They are interior, however, in the sense that they have an importance to us in the terms of our private perception and feeling. They have an *inner meaning* to us; and it is thus that they have consequences at the interior, qualitative level of our lives. They become the building blocks for the larger units of spiritual experience that eventually comprise our spiritual history.

These interior events may have an importance to us that is personal, but they are not merely subjective experiences. The paradox, in fact, is that an event or a situation can be said to have an inner meaning when it arouses in us something deeper than a personal emotion so that we feel it connects us to a context of life that is larger than ourselves. The inner meaning of an interior event comes from the fact that it is felt to have a more-than-personal significance. We do not see it as an event that just haphazardly happens. We see it as a significant link between ourselves and the universe. Its inner meaning is at a deeper-than-personal level, and comes by means of the traditions or beliefs or symbols that carry it.

Every day of our lives, for example, we are aware that the sun is in the heavens, and we see it there. But one day we see the sun move toward setting in a way that enables us to feel that we know the ultimate principle behind the setting of the sun, and that, beyond intellectual knowledge, we are one with it. That is an outer event with an inner meaning. We become more than ourselves in such an experience because we are connecting with the larger context of the cosmos. We become in that moment the single drop of water reconnecting with the cosmic ocean.

Such an event has an inner meaning to us because it gives us an intimation of transcendence. The paradox is that, while we think of it as *inner,* it is actually taking us *beyond* ourselves. But it is a qualitative and not a physical beyond to which we are carried. It is a connection to a larger context of life.

As an example let us consider another connective event in relation to the world of nature. I learn of a major earthquake in which great devastation is wrought and many innocent people are killed. Far from feeling connected to the beauty of life, my mind is overwhelmed by thoughts of the disharmonies within the universe, of the discord and destruction in nature, and the seeming absence of God. As a result of this perception of the earthquake and the questions that it raises, much new thinking and exploration may be stimulated. The catastrophe sets in motion a process of search that opens many questions about the nature of the physical world, good and evil, the role of divinity, and other riddles of human existence. Eventually it may lead us, like Job, to a new understanding and perhaps to a reconnective experience.

The events that may be included in our spiritual history are of many different kinds. Events may range from pleasant to unpleasant, connective to disconnective, secular to religious, *peak* experiences to experiences of despair. But the one common quality which they all share is that they are part of our individual effort to reach an awareness of meaning that will enable us eventually to feel connected to a larger context of life. They are all aspects of this effort in its various phases, and that is why we accept and record them without judgment. They are all contributing to the whole. With their diversity and sometimes with their seeming diffusion, they are building toward the unity of meaning in our lives.

In each person's life there is a continuity of process in the course of which a core of meaning gradually forms itself. One purpose of the set of exercises we are now beginning is to reconstruct our individual spiritual history so that we can identify what that core of meaning is in our individual life. A key to that lies in the relation between the specific interior events that have happened in our lives and the full cycles of our connective experiences.

Experiences of connection all have the effect of linking the individual human being with the larger-than-personal contexts of meaning in life. That applies to the experiences as a whole, but not necessarily to their individual parts. We thus have the paradox that the individual events that comprise connective experiences often do not have a connective or unitary quality themselves. The fact is that many different kinds of events are necessary in order to form a full cycle of connective experience. Inherently the individual events are not homogeneous. Since they occur at different points in the cycle, some of them express anxiety, a sense of isolation and despair; yet they are parts of a constructive experience that may eventually bring an initiation to a new sense of truth and an affirmation of life. These individual events are simply the early phases of a broad-ranging cycle. They must be understood as being inseparable and integral parts of a single unit of experience because the connective integration of the cycle could not take place without them.

This has very important implications for the way we carry out our work in this Gatherings subsection. Let us imagine for a moment that we are an artist and that in that capacity we have achieved recognition because we have a distinctive way of presenting color and form. Now we are trying to explain to friends how we happened to become creative. We recall a particular interior event that took place for us, and we describe it as a visionary breakthrough. We explain that it enabled us to see the outer world of sensory reality in a way we had never been able to see it before. We found that after that event had taken place we could paint differently because we now perceived the outer world in terms of an interior dimension.

That was indeed a connective experience. But if we tried to explain our creativity by referring to it alone, we would be telling only a partial truth. To tell the whole truth we would have to include in our account the fact that our visionary breakthrough was just one event in a cycle. It would not have been possible without the various interior events that preceded it.

To tell the whole truth, therefore, we would have had to move back in our personal history and recall the first intimations we had that life would feel good if we could become an artist. And then we would remember the terrible nightmare dream we had that said, in effect, it was not possible and that we could never be an artist. We would have to describe also the interior event that extended over quite a period of time in which we lived covered by a cloud of anxiety. During that time there was pain as well as fear, and our confusions sometimes became depression. We would have to describe the occurrences of that time as part of the cycle of our connective experience. At the same time, however, that we were describing the darkness of that long period of night through which we lived, we would be reminded of occasional awarenesses that came to us. When these appeared, they seemed to us to be great illuminations, perhaps in contrast to the darkness we were in. They were so fragmentary and transient, however, that we did not give them much importance at the time. And they did not give us anything tangible to use in our lives. We might then recount the painful feelings of emptiness and isolation when those brief moments of light had passed and left us in the darkness again.

All these interior events and more would have to be described as parts of the cycle of connective experience by which artistic creativity came to us. Each had an integral role in the continuity of the process, since the cycle could not move through its phases without each of them, or at least their equivalent. This observation is central to the work we do in Gatherings. We want to draw together as many of the interior events as we can recall in order to reconstitute the cycles of connective experience that have been meaningful in our lives. We try to remember and gather here events from all phases of the cycle, whatever their quality, whether pleasant or painful, since all are necessary. We seek to draw memories back to ourselves, but not just fleeting impressions of past happenings. We wish to remember the circumstances of experiences that were oɪ such depth and extent that as we recall them we reenter them. And these are experiences of such qualitative size that when we are once again inside their atmosphere, we can move around and explore them to see what else they may hold for us. There we may find our way to further perceptions and further understandings that will lead to new interior events in the cycle of our experiences. But first we must recall them so that we can reenter them.

The question then is how we can reinvoke these memories? How shall we draw them back to ourselves? And how shall we work with them in the Gatherings subsection?

We sit in quietness, our *Intensive Journal* workbook open before us. We keep a pen handy for the entries we may wish to make. Our eyes are closed, and as the quietness deepens within ourselves our breathing becomes slower.

Letting the Self become still,
Letting the breath become slow,
And slower.
Feeling the movement of life
Feeling my own life
As it moves through its phases
And changes
And cycles.
Feeling the movement of life
And seeking truth
Seeking the truth in my life.

Finding glimpses,
Glimpses of truth.
Wondering at the bits of truth
Knowing and wondering
And remembering
In the Silence . . . In the Silence.

As your silence deepens, and as you find yourself going back into the movement of your life, let memories come to you. And record them as they come, giving each its separate place. Leave at least several lines, perhaps as much as half a page, between each memory as you recall and begin to describe it.

Let these memories come to you in your quietness. Do not reach out deliberately to draw them into you, but let them come as you sit waiting for them, holding the atmosphere of the interior events in your life. In that atmosphere, memories will come from many parts of your life, and they will reflect the various phases in the cycles of your experience.

As these recollections come to you, describe them briefly, saying just enough to identify the content of what took place. You may write a few sentences but not more than a moderate-sized paragraph. We have found it helpful to follow the general rule of thumb that when a Gatherings entry reaches half a page in length that is a sign that we have written enough for the present.

Sometimes a memory will return to you with particular strength and energy. It may stimulate you so forcefully that you will have the desire to write about it at great length, even to the exclusion of other memories. If that happens, you should bear in mind the role of this exercise in relation to the larger purpose of our Process Meditation work. We are seeking to give ourselves access as broadly as possible to the full range of our inner experiences. And here in Gatherings we are collecting as many as we can.

In this context, if you find yourself particularly stimulated by the memory of an interior event, the best practice seems to be to write your half-page of description, perhaps adding a few notes for the future, and then turn your attention to receiving other memories. You will not be losing your chance to write at length about that experience. There will be an opportunity to return to it in a little while when we work in the Re-Openings segment of the Connections section. You will have ample time to enlarge it there. At point you will also have an additional perspective with which to return to the experience. The most important reason, however, for setting a limit on our present descriptions is not to distract ourselves from calling up and gathering additional memories of interior events that are related to the cycles of connective experience in our lives.

As we are writing our descriptions of particular memories, we may find that we are drawn up to the surface of our consciousness. To that degree, also, we may be drawn out of the quiet atmosphere of remembering. When that happens we should take the time to sit in quietness once again, letting our breathing become slow again, letting our self become still. In that stillness additional memories will come to us, and we add them, a half page at a time to our Gatherings. Now we proceed with our inward remembering in the silence.

✍

Since they come from all phases of the cycles of our connective experiences, the range of interior events that we may recall is very broad. These memories may be of the early anxious aspects of our experience, of the high plateau times when we feel permanent and secure, or of the later, ending times when we meet uncertainty again. All of these rememberings have their own integrity, and they are not the same for any two persons. Here are some examples that are indicative and that may remind us of circumstances in our own lives.

I remember the feeling of belonging that I experienced at the close of an Easter service when I was about eleven years old. I felt that everyone there in the church was part of one group. It was a spiritual thing but more a social thing, like a family belonging together. I remember that closeness and I think of it as what religion should be. But it hasn't been.

My grandfather was the cantor in a small orthodox synagogue. On Yom Kippur he wore white robes and only stockinged feet and lay down prostrate before the Ark of the Torah. When I was a small boy I saw him do that and I remember seeing a white light around his whole body as he lay on the floor praying. It was awesome and I felt it was very holy.

I was really afraid through most of the time that I did my first mountain climbing. I thought I'll never do this again. But when we reached a really high place where we could sit and rest and see what was around us, I felt I touched reality for the first time. The vastness overcame me, and draws me back to it.

Singing *The Messiah* for the first time. Singing in a choral group is always a good experience for me, but that time it was more than music. I felt I discovered what religion is about. And I was glad I could sing it.

At certain periods in my life it has been important to feel that I knew God, or that I knew about God. At those times I would wonder about it a lot, and listen to preachers. And then I would forget about it. Those have been each a different time, but they seem to be dealing with just one question.

Football isn't religion, but I have felt very connected when the team was really going right. Certain times in particular the whole team seemed to be like one person, and the spirit was such that everyone knew to do the right thing. It was like being one with the world.

I was in my teens and I thought I wanted to be a monk, so I decided to try to see Thomas Merton. I hitchhiked to Kentucky and I managed to get to his meditation hut. I didn't see him but I saw some empty beer cans on the floor, and I left in disgust. Later I realized I didn't really want to be a monk and I was ducking the issue. But I still need to understand Thomas Merton. Perhaps I was afraid to meet him.

When I was a little girl I saw my grandmother cover her face with her hands as she said a blessing when she lit the candles on the Sabbath. Everything seemed very safe when she did that. But I could never think of myself doing that. Now I wonder what kind of belief I would have to have. And what kind of woman I would have to be.

When my mother died unexpectedly my first thought was that there is no God and that life is pointless. Later I thought about it further, even considering the possibility of life after death, or reincarnation. I felt the separation very sharply when the death happened, but now I feel a relationship starting again. I seem to be thinking of death in a different way, as a connection perhaps. But to what?

When I joined the Communist Party it was like a conversion experience. There was a great wave of history going to take over the world and make mankind united and happy. And I was now part of it. Then I saw the cruelty within the party toward others. So I left disillusioned. But I still wish there was some way I could feel connected to mankind.

I used to fight and argue about practicing the piano. Then one day I was by myself and it came out just right, more than perfect. It was as though I hadn't played it but something in the world had played that piano just right. I felt it was a mystery. After that I played the piano my same old way, but I didn't argue about it any more. I just wondered if it would ever happen again.

The time when I felt unity in the presence of Swami—. I had never known it before, and although I have known it since then, it has somehow been different. That one experience remains a white light for me.

A variety of memories and awarenesses of such earlier experiences may come to you as you let yourself reflect on the interior movement of your life. Sometimes it will be specific and separated events that you will recall. At other times it will be a whole constellation of happenings or attitudes, an inner situation that extended over a considerable period of time. In either case, they are part of the larger cycles of your connective experiences. Therefore, as you recall them, describe them in your Gatherings. Giving them a place here, they can eventually show whatever their additional message and meaning may be in the larger context of your life.

✍

In recalling our Gatherings, it is not necessary to list them in chronological order. Our purpose in this segment is merely to give ourselves access to as many memories of connective events as possible. Therefore we record them in whatever order they come to us. We may list them very unsystematically, now a recall from a recent period, now one from earlier years, now a memory of a poetic experience of nature, now a political loyalty or concern, now a memory of a religious ritual in childhood, now philosophical thoughts and questions about a mystical experience, now a memory of devastating despair and disillusionment.

We record them as they come to us with no concern for their sequence or their subject matter. We simply describe them briefly, but fully enough to include their main elements, and then we go on to describe the next experience that comes to mind.

For some of us at certain points in our work of Gatherings, it will work better to begin with experiences from early years and then to move forward chronologically. On the other hand and at other times you may find that it is too arduous a task for you to move across long periods of lifetime to identify one by one the particular events that contributed to your sense of meaning in life. You may find that once you have made contact with recent experiences, you are better able to move back in time to the events that preceded them. This may also be influenced by your mood and by the pressures of outer circumstances. Sometimes you may find that it works best for you to begin with experiences that stand out in your memory as dramatic events either because they were beacons of light or because of the darkness through which you passed. Describing these standout events, the experiences of intensity that are the first to return to your memory may be a convenient way to begin because it sets the process into motion with something that readily presents itself.

Once we begin to record our Gatherings, the first memories will be followed by rememberings and awarenesses from all parts of our spiritual history. Each entry that we make tends to stimulate the process, for it gives us reminders of other happenings in the past. We find, therefore, that once we have begun the work of Gatherings, one entry leads to another. While we may have been slow in starting, the associations and reminders soon build a momentum in our stream of consciousness and additional entries suggest themselves to us without our seeking them. For a similar reason we find that when we are working actively in other sections of our *Intensive Journal* workbook, the writing stimulates us to remember events of our spiritual history that were lying dormant within us and which belong in Gatherings.

Be aware, too, that as we record the Gatherings of our spiritual experiences we are also re-creating the fullness of our life. Since many of the Gatherings represent events that were important in our life, we may describe each Gathering again in another Connection in the Life History Log. We may describe them particularly in filling out our descriptions of the various Steppingstone Periods in our life. The value in these remembrances is that they will tend to evoke in us memories of our experiences in the past. When we come to use the *Intensive Journal* method in its aspect as Journal Feedback we will see the greater value that comes to us when we describe a particular event in our life from more than one point of view.

When we have described all the relevant memories that come to our mind now, we leave the Gatherings segment open ended, available for continuing entries. We move on to further exercises, but we shall return with additional Gatherings from time to time.

23

Connections III:
Spiritual Steppingstones and
Inner Wisdom Dialogue

In this section of the Journal we turn our attention to the spiritual realm of our life experience. The word *spiritual* as we use it in this context has a large and general meaning. It is not restricted to any particular metaphysical teaching or belief, but it refers to our fundamental human quest for understanding of the ultimate truths of existence. Some find this understanding in the terms of the traditional religions, others in the modern language of the technologist and scientist, and still others are working toward new personal syntheses that reach beyond the old dichotomies.

The word spiritual . . . refers to our fundamental human quest for understanding of the ultimate truths of existence.

The categories, however, do not matter. The one thing that is certain about them is that they will pass through many changes for anyone who is actively engaged in a spiritual quest. The quest for abiding truth is the reality of the spiritual life, regardless of what particular metaphysic or doctrine is espoused at any moment. This ongoing quest in its permutations through each person's life history is the subject of the *Inner Wisdom Dialogue* section of the Journal.

We have learned from the history of depth psychology—and it is one of the principles of the *Intensive Journal* process—that untapped capacities of awareness are contained latently at various levels of our being. Many human beings know intuitively more than they rationally understand. The question, however, is not merely whether we have a strong enough belief, but whether we can actually gain access to the potentials of personal development and knowledge that are contained in the depth of us. How can we achieve increased capacities of direct intuition and awareness?

The way we collected our spiritual data in Gatherings was deliberately amorphous, but in the Spiritual Steppingstones section of the workbook (see Appendix C) our purpose is to make it possible for our inner life to take form, or to reveal the form that it already has. And we wish to do this without imposing upon it the desires of our conscious mind. We wish to make it possible for our inner life to express its own intention.

The work of Spiritual Steppingstones, we should note, does not involve the collection of historical data. We have collected the data of our spiritual history in Gatherings. In Spiritual Steppingstones we draw the past together qualitatively and cogently by means of its key points and not its details. The Steppingstones list contains the points of emphasis provided by the movement of our life itself as a means by which it can show us its inner goal and direction. In order for the exercise to serve this function for us truly, it is essential that it be carried out at a level that bypasses our conscious thoughts, our wishes and desires. If we manipulate our list of Steppingstones to suit ourselves, it will only be ourselves that we are fooling.

We require a means of increasing our interior sensitivity to make an expansion of consciousness possible in personal terms. In a far-reaching sense, the entire thrust of our work with the *Intensive Journal* process has this as its goal. The process of Journal Feedback that moves back and forth among the sections of the Journal achieves its results by moving on two levels simultaneously. On the one hand, it generates a movement within the person; on the other hand, it deepens the level on which all the contents of the psyche are experienced. It brings about this double effect by sending our inner attention and our psychic energies back and forth, up and down, in the inner space of our lives by means of the various sections and exercises of the *Intensive Journal* workbook.

The movement of material in the Journal corresponds to the movement of the life contents within the psyche of the person. It generates a momentum of inner experiences within the individual, first on the personal, subjective level of the psyche, and increasingly on the deeper-than-personal, the generically human level of the psyche. As this momentum continues both on the surface and on the depth levels, it draws the psyche as a whole together, forming new integrations of personality. As it proceeds, progressive reintegrations take place, so that a series of changes is observable in the inner structure as well as in the outer aspect of the individual. These changes, which accompany the Journal work, are cumulative. As they continue, they bring about a new quality of being and especially a greater sensitivity to the interior dimension of life. In particular, as the work of Journal Feedback multiplies its momentum, the subjective, personal contents of one's life are brought into closer relationship with the deeper, transpersonal levels. This progressive deepening enlarges the capacity of inner knowing with respect to the conduct and meaning of our human existence.

At this point in our Journal Workshop we are in a position to recognize how the process of *progressive deepening* takes place. We began our workshop experience at the rational surface of consciousness with our description in the Period Log of the recent unit of Life/Time. Following that, we had our first exercise in the use of Twilight Imagery. Then, by the practice of life correlation, we drew out the relationship between our imagery and our outer experience. These last two steps began the process of drawing the focus of our awareness to a nonrational, intuitive level beneath the surface of consciousness.

As we proceeded with our Time-Stretching exercises to reassemble our life histories, we combined the conscious use of memory with a cumulative prodding and prying open of the repressed levels of our unconscious psyche. This was the preparatory, ground-breaking work of loosening the soil of our lives which we carried through in the Life History Log, and to which we continuously add. Those entries activate our memory of repressed events, and our reentry into the Steppingstones and Intersections of our life further stimulates our nonconscious perceptions.

The data that we gathered in these Life/Time sections then provided the base for our dialogue experiences with specific contents of our lives. The dialogue work continues the process of deepening and serves as a bridge between the unconscious and conscious levels of our awareness. We see this mediating quality of the dialogue exercises in the fact that they frequently cause us to articulate a knowledge of things we did not know we knew. The dialogues reach into our unconscious knowledge and draw it up to conscious awareness in the form of language in the dialogue scripts.

We take a further step in our progressive deepening when we work with the procedures of Twilight Imaging and with our dreams. These enable us to move into the deeper-than-personal levels of symbolism and to experience our individual lives in larger contexts of meaning. This is especially so when we extend the seriality of our dream movement by Twilight Dreaming. Continuing beyond this, we find that our Twilight Imaging experiences enable us to move even more deeply than the dreams to the transpersonal level where the symbolism reflects a unitary wisdom of life. This takes us toward a direct knowing that is beyond intellect, but it does so in symbolic forms that are often ambiguous and difficult to understand. The symbolism that comes to us is often profound, but it is also obscure and thus liable to mislead us. It becomes essential, then, that we move back from our unconscious depths into consciousness again. We do this by following the feedback leads that have been given us by our dreams and our Twilight Imaging experiences, and by working with them in the dialogue sections which they suggest to us.

The exercises that we have carried out in our workshop so far have moved in two directions simultaneously. They have moved both down and up. The progressive deepening has taken us to a level where deeper-than-personal experiences become possible for us. And the dialogue work translates these experiences into the actualities of our life. Combining these is the specific role of our Inner Wisdom Dialogues. As we have worked in the context of our lives, we have cumulatively deepened our inward atmosphere and our level of depth contact. Now we take a further step. We hold ourselves at the deepest level to which our Journal work so far has taken us, and we now seek to establish a dialogue relationship with the quality of *knowledge beyond understanding* that becomes present to us at that depth. It is our attempt to enlarge our contact with wisdom and with the ultimates of meaning in life through the particular symbolic forms and contexts through which this may be accessible to each of us.

This section of the *Intensive Journal* workbook thus becomes the place where we work to establish a dialogue relationship with all the possibilities of spiritual contact and larger philosophical awareness that reflect the inner wisdom of our deep human nature. Our first step in this direction is to go back over our life history and to recapitulate the main experiences and beliefs by which we have each sought in our own way to relate ourselves to the ultimate truths of human existence.

WRITING OUR SPIRITUAL STEPPINGSTONES

We sit in silence and reflect on the range of faith and doubt and seeking that we have experienced since childhood. We wish to draw together now what can be called the Steppingstones of our spiritual life, understanding the word *spiritual* in its broadest sense as our total inner quest for wisdom in life. To give ourselves a frame of reference for this, it may be helpful to turn back to the list of Steppingstones that we wrote earlier in the workshop. Here we can review the main points and periods that we marked off with respect to the movement of our life as a whole. Working within the large context of the Steppingstones of our life, we can take ourselves back in memory and ask ourselves specific questions regarding the content and quality of our spiritual life in each of those earlier periods.

We open our Journal Workbook to the Meaning Dimension, a dimension of our lives with which we have not worked as yet. We go into the section called Connections and into the subsection for Spiritual Steppingstones. We go back into our Life History recalling in this section the Steppingstones of our inner life that come to our mind. We will write them down in the form of a list, describing them concisely so we will know what we are referring to when we read it back to ourselves later on. We recall the experiences that come to us out of our inner life as times of breakthrough when creative insights came to us, and equally we recall times of emptiness when it seemed that there would be no time of discovery for us.

We set the atmosphere for recalling the Steppingstones of our inner life so that we can reconnect ourselves with the meaningful experiences that have come to us. We place ourselves in an atmosphere of quietness.

As we sit and write in Spiritual Steppingstones, a new awareness opens to us regarding the problems we were tussling with and allows us to see them in a new light. Now we list in the Spiritual Steppingstones subsection all the instances we can recall of experiences that have involved breakthroughs for us whether in our religious or creative life. We describe these experiences briefly as we did when we listed the Steppingstones of our life as a whole earlier in the workshop. Now we add them to the list as we recall them and we order them as they come to us.

Our next step is working with our Spiritual Steppingstones. First we open a new subsection here in the Connections sections. Leave a few blank pages in the Gatherings subsection so that there will be room for additional entries as further memories are recalled to you. Now we write the heading *Spiritual Steppingstones,* and today's date, and we are ready to begin.

Bear in mind that one key to working with Steppingstones in any of their aspects in the *Intensive Journal* process is to stimulate the equivalent of the condition of dreaming and yet to remain on the conscious level. To achieve that, it is necessary first to establish the atmosphere of dreams and to place ourselves within it, but without leaving the waking state. To do that, we try to enter the twilight range in a manner that is direct and simple and as free from thoughts as possible. We move into the twilight range in an altogether neutral mode of consciousness, taking special care to influence neither the content nor the direction of movement of our twilight experiences.

We sit in stillness, our eyes closed, our workbook open to the Spiritual Steppingstones segment. Relaxing, we breathe slowly, slowly, letting the stillness establish itself within us. We have no special thoughts in our mind, but we let ourselves feel the movement of our life. We feel the passage of time, the changes in our life. We do not think about what they are, but we feel the movement that underlies the contents of our lives. We feel the flow of it, and especially we feel the movements of beliefs and our varied reachings toward meaning through the continuity of our inner life. Sitting in stillness, we feel the flow of our inner life. Nothing more specific than its continuity is in our consciousness, just the flow of it, a moving river at the depth of our being. We feel the flow of it, and we let it reflect itself to us in whatever forms of Twilight Imagery it chooses.

Now we maintain a quiet receptivity. Being in the stillness of the twilight range, we are open to perceive whatever is presented to us, images that we see, sounds or words that we hear, streams of thought that move through us unbidden, intuitions or insights that come to us as flashes of awareness.

There is a great need to balance the repression of personal spiritual experience in society.

The imagery and the memories that are stimulated in us by our preparatory twilight step now enable us to move at a deep level into our task of drawing together our Spiritual Steppingstones. In doing this we follow the principles of the Life Steppingstones exercise that plays a basic role in the Life Context *Intensive Journal* workshops. Here, however, we extend these procedures to the meditative level.

When we worked with our Life Steppingstones, we let the multiple events that comprise our life as a whole be consolidated into just a dozen Steppingstones, thereby reflecting the main line of movement in our total existence. Correspondingly, our Spiritual Steppingstones are the main events of our interior life. They reflect the way we seek, and occasionally find, a larger meaning in our personal and human existence. In saying that they are the main events, we mean merely that they are the most striking, the most remembered if not necessarily the most memorable, and that they are most indicative of our continuing, conscious and unconscious quest for interior significance.

In the lives of many persons the quest for meaning is left implicit and unarticulated. This is true not only of persons living in modern times, but was true of those living in earlier, seemingly religious periods of history. While the questions and the wonderings are there, the circumstances of outer life in most societies tend to discourage people from giving outer expression to inward sensitivities and to private intimations of truth. In earlier times these personal feelings and experiences were restrained by the pressures of institutionalized traditions and the powers of authority. In modern times they are repressed by the more informal power of the secular materialism of industrial society. There is a great need to balance the repression of personal spiritual experience in society, and that is one of the roles that the *Intensive Journal* work undertakes to fulfill. Our workbook becomes a place where a person's private intimations of meaning can be articulated, respected, and explored. More important even than the basic fact of acknowledging our spiritual feelings and treating them as realities, our method gives us a means of working with them in tangible ways so that their intuitions of truth can be nurtured, can be considered, altered, or brought to further development.

The work we began in Gatherings has this general purpose underlying it. It also has the specific purpose of preparing us for the crystallizing step that we take next in identifying our Spiritual Steppingstones.

In Gatherings we recorded as many memories as came to us of the inner or outer episodes that have been part of our quest for meaning. These Gatherings reflect both pleasant and unpleasant phases in our cycles of connective experience. In collecting this inner data, we were in the first place paying respect to our interior life as individuals by recognizing and recording the facts of its experience. In the second place, we were strengthening its intuitions by feeding it into the integrative process that will carry it toward further understanding.

In listing our Spiritual Steppingstones now, we use a procedure that enables these facts to draw themselves together and to wind themselves fine so that they can form and can show to us the thread of inner continuity in our lives.

An important facet of the Steppingstones exercise is that it is both spontaneous and selective. In order to carry it out in an atmosphere that is as free as possible from conscious controls, we take ourselves to the twilight level where imagery and the experience of making the list can take place in a spontaneous way. As we do that, we set a ceiling on the number of Steppingstones that can be included in any single list, limiting it to approximately a dozen, give or take one or two. The reason for this limitation is that the functioning of the Steppingstones exercise requires a list that is neither too short nor too long. It should be long enough to include the relevant phases and variations within the life, thus to convey the quality of movement and the cyclical changes taking place. And it should also be short enough to give a compact impression of the tenor of the life as a whole.

While the number of Steppingstones is fixed, the span of time covered by a list of Steppingstones includes the whole life of the individual. Some individuals may therefore have eight or even nine decades to compress into their dozen Steppingstones. And another person may have only two or three decades of experience from which to draw. Each life thus becomes a unit establishing its own context, regardless of its chronological length. The polarity of these two rules creates a tension within the person, and this often leads to unexpected recognitions regarding the individual's life.

Whether we are making these entries in private or at a workshop, it seems to be helpful for many people to speak them out while writing them in the Journal. In any case, whether speaking them aloud feels comfortable or not, we record them as they come to our memories, without censorship, without judgment, without comment, and at this point without amplification. We are interested at this point in recording concise entries that will indicate the varieties of inner experiences that have been significant in our development. We are gathering the data for the later steps in our work.

As though we are at a Journal Workshop, let us now speak aloud the Steppingstones of our inner development, as the other participants also do, recording them as we speak them.

Being told that God was watching so I'd better behave.

Thunder clapping very loud one night while I was saying my prayers.

The death of my mother. I prayed for an afterlife.

I doubted God and all the stories of religion.

My first communion experience. It was good but I thought it would be more.

A conversion experience. It was so strong I thought it would never change.

Realizing that Jesus loves me.

Feeling the presence of God.

Entering religious life. A door closing and a door opening.

Meditating on the Gospels and feeling the power of a truth grow stronger.

Being transfixed when my minister spoke. He had a light around him.

Reading Walt Whitman for the first time.

The presence of the Blessed Virgin. She was my mother too.

Reading Tom Dooley's books and wanting to live his life.

Meeting a person who really felt God's presence. After that I knew I could recognize the real thing.

Meditating in the Eastern way.

Feeling the silence deepen by degrees.

The waves in the ocean, the ocean in the waves, I wondered which was which. Then I gave up and felt it all wash over me. I was renewed.

Being inside the vision of Isaiah.

On a drug trip. I wouldn't go again, but I know it's there.

Realizing there was spiritual truth before Jesus. That shook me, but my world opened.

I fell in love with Socrates and I wished I were his wife. Poor Socrates, I thought.

Realizing that I was creating my own misery. Scales fell off my eyes.

One morning I suddenly knew what love is, and I felt connected to all things.

I discovered philosophy and realized that my mind could be an instrument of truth. I admired it, but I began to worry about faith.

I was walking into the ocean without hope. Suddenly something turned me around and here I am.

With nothing and alone and walking in the shadow. Then seeing the light. Even when it's dark, it never goes away.

We record these experiences in the order in which we recall them. We shall very likely find, however, that we recollect our more recent experiences before we remember our earlier ones. The result is that our list does not reflect the actual sequence of steps and stages and changes by which our inner development has taken place. A main purpose in making this list, however, is to recapitulate not only the broad range of content by the specific style and tempo of movement of our inner life. We are seeking to assemble our spiritual life history so that we can establish an active dialogue relationship with the process within it. Toward this goal it is essential that we experience the events of our inner development in the sequence in which they took place.

Since we listed our spiritual Steppingstones spontaneously as they came to us, we can now set them in chronological order by numbering them in the sequence in which they took place. Even as we do this, we shall undoubtedly find situations of overlapping where we cannot tell clearly which came first. We can leave leeway for this irregular development since we realize that it is inherent in the spiritual and philosophic life. The continuities of inner growth do not lend themselves to sharp demarcation particularly because they frequently pass through long incubation periods when they are not visible on the surface. We shall bear this in mind, and later phases of our Journal work will enable us to draw out the details and nuances of this elusive timing in our inner life.

CONTINUING TO WORK WITH OUR SPIRITUAL STEPPINGSTONES

At this point, having listed the various phases of our experience, we number them in approximate chronological order. By drawing our list together in sequence we enable ourselves to see the unity of inner development that has underlain the many changes and uncertainties in the cycles of our life. With it we shall be able to identify the thread of integrity that has been seeking to establish itself beneath the variations of attitude that show on the surface.

We now read our list to ourselves in chronological sequence. We may read it aloud if it feels comfortable for us to do so. Especially we read it to ourselves silently, and reread it several times so that the feeling of its flow, including both its smoothness and its irregularities, can come to us. As we do this, we take note of the feeling and responses that arise in us as we read it, and we record these as an entry following our list.

It may be helpful for us, in reviewing our own list, to have as part of our perspective the Spiritual Steppingstones that occur in the lives of other persons. With this in mind, I include some indicative lists of Spiritual Steppingstones in Appendix C. You can see from these how close the interrelationship is between our inner experiences and the external circumstances of our lives. Each life contains the necessities and problems that set the terms of its individual destiny as well as the possibilities of its integrity. For that reason we may not pass judgment on anyone's list of Steppingstones, not another person's and not our own. But we may draw from them a sense of the range of inner and outer events by which human lives reach toward meaning in the modern world.

Parallel with the events of our lives, there comes a sense of the meaning of our existence in its personal and in its larger-than-personal aspects. Sometimes the meaning we perceive is clear and definite; sometimes it is uncertain, problematical, and changing so that it places the person in a turmoil of inner confusions. A human life may move through all these phases. In listing our Spiritual Steppingstones, we are retracing the varied, sometimes painful path by which our life has moved toward meaning. Now we are in a position to pick up that movement and carry it forward to new understandings and experiences of the issues that our life has given us.

✍

In whatever way you read your Spiritual Steppingstones back to yourself, let yourself feel their import with the fullness of your being. Sitting in silence, you may sometimes read them back to yourself quickly in order to feel their inner movement or you may sometimes read them slowly in order to recognize and consider the implications of particular aspects. Read them as many times as they continue to be meaningful. And each time take note of the old emotions that stir in you, and new emotions that arise, and describe them following your Spiritual Steppingstones.

These additional entries can be as short or as long as feels right and necessary to you. Let each entry be first a response to the composite of your Steppingstones, their movement and place in your life as a whole. And also take note of specific changes and shorter cycles, as well as particular insights and realizations that come to you now. Especially as you read back your Steppingstones, try to be open to perceive the directions in which your inner experience is taking you, for these may not have been explicit and clear to you before. You may see that you have been reaching toward goals and desires of which you were not aware but which now become apparent to you as you read all your Spiritual Steppingstones together as a unit and can see them as a single life unfolding. The recognitions that may come to you in this way can be very striking, and often full of emotion. Most important, they can be very suggestive in giving you leads for your continuing work in the other sections of your *Intensive Journal* workbook. Record your spontaneous responses as they come to you, and let them expand of themselves. They will very likely provide valuable clues which, as you proceed, will help you select the material with which to focus the next steps in your meditative work.

As you are writing now, you may be reminded of additional events of your past that are meaningful to you for the role they have played in the cycles of connective experience in your life. You may not have thought of them before, but now they are recalled to you. These may be added to the Gatherings segment, which we left in an open-ended state when we began to list our Spiritual Steppingstones. If additional Gatherings come to your mind, record and describe them. This is part of our intermittent and cumulative work of building the resource of our personal spiritual history.

FURTHER WORK WITH SPIRITUAL STEPPINGSTONES:
THE INNER WISDOM DIALOGUE

After we have made the list and have read it back to ourselves, there is an important piece of data to be added. As we reread each of the entries and place ourselves back in that time of our lives, we think back to the persons who were of importance to us in a profoundly meaningful way during that time. These are not merely the persons who were with us at the time, or who were friendly to us, or in a personal relationship with us, but the persons who were of profound importance to us in specific relation to our inner experience and to the enlargement of our consciousness in that regard. As we become aware of such persons, we add them to each of the Spiritual Steppingstones that we have listed wherever they apply.

The persons whose names we record in this way may possess a great variety of qualities. Their principal characteristic is that they are individuals who represent wisdom to us with respect to some particular area of our lives and who, at least in our perception of them, embody a capacity of deep and direct knowing. They need not be people who are well-educated, nor people who possess a great deal of information. That is not the kind of knowledge we are seeking here. They are, rather, individuals who personify wisdom for us because of the way that the quality of their inner being speaks to our own being. They may not represent wisdom to us in every aspect of their life; and the same individual may not carry the same deep relevance for us in all areas of our life. Although they embody wisdom for us, other people will not necessarily think of them as wise.

In our earlier years, for example, it may have been a grandfather or an uncle who represented truth to us. Or it may have been our image of God, or Christ, or the Virgin Mary, or our local priest or rabbi. In later years the wisdom figure may have been embodied in a professor at college, in authors of books that influenced us greatly, Plato, Spinoza, or a contemporary author whose approach to life speaks to us. It may have become a missionary minister like Billy Graham or Mary Baker Eddy, a militant revolutionist like Che Guevera or Joan of Arc, political figures like Martin Luther King, John Kennedy, or Susan B. Anthony, depending on our areas of interest and commitment at particular times in our life.

As our experience proceeds and as our values change, the persons who personify wisdom to us will also change. They may be individuals whom we know personally and with whom we share an active interchange of ideas. Or they may be persons from history, St. Paul, Karl Marx, Gandhi, Van Gogh, Beethoven, and so on. Whoever has spoken to us in the depth of our being, whether through their spoken words, their books, their music, their paintings, or by their lives and the legends and symbolism that have grown around them, all of these may be wisdom figures for us in some areas of our life. Whoever they may be, living persons, persons who now live only through their works and words, historical personages, mythological figures, or divine beings, all may be among the persons who have served as wisdom figures for us at some point in our lives.

We can, however, make a distinction here from a certain point of view regarding the two types of persons who have the capacity to personify wisdom for us in a dialogue relationship. We note the *personal* wisdom figures and the *transpersonal* wisdom figures. In the first group are the individuals who personify wisdom for us but who are part of the world in which we live, whether they are present with us physically or not. These are persons in whom we find wisdom, but whom we understand to be human beings, just as we are.

The transpersonal wisdom figures, on the other hand, belong to history and the universe. They are persons whose lives, if they have indeed lived historically, have made them symbols for us of connection with the ultimate and encompassing truths of human existence. They are transpersonal wisdom figures by virtue of what they represent in the universe, and because of the power of personal being that is identified with their names. It is in this sense that God, in one aspect, is a transpersonal wisdom figure with whom we can establish a dialogue relationship, God by whatever name and in whatever form He is recognizable to us.

Having made this distinction between personal and transpersonal wisdom figures, there is a further point for us to note. The personal wisdom figures are human beings as we are and share our realm of life, but the quality in them toward which we reach is more-than-personal. As human beings they have activated within themselves an aspect of the transpersonal depths of inner wisdom. They have lived it, and it is this level of the universe, which has been actualized and made real by their experience, that we now seek to bring into our own lives. We can do that by means of an ongoing dialogue relationship with them, including progressive dialogue scripts. As we proceed to this active phase of our exercises, we should realize, however, that we are not establishing contact by dialoguing with the personal side of these inner wisdom figures. We are reaching toward the transpersonal depth of wisdom within them seeking to establish a relationship between that and the corresponding depth of wisdom in ourselves. It is in this fundamental sense that all persons may be spoken of as transpersonal wisdom figures, including ultimately ourselves.

For each of our Spiritual Steppingstones we list the names of one or two or three wisdom figures, or as many as come to mind. Take time now to do so. We know that the entries we make in this regard will by no means be complete at this time. As our work in the Journal proceeds, however, we can add the names of others who are recalled to our memory.

WRITING AN INNER WISDOM DIALOGUE

From the list of these various wisdom figures, we now choose one to focus on for our dialogue experience. In deciding upon our first figure for Inner Wisdom Dialogue, we should not necessarily choose one who is important to us at the present time (though we may choose a current figure).

What can be most valuable for our first Inner Wisdom Dialogue is that it be with a person the very thought of whom, the mentioning of their name, causes us to become quiet and feel centered within ourselves. Let our first dialogue be with one whose presence we have experienced in an atmosphere of profound understanding, perhaps also of warmth and supportive love. Perhaps it will be one with whom we have been in contact in times of prayer or solitude. What is most important is that it be a person to whom we can open our hearts fully on any of our deepest concerns, and that we can do so with no reservation, knowing it will all be accepted.

We are now preparing to let a dialogue script be written to carry forward the inner relationship between ourselves and that other person, that other Being. This first dialogue is to reopen contact and to clear the way for successive dialogues that will take place afterward in their own timing.

It is important for us to acknowledge to ourselves that this first Inner Wisdom Dialogue will not necessarily be profound, or poetic, or a great spiritual revelation. Dialogues in this section of the *Intensive Journal* workbook have indeed been just that, but dialogues in any section of the Journal can have those powerful and transforming qualities *only unexpectedly*. If we are deliberately looking for them to be wise or inspiring, we tighten the channel and the passageway becomes too narrow. For this reason we approach our first Inner Wisdom Dialogue with the attitude that it is merely an introduction. We are merely saying hello, but in a deep sanctuary part of ourselves. In this relaxed way we make the experience of deep inner dialogue available as a continuing, open-ended contact with the transpersonal wisdom of life.

We also may find that as we prepare for an Inner Wisdom Dialogue, as we are doing at this moment, that we realize we are uncertain as to the person with whom we actually wish to speak. In practice it often happens that our conscious mind decides to set up the dialogue with one particular person whereas the intention of our deep psyche is quite different. In that case we suddenly recognize in the midst of a dialogue that we are speaking with someone other than the person with whom we had started. It is not uncommon for the script of an Inner Wisdom Dialogue to shift its cast of characters while it is taking place. What is important then is that you be open and receptive to the change, and that you be flexible enough to go with it. Let the dialogue lead itself and go where it wishes. When this is happening, it is an indication that you are allowing yourself to be drawn into the nonconscious depths of your self, and that it is indeed your inner wisdom with which you are speaking.

Now we are ready to begin our dialogue script with the wisdom figure whom we have chosen. We sit in stillness. Our *Intensive Journal* workbook is open and we have dated a new page. The subsection in which we prepared for the Inner Wisdom Dialogue by listing the Steppingstones and the persons who were important in them, is left open ended so that we can add to it from time to time. Now we are ready for our dialogue. We are sitting in silence waiting for it to begin.

Our eyes are closed and we feel the presence of the wisdom figure with whom we wish to enter into dialogue. We feel their presence, but we do not think of them with conscious thoughts. We let our thoughts come to rest. Our breathing is slow. It becomes slower, softer. We are still.

In the stillness we feel the presence of this person, this wisdom figure, this being.

We are feeling their presence, feeling the inner quality of their being, feeling the deep wisdom, the unity and knowing of existence that is personified in them.

Sitting in quietness, we let images come to us. They may come to us visually upon our Twilight Imagery screen. More important, through our image of them we feel the quality of the person, their atmosphere, and especially their presence. We feel their life, their concern, their desires, and we speak to them. We greet them. We say what we feel of their life and of their quality of life. We say what we feel of our life, our concerns, and our questions. We speak of our relationship to them, why we come to them, why we call upon them, and what we have to ask.

All that we say we write as our part of the dialogue script. We return to silence and wait. When they are ready, they speak to us, and it is written. Whatever they say, be it casual or profound, we record it. We let the dialogue move along its own path, make its own turns, cover its own subject matter. We speak and the other speaks, and we let the dialogue continue as long as it wishes.

We are sitting in stillness, waiting in openness. We feel the presence of the person and their quality of wisdom. We speak and we are spoken to. And we let it be written through our pen. Thus the dialogue script is written between ourselves and the person of wisdom. We sit in openness, enabling the dialogue to take form through us, in the silence, in the silence.

Concluding the Inner Wisdom Dialogue

It seems to be more often true of the Inner Wisdom Dialogues than of other dialogue exercises in the Journal work that they come to points where they must stop although they are not actually finished. These stoppings are actually pauses during which the dialogue process seems to renew itself and gather new energy. It is as though the inner speakers are taking a second breath. When the dialogue script resumes its movement, it seems also as though it has moved to a deeper level. These pauses that occur in the Inner Wisdom Dialogues may therefore not be from fatigue or a diminution of energy in the dialogue process, but rather a deepening of the level. They are often the prelude to special profundities in awareness and expression.

When the pace of your dialogue slows, let it come to a stop if it wants to, but do not assume that it is finished. Let it rest. And while it is resting, let yourself become quiet. In the silence it will renew itself and continue when it is ready.

These pauses, renewals, and deepenings may take place three or four times during the writing of a single dialogue script. Each time you will move forward and then come to a stop. Eventually enough will have been said for the present, and you will know that by the way it feels to you. That will be the time to read what has been written. First you will read it silently; then, if the circumstances feel right, you will read it aloud, either at a workshop or in private, perhaps into a cassette recorder.

As you read, you take note of the feelings, the energies and emotional tone that become present in you. Compare these with the way you felt when the dialogue script was being written, and describe your observations. This is an additional entry to be made in the same section of the Journal. It is a further aspect of the Inner Wisdom Dialogue, extending the process now at a conscious level. All phases of the experience contribute to building the ongoing dialogue relationship.

With this entry the specific work with the dialogue script comes to a close for the present, but the dialogue relationship as a whole continues. In many additional ways it may be actively extended.

When you have recorded your observations regarding the side aspects of the experience, the dialogue script writing will come to rest. During that pause, while you are not deliberately trying to do anything further with this experience, a flow of additional thoughts, perceptions, insights, images, and awarenesses will very likely be activated within you. They will arise of themselves, and your role in the process at this point will merely be the neutral one of recognizing and recording them. As you write your descriptions a momentum will be generated, and a further stream of Journal entries will flow of their own accord. They may take the form of an inner monologue, but they will all be part of the ongoing dialogue relationship that builds and grows through many facets and phases. At a later time, in a week or a month, whenever its inner rhythm draws it to the fore again, the dialogue script also may spontaneously resume itself. All are part of the cyclic process by which a dialogue relationship continues and extends itself in the course of our life.

Each section of the Journal has its own style of approach to dialogue experience, but the inner relationships that we establish are not restricted to any one section. Quite the contrary, as they proceed they overflow their bounds and move in and out of the various sections and dimensions of Journal experience. At the close of each cycle of exercises in our Journal work, we ask ourselves the questions: Where else in the Journal can I go to explore and extend the material I have now recorded? What feedback leads do these entries give me? Do they lead me to memories that should be recorded in the Life History Log? Or to the realization of Intersections, of roads taken and roads not taken in our inner life? Or do they suggest to us connections to be pursued in other dialogue relationships in other sections of the Journal?

Most important, one Inner Wisdom Dialogue leads to another. Now that you have begun a dialogue relationship with a wisdom figure, you can initiate other dialogues of this kind as they are suggested to you by the further work you do in your Journal. Over a period of time we can establish a contact via dialogue with a number of individuals who personify for us a deep relationship to truth. As we extend our Inner Wisdom Dialogues, expanding their variety and their range, these become a major resource for the progressively deeper experiencing of our lives.

24

Connections IV:
Re-Openings of Spiritual
Roads Not Taken

When we have written our response to reading back our Spiritual Steppingstones and have added to our Gatherings the further memories that it stimulated, we are ready to work in the fourth segment of the Connections section. We start a new subsection, writing the title, *Re-Openings,* at the head of a page. We record today's date, and we are ready to proceed.

Unfolding Themes at the Twilight Level

The purpose of our work in the Re-Openings segment is to draw from the experiences of our past the raw materials for the spiritual experiences of our future. (See also Chapters 26 and 27 on modalities and mantras.) We have given ourselves two resources with which to do this. One is the data we collected in Gatherings, memories of the various phases of our connective experiences. The other is the perspective of our inner life as it presented itself to us in our Spiritual Steppingstones. Those two exercises reflect our interior lives from different angles of vision. The Gatherings focus on particular events of our past while the Spiritual Steppingstones present the continuity of our inner life in its ongoing movement. In this sense they are polarities: on the one hand, the individual occurrence and, on the other hand, the encompassing perspective of lifelong movement. They are, however, opposites that balance and complement each other. Because they come from different directions in time, their effect is to activate earlier experiences that had been forgotten or had seemed to have reached a dead end. Now they can be reentered and explored anew in a larger perspective of time. That is the key to the way we draw upon Gatherings and our Spiritual Steppingstones in the work we now do in the Re-Openings segment.

We begin by sitting in silence, breathing slowly and deeply. We sit relaxed in the silence, not thinking specific thoughts but feeling the atmosphere of our inner life, its cycles and changes as we have been reviewing it and reconstructing it. In the quietness we recall to ourselves the tone of our feelings as, a little while ago, we were reading back to ourselves our Spiritual Steppingstones. We place ourselves again in that atmosphere, and we feel again the responses and the recognitions that arose in us then. Our attention moves increasingly inward, feeling the continuity of our inner lives.

We are in the twilight range of perception now. At a deeper-than-conscious level we have the freedom to move about now in a large and open atmosphere of inner space and inner time. In the silence we take ourselves back to the Gatherings we described. We let ourselves feel them, simply remembering particular aspects that return to our minds, not directing our thoughts but letting those memories move through us. We do this until we feel that we are in their general atmosphere again. Then we go back to those Gatherings entries to read them once more. In the beginning we read them lightly. We might better say that we are perusing them than that we are actually reading them. We are touching them to reestablish our contact with them and to remind ourselves of their existence and of their content.

We are moving through our Gatherings now, touching them, and observing, as we pass from one to another memory, the emotions that stir in us and the thoughts that come to us. We find that some of our Gatherings arouse particularly strong emotions within us as we turn our attention to those old events and touch them again. Strong feelings may be stirred in us, and an active train of thoughts, rememberings and associations may be set into motion. New ideas, observations and intuitions may then come to us, as well as imagery and symbolic per-

ceptions that may provide the base for new departures in our next experiences. We record the flow of all of these, as they come to us, whatever their form or their content. That is the first entry we make in the
Re-Openings segment.

ADDING TO OUR SPIRITUAL HISTORY

With our next step we can have a further, a more considered response.
We can reapproach our Gatherings in the perspective of inner time that
we have established with our Spiritual Steppingstones. That will open
another range of understanding and possibility of experience for us.

When we have made our entry describing our spontaneous response to reading back the memories of our inner experiences, we return to our silence. We let ourselves become still again, our breathing
slower and deeper, our eyes closed as we return to the twilight range of
perception. We sit in stillness some moments, and gradually we focus
our attention on the ongoingness, the continuity of movement that we
have noted in our inner life. Listing our Spiritual Steppingstones has
enabled us to see the unity of that ongoingness. Without seeking to
define it specifically, we let ourselves feel the persistence of the elusive,
inner thread that has moved through our lives. It helps us identify to
ourselves our own private, interior individuality.

Sitting in silence, we recall the uneven sequence of steps by which
we have reached toward meaning, holding various doctrines and beliefs in the course of our life. We have moved through cycles in which
there were times of intensity with many contents, and times of emptiness when the main characteristic seemed to be an absence of experience. All of these together in their degrees and their many phases have
comprised our inner life; now in our silence we let ourselves feel the
wholeness of movement, the thread of continuity within it. This becomes a perspective in the background of our mind, and with it we
return to touch our Gatherings once again. We go over them lightly,
rereading significant parts, and recalling ourselves to the experiences
we had described there. We are turning our attention to them now, not
from the point of view of our emotions, but in the perspective of the
ongoing movement of our inner lives.

As we consider our Gatherings and Steppingstones from this vantage point, we find that certain of our earlier experiences now appear

to us in a new light. There have been striking events that have stood forth in our memory as impressive markers of our inner life. In our view of them they possessed qualities that set them apart as distinct moments in our experience. Now, in the perspective of our whole spiritual history, we see that those events are related to others that came at various times in our life. Each of them was so intense or dramatic an experience that we thought of it as being unique and self-contained at the time. Now we can see the connection of these events to one another, observing how a theme is carried in a particular experience, then dropped, and after some passage of time, resumes its development in another event. In this perspective, we find a continuity of connections moving not only through our past experiences but also extending into the possible experiences that lie in our future.

Now we perceive that there are experiences which we had not thought of previously as belonging to our spiritual history but we can see in our present perspective that they have each played their necessary role, however brief, and have each made their small contribution to the whole. As we reconsider the contents of our life in terms of interior continuity, we recognize many more events that belong in our spiritual history. We add them to our Gatherings, taking note both of the specific events and of their broader meanings in our life. We recall:

Early experiences of disappointments;

Feeling connected to the changing colors of the leaves in autumn;

Feeling connected to the rising of the sun, or the renewal of spring;

The time when we were not caught in a lie, but knew we had lied;

Trying to do good works and realizing how complicated that can become;

Our political ideals, our activities, enthusiasms, frustrations;

Perceiving the unity of nature in science, and its disunity;

Experiencing the unity of nature in sexuality, and its disunity;

Trying various philosophies, and believing them;

Being disillusioned in a belief, or in a hope;

Being alone;

Following a dream and finding it was not what it seemed to be;

Following a vision that is partially true;

Intimations of large truths that come in poetry-type statements;

Observing the imperfectness of life;

Degrees of understanding of God;

Experiencing the reality of other people.

Memories of experiences of this kind in their various individual aspects are recalled to us now as parts of our cycles of connective experience. As we record them we realize that the continuity of the whole of our inner life would not have been possible without events that we barely noticed at the time they took place. We may also consider the implications of the fact that some of the most meaningful of these were events that we would have avoided if we could.

Going back over our Gatherings a second time, we proceed in the perspective and by the light of our Spiritual Steppingstones. We find that the new perceptions coming to us now have broader overtones than our first, essentially emotional responses. They form new configurations of understanding we had not seen before. Of particular importance is our recognition that various experiences that have taken place at widely separated times in our life and that we have perceived as separate events distinct from one another were in fact phases of a continuing process unfolding beneath the surface of our consciousness. They were collectively forming a single theme of meaning in our existence. For that reason they have to be considered in contexts that are different from the circumstances that immediately surround them. They are not limited to any single moment in time but are part of unfolding contexts that move through all the periods of our life. Even though the individual occurrences took place at points quite distant from one another in terms of *chronological time,* they have to be perceived in terms of units of meaning that are progressively unfolding across *qualitative time.*

As we go back over the Gatherings that we have recorded, we perceive them now as part of the *unfolding contexts* moving through the inner continuity of our lives. We observe how particular events that outwardly seem to be separate are in fact inwardly connected to one another. With brief entries here in the Re-Openings segment, we describe the essential details of these events, but it is the inner continuity that moves through them that is of the greatest importance. We should describe our perception of this as fully as we desire. By means of these entries we gradually weave together the threads of the various mini-processes that comprise the contents of our inner life. As we proceed and as a number of threads accumulate, we begin to see patterns of meaning being formed of which we were not aware before. As we observe them taking shape, we realize that they have been establishing the direction of our individual destiny. They have been prodding us and drawing us, without our being aware of it at the time, toward the next steps of our inner and outer lives; and they have been drawing us especially toward extensions and further developments of our beliefs. It becomes apparent to us now that, while we are here working with events from our past, it is our spiritual *future* that is being formed.

Considering our spiritual history in this perspective leads to another realization. When those inner experiences originally took place in our lives, they were reaching toward a meaning that we did not know. Since our knowledge of them was incomplete, we could respond only to a part of their possibilities, perhaps a small part. Other possibilities that might have led us to a larger sense of meaning and to a deeper understanding were necessarily passed by. We did not know of their existence, or we were not able to explore them, and thus they have remained unlived and unexperienced.

EXPLORING THE INTERIOR ROADS NOT TAKEN

These are the interior roads not taken in our lives. They contain the possibilities of connective experiences that we never followed through to find and develop. And yet these may be the essential opportunities that we missed in the earlier phases of our personal spiritual history. When we read the individual events of our Gatherings against the background of our spiritual history as a whole, we can identify the interior roads that were not taken earlier and the possibilities that may still be available to us. In this Re-Openings segment we can return to those events in order to explore the spiritual roads that were not taken earlier. And as we carry what we find here into the further practices of our Process Meditation work, we may reclaim what might otherwise have been the lost opportunities of our inner life.

We come then to a practical question: How can we know which spiritual roads not taken earlier in our lives will lead to valuable experiences and to a larger sense of meaning if we explore them now? Not every road that was not taken earlier is worth taking now. In most cases the decisions that we originally made, choosing one and rejecting the other, were for good reasons that are still valid in our lives. In some cases, however, circumstances have changed and important understandings that we could not have conceived at the time may now be waiting for us to find in doctrines we rejected long ago.

But how shall we locate them? How shall we find which roads not taken in the past are worthwhile exploring at this point in our life?

When we reconsidered our Gatherings in the light of our Spiritual Steppingstones, we were able to see that many of our memories were part of a larger continuity of events. Certain issues or concerns were present in our experiences and would reappear from time to time. They contained themes that surfaced again and again in our inner experience. These recurrences indicate that, for whatever combination of reasons, our life intuition perceives that these issues are strongly relevant to the further development of our consciousness. They have an inner importance for our lives, and thus the inner wisdom that is present at the depth of our lives repeatedly calls them to our attention.

The fact of the recurrence of particular themes of experience also leads us to the realization that there is a difference between our more recent experiences and those that came in earlier years. Very often we find that among our earlier experiences there were some that possessed a marked intensity and validity for us. Indeed, it is very often the strength of an early experience that sets us onto a particular path of involvement, as we seek larger meanings within the terms it set. The fact, however, that it was an early experience usually implies as well that we had not attained at that time a sufficient capacity to appreciate the issues that were implicit there. We may therefore have been very much impressed and influenced by the experience, but there were aspects of it, or implications of it, that we were not equipped to absorb, or to understand, or to act upon. We therefore let those aspects of the experience pass us by. Although they possessed great significance, we either did not recognize the significance of those side aspects of our experience, or we ourselves were not in a spiritual position to act upon them. They therefore became spiritual roads not taken in our life. They may have contained the possibility of taking us to great profundities of spiritual awareness, but we were not able or willing to take or to see those possibilities at that time.

Patterns of meaning have been drawing us without our being aware of it toward the next steps in our inner and outer lives.

Ordinarily when we have had a moving inner experience at an early point in our development, we remember the event itself, but we are not concerned with the road-not-taken aspect of it. We may not even be aware that that side of it exists. As we become increasingly aware, however, of the spiritual continuities moving through our inner life, we recognize the large concerns for which we have spontaneously been seeking further understanding at a deeper-than-conscious level in the course of our life. Inevitably it becomes clear to us that while our early experiences may have possessed great intensity, they also possessed less understanding of the deeper issues than we have available now. We can appreciate the fact that in those earlier experiences there may well have been aspects that were beyond our ken so that they had to remain spiritual roads not taken. But we might now be in a position to learn a great deal from them if we could take those roads now.

The primary guidance that we can follow, therefore, is to identify, in the perspective given us by our Spiritual Steppingstones, the themes and concerns that recur in a sequence of experiences through the continuity of our inner life. Their persistence calls our attention to the lines of inner process, the various cycles of connective experience, to which we should return in order to find the spiritual roads not taken that might appropriately be taken now. As we go back into those earlier experiences we look to see whether, in addition to the intensity of the events themselves, they contain any implications that were beyond us at that time but which we might be able to understand now. That is one guideline in identifying which spiritual roads may be worthwhile exploring now.

Sometimes the issues that call our attention to the spiritual roads not taken in our life are not first stated in religious or philosophical terms. They are simply events in our life experience, and we do not at first perceive them as having a spiritual significance. Only after we have worked in the broader context of our Spiritual Steppingstones do we realize that they possess large implications, and it is then that we are alerted to look for the factor of meaning in earlier events. When we look, we recognize that something important is there. We also realize that the distance of time has separated us from the reality of the original experience. We are no longer in its atmosphere, and its atmosphere is no longer within us. We do, however, have the intuition that if we could restore our sense of the presence of that experience once again, additional events of connection and awareness would take place for us. If we approach these as spiritual roads not taken, it is not in the sense of opportunities that we have missed but as further experiences that have not yet taken place and which we now can open as new possibilities. It is with this purpose that we carry out the exercises of the Re-Openings segment in order to place ourselves back in the atmosphere of earlier experiences.

Mother of Earth and of Love

Let us follow the sequence of T. F.'s experiences to see some of the actualities that may be involved as we take the steps of working in Re-Openings.

One of the important events of T. F.'s personal history was the sudden death of his mother while he was in college. Although it was a shaking event, he had absorbed it in time and had continued to build his life. In his forties he came to a transition point involving both his career and his personal relationships, and it was then that he became engaged in the *Intensive Journal* work.

At the Life Context workshop where he made his basic listing of his Life Steppingstones, he naturally included the unexpected death of his mother as an event that had a major effect on his existence. At his workshop, however, he did not include it in the listing of his Spiritual Steppingstones since he thought of it as a strictly personal occurrence. He placed the material that dealt with his mother and his relation to her in the Dialogue with Persons section.

While listing his Spiritual Steppingstones as part of his work in the Meaning Dimension, however, he made the more general entry, "Questions of death and ongoing life," to describe one of the concerns of his inner life. Reading that back to himself in preparation for the Re-Openings exercise and considering the entries he had made in Gatherings, he realized that the questions he was asking about death and immortality were not limited to a single event in his life. They involved issues that had appeared to him at numerous times over the years, sometimes as a result of outer circumstances, sometimes as part of inner experiences. That recognition now led him to recall and to record additional memories in relation to that Spiritual Steppingstone. After reading back and reconsidering his Spiritual Steppingstones, he added to his Gatherings various memories that he would not previously have considered to be part of his spiritual history.

> The sudden death of my mother when I was in my late teens threw me into shock, but I tried to respond in a "rational" way. I was beginning to read philosophy at the time, and I remember referring to Schopenhauer and talking as a cynic about life and death, as Schopenhauer would. I also remember having feelings of a great extension of life, and thinking there was something profound to be understood about death. I did not quite know what that was, but I had vague feelings that in some way my mother's death would show me. I also remember feeling that I was under too much pressure at the time to deal with such complicated issues, so I just let it go and did not explore it further at that time.

Another Gathering:

> About a year after my mother's death, I wandered by accident into the church of a spiritualist religious group. A seance type of reading was taking place as I walked in, and because I was young and a stranger, the lady giving the reading looked up from her Bible and turned her attention to me. I was amazed when, never having seen me before, she told me that my mother had died not long before. And then she assured me that I was being protected by my mother "from the other side." I neither believed it nor disbelieved it; but I did feel some truth in it. I think I acted afterwards as though I believed it.

Another Gathering:

> Sitting in a rowboat on a small lake some years later. Sitting alone, just drifting under the shadow of the trees. No one else around. Suddenly a sense of nature comes over me. I feel connected to the world of nature and I have the inexplicable feeling that nature is my mother, my own mother. For some minutes I feel the presence of my mother, very close and very personal. It was a very warm and intimate, a very protected feeling. It was very personal and also much more than personal.

At the time of his mother's death, while he was living through the trauma of the sudden separation, he had also had the feeling that much more could be shown to him if he were able to handle it emotionally and if he were able to assimilate it intellectually and spiritually. But that was not the right time. He felt that he was under too much strain because of the pressure of events to be able at that time to absorb a profound new teaching or understanding about the mysteries of life and death. Therefore some other time; not now, but later sometime.

T.F.'s experience of postponing a deeper meeting with truth is quite common in the spiritual histories of many persons. "The world is too much with us," with its pressures of things that have to be done immediately, so that there are always valid reasons available to explain why we cannot deal with the profounder issues of life at the present time. We are, of course, very interested in dealing with them sometime later, whenever we shall have time. But the world is always too much with us, unless we discipline ourselves specifically to make the time. One of the functions of our work in the Meaning Dimension is to end our postponing by giving us a method and an atmosphere that enables us to work at deepening our inner experience while we are in the midst of the outer activities of our lives. Our work in Re-Openings is a means of moving deeper into those truths that we glimpsed in our earlier experiences but that we did not stay to learn of more deeply at the time.

Given the context of his Spiritual Steppingstones and the additional Gatherings that were recalled to him, there were two steps for T.F. to take in his Re-Openings work. The first step involved his re-entering the situation that immediately followed his mother's death, especially since he had the intuitive feeling at the time that there remained more for him to learn about the meaning of the death of his mother. Further understanding was waiting for him, he felt, whenever he would give the subject more time and attention. The second step involved his experience on the lake when nature and his mother became inseparable for him. Each of these events was an intersection in the continuity of his inner experience. The road of his life had taken him to the point of a choice. There were two roads to take. He took one and left the other untaken. If he wishes now at this point in his life, much later in time and circumstance, to learn the knowledge that lay on the road not taken, he must come back to the original road and proceed with it up to the point of the intersection. Then he can continue along the road he did not take before. Those are the steps we follow in the work of Re-Openings.

Let us take these steps with T.F. He is going to return to the time in his life immediately following his mother's death. He is going to re-enter the situation and let it continue to open itself anew.

He begins by sitting in quietness. His eyes closed, he feels himself to be back in the events that followed his mother's death. There was the initial shock and the feeling of disorientation. There were the emotions shared with relatives, but he was too numb then to feel the emotions. At that time he was mechanically saying things to relatives who were trying to comfort one another. But he did not really know what to say.

Reentering the experience in his silence, T.F. recalls this and he begins to feel again the emotional exhaustion he felt at that time. Eyes closed, he is back again with the mourning relatives. Finally they leave, and he begins to feel alone and quiet. Now he can reenter the experience in a way that takes him toward the depth of it.

The original event returns. He is there again in the room, in the silence. He has realized and assimilated the event that has taken place. And now he is feeling its implications. What else does it mean? Questions are being asked, and it is as though someone is speaking. That is how it was. Someone is speaking now in the silence. Things are being said about the nature of such experiences in people's lives. He is told that they happen all the time. But there is much more to it than meets the eye. There is more to be said.

Now T.F. has gone all the way down the original road to the intersection, to the point where the new road begins. Moving in the twilight range of perception, he is making it possible for twilight memory to re-open old events in order to move through them and beyond them. Now the original situation is reestablished, the atmosphere is there, the experience is being re-opened. T.F. is within it, and now, in the twilight range, it can proceed of itself. It can now bring forth as much as it wishes to provide at this time.

T.F. will record in his Re-Openings segment all that takes place as his experience continues. Later he will turn to other sections of his workbook and describe there the special aspects of the material that has come to him in his Re-Openings experience. In the sections of the Meaning Dimension as well as in the other *Intensive Journal* exercises, he will feed this information into the context of his life as a whole, and he will work with it in relation to other experiences that have come to him at other times. But more of this as we proceed.

In his Gatherings T.F. had recorded a second memory which he can now reenter. He can now return to his experience on the lake in order to re-open the events that were taking place there, to see if they are ready to carry him further along the road that was not taken.

Once again T.F. places himself in a condition of quietness. His eyes are closed, and he is drifting into the twilight range of perception. The memory situation is establishing itself, and it is placing him within it. He is on the lake, in the rowboat in the quiet place under the trees. It is memory, and he is perceiving it on the twilight level. Now the feelings and the tone of the original connective experience return to him. It is memory and more than memory. It is the re-opening of the original event. The original happenings return here on the twilight level. They reestablish themselves as they were, but something additional also becomes present. In re-opening the event, it becomes possible for the experience to move beyond itself and to open the way for further interior events. This is the enlargement of connective experience toward which our exercise of Re-Opening is reaching.

In the silence of *twilight memory,* T.F. lets himself again be drifting in the rowboat. The atmosphere of the situation returns and his sensitivity to the largeness and intimacy of nature becomes present again. There is the feeling of being close to all the natural world, of being supported and sustained by it. It is a feeling of encompassing peace, and of connection to both the animate and the inanimate realms.

Now an additional awareness becomes part of the situation as T.F. feels his mother to be present. She is there in the twilight space as she was at the boatside, hovering in the atmosphere, a presence, but not speaking. There is the increasing feeling that the world of nature and the world of the mother are not separate. In some way they are intimately connected to one another. It is a personal connection, and also more than personal. T.F. has a strong sense now of the personal qualities of his mother. He feels that, as they are being presented to him, they are being somewhat idealized with an emphasis on nurturing love and warmth and bountifulness. But he affirms it all. It is a personal reconnection and a connection with the world. Nature and mother are felt as one, but mother is personal also. She exists and is present. But her existence is now for T.F. a truth that is greater than her personal being. The phrase "Mother of earth and of love" comes to T.F. He feels the two realms brought together in a unity with a great surging of warmth and emotion within him. He is connected to the world of nature which is impersonal; he is connected to his mother, which is a very personal feeling. And the two are one. He is personally connected to the larger universe.

"Mother of earth and of love." It seems like the first line of a poem, but T.F. also realizes that it is a mantra/crystal. In the exercises that follow this chapter we shall have the experience of working with mantra/crystals and seeing the active role they play in our work. T.F., however, was already familiar with the use of mantra/crystals. He therefore recognized what it was when the phrase came to him, and he also recognized that, as a mantra/crystal, it would serve as a starting point for him in the further steps he would take in his inner experience.

T.F. could see the several ways in which his work in Re-Openings led beyond itself. By reentering his earlier experience on the level of twilight memory, he could establish contact both with the past and with the future, enabling his experience to move by its own momentum along interior roads that had not been taken before. He could thus have access to areas of inner experience that had been closed off before. Now they were open, and with them came the possibility of further experiences not only within this phase of his work but in other Journal sections and exercises.

One part in particular of T.F.'s experience, the phrase, "Mother of earth and of love," would provide a starting point for further practice in the Mantra/Crystal section of the workbook. And beyond that, the experiences that were re-opened here would draw forth material for a progressive enlargement of spiritual contact along various avenues in the Peaks, Depths, and Explorations section. While we may begin by reentering a single inner experience that calls to us from our past, we find that the work we do in Re-Openings reconnects us to inner resources which then unfold from experience to experience, providing energies and understandings that emerge unexpectedly out of their own depths. Our Re-Opening experiences often become pivotal points in our personal evolution because they provide the channel by which past experience leads to further experience in building our spiritual history.

25

PDE: Peaks, Depths, and Explorations

Our transpersonal leads take us to the *Peaks, Depths, and Explorations* section of the workbook. Whether we perceive our life in religious or in secular terms, this is the section where we each work with the questions which we feel as fundamental concerns in our life. Here we develop the themes that have the greatest personal importance to us, paradoxically, because their meaning to us is beyond our individuality. But that paradox lies at the heart of the definition of transpersonal themes. Such themes are issues that arise in areas like philosophy, religion, ideology, human destiny. They are larger-than-personal in their scope, and yet we feel them, think about them, worry over them, and eventually commit our lives to them—*personally*. In his neo-theological language, Paul Tillich spoke of them as *ultimate concerns*. We work with them actively, in detail, and especially in continuity in Peaks, Depths, and Explorations.

The Ongoing Use of the Meditation Log

This section is different in basic ways from the other Journal sections with which we have worked so far. The difference lies primarily in the fact that Peaks, Depths, and Explorations is solely devoted to extending and deepening our inner process. The other sections have been preparing us for this. Exercise by exercise, they have been providing the materials and teaching us the methods that would eventually enable us to continue our personal, self-directed spiritual development using the exercises of Process Meditation as our vehicle. Now we have arrived at the point where we can take that further step. The Peaks, Depths, and Explorations section is the place where we coordinate our use of the data and procedures that we have gained from all the other sections in our *Intensive Journal* workbook. We interrelate them, drawing them together in an ongoing format as we seek to evoke and experience more of their meaning.

We find that a large part of the work we have already done in other sections calls our attention to the transpersonal areas of our life. When we reread our earlier Journal entries, we see that we have been seeking to establish a larger contact with our transpersonal concerns both for emotional and spiritual reasons. Something within us has felt the need to know them and to experience them more fully. The transpersonal leads steer our deepening Journal work to these themes. They are able to indicate which areas of further Journal experience will be productive for us and will respond to our profound inner needs because, as original entries, they reflect the unpremeditated concerns of our life.

Now we take them as leads, as starting points, and enable them to unfold with the self-expanding format of Peaks, Depths, and Explorations. The exercises we carry out here essentially apply procedures with which we are familiar from our work in other Journal sections. It is the combining, the coordinating, and especially the continuity of these that is important here. Since each theme unfolds in obedience to its own principle, the sequence of procedures that we follow in Peaks, Depths, and Explorations is unique for each exercise. It is probably true that the work we do in this section is the most individualized and the most open to improvisation of all the sections in the *Intensive Journal* system.

While our work in Peaks, Depths, and Explorations draws upon the other Journal sections, using their customary procedures, there are special adaptations that have to be made in some cases. This is particularly true with respect to the Meditation Log since it has an expanded role as the supplier of transpersonal leads. At the beginning of our work in Peaks, Depths, and Explorations, our transpersonal leads tend to come directly from the other sections of our workbook. They involve our primary concerns and usually occupy a more obvious position in a person's life. As our practice of Process Meditation is continued and extended, however, we find that more of the transpersonal leads come to Peaks, Depths, and Explorations from the entries that we have made in the Meditation Log. Segments of the Meditation Log, such as Spiritual Positioning and Inner Process Entries, increasingly act as intermediaries between the contents of the events of our lives and the larger awarenesses that give us a sense of ultimate meaning.

In Chapter 21 we carried through an exercise that plays an important role in gathering resources for our work in Peaks, Depths, and Explorations. In the Inner Process Entries segment of the Meditation Log we recapitulated our work in Connections where we had begun the large task of reconstructing our spiritual history. In addition to the perspective which we drew from our work in the four segments—Cycles, Gatherings, Spiritual Steppingstones, and Re-Openings—we also built a resource for Peaks, Depths, and Explorations. Recapitulating the outlines of our spiritual history enabled us to recall the themes that spontaneously recur in the depth of our thoughts and feelings. That helps us identify the transpersonal concerns that are working in us beneath the surface of consciousness.

The segment for Spiritual Positioning in the Meditation Log also serves as a source of transpersonal leads, especially after we have had occasion to make several entries there over a period of time. When we began our work of Process Meditation, we set a base for ourselves by writing a first statement of our spiritual position. That statement was written as spontaneously as possible so that it would provide an honest and unpremeditated expression of our inner life. It was also deliberately made as a concise statement, since at that point our need was not for completeness but for a brief and focused statement that would enable us to dip at least one toe into the underground stream and thus get started on our inner work. We took for granted at that point the fact that, as our Process Meditation proceeded, there would be opportunity for further statements of Spiritual Positioning.

We do make such additional statements from time to time. We write them usually as pauses or at points of reconsideration in our interior process. We find that they are helpful in enabling us to see our situation from within. It is a convenient way to take stock of ourselves spiritually, to see where we are, and to consider where our inner life is moving.

Our speaking of Spiritual Positioning as a recurrent exercise may lead you to feel that now is the time for you to do it once again. Perhaps it is already time for you to write a new statement of your spiritual position; but perhaps not yet. There are criteria to consider.

If you have begun your Process Meditation work with these exercises, you should consider that it may still be a bit early for you to write a new statement. It is best to allow ample time between statements of Spiritual Positioning so that a sufficient number of new events and experiences can take place. It is also important to allow enough time for our new awarenesses and for changes in our beliefs to be absorbed into our inner life as a whole. We should bear in mind that absorbing our spiritual experiences into the tissue of our emotional life can be a slow process, much slower than having the experience itself or merely thinking about it. We should guard against making new statements too frequently or too close together. To do that can mislead us by giving importance to beliefs and attitudes that are only transiently passing through us.

Even though it is a matter of subjective judgment, there are objective considerations in determining what is the proper length of time to wait before you write a fresh statement of Spiritual Positioning. It depends upon your evaluation at each step of the movement of your inner life. One way to state it is that the right time to write a new statement of your present spiritual position is whenever you feel that so much has taken place within you that you need an opportunity to sort it out and make it clear to yourself.

Take notice in this regard that the criterion is not at all whether a dramatic new breakthrough has taken place in your experience, changing your beliefs and filling you with new enthusiasm. If you write a fresh statement of your spiritual position at such a time, the effect will most likely be to reinforce your new opinions. And the purpose of Spiritual Positioning is not at all to confirm you in your most recent experiences but rather to set them in perspective. The best criterion to follow, therefore, is the *muddy water* principle: when new inner events have multiplied in your experience, to the extent that you feel the need for clarification, this is a good time to write a fresh statement of your present spiritual position.

We thus have two balancing criteria to follow with respect to writing new statements of Spiritual Positioning. One the one hand, we wait long enough between statements to allow a sufficient number of inner events, experiences, changes in belief and awareness to accumulate. On the other hand, we proceed to write a new statement whenever the flux of interior life leads us to feel that it would be helpful to stabilize our viewpoint. At such times, you may pause in your Process Meditation work and turn to the Spiritual Positioning segment of the Meditation Log. Sit in quietness and make sure to allow sufficient time for a twilight experience to come to you. In that atmosphere the metaphors and symbols that come as twilight experiences can tell you a great deal in very cogent terms regarding your true spiritual position. Record what comes to you on the twilight level, and then proceed to describe your inner situation as you presently perceive it. The correlation between those two can be very instructive to you.

Whether you write new statements of spiritual position frequently or sparingly, from the point of view of Peaks, Depths, and Explorations it is valuable to have a number of them collected in the Meditation Log. After we have written a few such statements spread over a period of time, reading them back to ourselves in sequence gives us a sense of the movement of our inner life. Reading back enables us to recognize the themes, concerns, questions of belief that recur in various aspects in the course of our statements of Spiritual Positioning. Their reappearance indicates to us that these are the leitmotifs of our inner life. By the fact that they arise again and again as our deep concerns we are led to acknowledge them as requiring our further attention. Over a period of time these Spiritual Positionings in the Meditation Log become a valuable source from which we obtain transpersonal leads to Peaks, Depths, and Explorations.

A further important and ongoing source of transpersonal leads in the Meditation Log is the record that we keep in the segment for Inner Process Entries. After we have recapitulated the experiences we have had in carrying out the exercises of Process Meditation, we continue to record in Inner Process Entries the interior events of our lives on a current basis. This is the active recording of our experiences, our concerns, and our searchings, as we are engaged in them and as they are taking place within us.

The material that we record in the continuity phase of Inner Process Entries covers a broad range of experience. Some entries seem unimportant to us when we consider them by themselves. Succeeding entries, however, pick up and discuss varied aspects of the same concern. After a period of time, when we read back to ourselves a series of Inner Process Entries, we can perceive that a single theme has been building as it moved in and out of the other subjects we were describing. It is thus by their interweaving continuity among our Inner Process Entries that we can identify the transpersonal themes which, by their persistent recurrence in our spontaneous Journal entries, are telling us that they will have a still larger message for us when we transfer them to Peaks, Depths, and Explorations and work with them there.

Try not to prejudge any of your inner experiences as being unimportant, for that may cause you to eliminate them without knowing their full meaning or their possibilities.

We can also infer from this a valuable rule to follow as we make our ongoing entries in this segment of the Meditation Log. As much as possible we should try not to prejudge any of our inner experiences as being unimportant, for that may cause us to eliminate them without knowing their full meaning or their possibilities. It is better to record them, even if only briefly and with no comment beyond our basic description of them. In that way we have them on record. If subsequent experiences carry them further we can extend them and build upon them. If not, we can let them rest where they are.

The primary criterion of the materials that we record as Inner Process Entries in our Meditation Log is that in some aspect or degree they pertain to our personal quest and concern for deeper meaning in our life. The subjects of these entries may be of many kinds, reaching into diverse areas of our life experience. The following are examples of how such entries may begin, indicating all the subject matter that they may proceed to explore.

Sitting in silence waiting for the meeting to begin, unexpected thoughts and feelings stirred in me . . .

Listening to the music and thinking of nothing, images and awarenesses began to form before my mind . . .

Gathering the statistics for the research, I found myself wondering about the principles behind what I was doing. I began to think about the relation between God and science, and I was considering whether . . .

Reading the poetry of ——, I found myself sharing the imagery and having the feeling that I was in the same place as that in which the poetry was formed. Then my experience moved on, and I had the feeling that . . .

Sitting at the lake alone under a tree, I felt the quietness of nature all around me. Thoughts of life and a work that would be valuable began to move around in me. I found myself thinking that . . .

The text of the sermon was. . . . Reading it by myself later on I was especially struck by the passage that said . . .

The death of —— raises questions in me that reach beyond the personal aspect of my feelings. I should not continue to postpone the question of what I believe about death and what my attitude is toward the event of dying. And also aging and serious illness as part of a human existence. I think of the situation of ——. The feelings and images that come to me are . . .

These are instances of Inner Process Entries that we may make in our Meditation Log to express the various experiences that come to us in the course of our lives. Not infrequently, as we write them we find ourselves in a position where it seems that we have just taken the cork out of a geyser. That is an incongruous metaphor. But the point is that, as we do something simple like making a Mediation Log entry, we suddenly realize that a tremendous energy has been set free. We realize further that this energy is carrying many unknown contents, some of which will become resources for understanding and new experiences at a later point in our life.

Thoughts and feelings, intuitions and images as well as fundamental life concerns begin to articulate themselves as we write in the Meditation Log. It becomes apparent that we each carry within ourselves a quality of caring that reaches beyond our individual existence and contains intimations of truth beyond our personal knowledge. After we have started our Meditation Log entries and the process of our writing them has begun to build its own momentum, we begin to sense the possibilities.

The Steps of Deepening Experience

It is apparent that the Meditation Log serves as a great deal more than a spiritual diary. As our work in the Meaning Dimension deepens and as we enlarge the scope of our experience, the function of the Meditation Log grows with it. It expands its role so that it can eventually screen and select the transpersonal themes that we follow in Peaks, Depths, and Explorations. This progressive development of the Meditation Log makes it necessary for us to discuss some details of how we work with it at the further stages of the *Intensive Journal* process.

The principle underlying all the log sections in the *Intensive Journal* system is that they are fact gatherers. On that basis all entries made in log sections are to be as concise as possible. They should also be as objective as possible, considering that many of the facts being recorded in the log sections are in actuality subjective experiences that are taking place even as they are being described. Because they often are expressing inner events that are in the process of happening, Meditation Log entries have a tendency to be more expansive than other log entries. The movement of the writing is part of the progression within the experience. As we read back to ourselves, however, we notice that in certain entries there is a point where the nature of the content subtly changes. Without realizing what is taking place, we shift from the direct description of our inner experience to a more intellectual type of discussion regarding the significance of what has taken place. That should be a sign to us that we have gone far enough in the Meditation Log. Its function is to catch the raw material of experience. Whatever is to be done beyond that is for Peaks, Depths, and Explorations.

The essential reason for which Meditation Log entries are to be brief is to record the facts of our inner life as effectively as possible. If we find that, despite our desire to be concise, a Meditation Log entry insists on extending itself, that may be an indication that it has more to tell us. We should then treat it as a transpersonal lead and take it to the Peaks, Depths, and Explorations section.

If we find that over a period of time the entries in our Meditation Log continue to return to particular themes, perhaps addressing the questions from different angles but returning to the same general subjects again and again, that may also be a message. It indicates that the theme of those entries has a persistent inner importance to us and the we should therefore work with that theme in Peaks, Depths, and Explorations.

We should be aware that the transpersonal leads that we are following are not merely passive pointers. They are not simply road signs that indicate the direction in which a particular town is to be found while leaving it to the driver to decide whether to go there. These are active leads that contain an energy of desire and need within them-

Transpersonal leads contain an energy of desire and need within themselves which carries the work forward.

selves which carries the work forward. They do more than road signs that merely point the way. The transpersonal leads might better be compared to self-directed engines that take you where they themselves want to go. The differences among them lie mainly in the fact that some transpersonal leads move with large heads of steam giving them energy while others barely chug along.

The Ways of Using PDE

The work we do with some transpersonal themes proceeds with great strength when we take them into the Peaks, Depths, and Explorations section. As an example, if you have an ultimate concern regarding the question of whether you will be able to make a living as a musician, as was the case in the life of Pablo Casals, so that you will be able to make music your total way of life. In PDE, if Casals had been using the Journal during his lifetime, he would have made music the theme of an entire subsection. He would have gathered the factual history of his involvement in music up to that time. And he would have left the section of PDE in order to conduct an Inner Wisdom Dialogue with someone from the world of music whom he respected. He would, perhaps, have had a dialogue there with Count de Morphy.

After the dialogue had taken place in the Inner Wisdom Dialogue section, he could describe the net result of his dialogue in the PDE section, including any additional insights that came to him in experiencing the dialogue script. Thus, the PDE section would be a base point for exploration of an issue that was of ultimate concern to him.

If Eleanor Roosevelt had used the Journal process during her lifetime, she might have chosen the time of her decision about whether to remain with Franklin Roosevelt or to explore the whole issue of her marriage, the question then in her life of ultimate concern. She could have also gone out of the PDE section in order to investigate the various possibilities and could have chosen various other sections of the Journal in which to conduct these further investigations. She could have gone to the section of Dialogue with Events and there, after she had developed the history of her relation with Franklin Roosevelt and his mother, she could proceed to dialogue further with the event of her marriage situation. Or she could have taken it to an Inner Wisdom Dialogue with persons whose opinions she respected in order to obtain a further view of the event. Whichever dialogue she chose to have, the net result would be recorded in PDE, and in that section, she would follow through with her discussion of this, an event of ultimate concern in her life.

For Eleanor Roosevelt and Pablo Casals, these experiences of ultimate concern in their lives carried considerable momentum and moved directly into active experiences.

They carry considerable momentum and move directly into active experiences. Other themes may have the same potential, but their inner timing has not yet generated as great an energy. That may come later, depending on the rhythms within the life cycle of the themes that are being carried to us by the transpersonal leads. Some may be ready for active extension immediately after a workshop experience while others may go into an extended time of gestation before they are ready to take another step. In the Peaks, Depths, and Explorations section, it is essential that we be sensitive to the tempo of the themes with which we are working so that we can adjust our procedures to their needs and rhythms.

FURTHER WORK WITH TRANSPERSONAL THEMES

We have a guideline format to help us in carrying out our work in Peaks, Depths, and Explorations. It provides a framework for the variations that are required as we proceed in our open-ended exploration of transpersonal themes. The format consists of a few basic steps that we should keep in the background of our minds as we carry out the various combinations of exercises.

Our first step is to identify the transpersonal themes that we feel to be important for our inner development. We rely for this on the transpersonal leads which we draw from the entries we have made in our Meditation Log over a period of time.

When we have determined the transpersonal themes with which we shall work, we set up a subsection for them in Peaks, Depths, and Explorations. Each theme is given its own subsection so that the continuity of the varied exercises we carry out in relation to this theme can be coordinated.

Our next step is to choose the exercise with which we shall begin our work in Peaks, Depths, and Explorations. Our primary clues for this will undoubtedly come from the transpersonal lead that originally called our attention to this theme. Its tone will give us our starting point. Perhaps its first effect is to recall us to earlier times in our lives. If it is personal memories that are awakened here, we go to the Life History Log for our next entry. If it is transpersonal memories, we go to Gatherings. Possibly what we describe in Gatherings will evoke additional memories in us, and these will lead us to further exercises in other segments of the Connections section, in Spiritual Stepping-stones, and in Re-Openings.

After we have carried out an exercise, there is an additional reportorial entry that we would ordinarily make in the Meditation Log. But now, having established the subsection for this theme in Peaks, Depths, and Explorations, we make that entry here. From this point on, everything that relates to this theme is brought together in this subsection, at least from the point of view of reporting what has taken place and recording the development of its continuity. As we decide on the individual exercises that we shall use, we move out into the various sections of the workbook.

Following the indications of our transpersonal leads, we may use any or all of the techniques available to us through the Intensive Journal/Process Meditation system, applying them in ways that seem appropriate to the particular materials. These practices may include:

1. Twilight imagery in any of its aspects, including twilight thinking and twilight dreaming experiences.

2. Life history work in its various phases.

3. Personal and transpersonal dialogues.

4. Mantra/crystal meditation.

5. Journal interplay and cross-referencing.

Moving from exercise to exercise in this way with a theme in Peaks, Depths, and Explorations, we find that we are taken back and forth through many of the sections of our *Intensive Journal* workbook. In the course of this movement, a number of other aspects of our lives may be stimulated into activity and awareness. But a report, a response, and a further reflection is always brought back to the sub-section in Peaks, Depths, and Explorations. This is how we maintain and coordinate the continuity of our exploration. All the experiences that take place in us with respect to that theme are fed back into the subsection where we extend our consideration of it with imagery and thought and the full range of twilight experiences.

Proceeding in this way, we find that one experience and awareness leads to another. Each is drawn forth by what took place before it. We realize that the sequence of exercises for each transpersonal theme is unfolding out of the life and the needs of the theme itself. By the continuity and the interior reference of our exercises, we have set a self-contained process into motion. This process began with the intimation that came to us by means of the transpersonal leads indicating that we could have a deeper understanding and relation to a particular area of reality. We began to explore that, and now the process is moving from one exercise to another as though by its own power and direction. It is enlarging its scope, incorporating data and images of which we did not know at the start.

As we proceed, the process of transpersonal exploration expands out of its own nature, drawing us from one exercise and perception to the next. There is an open-ended creativity in the process as its continuity carries it at each step another length beyond itself. Time and again we are brought to a surprise. As these unpredictable insights are given to us, we recognize that the essence of our spiritual method lies in its freedom within a structure. Had we tried to set our agenda of exercises in advance, we would have eliminated the breakthroughs that cannot be anticipated.

Working in Peaks, Depths, and Explorations, we find that there is a uniqueness and creativity in the way that each transpersonal theme unfolds its life for us. Depending on the degree of receptivity with which we follow its leads from exercise to exercise and commit ourselves to helping it bring forth its message, it becomes an artwork. It proceeds out of the seed of its potentiality and, once we have enabled it to establish its life and its integrity, it moves with its own tempo and style. We have then become the servant of the quest that we ourselves began, as every artist must eventually become the servant of his or her artwork. We find that the spiritual work we do in Peaks, Depths, and Explorations parallels the principles and process that are involved in the artist's life of creativity.

26

Modalities for Next Experiences

In working with our individual spiritual histories, we have been re-calling to ourselves the experiences in which an awareness of meaning and of a contact with the larger aspect of reality has entered our lives. Whatever the form or the degree of these experiences, whatever the doctrines or the symbols by which they came to us, they have been the moments when we have been able to recognize our life as belonging in a more-than-personal context.

The intensity of these interior events was so great that they impressed us as being unique happenings in our life, complete unto themselves. As we consider them, however, we realize that by no means were they end-points finalizing our beliefs. No matter how convincing they were at the time they took place, more is implicit in them: a further possibility to which they can lead in time. In this sense, no matter how profound and complete it has seemed to us in the past, every connective experience is also a seed experience for further knowledge and contacts that can open to us by means of it. Although these experiences are now part of our spiritual history, their value is in what they can contribute to our spiritual *future*. We require a means of working with these past experiences of our inner life so that they are not left as end-points but can serve as starting-points and can lead to new experiences.

A major task of every methodology of the creative life, whether in the field of religion or in the arts or sciences, is determining how it can make the bridge between the last experience and the next experience, and how it handles what happens in between. Various persons coming from different directions have developed ways of approaching this issue, and have developed a valuable resource upon which we can draw. There are three that are particularly relevant for our work in Process Meditation. The first is the way of the Russian Pilgrim; the second is the way of the wise, old Lao Tse; the third is a working hypothesis that has emerged from Holistic Depth Psychology with implications not only for religious experience but for the larger range of creativity as well. We shall now consider each of these briefly, observing the modality of process that is at work in each of them. Then we shall proceed to our work with mantra/crystals which serves as the pivot between past and future in the practice of Process Meditation.

The Russian Pilgrim and the Prayer That Prays Itself

One person who tested in his own experience a *process model* for the inner life is the anonymous Russian Pilgrim. He pursued his quest for spiritual connection in the context of Greek Orthodox Christianity and he recorded his efforts in a book that is becoming a mystical classic, *The Way of a Pilgrim.*

Many modern readers will be familiar with the Russian Pilgrim from J. D. Salinger's popular novel, *Franny and Zooey.* In that tale of a modern American schoolgirl who is desperately looking for an inner principle that can guide her through her time of confusion, Salinger created a realistic parable of the modern quest for spiritual security. His heroine, Franny, tries to use the Russian Pilgrim's techniques as a means of maintaining her mental stability. She turns to them seeking a source of strength, but her efforts are fruitless if not altogether disastrous.

Working with the Pilgrim's methods, as Salinger pointedly and accurately describes her, Franny falls into a swoon. But that is readily understandable. The gap between the context of the Pilgrim's experience and the context of her life was very great, and since she had no intermediate experience with which to make the bridge, she collapsed under the internal pressure. The Pilgrim's way of spiritual practice was not related to anything of significance in her life, neither to her cultural nor to her personal existence. Franny's use of the Pilgrim's method therefore made her exceedingly vulnerable. She had used a technique for stimulating the depth of her consciousness without first establishing a place for it in the context of her life as a whole. Since she was attempting her spiritual practice without adequate preparation, there was nothing in which it could take root.

The Russian Pilgrim had a difficult existence, but he fared much better than Franny with respect to his interior life. After a personal misfortune that probably involved the premature death of his wife, this simple anonymous peasant of mid-nineteenth-century Russia devoted himself to seeking an ongoing spiritual contact. The manuscript from which we know of his life and his efforts was found in a monastery but with no precise information accompanying it as to who he was or when he lived. All that we know about him we have to surmise from his text. Although he had the substantial attainment for his time and place of being able to read and write, he was otherwise an unlettered man. He did possess, however, a very earnest spiritual disposition, so earnest, in fact, that he took seriously and literally the New Testament injunction in Paul's letter to the Thessalonians that a person should "pray without ceasing." When, however, the Russian Pilgrim tried to fulfill that commandment, he found that it was beyond his capacity. He did not know how. He therefore undertook as his special task a pilgrimage of walking across Russia inquiring wherever he could and seeking to discover a method by which he could learn to pray without ceasing.

In his seeking this, we should note, the Pilgrim by no means had a simplistic understanding of prayer. He did not mean by prayer the rote recitation of ritual formulas, nor the repeated request of special favors from God. Prayer rather meant to the Pilgrim a special condition of being, an inner state of unity, freed from the interventions of his conscious ego, in which the ground of his being was connected with and at-one-with the abiding reality of God.

It is apparent from his writing that the Pilgrim had known from time to time the experience of feeling himself to be intimately connected to God. But that state of unity had not lasted. It had been subject to a cyclical movement. He had been in a state of prayer, in a state of intimate relation with God, and then he had lost it. The condition of unity had ceased to be. And the desire of the Pilgrim was to have a method by which the state of unity with God would not be lost to him but would be maintained as a reality of his experience. That was why he wished to learn to pray without ceasing.

In his chronicle, the Russian Pilgrim tells of his efforts and his experiences as he walked across Russia in humility of spirit seeking an answer to his question. In the course of his search, he met a monk on the road and told him what he was seeking. The monk turned out to be a man of spiritual learning familiar with the *Philokalia,* the Greek Orthodox collection of texts of mystical wisdom and practice. As the Pilgrim interpreted it, that was a providential meeting. He describes how the monk took him into his cell and taught him from the *Philokalia* the doctrine that "the continuous interior Prayer of Jesus is a constant uninterrupted calling upon the divine Name of Jesus with the lips, in the spirit, in the heart." He told him the words of the prayer. In the Greek, which is undoubtedly the language in which the prayer was recited, it is *Kyrie Eleison,* which is a seven-syllable mantra phrase, as it is in English when it is translated as "Lord Jesus Christ have mercy." (Sometimes in English the words "on me a sinner" are added, but they are not inherent in the Jesus Prayer.)

The monk read from the *Philokalia* the instructions given in the passage by St. Simeon the New Theologian. "Sit down alone and in silence. Lower your head, shut your eyes, breathe out gently and imagine yourself looking into your own heart. Carry your mind, that is, your thoughts, from your head to your heart. As you breathe out, say, 'Lord Jesus Christ have mercy on me.' Say it moving your lips gently, or simply say it in your mind. Try to put all other thoughts aside. Be calm, be patient, and repeat the process very frequently."

The phrase "very frequently" was soon made more specific by the monk who now became the Pilgrim's *starets,* his spiritual teacher. "Start to say the prayer three thousand times a day." He was actually to count to three thousand but the discipline of counting the times of saying the phrase under his breath was not the ultimate goal of the method. The goal was to go beyond counting and to reach a point where the Jesus Prayer would be said continuously and without pause through all the hours of his life.

Once he had mastered that discipline, the prayer would not abate during strenuous physical activities. It would not abate during sleep. It would not abate even when he was talking with another human being. According to the *Philokalia,* as the prayer was said continuously it progressively developed its own power. Increasingly it moved by its own momentum. It became, in the language of another anonymous spiritual, the fourteenth-century English monk of *The Cloud of Unknowning*, a "prayer that prays itself."

The Pilgrim's basic and difficult task was learning to repeat the prayer so constantly that it repeated itself without his having to think about it. After that it was present as though it were part of his body, part of the circulation of his blood or the beating of his heart. There were times when he lost that constancy of the prayer, but he was invariably able to reestablish it. And it provided the encompassing atmosphere of his life, undergirding and sustaining whatever actions he was called upon to take.

The fact is that the Pilgrim was not called upon to take many striking actions or to make many strong decisions. A few months after he had mastered his method of meditation, his *starets* died, and the Pilgrim was back on the road again. Now, however, he was not seeking a new teaching as he had been before, for he felt that he had found what he had been seeking. Now he was simply living his life, walking through the Russian wilderness, studying the *Philokalia,* and continuing to use his unceasing prayer as the foundation of his being. From time to time he would have an adventure, as when he was beset by robbers and his copy of the *Philokalia* was stolen, or when he mysteriously lost the use of his legs. But each time something wonderful happened to enable him to overcome his troubles, like having his *Philokalia* returned to him, or finding a peasant who was able to cure his illness. In each case the Pilgrim was certain that his great good fortune came from the fact that he continued to say "that ceaseless spiritual prayer that is self-acting in the heart."

It is clear that the *self-acting* quality of the Jesus Prayer contributed a great energy and atmosphere of wisdom to the Pilgrim's life. We have also to recognize, however, that the conditions of his daily existence were markedly different from that of persons in the modern world. The events that filled the Russian Pilgrim with rejoicing were exceedingly simple when compared with the requirements and pressures of modern urban existence. Since his experiences took place within a very sparse cultural environment, we may have to concede that the Pilgrim's way may be limited primarily to a monastic type of life or to small communities in which all persons share a single framework of beliefs and traditions. The complexity and diversity of the secular, cosmopolitan society of modern times does not appear to provide congenial grounds for the Pilgrim's lifestyle and practices. Nonetheless there are elements in the Pilgrim's way that form a core of spiritual method and express fundamental principles that may be relevant for the modern world as well.

How shall we state the essence of the Pilgrim's way, considering it as a modality of subjective process and seeing it as contributing to a general methodology for the inner life? Underlying his approach was the recognition that mental consciousness cannot by itself give us a connective experience. The Pilgrim has already tried to achieve his unitary contact by the fervor of his belief, by the intensity of his desire and his will, by the powers of thought and the use of the mind. But none of these had availed, and thus he was forced literally to go on the road for his search.

The essence of his practice of the Jesus Prayer lies in the fact that at the point where the prayer took over within him and became "a prayer that prays itself," the mind of the Pilgrim, his will, and even his beliefs were superseded. The tone and quality of his being, then, was set at a level of his life over which he no longer had conscious control. In terms of the concepts we are using here, it was set at the twilight range of consciousness, and it was carried by an energy that moved at that level. The experience of the Russian Pilgrim makes it clear that the technique of regularly repeating a phrase in a fixed rhythm in conjunction with our breathing is able to establish an inner condition that is governed neither by the ego, nor the will, nor by the analytic intellect. It is centered, rather, in the twilight range of awareness. Thus an atmosphere is established in which a person feels connected to and supported by larger-than-personal powers of life. The combination of this atmosphere with the dedicated repetition of the phrase seems to have additional consequences, including a helpful and sustaining power in the conduct of one's life. That is why the Russian Pilgrim believed that his occasional good fortune in the face of adversity was in some way a result of his continuing to say the Jesus Prayer without ceasing.

One question we must ask is whether the power lies in the prayer itself or in the unremitting repetition of the prayer. The answer seems to lie in a combination of the two, and that takes us to the heart of the Pilgrim's method. Two factors are important. The first is the content of the phrase, or prayer, and the way that it is felt or perceived by the person. The second is the way that the phrase is used repetitiously.

It is apparent that the Jesus Prayer is no ordinary phrase. It carries multiple levels of meaning as well as emotional identifications that connect the individual to centuries of inner experience. It is equally apparent that the Jesus Prayer cannot be a relevant phrase for everyone since its meaning is contained within the culture of Christianity. People who have lived outside of that culture and who have absorbed other traditions into the subliminal levels of their consciousness will require another phrase. It is also true that the Jesus Prayer will not be an effective or appropriate phrase for many persons who have been brought up within the culture of Christianity but for whom the phrase will not have an inner relevance. We can see that there are a number of aspects to the question of what is the right or valid phrase for an individual to use. There needs to be an inner connection between the person and the phrase that is being used. But we need not assume that it has to be a firm or doctrinal belief. It may be that the connection between the person and the phrase is a linkage on the level of emotion; or it may be that the phrase carries a life intuition, an intimation that a larger meaning is to come by means of the experience of that phrase.

It is clear also that it will not work, that it will not be effective if chosen for external reasons. It will do no good to choose a phrase because one had learned it by rote during childhood. But if it is deeply felt and experienced by the person, that is another matter. In that case, childhood teachings and traditions have a reinforcing effect which should be honored. Further, it will do no good to accept a meditation phrase simply to comply with the authority of the spiritual teacher who has assigned it. It must come authentically out of the life of the person, not directed by the conscious ego nor by the emotions of will or conscious desire, but as an honest evolution of the individual's own inner experience.

Given a phrase that is appropriate for the individual, as the Jesus Prayer was for the Russian Pilgrim, consistent repetition can prove to be a highly effective practice. It tends to neutralize the factors of ego, willfulness and mental consciousness. It establishes perception at the twilight level. And it brings about the progressive deepening of the interior atmosphere in which connective experiences can take place.

We can see that the practice of the Russian Pilgrim, derived as it was from the *Philokalia,* contains at its core an effective and subtle modality of subjective process. It will be valuable for us to bear in mind the way the Pilgrim's process operated for him, and also to consider the implications it has for us. It has a significant contribution to make to our modern practice.

The Rhythm of Active and Passive

Muddy water, let stand, become clear.

LAO TSE

The saying attributed to Lao Tse that "Muddy water, let stand, becomes clear," has played an important role in the *Intensive Journal* work. As a metaphor of life it carries an implicit philosophy; more specifically it carries a sense of timing in human experience. It refers to the conditions in life and the way they change and move into one another.

Lao Tse's saying suggests a way of positioning oneself in relation to change. It is both passive and active, but a person cannot be both passive and active at the same time. The opposites alternate, but the changes take place at a deeper-than-conscious level. To be in harmony with the movement of opposites in the cycles of experience requires much more than a conscious decision or a desire to do so. It requires an inner event that happens to us. We cannot just do it but we can act in such a way outwardly and inwardly that it becomes possible for it to happen to us.

"Muddy water, let stand, becomes clear." But how did the water become muddy? And how can it become clear? In the course of the activities of our life, many inner events, the concerns, the thoughts, the projects, the beliefs, the fulfillments, the disillusionments, the emotions of many kinds all come into the water of our inner being. These thoughts and feelings are separate from the water, but they are inherent parts of our life. As they accumulate in the course of our life experience, they have the effect of clouding the waters, both by the simple fact of their being there and by their movements back and forth. The waters become muddied by the many contents and activities of our lives.

We might first think that the solution would lie in removing the contents of the water. Then the water would always be clear. The fact is, however, that without the contents, we would have no life. It would therefore be self-defeating. The waters would be clear, but they would have no purpose.

In the entrance meditation from *The Well and the Cathedral,* the symbol of the muddy water moved to a further phase, fulfilling the larger image. It became quiet and it became clear. When the waters were still, the debris of activity, the results both of the person's activity within the mind and the activity out in the world, could settle to the bottom. The muddiness gradually disappears. The waters become clear, progressively more placid and lucid until they become still as a quiet lake. Now it is peaceful. Nothing is there. At first when we look into the waters, they are transparent. They are clear, but all we can see is the water. As we sit in the stillness, merely gazing into it, the water becomes like a mirror to us. Images appear in it, images of many kinds. Some of the images are reflections of things that are outside of the water; others are reflections of things, and especially of qualities, that are within it, that are within us. They are in the depth of the water; they are in the depth of us. The quietness has brought a strikingly new situation into existence.

In the time of activity, we were engaged in doing things and the waters of our life became increasingly muddied. Now, in the stillness, it is not only that the muddiness settles but that a further source of information is brought to us. Through the clarity of the waters, images are shown to us that are in fact reflections of various aspects of our life. The images that we see in the waters are the symbolic forms by which the contents of our existence are reflected to us. We see images reflecting the external realm of life, images reflecting the inner depths of our being, and we see a large number of images reflecting the intermediary realm in which emotions and twilight perceptions relate our inner and outer worlds to one another. We find that the qualities and contents of our life are reflected to us in the symbolic forms of imagery. As we learn to perceive them, and as we recognize the messages that are being mediated to us by means of their symbolism, we gain access to a varied source of information for use in our life.

Now let us observe the way the rhythm moves with respect to the alternation of opposites in our life. When we were actively engaged in our life, many things accumulated in the waters of our inner being until those waters became muddied. The psychological equivalent of that is simply to say that we became confused. Because of the turmoil in our life, the water became clouded so that we could not see the images reflected in it. That meant that we were deprived of our inner source of information, and without its inner guidance our life came to a condition of stalemate. It is thus that the activities of life bring about a muddiness which forces the movement to come to a stop. A condition of quiet is then established. It may not come about voluntarily, but the net result is an absence of movement.

When our life becomes so muddied that we are brought to a stop, we have a choice before us. We can refuse to acknowledge it and struggle to keep the activity in motion; or we can accept the stoppage as part of the natural rhythm of our life and we can regard it as a message for our life. If we make the latter choice, we place ourselves in a position to follow Lao Tse's way. Since activity has muddied our life, we now become inactive. We take a passive, a waiting stance toward life so that the muddy waters can settle and become clear.

What will happen then? We sit in stillness. We have at our disposal a number of different techniques for quieting the movement of our mind and emotions so that all those thoughts and desires, plans and hopes and anxieties can come to rest. The Mantra/Crystal practices which we shall soon be describing can be helpful in this regard; so also can the entrance meditations of *The Well and the Cathedral,* and especially this meditation from the *Star/Cross:*

Quiet the movement of our mind and emotions so that all those thoughts and desires, plans and hopes and anxieties can come to rest.

Letting the Self become still,
Letting the thoughts come to rest,
Letting the breath become slow.
Breathing becomes quiet.
Breathing becomes slow,
And slower;
Breathing becomes regular,
Regular.
The unevenness
Of nonessential thoughts
Drops out of the breathing.
It becomes
The breathing of the Self.

As we sit, breathing slowly in that stillness, the muddiness of the waters within us begins to settle. The waters become clear as the atmosphere around us deepens in its silence. The waters are quiet and clear, transparent as we look into them. Now the waters become as a still lake, and the lake becomes as a mirror. As we look into it, images appear to us. These images are reflections to us both of the external circumstances of our life and of knowings that are in the depth of us. They are all reflected to us in symbolic forms, and we perceive them in the quiet waters.

These images that we perceive, what do they say to us, what shall we do with them? These images may carry the ideas for our next project. They may carry the emotions for our next friendship. They may carry the energies for our next activity. We were brought to the condition of stillness by a stoppage, a confusion, an apparent failure in the conduct of our life. Our activity came to a standstill, and thus we were forced into the opposite position. Activity stopped, and thus we found ourselves brought to a passive state.

We remain in this state, and we let the silence deepen. The muddy condition within us settles, our inner being becomes clear. We become like the still waters of a quiet lake, as images reflecting the surface and the depth of our life are presented to us. Knowledge we need to know, ideas we have long been seeking, come to us. They come in symbolic form, but in our quiet atmosphere their meaning is apparent to us. Now we have ideas for new projects, guidance for new tasks to fulfill. We are back in motion. The stoppage is over. The time of being in a passive stance is ended; indeed, it is reversed. We are active again. And most significant of all, we are able to be active again just because we were profoundly quiet. In that silence the effects of our last period of activity could settle so that we could inwardly become clear again as a quiet lake. In the mirror of those still waters, the contents, ideas, and energies for new activities were given us. And thus we were propelled from within out of the silence from our passive stance back into our active life again.

We may assume that we shall continue along that path of activity until the muddiness accumulates once again and draws us to a standstill. At that time we shall find our way to stillness and remain in the quiet place until the cycle that has moved from active to passive has provided the resources that return us to an active stance once more. As we move through that cycle again and again, sometimes in spans of short duration, sometimes in cycles of a longer range, we gradually recognize the rhythm that seems to fit best our individual nature. That rhythm is our personal rhythm. It is the rhythm by which the cycle of the opposites of experience, the active and the passive, moves through our individual life. This is the form in which hope and achievement, disappointment and renewal, all find their place in our life. It is the personal rhythm by which the universal cycles of opposites can find a channel in our life.

One of the important functions of *Intensive Journal* practice is the way it enables each person to fill in the details of these cycles. It is a means also for enabling each of us to work out and recognize our own rhythm so that we can be in harmony with the cycles of opposites as they appear and reappear in the course of our life. Lao Tse's sense of having a rhythmic relationship to the cycles of active and passive is a valuable contribution to our methodology of Mantra/Crystal practice.

MTI's: Molecules of Thought and Imagery

The third modality to which we look for information regarding the movement of subjective process is drawn from the concepts of Holistic Depth Psychology. This is a metaphor that has served as a prime hypothesis in our work, the MTI's, the molecules of thought and imagery. We shall describe it here not in the terms of the depth principles that underlie it, but as a modality that we can consider and apply in the active practice of the *Intensive Journal* process, especially in our Mantra/Crystal work.

Think of a piece of wood. It is solid, opaque, hard to the touch. We can pick it up, hold it, use it as a single solid unit. And yet we know from the science of physics that the apparent solidity of the wood is only its outer aspect. Its opaqueness and hardness are only relative. When we approach it from another point of view, we realize that the wood is not solid at all but that, among its other aspects, it is a movement of molecules. In addition to its outer facade, it has an inner dimension that is active and effective. But this fluidity within the wood is not visible to our commonsense perception.

Considering this, we can recognize a number of correspondences between physical reality and our human existence. Two are of particular significance. The first is that physical reality has its outer aspect concealing some subtle and elusive levels beneath it. When we move past the commonsense assumptions of our superficial perception, we come to qualities and energies of physical being that are much greater than we had imagined. That has certainly been the experience of chemists and physicists ever since the discovery that there are molecular structures beneath or within the apparent solidity of what we see on the surface.

In a parallel way, our human existence has its duality of outer appearance and inner reality. We have our social veneers, the various attitudes and behavioral traits that are visible on the surface. And, like the wood, we also have levels of reality within ourselves that cannot be seen. There are very powerful forces working in our depth, but, since they are concealed from our view, we are not able to perceive them, much less gain control over them, unless we have a special knowledge and training. In that regard, the hidden level within ourselves, our psychological depths, is comparable to the molecular level of physical reality.

There is a second correspondence between physical reality and human existence that is of even greater significance. In the depths of matter, the molecular level is *in motion*. That was a most surprising realization when it was first discovered. But the same is true of the hidden depths within the human being. A movement of images and subliminal thoughts is actively taking place beneath the surface of our consciousness. Included in it are not only visual images, but ideas, hunches, intuitions, things we feel and hear inwardly, the perceptions and awarenesses that come unguided from within. They all move as molecules move, as images and thoughts coming together to form new combinations.

Both in sleep and in the waking state, imagery moves within us at levels deeper than our mental consciousness. Experiments have repeatedly verified the fact that a movement of imagery and thoughts takes place during sleep. We know that these involve the significant contents of our lives, the situations about which we are concerned, the problems we are seeking to solve, the emotions we are feeling. They continue to move around in our inner space while we are asleep. It may well be, therefore, that the making of dreams during sleep involves essentially the patterning and repatterning that takes place as part of the flux of the molecules of thoughts and imagery as they move about within us. This possibility opens a number of implications to be explored with respect to the relationship between dreams and the MTI's.

The phenomena that occur during sleep are even more markedly and observably present in the intermediate waking state that we have described as the twilight range of experience. In twilight imagery, as we have seen, the definition of imagery includes all the perceptions that reflect to us in any form the varied aspects of those contents of our life that we experience at levels below our mental consciousness. In addition, an important quality of twilight images is that they are perceptions that come by any of our inner or outer senses, and that they take place without our conscious direction.

In both the sleep and twilight states, patterns of imagery move, change, regroup themselves, and form new patterns again and again. It is very similar to the way that molecules move, interact with other molecules, and repattern themselves into new constellations with new characteristics. When these new qualities appear, they are visible on the surface; but the changes that brought them about occurred at invisible levels. The regrouping of the molecules is the factor that effectively brings about changes which then become visible at the outer level.

The correspondence now is apparent between the molecules that move within the chemistry of a piece of wood and the MTI's, the molecules of thought and imagery, that move at the subliminal levels of our psychological nature. Motion is characteristic of both of them, sometimes a flux, sometimes orderly motion. The coming together into clusters and constellations to form patterns with particular traits and systems of energy is also a characteristic of both types of molecule, the physical and the psychological. And changes in the clustering of both types also lead to changes in the derivative qualities, the outer traits that become visible on the surface. This is particularly true with respect to the molecules of thought and imagery because, when the images regroup into new patterns, new qualities of behavior and action soon are reflected at the surface of our lives.

To think of the depth levels of our being in terms of the metaphor of MTI's the molecules of thought and imagery, may provide one clue to understanding how change takes place in human personality. It may be that when abrupt changes occur in people's attitudes or beliefs, as in the transformation experiences of rebirth that often happen unexpectedly and without explanation, the outer events are reflecting sharp inner changes in the clustering of the MTI's. Most probably it is not relevant to ask the question of which comes first and which is the cause of the other. Beyond cause and effect, what we observe is a fact of correlation between the outer and the inner. In some synchronistic way, outer experiences and the inner constellation of the MTI's go together. In their interaction upon one another, they set up new units of outer/inner circumstance which then become the next set of contents and conditions in our life. Considerations like these open the possibility that there are ways of personal practice and spiritual discipline that will be more conducive to the creative self-combining of the MTI's. This hypothesis is in the background of several of our *Intensive Journal* procedures.

When we move past the common-sense assumptions of our superficial perception, we come to qualities and energies of physical being that are much greater than we had imagined.

Our observations in Holistic Depth Psychology have enabled us to draw several inferences regarding the qualities of the MTI's. They are apparently reflectors of the whole range of our human existence. The personal situations of our lives, our desires and frustrations, are reflected in them; and the more-than-personal symbols of poetry and religion that carry our intimate feelings of meaning in life are also reflected in them.

The molecules of both types of imagery—the personal and the transpersonal—move about together, intermingling in the depth of us. Sometimes the various MTI's fuse freely with others to form new constellations. At those times there is a marked fluidity in a person's thoughts and imagination, usually leading to a period of great productivity both in ideas and actions. At other times the MTI's are restrained and seem to repel one another. They do not intermingle then and it seems that very few new combinations of molecules are being formed. This, of course, is not creativity but its very opposite. It is experienced as a dry time. Instead of fluid movement, there is tightness and rigidity. Instead of creative fulfillment, there is frustration. An atmosphere of tension then builds in the depth of the person, and this further hinders the free movement of the MTI's.

This negative aspect suggests the need for a constructive approach that can assist the process by which the molecules of thought and imagery form their larger configurations. It would seem that the MTI's require an atmosphere in which they can be free from constraints upon their movement. They should be as free as possible from pressures that are external to their own nature, whether these are the pressures of social demands or of personal emotions. Then the capacity of intuitive knowing and self-guidance that seems to be a quality of the profound patterns of symbolism can be expressed in the MTI's. As they come together, combining, breaking apart and recombining, they form new groups and constellations which take expression in new ideas, awarenesses, plans for action, poetic visions, and inspirations for belief. That is one reason why we seek a quiet atmosphere. The reason for stillness is not merely to bring about a subjective condition of inner peace and tranquillity. It is to establish a profound field of harmony at the depth of our being so that the MTI's within us will be as free as possible to find their way to the most meaningful new combinations. This seems to be the inner ground of creativity and spiritual awareness.

Aspects of the three modalities of process that we have described—the Jesus Prayer that prays itself, the rhythm of active and passive, and the MTI's—are expressed in various forms at several points in the *Intensive Journal* work, and especially in the Twilight Imagery phase of Process Meditation. The principles underlying them come together, however, in making possible the conception and practice of Mantra/Crystals as an instrument for creative spiritual practice. To work with Mantra/Crystals is the next step in our practice of the *Intensive Journal* process.

27

Mantra/Crystal Experiences

The Meaning of Mantra and Crystal

We can now take the steps that will enable us to make Mantra/Crystals and then progressively to work with them.

What is a Mantra/Crystal? And why is that the term chosen to refer to a procedure that plays a pivotal role in the active experiencing of Process Meditation, and thereby in our *Intensive Journal* work?

In the course of creating the *Intensive Journal* system and of adding to it over the years, I have had the task of choosing names for the various Journal sections and procedures. In doing this, one criterion that I have followed is to try to find terms that are as descriptive as possible of the operations they embody within the *Intensive Journal* structure. An even more important criterion has been to find terms that reflect the *style of movement* of the procedures they represent; and, if possible, to find terms whose varied nuances and cultural overtones will help carry that movement. This is particularly true with respect to the Mantra/Crystals.

In the case of the word *mantra,* we utilize a term that has an Oriental derivation. While there are a number of other terms to describe the meditative process of making deeper contact, they tend to refer to practices that depend on doctrines within their own framework of belief. Because of the pluralistic nature of religious experience, especially at this point in history, it has seemed to me to be essential to have a term that would not be identified with any particular doctrine.

It is with this thought in mind that the first word in our Mantra/Crystal phrase is taken from its primary Oriental usage. It has a large place in Hindu/Buddhist religious practice, appearing in many forms in that broad tradition. In its most general and fundamental meaning, however, a mantra has a universalistic sense. It refers to anything that serves as an aid to meditation in the general sense of quieting the self. Mantras may be of many kinds, not only Eastern, and they may be used in diverse ways as they serve different purposes. They may call upon a single sense or upon several of the senses. They may use the various modes of perception in different combinations and patterns according to the purpose of the particular discipline and the customs of the time. For example, a mantra may be a single word or a group of words used as an aid in the practice of meditation. Equally, mantras may not be words at all but a sound, a musical note, or a chant. They may be a painting or a sculptured object. Various works of art in the East serve as mantras. Mandalas, for example, which are the symmetrical and symbolic designs presented in the East in many forms, in paintings, in carpets, in woven tapestries, are often used as mantras. They serve in diverse combinations of ritual and religious discipline as aids to meditation in the several Eastern traditions.

Very often the mantra is part of a special initiation ceremony. At those times it is given by the guru as a secret which the disciple is to guard very closely. Its significance may then also be as an object of private knowledge, usually described as an arcane wisdom known only to the master and disclosed to his student. Mantras given in this way are regarded as a special secret key by which the student will be enabled to unlock spiritual mysteries.

Used in such an atmosphere, mantras tend to draw an aura of holiness around themselves. They come to be treated as sacred or numinous objects. Special spiritual powers may then be attributed to them, and psychic phenomena of various kinds may be felt to occur in their presence. Gradually, as the mantras reach the point where they are venerated as holy objects, a subtle shift takes place. The mantra ceases to serve as a means of spiritual enlargement, but it becomes an end in itself. Not infrequently it has become an object of personal pride and cultism. In fact, one of the commonly noted causes of idolatry and superstition within the Eastern religions is the popular misuse of mantras. But none of these misuses negates the basic validity of working with the mantra principle in meditation as a means of stilling the self.

We also use mantras as a means of stilling the self. To that degree our use of mantras is in accord not only with the Oriental use of mantra but also with comparable practices in non-Eastern spiritual disciplines, like the Jesus Prayer of the Russian Pilgrim, that also seek to achieve an inward quieting.

It is significant that this modernized use of mantra helps to fulfill some of the fundamental concepts of depth psychology. One of my goals for many years has been to develop, on the basis of depth psychology, a methodology that would provide a psychotherapeutic effect while it was engaged in the larger task of providing a way to personal meaning that could meet the special needs of persons living in the modern age. It was that effort that led me to formulate the Holistic Depth Psychology described in *Depth Psychology and Modern Man.*

Crystal is the second word in the name Mantra/Crystal because the phrase presents a crystallization of a segment of the person's life history. The Mantra/Crystal contains the essence of an individual's experience of a connecton with a larger-than-personal reality. Very often it is an experience that began with an individual's expectation that it would lead to a deepening contact, but something in the nature of the experience led the person onto a different track. The Mantra/Crystal phrase, containing in its crystallization the essence of the person's experience, is an attempt to get back into the original experience and extend it.

The Nature of a Mantra/Crystal

There are several characteristics of Mantra/Crystals in our modern usage that must be borne in mind. The first is that the Mantra/Crystals we work with are seven syllables in length. The Mantra/Crystals may be any number of words, provided that the total syllable count is seven. Another necessary quality of Mantra/Crystals is that they be smooth and rhythmic enough so that we can easily speak and repeat them under our breath. It usually works out more harmoniously if the individual words are no more than three syllables and mostly only one or two syllables each. We try to compose our Mantra/Crystals of words that fit together smoothly so that each Mantra/Crystal will establish its own rhythmic flow within its own unity. This rhythm eventually becomes an important factor in conducting our meditations for it enables us to repeat the Mantra/Crystal without conscious effort or thought. Once the meditation gets under way, the rhythm itself carries it. Especially when it is combined with rhythmic breathing, the continuous repetition of a seven-syllable mantra phrase builds a self-sustaining rhythm that strengthens it and enables it to maintain itself under its own power.

Working with seven syllables enables us to establish the necessary length and rhythm in our Mantra/Crystals. These two factors, length and rhythm, are of central importance because of two primary relationships: the first is the relation between our regularized breathing and the inner rhythm of our Mantra/Crystal; the second is the relation between a significant inner experience drawn from our life history and a Mantra/Crystal that reflects in a concise way the atmosphere of that experience. Together these determine the qualities of the Mantra/Crystal and they provide us with our main criteria in constructing them.

The connection between breath and spirit is a fact that has been widely recognized in religious history. Wherever people have worked seriously with spiritual disciplines, they have noted the close relationship between the movement of the breath and the quality of inner experience. Much of this understanding is stated metaphysically in cosmic conceptions that are largely symbolic or mythological. The concepts are symbolic because the perceptions they express are largely intuitive or poetic and are very difficult to demonstrate in detail. We see a major example of this at the very beginning of the Old Testament where the *Ruach* is the breath and/or Spirit of God. Breathed into human beings, it is also the carrier of life and of intelligence for mankind. There are many correspondences to this with rich variations in the cultures both of preliterate and advanced civilizations. Especially in the Hindu-Buddhist traditions the the symbolic understanding of the relation between breath and spirit is developed in many sophisticated ways. In the forms of Yoga it becomes a fundamental discipline for spiritual development.

We can see from the uses of Yoga that once it goes beyond social beliefs and symbols the relation between breath and spirit becomes a matter of personal practice. Without practice, it becomes merely talk and intellectualization; with practice, it expands the possibilities of awareness and action. By means of particular techniques that vary with each religion and culture, breath and spirit are brought together in special ways in each individual's experience. The regulation of the breath plays an important role in balancing the inner and outer aspects of a person's life. In particular, the quieting of the self is related to the stabilizing of the breathing especially in the way that it helps neutralize the hold that habits have on us. It helps us establish at least a degree of freedom from being controlled by our conscious ego. The linkage of breathing and the Mantra/Crystal is an essential step first in establishing and then in progressively deepening the process of our meditation.

It is important to bear in mind as we construct our Mantra/ Crystal that eventually, when we come to work with it in practice, it will be specifically coordinated with the movement of our breath. At that point we shall establish a regular rhythm in our breathing, and we shall coordinate that with the saying of the Mantra/Crystal under our breath.

The cycle in a unit of breathing gives us a natural criterion and measure. *Breathing in and breathing out.* In fact, that phrase itself with its seven syllables is a good indication of the length and rhythm that a Mantra/Crystal should have. Breathing in and breathing out. The phrase naturally coordinates with the systole and diastole of our breathing and reflects the underlying cycle. That cycle is a natural unit and it serves as a model for us in making our Mantra/Crystals.

Experience indicates that a Mantra/Crystal of seven syllables carries its inherent rhythm so that, as we continue to say it under our breath in conjunction with our breathing, the rhythm establishes and maintains itself. We can each work out our own balanced rhythm of breathing in and breathing out, fitting it to the seven-syllable phrase. Thus we can breathe in on the first three syllables, hold on the fourth, and exhale on the last three syllables. Or we can breathe in on the first three syllables, breathe out on the next three, and maintain a state of emptied breath on the seventh syllable. There are also alternate rhythms that are possible within the seven-syllable unit. As we proceed in our individual work, we each can devise additional ways to coordinate the breathing with the Mantra/Crystal. But we can discuss these at another time in the context of our actual practice. Here we wish merely to set the background and to explain the functional reasons for making our Mantra/Crystals of seven syllables.

The possible combinations of in-and-out or back-and-forth

rhythms that are inherent in the number seven greatly facilitate the process by which we coordinate our breathing with our Mantra/Crystal. It may well be that the factors behind this are not to be rationalized, but in my understanding of it the *rightness of size* seems to be very important. Being not too long and not too short, the seven-syllable phrase corresponds to a full cycle of breath. Thus it is sustained and continued at a physiological level even when it becomes very meager with respect to both its conscious and its nonconscious contents. An important consequence of this is that, at those times when the energy and the motivation of our meditation dip to a low level, the natural rhythm of the Mantra/Crystal itself can continue the meditation for us. It serves as a riderless horse that knows where to go, continuing through the valley with only the guidance of its inner nature until it comes to the next valid phase of its journey. Many times, when the disciplines of meditation lag in a person, the momentum and rhythm of the seven-syllable Mantra/Crystal carry the process so that it does not come to halt before it contacts new energies and can resustain itself. In practice this is of tremendous importance.

Quite often the Mantra/Crystal changes by itself in the midst of the meditation. It frequently happens that the original one is replaced by another, even as the rhythmic breathing and the process of silent meditation are continuing. The observation that has been most interesting to me in this regard is that invariably the new Mantra/Crystal that is not consciously made but simply emerges in the course of the meditation fits the criteria for making seven-syllable Mantra/Crystals, and does so without any thought or planning or editing or fixing. Most of the time, in fact, the new form and content of the Mantra/Crystal is more appropriate to the evolving inner situation of the person than the original one that was consciously made. There is apparently a factor of inner wisdom that expresses itself at the depth of human beings whenever the circumstances are right for it.

An example of a Mantra/Crystal phrase that carries a back-and-forth rhythm inherent in its structure is

The waters beyond the well.

Let us set to one side for the moment the question of the content of this Mantra/Crystal (which comes from the *The Well and the Cathedral*) and consider merely its structure and its sound. Although it is not your own Mantra/Crystal, try repeating it at least half a dozen times under your breath just to feel the kind of rhythm it establishes. As you say it, let it set its own balance and tone, with your conscious mind interfering as little as possible.

This is an example of the simplest and the most effective form in which to compose a Mantra/Crystal. As much as possible let it be a phrase that has a single identity, a phrase that is not broken into separate words that are in sequence or in apposition to one another, but a phrase that can be *spoken and breathed as a unit.* That combination contained within a unity is its most desirable quality. It does not break apart into separate words but maintains its wholeness as we repeat it in conjunction with our breathing. It thus supports and builds the rhythm of our breathing in a self-sustaining way. Doing this, it contributes to building the cumulative effect that establishes the deep atmosphere we are seeking.

Some other examples of this unitary balance within the form of Mantra/Crystals are:

Feeling the movement of life.
Holding the stillness within.
In the chapel of the self.
The silent work of the monks.

In addition to the inner rhythms of seven and its correspondence to a cycle of breathing, a Mantra/Crystal is composed of seven syllables in order to serve its function as a crystal of our individual life in the process of meditation. As a crystal it is a concise but representative excerpt drawn from an inner experience in our life history that is meaningful to us for whatever reason, personal, emotional, social, cosmic, metaphysical. Taking a crystal from the whole experience in our past and making it into a Mantra/Crystal enables us to use it as an instrument for opening ourselves to new experiences and awarenesses. As a crystal, it needs to be large or full enough so that it can contain or reflect the essentials of that past experience. It must be concise, but not too concise. If we make a mantra phrase that has much fewer than seven syllables, it will be too brief an excerpt to give sufficient expression to the content and quality of the experience we are reinstating. And also if it is too brief, it will not have the requisite quality of rhythm and flow. On the other hand, if we describe the excerpt in much more than seven syllables, it may not be a concise crystal any more. It may then become bulky and even become a hindrance to our rhythmic breathing. Just as if it is too brief, a Mantra/Crystal that is too long can negate its quality of rhythm and flow. The mantra phrase needs to be able to function as a crystal. But it should not be too long, and it must not be too short.

We shall eventually be using the Mantra/Crystal under our breath, repeating it in coordination with our breathing, so we require a phrase that is soft and flexible. It should be a phrase that lends itself to being coordinated in a balanced rhythm. It should, whenever possible, be a phrase that carries its own rhythm, preferably dividing naturally into halves to correspond to the rhythm of inhaling and exhaling. It becomes like the Russian Pilgrim's "prayer that prays itself." At first it requires commitment and discipline, but once rhythm and momentum have been established, it is able to continue by itself.

We require words in our Mantra/Crystals that are easy to say. We find in practice that words of one or two syllables carry an advantage in this regard, since longer words may be difficult to repeat in a rhythmic way that can easily be coordinated with our breathing. While our Mantra/Crystals should be seven syllables in length, they may contain any number of words. It is the self-balancing rhythm of the whole that is important. The words should make the Mantra/Crystal phrase a natural unit so that we find ourselves saying it as a whole, as for example:

The river reaching the sea.

As we are making our decisions in choosing and forming our Mantra/Crystals, there is a question that we must carefully consider. At what level of our inner space can we expect our use of that Mantra/Crystal to place us? Will it take us up to the surface of mental consciousness? Or will it take us into the deeper levels of the twilight range of perception? There are particular kinds of words and structure in Mantra/Crystals that tend to draw the experience to the surface; and there are others that have a deepening effect. We can learn to identify them.

BEGINNING WITH YOUR OWN MANTRA/CRYSTAL

Let us visualize the basic sequence of steps involved in setting a Mantra/Crystal experience into motion. When we have formed and chosen a

Mantra/Crystal we use it first to quiet and center ourselves. We do this in coordination with our breathing in order to establish a balanced and self-contained unit of experience. The Mantra/Crystal contains its own rhythm, a rhythm that derives from its structure. As we speak the Mantra/Crystal, it establishes itself and becomes coordinated with our breathing. If the Mantra/Crystal is right for us and if our breathing is smooth, this coordination of the two will take place easily and naturally. We will not need to do anything consciously or deliberately in order to bring it about. The Mantra/Crystal and our breathing will come together as though by themselves while we are maintaining our steady and continuous practice. Presently, imperceptibly, a stillness will be established within us. At the same time our rhythmic breathing together with the saying of the Mantra/Crystal will continue and each will be assisting the other. In the course of this, the thinking processes that are directed by our conscious egos are progressively neutralized and are gradually brought to a quiet stop. The quality of our inner being is then no longer focused at the surface of our psyche where the conscious mind is, but is focused inward toward the depth of us.

What follows in our practice of the *Intensive Journal* process comes not from our surface mind but from depths in us that are beyond our personal or conscious direction. We have noted earlier that between waking consciousness and dream sleep there is a large realm of nonconscious perception that is the twilight range. It is here that we find and incubate the materials that eventually become the products of our creativity and the expressions of our enlarged awareness. One of the important functions of our work with Mantra/Crystals is that it puts us in touch with the depths of the twilight range in a manner that enables new contents of consciousness to become accessible to us. Even more important, our Mantra/Crystal work draws up this material from our twilight depths in a way that is beyond the intervention of our conscious mind. It is neither guided nor manipulated by the purposes or desires of our personal egos. At least that is the principle and the goal that underlies the Mantra/Crystal work. We seek to draw new experiences and awarenesses from the depth of the twilight range within us beyond the limitations and inhibitions of our personal habits, beyond our egos and our emotions.

For this reason the qualities of our Mantra/Crystals must be such that they take us into the twilight range of our inner space with a minimum of hindrance. One way to focus on the issue of creativity is to ask ourselves the question: Will it draw me toward the deeper levels of the twilight range where the silence can deepen? Or will it draw me up toward the surface where my emotions and my analytical thoughts will continue to go around in their circular movement? If we can answer that question truthfully we will be on the right track for creating Mantra/Crystals.

Working with Your Mantra/Crystals

When you have constructed a Mantra/Crystal that feels right to you and you are ready to proceed with the active us of it, there is one final test to make. Speak it aloud. Even though it is only in your own presence, speak it aloud so that you can have the experience both of saying it and of hearing it. And let yourself respond with your whole being to the way it sounds to you and the way it feels to you.

Eventually, when you work with it, you will speak the Mantra/Crystal under your breath. Speaking it aloud, however, is a way that you can verify for yourself that it is a Mantra/Crystal that feels comfortable to you. By speaking it aloud you can also double-check the fact that its words and sounds will move smoothly through your lips, and that there are no harsh sounds to get caught between your teeth and break your rhythm in meditation. But that is not the most important test. It is essential that it feel right to you, for a Mantra/Crystal is a very private thing.

Once you are satisfied with your Mantra/Crystal, you can turn to the Mantra/Crystal section in your workbook. (See Appendix B for a listing of the wide variety of Mantra/Crystals spoken at workshops.) Our first step will be to give our Mantra/Crystal a definite, recorded place, and then we can proceed to work with it actively.

The Mantra/Crystal section is divided operationally into two segments: the *Mantra/Crystal Index* and *Workings.*

The Mantra/Crystal Index is at the front of the section where we use it to keep track of those Mantra/Crystals that we have used more than once, and especially those that we feel we shall use from time to time in the future.

People who find Mantra/Crystal meditation to be a congenial way of spiritual practice tend to accumulate a number of Mantra/

Crystals over a period of time. They therefore have various Mantra/Crystals available to them, and they work with different ones according to the circumstances and the inner promptings that come to them. Sometimes, however, when you are in the midst of a tense or troubling situation, you may wish to practice a Mantra/Crystal meditation in order to quiet yourself in a meaningful way, but because you *are* tense you cannot decide on a Mantra/Crystal with which to work. Having the Mantra/Crystal Index before you can be very helpful at such a time.

We often find that certain experiences in Mantra/Crystal meditation are particularly memorable and meaningful to us. After some time has passed we may recall the experience in general but not remember it specifically, and not remember which Mantra/Crystal we used. It is helpful then to have a quick means of identifying our experiences and the Mantra/Crystals which helped bring them about. When we make our Index, therefore, we do not simply list our Mantra/Crystals one after another, but we leave ample space between them. Depending on your individual taste and on how much time you spend working in your inner experience, you will probably not want to have more than two to a page. In the lines between the Mantra/Crystals we record concisely such information as when we first developed this Mantra/Crystal and the dates of using it. If anything of particular significance took place during the experience of that date, we add a word or a phrase to remind us of it. We may also add a note to indicate cross-references to other Mantra/Crystals or to other Journal sections that are related to the Mantra/Crystal; for example, when it is related to a particular memory in Gatherings or to an experience in Re-Openings, as in the case of the Mantra/Crystal, "Mother of earth and love." Or when the Mantra/Crystal is drawn from a dream or a twilight image.

As they accumulate over a period of time, these small bits of data can say a great deal to us as they remind us of inner events that were intense when they happened but that have since dropped from consciousness. It is important to note in this regard that since deep inner experiences take place on the twilight level, they are as easily forgotten as dreams if they are not recorded soon after they occur. Once they are recalled, however, they can be remembered in vivid detail. The small bits of information we record in our Mantra/Crystal Index are intended to provide the cues we need.

The composite of information that will gradually fill the Index will be a concise way of making us aware of the extent and breadth of our inner lives as our Process Meditation proceeds. During those inevitable times when we feel separated from the depths in us, that awareness is an important factor in our being reconnected.

The Workings segment of the Mantra/Crystal section is the place where we carry out our Mantra/Crystal exercises, and where we record our experiences as best we can while they are taking place. As the name suggests, Workings is where the core of the Mantra/Crystal practice takes place. Or, better said, Mantra/Crystal practice takes place in the depth of ourselves, but Workings is the segment of our *Intensive Journal* workbook where we give our interior experiences a definite form so that they can continue on the outer level of our life.

Our Mantra/Crystal work becomes a process of transforming intangible inner experience into tangible new awareness and actions and we have a core of procedures for doing that. Whenever we are engaged in a Mantra/Crystal meditation, we write the Mantra/Crystal phrase at the head of a page together with the date. We then record all that transpires in our experience on that page and on the pages that follow. If at any later time we use that Mantra/Crystal again, we continue in that same part of the Workings segment. When we begin another time of practice with that Mantra/Crystal, we write the date of the new experience following the first one and we then record the occurrences that take place.

Sometimes a particular Mantra/Crystal is intensely felt in relation to an outer circumstance or an inner experience, and its use may then be concentrated into a short period of time. More generally, however, the use of a Mantra/Crystal tends to be intermittent and to stretch over a longer range of time. It will be intermingled with the use of other Mantra/Crystals, and there may also be times when no Mantra/Crystal meditation takes place at all. The fact that there is irregularity in a person's practice does not mean that there is not a continuity of process within the person corresponding to that Mantra/Crystal. That continuity of process may indeed be present, but since it is within the person it is taking place by inner time; and that may appear to be very irregular and inconsistent when judged in the light of external or chronological time.

One principle that underlies the structuring of the *Intensive Journal* system as a whole is the effort to provide an instrument for recording the intangible and irregular movement of inner time, and for drawing it into such a form that its data can be worked with. This is especially important where the practice of Process Meditation is concerned, since the primary means that we have for maintaining the continuity of our inner process is the way we make our Journal entries.

In the Workings segment, each Mantra/Crystal that we use retains its own continuous subsection so that whenever we work with that Mantra/Crystal our experience is recorded there. For example, we may work with a particular Mantra/Crystal on two consecutive days, then a week later, then a month later, then not for four months, then six months later, then on three days in the following week when something in the content or the atmosphere of the Mantra/Crystal has become inwardly important again. Each of these times of practice with that Mantra/Crystal will be recorded in the same subsection, one following the other. The dates will be irregular, but as the person whose experiences they are, we can easily recognize the continuity of the process that moves among them and that is working in the depths of ourselves.

As we continue in our meditation practice, those Mantra/Crystals that we use again and again soon accumulate substantial subsections containing the sequence of the various times that we have worked with them. Over a period of time these Mantra/Crystals, being well and productively used, seem to develop their own life history with their characteristic style and atmosphere. They also seem to acquire—or you will tend to associate with them—a particular quality of energy and an emotional attachment. The relationship with a Mantra/Crystal can become very intimate and profound, with many overtones, as the actualities of inner experience accumulate. It is all part of the process by which we deepen and extend our experience of Mantra/Crystals here in Workings.

A MANTRA/CRYSTAL MEDITATION

Now let us proceed with our active practice of Mantra/Crystal meditation. Having formed and decided upon a Mantra/Crystal with which we can at least begin, our first step is to write the Mantra/Crystal at the head of a fresh page. We add today's date, and we keep our workbook open, holding a a pen handy as we move into the quiet of the twilight atmosphere. (Perhaps you will want to read through to the end of the chapter and then proceed with this exercise.)

Preparing for a Mantra/Crystal experience, we sit in stillness, our eyes closed. The first thing we do is nothing. Just sitting in stillness. Not thinking. Not planning. Not actively preparing. Just sitting in stillness, letting the muddy waters of our spirit settle and become quiet. Starting in stillness, these inner waters can become quieter than they were. But perhaps not yet quiet enough to become clear.

We sit in stillness doing nothing, letting our whole being just be. As we remain that way, in whatever position we are sitting, we find that our breathing becomes slower and softer. We try not to be conscious of our breathing, just sitting in stillness and observing our breathing as though we were outsiders to it, looking at it furtively as though we were peeking in at our breathing through the window. We want our breathing to continue by its own inner principle so that it can balance itself and establish its own rhythm without our interference. We let it be. Our breathing proceeds by itself while we are doing nothing. The longer that the muddying movements of our inner waters are still, the more those waters become clear, and the freer our breathing is to find its own rhythm. We notice that this takes place of itself. As we remain quiet, doing nothing, our breathing gradually settles into a slower rhythm. This is not a rhythm that we give it, but a rhythm that our breathing finds and establishes for itself. It is a relaxed and steady rhythm, breathing in and breathing out, breathing in and breathing out at a gentle and regular pace. We let that rhythm continue to establish itself, as we sit in stillness, giving it as much time as it desires.

When our breathing has settled into a regular rhythm that feels comfortable to us, and when we feel that the pattern our breathing has established is strong enough to continue of itself, we are ready for our next step.

Now we say our Mantra/Crystal under our breath. We repeat it and repeat it, again and again, continuously. As we are saying it under our breath, we link our Mantra/Crystal with the movement of our breathing, connecting it with the rhythm that our breathing has established. It may require three or four times or even more of saying our Mantra/Crystal together with our breathing to draw the two into connection. Gradually they fit together, until their rhythms become intertwined and balance each other. At that point we find that our Mantra/Crystal and our breathing are actually carrying and supporting each other. Once they fit together, our Mantra/Crystal and our breathing bolster each other and carry each other along.

> *The mantra carries the breath:*
> *The breath carries the mantra.*

This is a rhythm that establishes itself as the two move back and forth. The regular breathing and the rhythm of the seven syllables of the Mantra/Crystal become a self-sustaining movement that draws itself inward. The two together sustain each other, each drawing the other forward into its next movement. The mantra carries the breath through its next cycle of breathing in and breathing out. The breath carries the Mantra/Crystal through the cycles of its own seven syllables. And each supports the other. Each draws the other forward.

> *The mantra carries the breath:*
> *The breath carries the mantra.*

As it continues we realize that this self-balancing movement is building its own momentum. Its continuity is derived from itself. The Mantra/Crystal and the breathing have formed a unit that is self-contained. Each supplies the other so that the energy for the continuous back-and-forth movement of the whole is provided by the mutual movement itself. Nothing else is required. Just the mantra and the breathing fitted together into each other. Together they are self-contained, as they draw each other along. Our breathing, fitted together with saying our seven-syllable Mantra/Crystal under our breath, creates a pendulum movement, continuously swinging back and forth, each cycle of movement leading to the next one.

Mantra/Crystal meditation sees itself as part of a process that contains cycles of changing experience within its continuity. Our Mantra/Crystal phrase sets itself into motion as a prayer that prays itself and it continues in repetition by its own power. Since we know that it is part of a cycle of experience that is contained within a larger process, we do not regard our Mantra/Crystal meditation as a final or unchanging event. We expect it to change, even though we do not know what to expect—and do not try to predetermine—what will come when it changes. We do, however, have some indication of the general sequence of cycle and process that will take place if we are able to continue as diligently with our Mantra/Crystal meditations as the Russian Pilgrim continued with his Jesus Prayer.

What will take place if we are able to continue the pendulum movement without interruption and without the intrusion of our mental consciousness? As our Mantra/Crystal and our breathing carry each other in their self-balancing continuity, our ego and our consciousness of what is taking place become superfluous. The event is happening without them. Therefore they can drop away. As we continue the pendulum movement of our Mantra/Crystal and our breathing, our ego-consciousness does drop away. Only the back and forth movement remains.

We continue the pendulum movement, or, better said, the pendulum movement continues itself. The regular rhythm of our Mantra/Crystal in balance with the continued repetition of our Mantra/Crystal, now without the presence of our ego-consciousness, creates an atmosphere of its own. It is a twilight atmosphere, deep and still. The pendulum movement with its repetitious sound adds to the stillness. As it continues, it becomes like the soft sound of lake waters lapping at the shore while the waters at the center of the lake become progressively still and clear. The pendulum movement establishes the equivalent of the cycle that Lao Tse described, "Muddy water, let stand, becomes clear," without our seeking it. For our attention has been directed only toward maintaining our mantra-breathing pendulum, a core of quiet has formed itself and has become present to us. It is like the clear waters of the lake, except that it has no specific symbol or image. It is simply a core of stillness, a quiet center, an absolute openness in which images and thoughts of every kind can take shape and show themselves to us.

The repetitive practice of our mantra-breathing pendulum leads to silence beyond ego-consciousness. And that, in turn, enables the deepest parts of the twilight range of our being to open themselves to us. Molecules of thought and imagery take shape in that twilight range. Freely forming, without our conscious intervention, they reflect themselves to us in the clear waters of our silence. At first we do not realize that something is being shown to us. The repetitious inner sound of our mantra-breathing pendulum has placed us in a glazed state of empty-mindedness, separated from our ego-consciousness. It is similar to the experience of being in a heavy sleep when we suddenly become aware that a deep dream is unfolding before us. In the first stages of surprise, we miss the early parts of the dream. They have slipped past us before we could realize what was happening. Gradually our consciousness returns and we may have the presence of mind to realize that, if we do not now record what is being shown to us, we will probably forget it forever. If it is a deep dream that is taking place, we have to draw ourselves out of sleep in order to record it. If it is a Mantra/Crystal meditation, however, we can learn to record it while we are perceiving it and while the experience is still happening. We can even learn to record it without leaving the deep atmosphere of twilight space in which the interior event is taking place.

The key lies in the difference between recording the essentials while they are happening and describing an inner experience in full detail. As you become aware in the midst of your Mantra/Crystal meditation that something is being presented to you at the twilight level, you will experience a tugging at your capacities of attention, as though something is pulling at you. It is similar to being drawn to a waking state by the impact of a strong dream. Having been in a deep sleep, suddenly your interior cognition is activated. You realize that you are being called to pay attention to something that is taking place within yourself. The dream awakens you from your sleep, and the effect is similar in your Mantra/Crystal meditation.

It is not necessary, however, for you to be drawn out of the deep twilight level as you recognize your inner experience and as you proceed to record it. The act of Journal recording may actually help you remain in the deep place so that the inner experience can be extended.

With your Journal Workbook open to the Mantra Workings section and pen available, you may have to open your eyes only very slightly in order to record what is taking place. A few words, a phrase or two, will suffice at the start to record what you have just perceived. The first written words establish a point of contact for you so that you can now function in both realms. You can remain quietly placed in the twilight range where new perceptions and awarenesses, new combinations of MTI's, continue to be presented to you. And you can record them as they are happening, letting the brief entries that you make serve as tangible embodiments of the inner exercises while they are taking place. In this way, your Journal recording does not diminish the inner process. It strengthens it because it gives those ephemeral experiences a permanent form. The fact that the experience actually occurred is now incontrovertibly established no matter how it may eventually be judged or regarded. Its existence is proved by its contents as they are being recorded.

You find yourself now in the position of being an intermediary between the inner and outer realms. The side of you that faces inward, your interior cognition, is engaged in observing a self-moving process that continuously brings new material to your attention. The side of you that faces outward is engaged in recording it. After you have become accustomed to it, you will find that playing the role of intermediary between the two realms has the effect not of separating but of connecting them so that your outer recording stimulates and assists the flow of inner experience.

When you are first made aware that an interior event is taking place, begin by writing just a word or a phrase with your eyes barely open, and with the paper just visible enough for your pen to find it. As you are coming up from the twilight range, that first writing will establish your contact with the physical fact of the Journal paper and the act of recording. When you start, write only what is essential to be written. The rest can be filled in later since you will have written clues to remind you. As you proceed you will find that you are able to record with increasingly fluidity while still maintaining your inner contact.

After a few times at it, you will very likely be able to record your experiences even while your mantra-breathing pendulum continues to be in effect, just as the Russian Pilgrim continued to say his Jesus Prayer while he went about his chores. Even if you have to stop the saying of your Mantra/Crystal in order to record your experience you can nonetheless remain in the midst of the atmosphere. In whatever forms they come, whether as visual experiences, as words that you hear, as intuitions or as body feelings, let the MTI's that present themselves move through you directly to the words you write. Make of yourself merely an instrument for your experience, and nothing more. Do not interpret it, nor explain it, nor elaborate it; merely be an instrument for it so that your experience can be transformed into words and can be recorded for your later use. If you remain only an instrument and do not become an interpreter, the atmosphere can retain its hold on you and keep you within it. In that way it becomes possible to record your experience even while you are in the midst of it and while the movement of interior events is continuing.

As you proceed with it, you will find that working with Mantra/Crystals has many aspects and varied applications. Sometimes it leads to large and extended experiences, rich with symbolism, carrying messages of profundity and inspiration. Sometimes it deals with current situations in our lives as dreams do, although it tends to do this more directly with less obscure symbolism than dreams. Sometimes it brings creative new ideas, solutions, or suggestions for problems that we did not realize we were thinking about. These new awarenesses may come in visionary forms, as simple thoughts directly stated; they may come as phrases or lines of poetry, as a feeling or as an intuition that has no words. They may carry messages that have great meaning for us, but we should not approach our Mantra/Crystal practice with the expectation or desire that it achieve any preconceived goal for us. To do that tightens and restricts the work by making it self-conscious. We should rather approach our Mantra/Crystal experience as a self-quieting process that sometimes evokes the depth of us, opening limitlessly from within.

The primary role of Mantra/Crystal practice is to give us a means of stilling and centering ourselves in relation to the continuity of our lives. Once we have constructed a Mantra/Crystal or two, we have a means of pausing in our life and quieting ourselves at any time. It is always available to us as a method for centering ourselves in the midst of the activity, and in relation to the unfolding contents of our life. We may adapt a Mantra/Crystal to particular circumstances and uses. Most practice with Mantra/Crystals is done in a sitting position, but there is no reason to limit it to that. For example, "Walking at one with the world" is a Mantra/Crystal that I have used considerably in walking meditations. I suppose it could have a jogging or a running version for those who are more energetic. Naturally, the pendulum aspect of the meditation has to be greatly modified when it is used in this physical form.

Various adaptations will occur to you after you have built up sufficient experience in your personal work with Mantra/Crystals. You will find that there are certain Mantra/Crystals with which you work again and again. Over a period of time these tend to establish a particular quality, an atmosphere or an aura around themselves, expressing your cumulative experiences with them. They become like old friends available to you as you need them. You may find, for example, that on a number of occasions a particular Mantra/Crystal serves as the means by which you become deeply centered and aware. You grow accustomed to working with it when you are sitting in stillness, but a crisis carrying great tension arises one day in the course of your life and you find that you spontaneously call upon the Mantra/Crystal. By means of it you establish your own atom of silence in the midst of the pressures of your world.

The core of each Mantra/Crystal experience is established at the point where our rhythmic breathing combines with the Mantra/Crystal to establish the pendulum effect. This is when we are taken into the twilight range, a restful and a freeing place to be. To be there is good and valuable and renewing in and of itself. That is why, when we have worked in Mantra/Crystal meditation to a degree sufficient to establish the pendulum effect, even if nothing additional transpires in the form of a definite twilight experience, we must recognize that a great deal has already happened. The deepening of silence, the neutralizing of mental consciousness, the movement of the Mantra/Crystal, are all substantial interior phenomena. They establish their atmosphere and they place us in the twilight depth. That is why the practice of working with a Mantra/Crystal until we experience the mantra-breathing pendulum moving within us is valuable for us to do whenever we feel called to it. In addition to the atmosphere it establishes within us, it opens the way for new awarenesses to come to us.

There is a great range and flexibility in the times and forms of working with Mantra/Crystals. Some individuals prefer to establish a definite discipline and fixed times for their practice. Others prefer to follow their spontaneous promptings and to work with their Mantra/Crystals when an inner stirring calls them. Either way, or a combination of both, is valid. After your first several times of working with Mantra/Crystals, as you are building a resource to draw upon in your Mantra/Crystal Index, you find that this area of your inner life seems to generate its own energy. Certain Mantra/Crystals not only sustain themselves by reappearing our experiences but they seem to be moving toward a further awareness in the course of each time of practice. While we may set regular times for our disciplined Mantra/Crystal meditation, we should also be responsive to the irregular times when these Mantra/Crystals call to us spontaneously.

As your resource of Mantra/Crystals grows, you may soon feel that you are suffering from an overabundance of riches. You find that you possess several Mantra/Crystals in your Index, each of which has good potentialities. Which shall you choose?

Since your life has many facets, it is appropriate for you to have many Mantra/Crystals available for your use. Each suggests its own directions of emphasis and experience. Thus you will work with different Mantra/Crystals according to the varied circumstances of your life. In choosing a Mantra/Crystal for a given time of practice, there are two main criteria to consider: the first is your feeling that this is a Mantra/Crystal that will enable you to reach a condition of centeredness in which the mantra-breathing pendulum can take effect; the second rests more on your intuition that the subject matter or the area of your life from which a particular Mantra/Crystal is drawn contains something to be unfolded further and to be disclosed to you at a deeper inner level. It is your intimation that something more is contained here and that it will express a message for your life when you give it the opportunity.

In considering these two criteria, we recognize that the first is concerned with establishing a stillness within yourself while the other concerns the evoking and creativity that can be a by-product of Mantra/Crystal work. Let the first consideration be your primary one. Choose a Mantra/Crystal that feels especially congenial to you as a vehicle for achieving a quietness of being. The rest will come of itself, if not this time in your meditation, then in the course of your further practice. When you work with your Mantra/Crystal, let it not be in the hope of achieving some predetermined purpose but rather to establish the continued movement of the mantra-breathing pendulum within yourself. When that has taken place, you will have set a process into motion that has its own autonomy. It brings about first an inward stillness, and then a quiet activity that opens from within. The second stage in your Mantra/Crystal experience corresponds to the second half of the cycle of active and passive, the phase in which new movement stirs in the depths of that which lies passively at rest. That is when images take shape and disclose themselves on the quiet lake of our consciousness, in accordance with the modality we have adapted from Lao Tse regarding the rhythms working at the depth of life. Our Mantra/Crystal meditation draws us into harmony with the timeless principle that underlies that rhythm so that we can experience it in the particular terms of our individual existence. That is how new molecules of thought and imagery, new MTI's relevant to the conditions of our lives, take form and emerge as though by themselves out of the depths of us. They are expressions of the creative principle of life reaching toward meaning and disclosing its intimations of truth to us in the midst of our stillness.

Our Mantra/Crystal meditation may bring forth new ideas and understandings as products of creativity, but we do not regard that as its purpose. Stillness in the midst of our active and committed life is the purpose of the total practice of Process Meditation of which our Mantra/Crystal work is a part. Creativity is merely one of its occasional by-products, an extra gift that is sometimes given to us to encourage us in the continuity of our life.

28

Testament

We turn now to the *Testament* section in our *Intensive Journal* work-book. This is where the varieties of our Process Meditation, or Meaning Dimension, explorations come together, where we crystallize and find their essence that gives the message of the whole. It is here that we restate our beliefs and awarenesses as they are shaping and reshaping themselves within us. Our philosophy of life takes form here and adds its increments to the building of our spiritual history, thus taking the first step into our spiritual future. When we are involved in the *Intensive Journal* process, our Testament practices draw together the unit of inner experience through which we have just passed.

The concept of a workshop in the *Intensive Journal* system does not require that a number of persons be present. A workshop is taking place whenever our attention is concentrated for a period of time in following a focused agenda for working in the depths of our life, whether in the company of others or in private. By that definition, it can surely be said that those of us who have been practicing the procedures described in this book have been engaged in a workshop. And it is now time for us to draw together the fruits of that unit of our experience.

We take a moment of quiet to pause in our inner process. We sit in silence with our journal open to the Testament section. Many thoughts and memories, emotions, images, and new realizations have been brought to our consciousness in the course of our Process Meditation work. Much is intermingled here, but the metaphor of muddy water does not seem appropriate now. Our water is not muddy; it is, however, full of things. It is full of the contents of the inner experiences that have been stirred to life in us. We do not wish these to settle to the bottom like formless mud. We have activated these varied contents from the depths and heights of our consciousness so that they can come together in new forms and combinations, as new MTI's, as molecules of thought and imagery that carry new patterns of awareness for our consciousness. This is their time to come together and show us the new shapes they are taking.

As we become quiet, we let ourselves feel the presence of the varied contents that have been stirred to life in the course of our workshop. We do not think of any of them specifically. We do not try to identify any of them individually. We merely feel their presence and we let them move around within us in the twilight range of our consciousness. There is a moving flux in the depth of us beneath our surface self. In the metaphor that we used earlier, it is like the molecules moving within the apparent solidity of a piece of wood. These molecules contain the contents of our beliefs, our visions of what can be painted or sculptured as art, our understandings of what can be stated as truth, our hopes of what may be possible in the activities of our lives. These are the things we feel so full of, especially now that we have stimulated them to experience with our Process Meditation exercises. We feel their presence and their movement as we sit in the stillness.

Gradually we let ourselves drift into a twilight state. The various symbols and images, memories, ideas and intuitive knowings are there within us, moving about, looking for new combinations that will feel right to them. The molecules of thought and imagery are seeking to fit together with others to make new forms, new joinings at the twilight level, to bring new perceptions and new understandings to us. Presently we become aware that new combinations of thought and imagery are being set before us. They may take the form of symbols that appear visually, phrases that are spoken to us, concepts that we find ourselves thinking, a statement of an idea or a doctrine or a belief. Mantra/Crystal phrases may present themselves to us, or lines of poetry or a prayer or a metaphor that states our inner perception of reality, our sense of what is becoming true for us.

We record whatever comes to us in this silence. Our perceptions may be of many kinds, but we give each its place and describe as much as is given to us. As they move through us, coming together in new combinations that may seem strange at first since we are not accustomed to them, we recognize that new units of thought and imagery are being formed within us. As we describe them, we find that more of their meaning declares itself to us and we begin to sense what they can eventually become in our lives. We find that, as we are describing what is being manifested to us, the possibilities of the future increasingly become present. They are taking *shape*. Images that were vague at the outset come into sharper focus, taking a definite form so that they can become the base point for an artwork. Ideas and beliefs that were little more than hunches before now articulate themselves as we describe them. Their outlines are being filled in with content. This is because, as we proceed in the silence at the twilight level, the various molecules of thought and imagery are moving about and coming together within us. New structures are being formed, combining symbol and idea with the actualities and needs of existence. As these elements are integrated into a single unit, they become the interior molecules that will provide the new content for our beliefs and our actions.

Like molecules forming and reforming themselves, new integrations of awareness both symbolic and conceptual are taking shape in us. This is a silence that should be allowed to continue long enough to establish itself and to hold in its atmosphere all the contents of our Process Meditation experiences. We are feeling the fullness of our Process Meditation work in the silence, letting the many aspects come to expression in a symbol or a phrase and articulate themselves further if they wish. We are open now to all that has taken place within us, letting it re-present itself in order that we can take a further step with it. We are sitting in stillness, writing in Testament, in the silence.

The Essence of Testament

We have allowed as much to be presented to us as wished to come, and we recorded all that we could. In that silence we have held ourselves open in the twilight range in order to gather as much nonconscious material as possible. Now, however, we reapproach what we have written from another point of view. Rather than encourage the movement to enlarge itself further, we seek to winnow it down to its essence.

We are adapting for our *Intensive Journal* use the doctrine from the history of philosophy known as Occam's Razor. "Principles should not be unnecessarily multiplied," said William of Occam at the turn of the fourteenth century. We now take his razor in hand as we read back to ourselves the extended entry we have just recorded. As much as possible we reapproach it as an impartial third party. What is the heart of the matter? What has been unnecessarily multiplied in it? We cull out the images and thoughts that are essential, and we draw them together into a single, concise statement, a sentence or two or three, not much more. It need not be prose. It may be poetry, some phrases of a prayer, a mathematical formula that is deep in your consciousness, some bars of music that express the core of your inner vision. Whatever language takes you closer to life/reality as you are now perceiving and experiencing it is the language you should use in making your crystallizing statement.

You will very likely find that a number of different experiences are coming together in what you write now. You are drawing together and consolidating into one unit the various elements that are adding to and reforming your view of what life is and what truly matters to you now in the atmosphere of your Process Meditation work. What is consolidated may at a later time need to be refined and integrated more sharply. Or you may recast it into an altogether new form. What is important is that you express now, in however compressed a form, the essence of your present view of life/reality. To that degree it may bear resemblances to a Mantra/Crystal, but your statement should be much more fully articulated. A Mantra/Crystal may, however, be contained within it.

You may bear in mind, as you read back what you have recorded, that the two steps we are now taking in Testament are modeled after the sequence of movements that we perceive in the molecules of thought and imagery as they form their integrations within us. First they reach out to a broad range of elements, as many as may fit into the formation of the new units they are seeking; then they proceed to integrate these into a consolidated form. In our twilight experience we made contact with as many interior contents as we could. And now we are applying our discerning intellect to assist the integrative process.

The statement at which we now arrive should be a concise articulation of our present envisioning of life/reality as we perceive it in its personal and transpersonal aspects.

Now we sit in stillness, turning our attention to the many contents we have recorded as they were presented to us from the twilight range. As our conscious mind moves through this material, discerning and separating, emphasizing and discarding, it is acting as the instrument of the process of integration. It is acting on behalf of the organizing factor within us that is drawing the molecules of thought and imagery together into meaningful forms. The resources have been drawn from the twilight depths. Now it is our conscious mind that does the organizational work.

We review and consider the various symbols and ideas, memories and emotions that have spoken to us most strongly in the course of our practice of Process Meditation. We have sensed a factor of meaning moving through our experiences and establishing itself as the reality of our lives. Now we seek to identify that factor in order to describe it and articulate it in the concise cystallizing statement that we are preparing to write. We write our statement now in the silence.

Ongoing Process Meditation Work

The best thing to do with this statement, once we have completed it to our present satisfaction, is to set it to one side. Keep it in the Testament section, of course, but try to resist the temptation to read it back to yourself—at least for a few days. It is good to let some time pass after the intensity and inner concentration of our Process Meditation experience. Even spiritual work has to be followed by a Sabbath!

After we have rested from our Process Meditation work and sufficient time has passed to place some distance and objectivity between us and our subjective work, we may return to it. The post-workshop use of Process Meditation is of great importance, especially because it sets into motion the continuity of our lifelong meditation. Very often we find that the best point at which to resume our Process Meditation work is by reading back to ourselves the crystallizing statement we made in Testament, and moving from there into the ongoing process of our inner work.

Let us speak, before we part, about the first steps you take following a Process Meditation Workshop. Those first steps will set you into motion, and after that the practice of Process Meditation is freedom, disciplined freedom

When you read back to yourself your crystallizing statement in Testament, there will undoubtedly be additional responses that will arise in you. Take note of these, but do not record them in the Testament section. You now work in the Meditation Log again, and your response to reading your Testament statement should be recorded here in the Inner Process Entries segment. As you describe the stirrings within you it may occur to you that you would now like to alter your original statement or at least add to it. Record these thoughts here in the Meditation Log and let your Testament statement remain as it is, unchanged. You may, however, add a cross-reference in the Testament section indicating the date of the additional entry you are making in the Meditation Log.

As you are responding to your statement and considering it, the question of Journal Feedback is bound to arise in you: Where else in the *Intensive Journal* workbook can I go to explore the life issues and concerns that are raised in my Testament statement? What personal leads are given to me there? And what transpersonal leads? To which Journal sections do they take me?

As the answers to these questions come to you, record them in the Inner Process Entries segment together with your other considerations. You may wish to follow those leads now, at least some of them, and carry out their full additional exercises while their energy is still strong. Or you may prefer to make a brief indicative entry in the appropriate section and return to it later. Generally these decisions are determined by the momentum of the Journal work as you are continuing in its process.

You may now be ready to take a further step in your post-workshop process. You may now read back to yourself, proceeding either systematically or by browsing through the Journal sections, choosing any or all of the experiences that you recorded in the course of your Process Meditation workshop. Take note of the responses that stir in you as you read them back to yourself. In many cases you will find that thoughts and feelings and awarenesses will come to you now that were not present in the original experience. Be sure to record all that comes to you now. As you return to each section it is especially important that you remember to ask yourself the Journal Feedback questions: Where else can I go with this material? What personal leads, and what transpersonal leads, does it give me?

With the perspective we have now after having worked in Testament, we observe another possibility as we read back the experiences we have recorded. Some of them, most of them probably, seem to be incomplete, still developing, still in quest of and in need of further work and exploration. These are the experiences that give us the personal and transpersonal leads to other Journal sections where they can be carried further. There will be other experiences, however—perhaps only a very few at first—where the experience seems to have had a wholeness, a completeness in itself. These will be experiences in which our statement of our view of life/reality took place spontaneously, emerging out of our Process Meditation practice as an awareness of an essential truth. We may come upon such statements interspersed as random jewels of poetry among our *Intensive Journal* process. These should be copied and added to our Testament section following our original crystallizing statement. As we copy them over, we find that we wish to add to them, perhaps inserting comments and explanations as well as elaborations. It is good to do this, but keep the identity of the original experience and entry distinct, adding your new material separately. When you copy these over into the Testament section, make sure to enter both dates, the date of the original experience and the date of the transcription. And insert a cross-reference indicating the Journal section from which it was taken.

As we proceed in our Process Meditation work we find that such integrative statements expressing our perceptions of essential truth increasingly enter our experience. They are part of the new events that take place as we continue our practice in the *Intensive Journal* process. We find more and more of them especially as we extend our explorations in the Connections section, since it is there that we uncover and remind ourselves of the connective experiences in our spiritual history. Sometimes we come upon integrative statements of this kind that are fully written and complete unto themselves as of the moment they took place. Such entries seem just to be waiting for us to copy them over into the Testament section. At other times, the experience that we described was integrative, but our statement of the essential truth that it carried was not adequate to convey the fullness of what was involved in it. Now we write that statement, whether in prose or poetry, and we place it in Testament.

As we proceed in our Process Meditation work, then, we gather together in the Testament section two types of statements. The first are the integrative statements that crystallize our experience at a workshop in the *Intensive Journal* process. They come to us one workshop at a time. Those of the second type, which become more numerous as we proceed in our Process Meditation work, are statements that express our experience or perception of an essential truth as these realizations are given to us at any point in the course of our life. Going back over our Process Meditation entries, we may find at first just a few statements of this second kind. We add them to the Testament section as we discover them in pages that we have already written, or as they come to us afresh as we continue in our work.

As we proceed in collecting into our Testament section the record of our experiences and our statements of essential truth, we find over a period of time that a significant spiritual resource is being brought together. Its contents are very personal to us as individuals, but they are also much more than personal. They are the events in which we transcend ourselves because we are experiencing our lives and our consciousness in relation to realities larger than ourselves.

Each of these interior events that is a connective moment in our life is an increment to our spiritual history. Taken by themselves, like individual bricks, they have little strength or significance. But taken together, like many bricks that have been properly arranged, they become a substantial edifice. Working in the continuity of the *Intensive Journal* process, unitary experiences of essential truth will inevitably accumulate. They are the fruit and the flowers of our interior practice. They give us both truth and beauty. They are the personal scriptures being created from within us, out of the substance of our lives with the help of our commitment and our inner desire.

As our experiences continue and are gathered together, we extend our spiritual history into the openness of our spiritual future. In this we can recognize the meaning of the term *Process-plus-one*. All that we have experienced in the past and all that we are working at in the present are part of process in the universe. But as individual human beings living with an intention toward essential truth, we add to the totality of process, experience by experience. Abstractly we add to process in the universe. Specifically we add to process in our civilization. And concretely we add to process in our individual lives, particularly with respect to the dimension of meaning, the spiritual essence of human existence.

Process-plus-one means all of our past, plus the next experience for which we are now preparing. Since that next experience is still un-known, indeterminate, unpredictable, infinite in its possibilities, the *plus-one* factor is our doorway to freedom and creativity. We do not know when, beyond all the determinism contained in process, the bonus of an *extra* will be given us, an *emergent*. Both the evolution of life and our individual human condition wait for such emergents. And better than waiting, we each do our interior work.

When we began our practice of Process Meditation, we possessed the past experiences that our life had given us up to that point. Since then we have had the additional experience of actively recalling some of those events, drawing them together into accessible formats, re-entering some, re-opening others, and especially we have had the additional experience of reaching into our twilight depths where new constellations of awareness have taken shape for us beyond our conscious knowledge. All of these are part of the vital process that adds to itself in freedom one present moment at a time as it creates our personal spiritual history. Now, with our Process Meditation experience added to it, we have given ourselves tools and a methodology by which we can continuously add to our spiritual history, one *next experience* after another.

29

Now: The Open Moment

We come now to the closing experience of our workshop. We turn for it to the last section in the Meaning Dimension, *Now: The Open Moment.*

When we began the workshop we took the last part of the past as our starting point. We marked off the unit of experience that immediately preceded the present moment in our lives. It was the contents of this period that we described with our first Journal entries in the Period Log.

Since that time we have no longer been in our past, but we have not yet entered our future. While we have participated in this workshop, we have been at a midpoint of time between our past and our future. Everything that has transpired in our life prior to the workshop is our past. Everything that will take place in it after the workshop is over is our future. Our Journal Workshop is the quiet place in between the past and the future. Being here, we have been protected, at least temporarily, from the outer pressures of our life. We withdrew to it as a Sabbath in order to give ourselves an opportunity to reposition ourselves in the movement of our lives as a whole. In the terms of our metaphor, for the duration of the workshop we went down into the well of our lives to work in the deep places of the underground stream.

And now, as our experience of the workshop comes to a close, we return to the surface of our life again. We come up from our well ready to go forth into the movement of our lives again.

As we prepare for this, we turn our attention to the first period of the future that we shall enter when we return to the world. This is the Open Moment dawning before us as we come to the close of the workshop and to the beginning of a new unit of time in our lives.

Let us sit in stillness now as we prepare to enter this Open Moment. With our eyes closed, we go back over the varied entries we have written in the Journal and the experiences we have had in the course of the workshop. Some of us may wish to go through the Journal pages quickly to remind ourselves of all that has taken place. For others it will be sufficient to take ourselves back mentally through the experiences we have had as we worked in the sections of the Journal. In either case, as we let it all come together within ourselves we can feel the wholeness of the perspective of our life that has been progressively crystallizing.

We can recall now how we thought of our life when we began by placing ourselves in the most recent unit of our experience and described it in the Period Log. We think back to the entries we made in the Daily Log recording the happenings and especially the inner phenomena of our minds and emotions. We began the discipline of recording them as they take place day by day.

Working on a larger canvas, we recall also how we began the Time-Stretching procedures, reaching down the track of inner time and recapitulating the cycles and continuity of our lives. As we listed our Steppingstones and elaborated the contents of the Steppingstone Periods, we took ourselves back over our childhood years, moved up through early adolescence and into physical and psychological maturity. Eventually, beginning with our birth and continuing to the present moment, we have reentered and explored as many units of Life/ Time as we have individually experienced so far. Some of us who have lived through several decades have recapitulated the cycles of later maturity leading to the ultimate transitions of life. Others of us, still in our early decades, have reflected in our Steppingstones the uncertain groping of life potentials that have not yet found their channel and are seeking a direction by which they can be fulfilled. For each of us, the continuity of our lives has moved toward a more unified focus and thus has taken a further step in its self-integration.

Our active work in the Life/Time Dimension opened the way to dialogue with various important contents of our lives. We have begun what can now be ongoing inner relationships with the personal aspects of our life, with other individuals, with the artworks and activities in which we are engaged, with our body, and with the various events, situations, and circumstances of our life. We have also opened an avenue for expanding contact with the more-than-personal aspects of our experience, society, the arts, and especially those institutions and beings who embody the larger wisdom of life in our individual awareness. We have laid the foundation for continuous contact with all of these by means of dialogue as well as by the dynamic extension of our dreams and twilight imagery.

By working with all these procedures while using the *Intensive Journal* workbook as our instrument, we have repositioned our life with respect to our past and our future. We have arrived at a new Now, and this is the Open Moment of our life. In the course of our experience at this Journal Workshop, an inner perspective has progressively formed in us, enabling us to *feel from within* the movement of our life as it proceeds through its cycles of difficulty and achievement. It brings us into intimate and ongoing contact with the elan vital of our life.

Beyond this perspective are the images of the future that form within us. They arise out of the depth of our continuing experience, and they reflect the results of the self-integrative process that has been taking place in the background of all our work. While we have been carrying out our exercises and making our entries in our Journal, a self-balancing and self-integrating principle has been progressively at work within us, recrystallizing the contents of our life at the deep level of knowing that is *behind our mind*. It has been working in the depth of us unseen, while we have been working in our lives on the visible level of our Journal. The process of Journal Integration has been stimulated and sustained by the entries we have fed into the Journal; and the Journal Feedback procedures have served as the medium by which the larger integrative process could establish itself and bring forth its new products of awareness and guidance for our life.

Out of this life-integrative process comes our vision of the Open Moment which is our future. Let us now, therefore, close our eyes and turn our attention inward so that what has emerged from the integrative process in which we have been working can now reveal itself to us. Our eyes closed, we see again the varied experiences through which we have moved, the recapitulation of events of the past, our dreams, and our dialogues. Out of all of these as a new crystallization, a further flow of thought and imagery opens for us. Sometimes in symbolic form, this flow of consciousness presents to us the possibilities of the Open Moment of our future. It enables us to focus upon our future in the context of our life history as a whole.

In our silence we experience this present moment as the moment of our life history that opens into the future. Out of our nonconscious depth it presents itself in the variety of possibilities it holds for us. We let it express itself in whatever form it wishes to take so that we can be guided by it.

It may be that it comes as a fresh flow of Twilight Imagery. We behold this imagery, take note and record it as part of our open moment.

It may be that it takes the form of a conscious recapitulation of the experiences we have had during the workshop, and these then lead us to a projection of thoughts as to what the future may hold. We record these as they come to us.

It may take the form of a summary statement of the situation of our life as we have seen our life come into focus in the course of the workshop. Having repositioned ourselves between the past and the future, the possibilities of our Open Moment may now be clear enough to delineate and think about specifically.

In all the forms in which it presents itself now in our silence, we record it and describe it. Let it be as a conscious recapitulation, as a summary statement, as a refocusing, as a movement of imagery, as a stream of thoughts, as a hope that we project as a strong wish into the future, as a prayer for new conditions and a larger vista in our life, as a blessing offered by our deep self upon the movement of our life, and as a benediction that our whole soul places upon the open unfolding of our self. It may be a prayer that prays itself, a meditation that makes itself, a poem that writes itself, a vision that comes of itself, a brief focusing phrase that can give us a point of contact and a reminder through the continuity of our life. Whatever form it takes, we record it as the present expression of Now, our Open Moment.

We hold it in the silence. We do not speak aloud the statements that we write here. Rather we maintain our silence so that our newly generated energies can move inward, incubate, and multiply their power. At a later time we shall reread to ourselves in sequence the various Open Moment entries that we have written at successive workshop experiences. That, and other uses of this section, are part of the advanced Journal Feedback procedures that we shall practice at another time. Meanwhile we hold in the silence of prayerful focus the new intimations of purpose and meaning and life potential that have come to us.

Thus we draw our Journal Workshop to a close in peace. We re-emerge from our well with the waters of life that we have found there, and we go forth again into the world.

Part 7

CONTINUING YOUR JOURNAL WORK

30

Resource and Continuity

Now that we have completed our basic experience at a Journal Workshop, what shall our next step be?

When we began to use the *Intensive Journal* process, there were a few definite and attainable goals that we set for ourselves. One was that we would develop a *perspective* of the movement of our life history as a whole as it appears from the vantage point of the present moment. Second, we wished to *position* ourselves between the past and the future in such a way that we could refocus our current actions to support the unfoldment of new potentials in our life. And while we were working toward these two goals of perspective and positioning, we were learning the techniques for working with the various sections of the *Intensive Journal* workbook. We were seeking to become familiar with their procedures so that we can feel comfortable in using them by ourselves after the workshop is over. Now that time has come. How shall we work with the Journal in the future?

An important question that is often asked at workshops is, "How often should I make my entries in the *Intensive Journal* workbook?"

There are no fixed rules or requirements. The purpose of the *Intensive Journal* method is not to give us one more thing to feel guilty about not doing. We already have enough of that, and enough regulations for our life. But the purpose of working with the Journal is to give ourselves the means and the freedom of expressing the inner process of our lives when it wells up in us and desires expression. Writing your entries in your *Intensive Journal* workbook should not be a chore. Once you have established a dialogue relationship with your Journal, your inner self will tell you when there are things to be written and it will become natural for you to do so. Recording Journal entries when they are there to be written will become an accepted part of your life.

We may recall in this regard a metaphor that is very indicative of the Journal Feedback process. It is a fact of nature that water finds its own level. This self-balancing principle is true of the entries that we make in the *Intensive Journal* process.

What is most important is that the process be started, and that it be carried far enough so that it generates its own energy. Once that has been done, the Journal Feedback process will operate of itself. The material that has been fed into the Journal will be given back in new forms, stimulating additional experiences and thus calling forth a further continuity of entries. It is necessary, however, that we begin by feeding enough basic entries into the Journal so that the dynamic of the feedback process can build its momentum.

There is a larger context of time which we should bear in mind when we think of the self-balancing factor in the *Intensive Journal* process. As we work with the Journal through the continuity of our lives, moving through one life period after another, the multiple interplay of the entries and exercises has a cumulative effect. It generates energies and movements of various kinds, and these balance one another. Over a period of time, as a person lives through more than one cycle or time-unit of his life, the self-balancing process becomes multiple. It works upon itself and thus it brings about a larger integration of the contents of the life as a whole. Beyond the self-balancing process which takes place within particular short-range periods of our experience, there is a larger process of *life integration* that builds and establishes itself over longer units of time.

As you continue your Journal work, it will be helpful to bear in mind the distinction between these two types of processes. The self-balancing process applies to the short run of our life experience. The life-integration process applies to the long run of our life movement, including within it and drawing together several short-run time-units.

When we work in the *Intensive Journal* process, we are always engaged in situations that express the immediacy of the moment; but we are also working in the large encompassing context of our life as a whole. We therefore have two perspectives of time: the short run of the particular period in which we find ourselves and the long run of the total movement of our life. Each time-unit or individual period carries the possibility of coming into balance within itself. We experience this in the moment of its happening as a feeling that the problems of this period are being resolved and that its tensions have been harmonized. At such times, therefore, we feel that we can relax. We feel satisfied that a unit of our experience has been brought into balance within itself. A natural unit seems to have been completed. We thus feel free to enter a new period in our lives.

Each time-unit of our life passes through such a cycle of problems, tensions, and resolutions by a process that self-adjusts within the context of the period. Our Journal work serves as a vehicle for this self-balancing process in the short run. The long-run movement of our Journal work, however, includes a succession of such time-units in our life. Each achieves a degree of self-balancing within itself. As an individual continues to work with the *Intensive Journal* process over a number of years, the succession of these self-balanced time-units builds a cumulative effect. The movement of the life as a whole restructures itself again and again to incorporate the meaning of new situations; each time this takes place our total life history is progressively recrystallized. This is the larger process of life integration proceeding in the background of our Journal work.

The distinction between self-balancing within the short-run time-units of our life and life integration in the ongoing movement and larger scope of our Journal work is important for the perspective it gives us in continuing our use of the Journal. Given the pressures of the modern world, it is fair to assume that most people who begin to use the *Intensive Journal* process do so because there is a problem in their life that urgently needs to be resolved, an intense and difficult transition through which their life must pass, or a critical decision they must make. Because of the self-balancing process that underlies it, the Journal feedback procedures facilitate the solving of problems and the making of decisions. The approach of activating the depth of a person while maintaining the context of each unique life stimulates the finding of answers that are specific and relevant. In the short-run work, moreover, these answers tend to be found sooner rather than later. As the needs of the immediate situation are met, however, and as ideas begin to flow for the next step in our life, there is a strong temptation to take these first fruits and rush off with them before a fuller harvest can be gathered. Once you have begun to use the *Intensive Journal* process, however, it is a great waste not to do the follow-up work that will give you the accrued results that come from staying with the process.

Since the principle underlying Journal Feedback is that of cumulative movement, maintaining the Journal work has a multiplying effect if it is allowed to continue over significant units of time. As we extend its use, the scope of the *Intensive Journal* process enables us to build a context for decisions that encompass our whole life history. Beyond the factor of self-balancing, the principle of life integration is then able to operate on the scale of the full movement of our life history and reconstellate our life for us in a perspective that neither our conscious minds nor our imagination could conceive or create. We could not have figured it out with our intelligence, but continuing the Journal process draws a *reintegrative factor* into our experience. It progressively calls into play a dynamic of inner direction that restructures our unfolding experience in ever new contexts, opening new possibilities and meanings for our future. Neither consciousness nor the unconscious, but the reintegrative factor which is brought into play by the continuity of Journal work makes this possible. This carries the operation of the life-integrative process and is the reason why we often find it to be true in our Journal work that specific and immediate problems are most meaningfully solved by Journal Feedback not when they are concentrated upon directly, but when they are allowed to take their place in the movement of our whole life history. The Journal exercises carry this movement, and our indirect way of working with them makes it possible for solutions and new guidances to come to us *as though by themselves.* These new life answers emerge as though they were merely by-products of our basic Journal work. And, in a sense, that is what they are. They are the by-products that emerge when the process of life integration is given a time and experience in which to do its organic work using the *Intensive Journal* workbook as its instrument.

The key to working with the *Intensive Journal* process productively lies in the quality and quantity of the material that we feed into it in the continuity of our work. As we sustain our use of it, the Journal can feed back to us in self-transforming ways the material that we have recorded in it. It is essential, however, that we supply it with sufficient data, and that we maintain this on a current basis. The longer we work with the Journal in continuity, the more we can reap the benefit of its progressive and cumulative feedback effect.

Ongoing Journal Work

After a workshop, a primary means of building the continuity of the Journal work is with your entries in the Daily Log. It is not necessary to write in it everyday, but just often enough so that when you read the sequence of Daily Log entries back to yourself at a later time they will reflect the day-to-day movement of your life. In this way, the Daily Log can fulfill its basic function of supplying life data that will become the starting point for further feedback extensions.

In the beginning, in order to gather a basic resource of life material and to set the Journal process into motion, it is good to make daily entries. At least for the first three or four weeks in which you are using the *Intensive Journal* workbook, try to record at least some inner experience each day. This will establish your relationship to Journal work and make you secure in using it. Eventually, as it builds its own momentum, you will be able to continue it more flexibly and let it adjust itself to your life tempo.

In addition to our continuing entries in the Daily Log, a great deal of work remains for us to do in the Life/Time sections. The time at a workshop is sufficient only for us to begin the large task of filling in the details and elaborating the contents of each of the Steppingstone Periods. Extending the work of Time-Stretching as it leads to the progressive reconstruction of our autobiography, working in the Life History Log, and exploring our Intersections: Roads Taken and Not Taken has the effect of feeding a great deal more life data into our Journals. Thus the more we do here, the more we contribute to the self-balancing process and to the working out of the integrative principle in the background of our life.

In this same context it is important that we continue to make our entries in the Dream Log and the Twilight Imagery Log on a current basis. Whenever we recall a sleep dream it is important to record it so that, at a later time, we can work with the seriality of our dreaming and thus draw ourselves into contact with the energies and the meanings that are unfolding in us at an unconscious level. Whenever we become aware, also, that we are having a spontaneous Twilight Imagery experience, these are to be recorded and added to the flow of our depth material.

As we record our dream and Twilight Imagery experiences and while we are filling in and extending the Time-Stretching exercises, we find that we are building a large resource for the Journal Feedback work. We make our entries as they come to us without judgment and without analysis; but when we read them back to ourselves we become aware of the feedback leads they give us for working elsewhere in our life via the various sections of the Journal. We have learned in our Journal work that the question "What is the *meaning* of this experience?" is not well answered when we turn back to look analytically at the events of our life. We find the meaning of our dreams and other life experiences not by interpreting them but by following their feedback leads to other sections of the Journal. As we work with them in the Depth and Life/Time Dimensions, whatever their specific content, they lead us toward a fuller dialogue relationship with a particular aspect of our life. The feedback leads direct us through a succession of Journal experiences, culminating eventually in a dialogue script. It is here that the meaning of our experience discloses itself, not in terms of an abstract or interpretive concept, but in the context and language of our own life as it is unfolding.

Following the feedback leads is the primary means of extending the Journal Feedback process in the continuity of our life. It makes possible the interplay among the sections, and this in turn builds the multiple and cumulative effects of self-balancing and life integration. Thus we proceed in an open-ended way to extend the range of our inner experience and to find practical ways of expressing it in the outer world.

The concept that underlies the *Intensive Journal* approach is that the potential for growth in a human being is as infinite as the universe. This refers not to physical growth, of course, but to the qualitative growth of persons. It refers especially to the development of our inner capacities of awareness and our outer capacities for living as full human beings among our fellows.

Personal and Transpersonal Leads

Each of us who has carried out the practices described so far in this book has done a great deal of work. Many pages have been filled by now in our *Intensive Journal* workbooks. We use the word *work* with a number of different connotations in the course of our practice of the *Intensive Journal* process, but here we can speak of work in its ordinary, everyday sense. Much of what we have done has involved arduous and difficult effort, and we know that more of the same will be required as we continue. It has been *work*, and it will be again.

Having come this far, however, we may have reached a point where our work will become less arduous as we proceed. This is for various reasons. One is that, as the pieces of our inner lives come together, we begin to see not only patterns forming but purposes and new directions disclosing themselves. Now we have indications of where the movement is heading, and that makes it easier to go ahead. One of the special capacities that we develop in the course of our Process Meditation practices is the ability to proceed toward goals that have not yet been announced to us. We do not know what they are, but we can press on toward them because we have already had the experience of having new meanings disclosed to us in the course of our work although we had not envisioned them before. That has undoubtedly happened to a number of us in our work until now, especially in the Mantra/Crystal meditations.

Another reason that our Process Meditation or Meaning Dimension Journal work may be less arduous in the future is that we have had to pass through a preliminary time of laying the foundations for our ongoing work; and that is mainly completed by now. The practice of Process Meditation divides into two general phases. The first is the time of gathering the data of our personal spiritual history and also of learning to work comfortably with the various Journal sections and procedures that comprise the Meaning Dimension methodology. This is the resource phase of the work and it provides the basis on which we can proceed to our ongoing and deepening practice of *Intensive Journal* work.

As we have carried out the exercises of Process Meditation until now, working in the Meditation Log, in Connections, and in the Mantra/Crystals section, we have seen that each procedure generates new experiences. Consequently it increases the inner data available to us. It gives us a spiritual resource that we did not have before. It also raises the question of how we shall utilize this new material in extending and deepening the contents of our inner lives. This is the essence of Process Meditation as a method of continuity in spiritual experience.

In speaking of a *continuity phase* in our Journal process we do not mean simply that it keeps on going. Continuity has a much larger significance in the context of *Intensive Journal* work. It means that, after we have established as our foundation a resource of information drawn from our spiritual history, and after we have established a framework of structure and practices in our *Intensive Journal* workbook, we have a means of working continuously at our own pace and tempo whenever and for as long as the quest for deeper meaning personally involves us. The quest for meaning in life in which we are engaged is, after all, not like a task that we can expect to complete in a definite time, or an illness that we shall cure and then be finished with. Process Meditation is as infinite as the meaning of life is infinite. It is as open in possibilities as our personal potential for wisdom and sensitivity is open, and it increases with our capacity for finding the poetry of human existence.

In this perspective we can see that what we are engaged in here is a process of lifelong meditation reaching toward what is qualitative in human existence. Many of us have already had the experience of discovering that this process of lifelong meditation draws us into mysteries as profound as they are obscure; but from time to time they may open for us and they become like a bud that has iridescent jewels in its flower. As we work in it, we gradually recognize that the quest for meaning which is at the heart of the meditative life is not a quest for a fixed object. It is not like seeking a new land or a gold mine or an oil field; nor is it even like seeking a truth that objectively exists and is waiting for us to find it. It is a quest, rather, that builds and grows as our capacity to experience grows. The meditative life is a cumulative reaching toward meaning that is its own goal. Ends and means are a unity in it. The apparent paradox which becomes clear to us as we experience it is that meaning grows in and by the process of what we do as we are actively engaged in seeking it. Another way of saying this is that meaning is being created and is being added both to our lives and to the universe as we proceed in deepening and in extending our individual inner experiences.

This is the large context in which we should think of the continuity aspect of Process Meditation and our *Intensive Journal* work as a whole. It involves our individual experience in a way that makes it a process of lifelong meditation. It is a personal quest, but it reaches beyond itself since its essence is more than personal. There is, in fact, a very significant parallel that can serve as a metaphor for continuing inner work. Just as a process of qualitative evolution takes place across the millennia in the life of the cosmos, so it may also take place across the decades in the lives of those persons who are actively engaged in the quest for meaning. The evolution of the individual parallels that of the cosmos, and occasionally the two may intersect and reinforce each other as well.

Continuing Work in the Meaning Dimension

We want now to take our first step in the continuity phase of Process Meditation. The exercises in this chapter will help us continue. In addition to continuing our work in other sections of our Journal, having begun with the Daily Log, we now move out into the full range of the *Intensive Journal* system. This will enable us to experience in actuality the implications of conducting our spiritual practices in a framework that includes the history and contents of our life.

We began our Process Meditation work by making a brief statement of our spiritual position, describing spontaneously what we felt to be our interior situation. That was our starting point. Since that time we have had many additional experiences, stirred memories and emotions, opened the way for new awarenesses. What is our interior situation now? What have we learned? What do we now believe? And what further steps have been indicated to us?

Having collected considerable information in the course of our Process Meditation work, it is not necessary for us to make another spontaneous statement of position. We are, in fact, engaged now in re-positioning ourselves in the movement of our inner process, but we can do that now more empirically. We have already gathered a resource of our life facts so that, as we draw these facts together in the next steps of our Journal work, they will indicate to us what our present spiritual position is, and they can direct us toward our further experiences.

To do this, let us now turn to the Meditation Log section, and particularly to the segment for Inner Process Entries. This is where we draw together the facts that pertain to the present situation of our inner life.

We begin by sitting in stillness. We write today's date to start our entry in the Meditation Log. We begin by describing directly and simply the facts of our present situation. We report on the fact that we have carried through at least one Mantra/Crystal meditation since we last wrote here. We may take note of the Mantra/Crystal that we eventually used, perhaps adding some brief comments at this point on our Mantra/Crystal experience. We wish to reach back beyond our Mantra/Crystal work, however. We want to recapitulate the main movement of our Process Meditation work as a whole up to now, so that we can consider our present spiritual position and determine what our next moves shall be.

Sitting in stillness, we go back in our minds over the way we felt when we began to record our Gatherings, the specific memories of our inner life. Time has passed since we wrote them, and that distance gives us some perspective. We are not interested now in recalling the contents of those Gatherings but the emotions we felt when we wrote them. In particular, we note that some of the memories we described in Gatherings have a greater emotional intensity than others. There may be some also that we now feel more strongly about than when we first recorded them. In making our Inner Process Entries, we especially take note of our emotions and the changes in our emotions.

As we proceed we recall also the feelings that came to us as we were listing our Spiritual Steppingstones. It may be that additional thoughts or considerations come into our mind now, and that we find ourselves reflecting further about particular aspects of our spiritual history. We include these reconsiderations in our Inner Process Entries.

We take ourselves back also to recall the experiences we had in Re-Openings. It may be of interest to us now to note which event we chose to reenter and to re-open. We recall the emotions that stirred in us then as we were engaged in that exercise. As we think of that, other events may suggest themselves to us as containing unexplored aspects that would make it worthwhile re-opening them at some later time.

Having gone back over the varied exercises that we did in the Connections section, we may now take note especially of the feelings that stir in us with respect to our spiritual history as a whole. Writing now, we may find that there are new perspectives taking shape in us, that our standards of evaluation and our responses are changing. We should record these observations and reflections now as expressions of our inner process in motion.

We come now to make the Inner Process Entry that records our feelings with respect to our Mantra/Crystal meditation. We have recorded the details in the Workings segment of the Mantra/Crystal section, but now we want to write a spontaneous overview. The spontaneous quality of the summary description that you write now is an important aspect of it. Do not analyze what took place. Just describe your emotions and especially refer to the thoughts and images that stirred within you and that came to your attention in the course of your experience. Perhaps a metaphor now occurs to you to describe the movement as a whole as it was taking place in the course of your Mantra/Crystal meditation.

In reviewing the experiences of the resource phase of our Process Meditation work, there are a number of entries to make. Most of them should be brief entries, but some may stimulate us to greater elaborations. Let those entries move as freely as they wish. At this point in the work, entries that seek to extend themselves by their own power are very likely bringing us information that will contribute to our next experiences. We let them say all that they have to say.

The important question to which we come next involves the possibility that these entries, with the symbolism and the imagery of the events they are describing, may be opening paths for us to a deeper awareness. They may contain hidden messages and clues to our next experiences. The practical question then becomes, Do we have a means of discovering what these clues and this information actually are so that we can make use of them? To do this we draw upon a procedure that plays an important role in the *Intensive Journal* method. We look for the Journal Feedback leads.

The Process Meditation exercises with which we have been working up to this point have primarily been directed toward the possibilities of evoking meaning in our lives. They have involved experiences of connection, the development of our beliefs, and the varied practices by which we have sought a larger understanding of the mysteries of our life. They are reaching toward what is more-than-personal, but they take place within the context of our personal existence.

Working with Journal Feedback

In setting the Journal Feedback principle into operation, the step of primary importance is the move we make in taking a life experience to the Journal section that is most appropriate for it. This is not a question of finding the proper category as might be expected. It is a question not of classification but of process. We want to feed experiences into a

Journal section where the exercises will draw them into a larger life movement while evoking additional energies and awarenesses from the depths of ourselves.

The best way to proceed in setting up the Journal Feedback movement seems to be not to try to figure out the answers ourselves. In fact, a good rule of thumb to observe is that if you feel definitely convinced that you are sure of where the contents of this particular life experience should go, pause. The chances are very great in that case that your judgment has been made at the level of mental consciousness and that it has in its background some analytical concept drawn from the habits of psychologism in past times. Therefore pause and do not rush to judgment. If we move more slowly, we can proceed in the empirical way of letting our experience itself tell us which area of *Intensive Journal* practice it desires for its next step. It will show us the Journal Feedback lead to the next exercise that its own nature requires. But we must first clear a path for it, and keep the way open without intruding our premature opinions.

To find our next Journal Feedback lead, we begin by sitting in silence. With our eyes closed, we inwardly consider the movement of the Process Meditation work we have done so far, the reconstruction of our spiritual history, our Mantra/Crystal meditations. We do not interpret them nor analytically think about them, but we let ourselves feel the whole of our life in the atmosphere of our Process Meditation. In this atmosphere we find that, without trying to understand the contents of our various experiences, some aspects of them fit together with especial harmony. Others do not seem to fit together at all. Where they do fit together, forming pairs or clusters, we are given an indication that something is trying to form a new integration of various factors within us.

We have noted in another connection that there appears to be a holistic principle in the world of nature that moves toward the formation of ever more focused integrative units. It is a phenomenon that takes place irregularly and unpredictably, but the holistic principle is nonetheless an understandable factor as it occurs in the physical world. When it is expressed, however, in the subjective contents of our individual lives, we tend to think of it less naturalistically. We attribute it then to the inner wisdom that is in the depth of the human person. So be it. The term we use is not important; but it is important that we place ourselves in a quiet, an essentially passive, interior attitude, with the contents of our varied meditation experiences moving around inside of us. It then becomes possible for our *inner wisdom* or the *holistic principle*—whichever you prefer—to draw together clusters of contents from our experiences and to form them into new integrative units within us.

These new integrative units are *wholes* in a special meaning of that term. They do not include all the parts of our previous experiences, and thus they are not wholes in the sense of including the whole of everything. But they are whole in the sense of being integral. They are whole in relation to the total movement and intention of our varied experiences. They express the essence of their direction, and they reflect their integrity. The varied contents of our experiences come together to form these new wholes. They are the emergents brought forth by the movement of our experiences.

As we have had many experiences, we let their varied contents move around inside of us. Sitting in stillness, we let these contents come together. Some of them fit together and join one another as though they are finding each other. Others do not fit together and drop away. Of those that do naturally come together, new clusters are formed. As you remain with them in quietness, they refine themselves further and new integrative units are formed. It comes about, then, that the multiple contents of your sequence of experiences have now been reconstructed by a natural, integrative principle. They are available to you now in a concise form. You may very well be able to find in them the essence of your experiences, their direction and their implicit meaning, while the extraneous contents have eliminated themselves. The tone as well as the contents of these new integrative units that have formed within you give you a means of recognizing the intention and larger purpose that lies in the background of your life experiences. It also provides the materials with which that purpose can unfold as the work proceeds.

One way to think of these new units that have formed at the twilight level is as MTI's, new molecules of thought and imagery. We consider them, therefore, not only from the point of view of their role and meaning in the inner development of our life but also in terms of their own intrinsic content. In addition to their significance for our life, new MTI's may also be carriers of a new hypothesis for our scientific work, a new image to use in our painting or poetry, a new idea for a project we would pursue in the world. As we become conscious of their formation within us, and as we describe them in our Meditation Log entry as part of our interior and subjective life, we should not overlook the objective contribution they may contain for our creative work.

When a new awareness, a new MTI, is presented to you in word or thought or image, record it without judgment in the Inner Process Entries segment of your Meditation Log. It may be brief or extended. There may be a single one, or there may be several. Record it as it comes to you, and remain in your silence.

Out of your varied and extended experiences there has now come a crystallization; one or two or three new integral units have been formed. They contain the essence of your experiences, as the message of their movement has been brought together by the holistic principle working in your life, which is your inner wisdom. This will become the starting point for your next cycle of experience. Now that they have been formed and recorded, we can look to these new crystallizations for guidance. As they become Journal Feedback leads, they will show us how to proceed.

Proceeding from Feedback

There are two general directions in which our Journal Feedback leads can guide us. As personal leads, they can take us to the Journal sections that deal with the private issues of our individual life. As transpersonal leads, they can direct our attention to those areas of human existence that have a significance beyond the needs and the desires of our individual life. These are more than personal, but they may be the primary concerns of our life as we are reaching toward meaning.

In the personal sections, we work in more pragmatic terms. We deal there with the pressures and the problems of our lives in terms of the immediacy of the issues. When, for example, we have to make decisions relating to our body—to deal with an illness, to participate in athletics, to choose a diet regime—the frame of reference is altogether in terms of the particulars of our individual life. It is personal in that sense. At such a time the Journal Feedback lead that would come to us would very likely be a personal lead directing us to the various procedures we follow in the Dialogue with the Body section.

In comparable terms, there are several other Journal sections to which personal leads might direct us for particularized work. They are personal in the special sense that they involve issues and decisions that are unique to us as individuals in that they can only be decided within the context of our own life. There may be questions, for example, of how we should seek to earn our livelihood, of the kind of role we shall play in society, of marrying and raising a family, of friendships and relationships with other individuals, of the tasks and responsibilities we will undertake in our work and in our life. All these are issues that arise and can be decided only within the context of an individual's own existence.

The personal leads that will be calling our attention to these areas of our life experience may be directing us to several sections in the *Intensive Journal* workbook. In addition to Dialogue with the Body, they may be pointing us toward Dialogue with Works, or Dialogue with Persons, or Dialogue with Events. Especially, if you are at a crossroad of decision in your life, they may be directing you to the procedures in a very important personal section, Intersections: Roads Taken and Not Taken.

In general, when personal leads emerge from our Process Meditation work, it is because our life intuition is calling our attention to specific situations that need care. It is setting our priorities for us.

On the other hand, our life intuition may also give an opposite type of guidance. People often feel convinced that if some particular situation in their lives were changed, all their difficulties would be solved. They see their lives in terms of personal-type problems. They are surprised, then, when a transpersonal lead comes to them and directs their attention to another area of their life. That is only an indication, however, that their inner wisdom knows better. It is indicating that in their present life situation, the sequence of concerns should be reversed. For them the priority is to work first with the questions that involve their sense of meaning in the transpersonal contexts of life. After that, their specific circumstances can fit into place and the problems can be worked out in the personal sections.

We might assume that the strongest emotions occur in the personal areas of life where individuals are moved by love and anger and jealousy. We find, however, that emotions of the very strongest power arise in the transpersonal area of experience. It is merely that these emotions are felt in a range of reality that reaches beyond the individual life. The emotions are felt personally and with great intensity, but insofar as their subject is God or immortality or truth or science or nature, the framework of the emotions is more than individual and therefore more than personal. Even in our secular and highly rationalized modern society, it is not uncommon for individuals to express a tremendous intensity of energy and emotion in relation to a transpersonal dedication. They feel it very personally, but its object is transpersonal.

We should bear in mind the additional implications of transpersonal experience. Its spiritual significance is only one aspect of it. Because of the great power of the emotions and the tremendous energies that may be generated by transpersonal experiences and dedications, they have a major social and historical importance. Since experiences and beliefs with regard to meaning in life seem to be essential for human beings, we know that they will inevitably arise. The only question is whether they will be thrust up in history as overarching passions that take over large groups of people and lead to violent events, or whether they can have an orderly and constructive development person by person. And whether in the individual life they can lead to a deepening of meaning as we seek in our Process Meditation work.

If the leads that are given to us are personal leads, we can follow them to several different sections of our workbook, depending on their special content. If they are transpersonal leads, however, we have one main section to which we take them. We go to PDE, the section for Peaks, Depths, and Explorations, where we draw upon whatever leads and hints and clues are given to us and whatever resources our basic *Intensive Journal* work makes available. This is the Journal section where all our interior efforts are consolidated, all our inner experiences and our most intimate intimations of truth brought together, so that we can see what larger understanding they can bring. PDE is the section for the continuity and progressive deepening of our spiritual work, whatever its contents of doctrine and symbol.

With these varied considerations in the background, aware of the multiple possibilities of interior knowledge that are open to us, we sit in stillness. Our eyes close and we let our breathing become slower, relaxed and deeper and slower. We sit in stillness, considering. We review within ourselves the new units of experience that have shown themselves to us. Certain aspects of those interior events speak to us more strongly now. They have more to say to us in words. They have more to show us in images and symbols. We let them be free to continue to add to what they have been, to continue their development within our experience.

Sitting in the stillness, we are asking them what their desire is. In the silence we are not seeking answers from them, only indications as to where their interest lies. What is the direction of their next development? We are not seeking answers, only leads. We are prepared to do the rest of the work ourselves in the continuity of our interior life.

Through our pen they can speak and tell us. Which are the areas of our life, what are the issues and concerns, that we wish to consider more deeply? That have more to say to us and to show us? We are willing to receive even those guidances and directions that we do not desire to hear. And we will explore whatever is shown to us.

We let the leads of every kind come to us in the silence. And we prepare to follow them on both the personal and the transpersonal paths of our *Intensive Journal* work as we proceed.

In a profound sense, each human life has the potential to become an artwork. To that degree, each of us can become an artist-in-life with our finest creation being our own self. Just as the true artist, like Casals or Einstein or Picasso, never ceases his creative work while he is alive, so we continue the creative development of the person within us. Whenever a phase of our life completes itself and we reach a particular level of integration or awareness and achievement, that in its turn becomes our new starting point. In this perspective, all those life difficulties that we might otherwise think of as problems or pathologies become the raw material of our next development. When a phase of our life completes itself, only that phase is finished. We ourselves are not finished. Our life history continues to unfold.

A principle comparable to this is true of the process of evolution in the universe at large. When a season or a geologic period ends, when an individual animal or an entire species dies, that is not the termination of things. It is rather an event that feeds into the total process of evolution. From one point of view and on one level, it is an ending. From another point of view, it is the material for a new beginning. In the unfolding context of evolution, what appears as death and termination becomes on another level the occasion for a further renewal of life.

As this is true of the universe, it is also true of our lives as persons. On the qualitative level of our inner experience, our endings provide the material for new beginnings. In the midst of the everyday pressures of anxiety and pain, we often lose the perspective of knowing this and we forget that our individual lives are each an inner universe in which a process of evolution is seeking to unfold. Our Journal work seeks to give us a practical way of maintaining this large inner perspective.

A primary purpose of the *Intensive Journal* process is to provide an instrument and method by which the qualitative evolution of life can take place within us as individuals. It seeks to maintain for the elusive subjectivities of our inner life an open space in which the processes of life integration can proceed objectively in the context of each person's experience. The *Intensive Journal* workbook becomes the outer embodiment of our inner life. It thus serves for many of us as the laboratory in which we explore experimentally the possibilities of our life. It also serves as the sanctuary to which we go for our most intimate and private, our most profound and universal experiences. But most fundamentally, the *Intensive Journal* process is our inner workshop, the place where we do the creative shaping of the artwork of our life.

Appendix A:
Entrance Meditations

In the *Intensive Journal* program three small volumes of Entrance Meditations are used to help establish an atmosphere of stillness and depth at Journal workshops.

The essence of the Entrance Meditation is expressed in its name. It is a means of moving through the entryway of consciousness. Once we have gone through the entrance, entered the mansion, and have begun to moved inward, we may experience whatever we find in the depths of ourselves. It may be pleasant; it may be exalting; it may not be pleasant at all. The Entrance Meditation is a neutral procedure, which does not specify what we shall experience. It merely takes us through the doorway at the surface of consciousness, and establishes an atmosphere that is congenial to further inward movement.

We have included a meditation from each of the Entrance Meditation volumes, to give us a taste of what is involved in an Entrance Meditation. Each closes with the repeated phrase, "In the silence, in the silence," which is the cue for each person to go into his or her own silence to allow for additional experiences. Each was chosen for its appropriateness in setting an atmosphere that would lead toward our goal of total centering, which is inherent in all meditation. Since the purpose of the meditations is to help us move inward through the entryway of consciousness, each may be used in whole or in part. Let your own experience be your guide.

Muddy/Clear: The Mirror of the Water

1. I remember the saying
   Of the old wise man, Lao Tse:
   "Muddy water,
   Let stand
   Becomes clear."

2. Thinking of that,
   I look within myself.
   I see,
   On the screen of my mind's eye,
   A stream of water,
   Moving,
   Swirling,
   Murky,
   It is full of things.
   I cannot look into this water.
   I cannot see my reflection
   In this water.

3. Now the movement stops.
   The water is in one place.
   It is heavy colored,
   Muddy
   But it is becoming quiet,
   The water is at rest.
   In its stillness
   The muddiness
   Is settling to the bottom.

4. At the surface it becomes clear,
   Transparent.
   I can see into the water
   More and more.
   Now I can see through

To the very depth of it.
There it shines
And it reflects.

5. The heavens are reflected
In the quiet water.
It is clear.
I see the reflection of a tree
In the quiet water.
The muddy water
Has become clear.

6. As I continue to look
Into the stillness
A reflection of myself
Begins to appear.
Deep in the quietness
Of the water,
I see
A reflection of myself,
Myself
In many different forms.

7. I sit
In the stillness
And let the image shape itself.
It becomes many things.
Many images
Appear in the still water,
Many things
Come up for me to see.

8. In the depth of the water,
The images
That open the greatest vision
Within me
Are not those that are visible.
I do not see them;
I just know them.
Something within me

Recognizes them
In the still water.

9. The muddy water has become quiet.
   I sit gazing into it,
   Seeing images,
   Visible and invisible,
   Letting them take form,
   Letting them change
   And re-form themselves
   In the depth of the still water,
   In the mirror of the water,
   In the depth of my Self,
   Moving, moving,
   In the Silence . . . In the Silence.

(From Ira Progaff's *The Well and the Cathedral*.)

Standing at the Altar/Tree

1. I am standing before the altar
   Of the underground chapel,
   The stump of an ancient tree,
   Massive,
   The power of ages
   Compressed within it.
   Ancient,
   Alone,
   It stands self-contained.

2. The altar/tree
   Is centered in itself.
   I feel the primeval depths
   Of the beginnings of life
   Move through the rings
   Of the aged wood.
   How far back they go,
   How present they are.

3. I feel myself entering
   The center of the rings
   Of the aged wood.
   They quiet me,
   They focus me.
   I feel myself to be
   At the center
   Of the circles of time
   There in the circles
   Of the altar/tree.

4. I feel the movement of time
   There in the circles of the tree,
   I feel the movement of time
   In the center of my Self.
   I stand before the altar/tree
   Centered in its circles,
   Swirling inward
   In the rings of time,
   Time before time,
   Time beyond time.

5. I go into the swirling circles,
   Into the timeless circles
   Of the tree of life,
   I stand before the ancient remains
   Of the tree of life,
   The altar/tree
   Of the underground chapel.

6. I am standing before it now
   Feeling my life.
   Feeling my life
   With all else that lives
   And has ever lived,
   There in the rings of time
   At the center of the altar/tree.

7. I stand before the altar/tree
   Entering its circles,

Moving into it,
Feeling time beyond time
Present now,
Here
In the movement of my life.

8. Feeling the years of my life
   Passing through time,
   Feeling the timeless in my life
   Present
   In this moment.
   Feeling the timeless in time,
   Knowing it,
   Being it . . .
   In the Silence . . . In the Silence.

(From Ira Progoff's *The White Robed Monk*.)

In the Presence of the Word

1. Quiet breathing
   In the stillness,
   My eyes closed.
   Not looking at things,
   I am free to see
   With an inner awareness.
   In the stillness of the Self
   I move nowhere
   But I reach beyond boundaries.
   I perceive
   By an inner perception.

2. I find myself in a forest.
   The trees are tall
   And very close together.
   The trees overlap one another,
   Their leaves intertwining.
   On the ground

There is space for me to walk,
But above
There is no space
For sunlight to come through.
I know there is sunlight above
But none comes through the trees.
It is dark in the forest.

3. Standing in the forest
    A stillness around me,
    A stillness
    Deepening,
    Surrounding,
    Reverberating around me.
    The stillness
    Echoes through the trees,
    The sound of it
    Returns and continues.
    It is a stillness
    And yet it echoes.

4. I stand in stillness
    Not moving at all.
    A presence is here
    Near me
    Yet not touching.
    Hovering above
    And about me
    In the darkness of the forest,
    It is an encompassing sound
    Enveloping everything.

5. This shapeless sound
    Pervades the forest.
    It is a Presence,
    Vast beyond form
    But taking form.
    Taking form
    In a word,

A strange, archaic word,
It is spoken
In a resonant and echoing voice . . .
Tremendum.
Tremendum.

6. The word resounds,
   It echoes over my head,
   Tremendum.
   Tremendum.
   I hear the word again,
   Tremendum.
   It is spoken
   But beyond speech . . .
   Tremendum.
   Tremendum.

7. The vastness of a shapeless sound
   Primeval
   Beyond mankind
   Beyond all words and purposes
   Beyond all beliefs,
   The vastness of a shapeless sound
   Taking form in a word,
   Tremendum.

8. I listen to the word.
   It continues to speak,
   Tremendum.
   One word
   Implying many meanings,
   Tremendum.
   The movement of the sound
   Raises me
   Inwardly,
   I am carried
   As by a soft inner wind
   Letting the word speak on . . .
   And listening.

9. Letting word speak on . . .
   Tremendum.
   One word is spoken,
   I hear many words,
   Carrying many thoughts,
   Mysteries of life,
   Paradoxes of truth
   Contained within one word.

10. Direct knowing,
    Knowing the oneness of life
    Comes while listening,
    Listening in the silence,
    Listening to the word,
    Letting Tremendum speak on
    Letting the word speak on . . .
    And listening,
    Listening . . .
    In the Silence . . . In the Silence.

(From Ira Progoff's *The Star/Cross.*)

Appendix B:
Mantra/Crystals from
the Workshop Floor

A main way that participants in workshops can check the Mantra/ Crystals they have drawn from their lives is by the exercise of *speak out.* By articulating their Mantra/Crystal they can test how it will feel when they use it as a basis for their meditation. A sampling of the Mantra/Crystals taken from the workshops follows.

> A tree of many flowers
> > *(An excerpt from a twilight image.)*
>
> The secret place in the house
> > *(A dream image carrying a sense of something in the past to be discovered.)*
>
> Feeling the pain of my life
> In the hollow of a tree
> > *(From a twilight image.)*
>
> Circle of friends and lovers
> Doors close and others open
> > *(Formed during a time of personal disappointment and life transition.)*
>
> Deep swimming with my brother
> > *(An image of spiritual friendship in the context of the metaphor of the underground stream.)*

The sea gulls floating at rest

(An image of nature in tranquillity. It could be an actual physical perception or a twilight image, equally valid in either case.)

My life for the love of God

(Suggested by reading the text of Brother Lawrence and considering his life.)

Kingdom of God receive me

(A spontaneous outcry in the course of an inner experience.)

Out of the silence it comes

(An experience of finding renewal when there seemed to be no further possibilities.)

Dark smoke in the chimney

(A dream experience that reflected a time of great personal difficulty.)

I'm flowing into the tree

(A twilight image that carried a connective experience.)

All the treasures in the trunk

(An indicative excerpt from a dream experience.)

Watching the waves rolling in

(A waking experience of closeness to nature. The difference in style and tone between this and the preceding mantra/crystal indicates how each mantra/crystal reflects its own experience in its characteristic way.)

A rose on purple velvet

(An excerpt from a twilight imagery experience.)

The old and the new both go

(This mantra/crystal is an observation of a phase of process. It came at the close of a twilight imagery experience.)

Sweet love of the universe

(The mantra/crystal helps reestablish the atmosphere of this private inner experience and move further into it.)

The morning song of the birds

Hearing the rain on the trees

(These are mantra/crystals that may recall particular life situations, and then enable us to go beyond their personal aspects.)

In stillness on the mountain

(Essentially a biblical theme, this may, however, be recalling an outer physical environment establishing an image as the basis for an inner environment.)

The Yom Kippur glow of light

(A mantra/crystal arising from an experience in the synagogue on the Jewish High Holy Days.)

Saul of Tarsus marching through

(A mantra/crystal of a theological student placing himself in the atmosphere of New Testament days. It is an excerpt from his own experience.)

Doing the work of the Lord

Being at one with the Lord

(Adaptations from the scriptural texts.)

I am like an olive tree

(Drawn from the larger phrase and image: "I am like an olive tree in the house of the Lord." After a year of general personal use, this mantra/crystal served as an anchor to reality in the crisis of a severe, disorienting illness.)

Soul of Christ sanctify me

(A Christian text mantra/crystal.)

Corpus Christi salve me

(A Christian mantra/crystal in Latin.)

Passion of Christ strengthen me

(A Christian prayer mantra/crystal. Note that the three preceding mantra/crystals have sometimes been used in special situations as a mantra/crystal series to serve as a means of religious dedication within a particular framework of symbolism and understanding.)

A faceless girl in the field

(Andrew Wyeth's famous painting becomes the equivalent of a twilight image and thus a profound representation of life to this person.)

Clean clothes hanging on the line

(A twilight image that carried great meaning for a person at a turning point in life.)

Being silent to listen

(Derived from the Mosaic injunction.)

Singing new songs to the Lord

(Based on the psalm that says, "Sing a new song to the Lord." Note that the mantra/crystal does not retain the commandment style in which the statement was originally given.)

The ground of naked being

(Drawn from the text of The Cloud of Unknowing.)

Who are you, Lord, who am I?
(A prayer phrase attributed to St. Francis.)
A straight road going uphill
(Reflecting the present situation in a life.)
Feeling the presence of God
Holding the finger circle
(A statue of the Buddha appeared in an image in which the fingers were held in a particular way. The finger circle became of symbolic importance to the person and is the subject of the mantra/crystal.)
The third eye of the Buddha
(In a dream, the Buddha appeared with a third eye that was felt to be a special source of wisdom.)
Crying in the wilderness
(An image from the Old Testament prophet applied to one's own life.)
Charged with the grandeur of God
(Drawn from a poem by Gerard Manley Hopkins.)
The point of hollow water
(A paradoxical teaching that came in a twilight image.)
Taking the path to the depth
Rocking gently on the sea
In the running stream of time
A tree planted near water
Footprints in the sands of time
(From the poem by Longfellow.)
Father, Son, Holy Spirit
My life is now becoming
Walking toward the midnight sun
Gardening in the holy place
Seeking wholeness on the Cross
Relinquishing to the Lord
(An interior decision and spiritual commitment is carried by this mantra/crystal. The four-syllable word at the beginning has a marked effect on the breathing rhythm. In this case the effect is salutary because it fits well with the atmosphere and content of the mantra/crystal.)
Lying down in green pastures
(Adapted from the psalm and retaining its famous image. For some persons, meditating with a mantra/crystal of this type can provide an equivalent to reading psalms.)

A jade teardrop on my cheek
In my house are many rooms
A red sunset on the beach
At the center of myself
Breathing the movement of time
In the very soul of night
Chanting on the way to faith
Rocking the baby within
In the forest of my life
The undertow of the sea
A flower opens to me
Seeing the rock from the hill
Taking the hand of a child
With an everlasting love
Sun shining down from above
The flux of life around me
Now the Christ from darkness comes
Standing on the mountain top
Quiet stillness nurtures the soul
The beads of life in the grass
The sound in the cathedral

Appendix C: Spiritual Steppingstones

What follows are examples of Spiritual Steppingstones recorded by various workshop participants.

The Spiritual Steppingstones of R.A.

1. Birth. I was born into an old-fashioned Christian home, and I believed that everything was true just exactly as I was told.

2. Early farm life. Being on the farm as a little girl, I became very close to the animals. I noticed what was natural in them, and I felt there was something spiritual about it.

3. Teen religion. In my teen years I felt very strong natural urges, and these came up against very rigid prohibitions. I identified religion with rules of moral conduct, mostly with restrictions on things I was not allowed to do. At that point I associated religion with rigidity.

4. Rejection. I reject religion. I don't go as far as being an atheist, but I end my religious affiliation.

5. The time of shopping. I feel that something is missing in my life so I go shopping for another religion. At that time I didn't know that Eastern religions existed, or that they were anything more than paganism, so I just shopped all the Christian religions I could find.

6. Conversion. I decide to become a Catholic because it has a religious quality that appeals to me and I feel deeply at home in it.

7. Disappointment. I become disappointed in Catholicism and become nonpracticing.

8. Alcohol. I become involved with alcoholism and various drugs. Somehow this seems to be connected with my religious desires, but it is not satisfying. I realize that it is destructive, and when I become ill I manage to stop.

9. Depression. A terrible period of depression. At this time life seems to be a barren desert. All I can think of is that I want to get out of it.

10. A new discovery. I have an inner experience in which I discover the reality of my life beyond all the suffering I have had and all the joy. I realize that I have had more than my share of both, and that my spiritual life is the reality beyond them.

11. Prayer. I learn to pray as a thankful connection to life. It seems strange not to be asking God for favors all the time. But blessings seem to come when I don't ask. This is a time of peace.

12. Christianity. My various inner experiences of Jesus as the Christ. Sometimes these have been too intimate and intense to bear, but it enables me to know how fundamentally I am a Christian. That seems strange to me as I write it. But it is a very warm as well as a surprising feeling.

    I realize also that these feelings of Jesus give me an especial love toward all the non-Christians in the world. I feel freed from the prejudice I was taught as a child. Perhaps that is the love my whole journey has been for. I feel peace.

The Spiritual Steppingstones of M. T.

1. When I was a young man I wondered about life in my phi-
    losophy courses, but I was not concerned in a religious way.

2. The first religious feelings I remember came while listening
    to music, especially Beethoven and later Bach. At that time I
    became convinced that the truth of life lies in the beauty that
    the arts can give us. I especially became religiously devoted to
    music.

3. With the depression of the nineteen-thirties, I felt the pres-
    sures of poverty. That was when I concluded that the arts are
    not sufficient to meet modern problems. I decided that the
    arts, like religion, are a means of escaping from the economic
    realities of life.

4. I became a Marxist. It is not too much to say that I undertook
    my new belief with religious fervor. I became actively en-
    gaged.

5. I became embroiled in doctrinaire disputes and changed my
    allegiance. I still remained a Marxist, but now I was devoted
    to a particular group within Marxism. Looking back I can see
    that in my devotion to this sectarian group I was even more
    religiously devoted than before.

6. I became embroiled in disputes within the party. Charges are
    brought against me, and I am thrown out of the party. I think
    it is very unfair, but I am really glad it happened. I think I felt
    like a religious heretic, and I realize now that I liked the
    feeling.

7. I become a business man and am quite successful at it. Mak-
    ing money is a kind of religion in itself, and not a bad one. I
    find that I like it.

8. I discover pyschoanalysis of the classical Freudian type and
    become involved in five-day-a-week analysis for several years.
    My business was doing well enough to pay for it.

9. Although I believed in psychoanalysis, I vaguely felt that it was shallow and inadequate. I remained loyal to my various therapists since I felt that they needed me (as I now am convinced they did) and I was beginning to look for new ideas.

10. I continued to search in the spiritual field even while I remained in psychoanalysis. I explored Buddhism and Yoga, but I rarely told my therapist.

11. I became especially interested in Buddhist philosophy and I studied it as much as I could. I was particularly intrigued by the Eastern conception of opposites in life, and it led me to reexamine the dialectical philosophy of Marxism. I thought I might achieve a union of the two philosophies, but instead I reactivated a great many emotional questions from the Marxist phase of my life.

12. I have recently realized that my philosophical studies of Buddhism and Marxism are only on an intellectual level, and that to that degree they are not adequate. Perhaps as a result of those thoughts, I find myself now thinking a great deal about the vanity of human existence, and this in very fundamental terms. Both Buddhism and the Bible speak of it, but I wonder whether it really has an answer. That is why I am now reconsidering the whole of my life history with an open mind.

The Spiritual Steppingstones of Y.P.

1. My family belonged to a church but they only went on holidays.

2. They sent me to Sunday school, but I decided that nobody really believed in it, so I didn't either.

3. When I found out about sex I decided not to take religion seriously.

4. I got onto drugs and went on experimenting from one thing to another. I think I wanted to believe in something, but I didn't know what it was. So I kept on looking.

5. I had some drug experiences that shook me up. I saw the universe breaking open, and many other visionary things. It convinced me there is a reality I didn't know about.

6. My physical condition became very serious, and for the first time in my life I was close to death. I thought I was too young to die and it frightened me. I decided that if I lived I would change my way of living. I did get better, but changing wasn't easy.

7. I found Swami —— and did Yoga. That was a help, but I couldn't stay with it.

8. I tried a lot of different teachings, mostly Eastern, Buddhism, Sufi, whatever. I couldn't really understand what was being said but the vibes of the people were good, for the most part. In most places it was like being high, only it was healthier. I didn't have one place to stay, but going to lots of different places made it a good in-between time.

9. I thought I understood what the single reality is and I was really seeking to experience oneness. Then I joined up with R—— and I really made that my dedication.

10. That was four years ago and I have stayed with it. I feel much stronger as a person, but I don't feel any closer to truth. Sometimes I feel very grateful, and sometimes I feel that I have been used. Lately I sometimes think that I have been had.

11. I have dreams now that seem to encourage me to take a further step toward truth. But right now I don't know what that step is. I may have to clear out some old things before I can take a step forward.

Appendix D:
The Registered
Intensive Journal Workbook

The registered *Intensive Journal* workbook, has served as the corner-stone of the Dialogue House program for individual growth for twenty-five years. Working with it is essential because it is the instrument that makes possible the method of Journal Feedback with its continuous and cumulative interplay of experiences. And it is this active interflow of Journal Feedback that enables the self-balancing process of life integration to establish itself in the course of our continuous and open-ended experience.

The indispensable function of the *Intensive Journal* workbook is that its structure provides a tangible equivalent of the inner space in which the mini-processes of our life can move about until they find their appropriate level and form of self-integration. The *Intensive Journal* method thus serves as the vehicle of our individual initiation into the larger process of existence. It enables us to draw our personal life into focus while opening an inner window to the transpersonal mysteries of human destiny. Since it serves so intimate and profound a role, it is inevitable that many people have found that over a period of years the *Intensive Journal* workbook becomes a symbol to them of their contact with the larger meanings and possibilities of their life. It becomes the embodiment of the movement and the unfolding of each person's unique existence. Its very presence thus becomes a token of the reality and the continuity of the inner person whom we each are and are progressively becoming. Small wonder, then, that many people like to carry their Journals with them even when they do not expect to write in them. Seeing their Journal reminds them that their inner process is real, and is continuing even when their outer life seems bleak and difficult. Beyond its functional value as an instrument for emergent growth, the *Intensive Journal* workbook develops a symbolic value of inner life continuity that becomes even richer with its overtones of energy and meaning as it is used through the years.

This symbolic as well as functional role of the *Intensive Journal* workbook is a major reason for working with it in the structured form that it has developed through its years of use. If, after carrying out the basic procedures that have been described in this book, you find the Journal Feedback method to be congenial to you, and if you feel it can help you focus and deepen your life, your next step should be to have the actual experience of participating in a Dialogue House Journal Workshop. When you attend that, you will receive a registered and numbered copy of the *Intensive Journal* workbook, and this will be yours to use in your privacy as well as at successive workshops.

In the meanwhile, if you have not yet attended a Journal Workshop and are undertaking to learn the Journal Feedback procedures while working by yourself, you will need a model of the *Intensive Journal* workbook to follow. With this in mind, the following pages contain a facsimile of the registered *Intensive Journal* workbook as it is issued in numbered copies to participants taking part in their first Dialogue House Journal Workshop.

One of the important functions of Dialogue House as a public organization is its role in making Progoff Journal Workshops available in appropriate formats at various levels of society, in education, in religion, in the arts, in drug and urban tension areas, and especially for the general population. In supporting these programs, Dialogue House seeks to monitor the issuance of *Intensive Journal* workbooks as carefully as it is able so as to maintain professional standards of responsibility in the use of the *Intensive Journal* method. Consequently, only those who are approved as Journal Consultants on the basis of their training and experience in the Journal Feedback procedures as well as their other professional qualifications are authorized to issue these registered Dialogue House *Intensive Journal* workbooks.

When you participate in a Journal Workshop, one way that you can check the credentials of the leader is by his authorization to issue you a registered and numbered copy of the published Dialogue House *Intensive Journal* workbook. This will be verification that you are not talking to a self-appointed Journal Consultant, but to a person who has studied the Journal Feedback procedures, whose basic competence has been recognized, and who is engaged in ongoing study. Such a qualified Journal Consultant will also have available to him new Dialogue House materials and procedures as they are developed, as well as whatever guidance and support he may require from Dialogue House staff consultants.

The facsimile copy of the *Intensive Journal* workbook includes sections that were added for the Meaning Dimension when *The Practice of Process Meditation* was published. The *Intensive Journal* workbook currently in use includes the four dimensions of human existence.

For your use now, you can create your own pages using the sample pages as guides, and put them in a looseleaf binder or notebook(s). Assemble the journal before you begin. It is best to use color-coded paper or at least color-coded tabs for each section.

(white)　　　　　　　　　　　　　　　　**(green)**

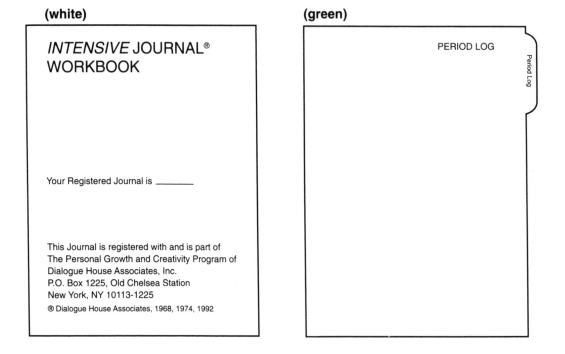

INTENSIVE JOURNAL®
WORKBOOK

Your Registered Journal is _____

This Journal is registered with and is part of
The Personal Growth and Creativity Program of
Dialogue House Associates, Inc.
P.O. Box 1225, Old Chelsea Station
New York, NY 10113-1225
® Dialogue House Associates, 1968, 1974, 1992

PERIOD LOG

Period Log

(yellow)

DAILY LOG

Daily Log

(orange)

DIALOGUE DIMENSION
Special Personal Sections

Dialogue Dimension

(orange)

DIALOGUE WITH PERSONS

Dialogue with Persons

(orange)

DIALOGUE WITH WORKS

Dialogue with Works

(orange)

DIALOGUE WITH SOCIETY
Group Experiences

Dialogue with Society

(orange)

DIALOGUE WITH EVENTS
Situations and Circumstances

Dialogue with Events

(orange)

DIALOGUE WITH THE BODY

Dialogue with the Body

(blue)

DEPTH DIMENSION
Ways of Symbolic Contact

Depth Dimension

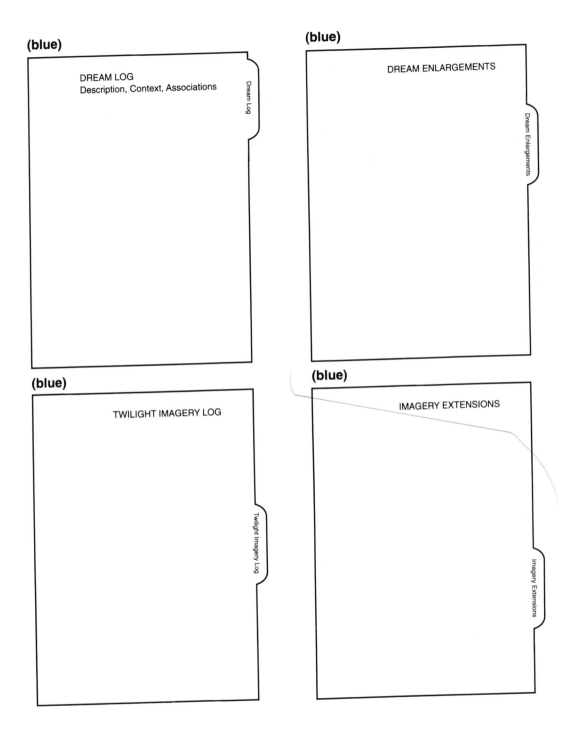

(blue)

DREAM LOG
Description, Context, Associations

Dream Log

(blue)

DREAM ENLARGEMENTS

Dream Enlargements

(blue)

TWILIGHT IMAGERY LOG

Twilight Imagery Log

(blue)

IMAGERY EXTENSIONS

Imagery Extensions

(blue)

INNER WISDOM DIALOGUE

Inner Wisdom Dialogue

(red)

LIFE/TIME DIMENSION
Inner Perspectives

Life/Time Dimension

(red)

LIFE HISTORY LOG
Remembrances
Steppingstone Periods

Life History Log

(red)

STEPPINGSTONES

Steppingstones

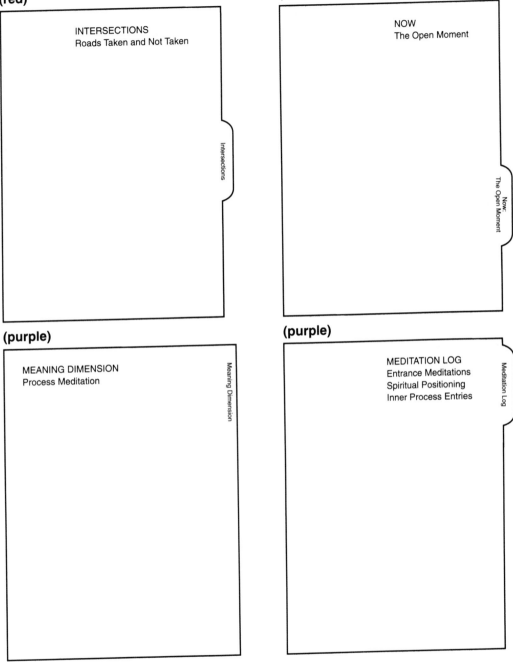

(red)

INTERSECTIONS
Roads Taken and Not Taken

Intersections

(red)

NOW
The Open Moment

Now:
The Open Moment

(purple)

MEANING DIMENSION
Process Meditation

Meaning Dimension

(purple)

MEDITATION LOG
Entrance Meditations
Spiritual Positioning
Inner Process Entries

Meditation Log

(purple)

CONNECTIONS
Gatherings
Spiritual Steppingstones
Re-Openings: Spiritual Roads Not Taken

CONNECTIONS

(purple)

MANTRA/CRYSTALS
Mantra/Crystal Index
Workings

Mantra/Crystals

(purple)

PEAKS, DEPTHS, and
EXPLORATIONS

Peaks, Depths and
Explorations

TESTAMENT

Testament

Other Books by Ira Progoff

ON THE *INTENSIVE JOURNAL* METHOD

Life-Study: Experiencing Creative Lives by the Intensive Journal *Method*
(1983)

ON ENTRANCE MEDITATION

The Well and the Cathedral: An Entrance Meditation (1971, 1977)
The White Robed Monk: An Entrance Meditation (1972)
The Star/Cross: An Entrance Meditation (1971)

ON DEPTH PSYCHOLOGY

*The Death and Rebirth of Psychology: An Integrative Evaluation of
Freud, Adler, Jung, and Rank and the Impact of
Their Culminating Insights on Modern Man* (1956, 1984)

*Depth Psychology and Modern Man: Holistic Depth Psychology
and the Magnitude of Human Personality* (1959, 1987)

*The Symbolic and the Real: A New Psychological Approach to
the Fuller Experience of Personal Existence* (1963, 1991)

*The Dynamics of Hope: Perspectives of Process in Anxiety and Creativity,
Imagery and Dreams* (1985)

ON JUNG'S PSYCHOLOGY

*Jung's Psychology and Its Social Meaning: A Comprehensive Statement of
C.G. Jung's Psychological Theories and an Interpretation of their
Significance for the Social Sciences* (1953, 1981)

*Jung, Synchronicity, and Human Destiny:
Non-Casual Dimensions of Experience* (1973)

ON MYSTICISM

The Cloud of Unknowing (1957)

*The Image of An Oracle: A Report on Research into the
Mediumship of Eileen J. Garrett* (1964)

Index

Acknowledgment of life
    experiences, 227
Active method, Intensive Journal
    process as, 20
Activity/passivity, cycles of,
    319–323
Adler, Alfred F., 212
Alienation, 247–248, 253
Anderson, Robert, 128
Arts, relationship with, 186–187.
    See also Dialogue with
    Works
At a Journal Workshop (Progoff), 10
Autobiography. *See* Life history

Balancing, interior, 219–220
Beliefs, 247–250, 253–256
    changes in, 254–256, 325
    inner meaning and, 258
Bergson, Henri, 32
Bible(s), 3–5, 12
Body, human. *See also* Dialogue
    with the Body
    life history of, 155–157

wisdom of, 155
Breathing rhythm, and Mantra/
    Crystals, 331–335, 341,
    343, 347
Buber, Martin, 125

Centeredness, 281
    achieving, through meditation,
    226, 229
Charismatic elements, 185
Checklist, Intensive Journal,
    54–56, 96
Cloud of Unknowing, 104–105
Coincidences, 171–172
    message of, 171–172
Color coding, 27
Connections section, 30,
    247–300, 371
    main function of, 249
    subsections of (*see* Gatherings;
        Inner Wisdom Dialogue;
        Spiritual Steppingstones;
        Re-Openings of Spiritual
        Roads Not Taken)

Connective experience(s),
    249–256
    conversion (entry) phase, 254
    cycles of, 247–256,
        260–261
    effects of, 258–260
    exit phase, 254–255
    reentering, 255–256
Continuity feedback, 24
Continuity of life
    of the body, 156
    fluidity of inner movement
        and, 20
    inner and outer, 220
    Intensive Journal structure
        and, 7
    observing, 77–78
    recognizing, 14
    reconnecting with, 13
    reconstructing, 15
    renewal of, 14–15
    spontaneous mourning and, 39
    Steppingstones and, 77, 80, 81,
        83–84, 88

Continuity of time, and self-
balancing principle, 166
Correlation, inner. *See* Life
Correlation
Creative persons
Drew University studies
of, 19, 20, 22, 27
experience of unfolding of life
in, 23
as model for Intensive Journal
process, 19, 20, 22, 23
processes of their lives, 22
Creativity/creative process,
142–143. *See also* Creative
persons; Dialogue with
Works
in Daily Log, 66
Mantra/Crystals and, 337, 349
in transpersonal exploration, 311
Twilight Imagery and, 58
Cross-referencing, 66–68,
199–200, 310
Crossroad situations. *See also*
Decision-making; Inter-
sections: Roads Taken and
Not Taken
recognizing, in retrospect, 111
Steppingstones and, 83, 87, 99
Culture, 248–249, 250
Current Recording, in Daily Log,
67–68. *See also* Daily Log

Daily Log, 65–72, 369
brevity of entries in, 66
cross-references to Dream Log
in, 199–200
dreams in, 68
entries in, 66, 67–72
guidelines for making entries
in, 67–71
primary function of, 65
Recapitulation in, 67
two ways of working
in, 67–68
Death, prospect of, 163

Decision-making. *See also*
Crossroad situations;
Intersections: Roads Taken
and Not Taken
perspective on life and, 17
using Twilight Imagery in,
117–120
Deepening awareness, 9, 269–271
and Journal Feedback method,
21–22, 65–66
Depth Dimension, 27
contents of, 29
Dialogue exercises and, 196–297
introduction to, 196–208
mini-processes of, 28–29
sections of (*see* Dream Log;
Dream Enlargments; Imagery
Extensions; Inner Wisdom Dialogue; Twilight Imagery Log
symbolism of, 28, 30
symbols in, 197
and Life/Time Dimension, 119
Depth psychology. *See* Holistic
Depth Psychology
Dialogue, meanings of term,
125–126
Dialogue Dimension, 27, 29
sections of (*see* Dialogue with
Events, Situations, and
Circumstances; Dialogue
with Persons; Dialogue
with Society; Dialogue with the
Body; Dialogue with Works)
dialogue relationships as basic
units of, 29–30
introduction to, 124–126
Dialogue House, 41, 403
Dialogue relationships, 29–30
criterion for choosing, 127–128
defined, 125–126
with Intensive Journal, 366
as I-Thou relationships, 125, 126
Dialogue scripts, 125, 138
continuing, 139
first segments of, 152
writing, 164–165

Dialogue with Body. *See* Dialogue
with the Body
Dialogue with Events, Situations, and Circumstances, 30,
167–181. *See also* Events of
our life; Relationships with
persons
background for, 172–177
beginning, 177–178
developing, 179–180
Dialogue with Persons and,
173–175
Dialogue with Works, 175
goal of, 176–177
Journal Feedback and, 175–177
Steppingstone Periods and, 97
writing dialogue script for,
180–181
Dialogue with Persons, 30,
127–140
beginning, 130–132
concluding, 138–140
deep, establishing, 134–137
describing relationship in,
132–133
Dialogue with Events combined
with, 173–175
Journal Feedback and, 133–134
listing persons for, 130–131
reading, 139
speaking and listening,
137–138
starting dialogue, 137
Steppingstone Periods and,
96–97
subsections, 139–140
Dialogue with Society, 30,
182–194
beginning, 187–191
building, 191–193
concluding, 194
relationship to political events,
185–186
Steppingstone Periods and, 97
writing dialogue script,
193–194

Dialogue with the Body,
    30, 154–166
  Daily Log subsection, 165–166
  developing, 160–165
  extending, 165–166
  focusing statement for, 159–160
  goal of, 155
  Steppingstone Periods and, 97
  reading, 161
  relationship with physical
    universe and, 154
  wisdom of life in, 163–165
Dialogue with Works,
    30, 141–153, 187
  concluding, 151–153
  describing work in, 147–148
  Dialogue with Events and, 175
  extending, 152
  listing works for, 145–147
  reading, 151–152
  speaking and listening, 150–151
  Steppingstone Periods and, 97
Diaries, feedback leads from, 67
Diet. See Dialogue with the Body
Dimensions of experience,
    meaning of, 27–28
Dream(s). See also Dream Log;
    Twilight Dreaming
  ambiguity of symbolism in,
    214, 216
  in Daily Log, 68
  difficulty in remembering,
    213–214
  emotional tone of, 218
  extending serial movement
    of, 213
  feeling emotions of, 203–204
  importance of not interpreting,
    203, 204
  inner movement of, 203,
    205–207, 218–219
  leads from, 215–219
  limitations of, 213–214
  and molecules of thought and
    imagery, 324–325
  nightmares, 205

  of past, 201–202
  problem of misinterpreting, 214
  reading, in series, 206–207
  recording, 200–202
  reentering and continuing,
    203–204, 205–207
  remembering, 198–199
  seriality of, 200, 204–207,
    213, 220
  significant, 198, 201–202
  sleeping, 29
  time-guidance of, 105–106
  titling, 68
  using as starting points, 216
  waking, 29
  working with, 202–221
  working with, on Twilight
    level, 207–221
Dream Enlargements, 29, 197, 220
  levels of depth, 220
  life correlation experiences
    in, 220
  recording Twilight Dreaming
    experiences in, 209–211
Dream leads, 215–219
  finding and following, 215–217
Dream Log, 29, 68, 197, 198–208
  continuing work in, 369
  recording, 198–200
  Steppingstone Periods and,
    97–98

Elan vital, 32
Emerson, Ralph Waldo, 18
Energy, psychic
  cycles of connective energy and,
    253–254
  of dreams, 218
  emotional or intellectual
    meaning and, 250
  group atmosphere and, 35
  Intensive Journal work and,
    6, 23
  Journal Feedback and, 31–32
  from unconscious mind, 118

Entrance Meditations,
    225–231, 321
  atmosphere for, 230–231
  as form of Process Meditation,
    225–226
  passages, 384–391
  samplings from volumes of,
    383–391
  spiritual position and, 234
  using, 228–230, 245
Events of life, 168–172. See also
    Dialogue with Events,
    Situations, and Circum-
    stances; Relationship to
    events
  broad meaning of, 168–169
  establishing contact with, 167
  inner, 255
  with inner importance, 169–172
  interior, 255–256, 257–258
  life history of, 172–173
  narrow meaning of, 168
  perspective on relationship
    to, 14
  political, 185–186 (see also
    Dialogue with Society)
  specific, in Period Log, 51–52
  synchronistic, 171–172
Evolution, process of, 381–382
Experiential feedback, 25,
    124–125

Family relationships, 183. See also
    Dialogue with Society
Feedback effects, 20, 24–25. See
    also Continuity feedback;
    Experiential feedback;
    Operational feedback
Feedback Interplay, 92
Feedback Leads, 100
Feedback procedures, 31–32,
    121–122
Feedback sections. See also Journal
    Feedback
  Log sections as data for, 26
  transformation of data in, 26–27

Francis, St., 161–162
Franny and Zooey (Salinger),
    313–314
Freedom of expression, 35, 40
    in Daily Log, 71–72
Freud, Sigmund, 212

Gatherings, 257–266, 374
    dates recorded in, 257
    entries in, 257
    focus of, 257–258, 259, 261, 286
    length of entries in, 262, 263
    purpose of work in, 257–258,
        273–274
    Re-Openings and, 286–288,
        289, 290–291
    recording, 262–266
Group atmosphere, 36–37
    as part of Intensive Journal,
        43–44
    reading Steppingstones and,
        82–83
    solitary work in, 33–37, 43
Growth, inner, 141
    new relationships and, 128–129
    outer work and, 141–142
    outward movement of, 143
Guidance, nonconscious, 14

Health. *See* Dialogue with
    the Body
Holistic Depth Psychology, 10, 31,
    267–268, 313
    formulation of, 330
    and metaphor of molecules of
        thought and imagery, 323
    on molecules of thought and
        imagery, 326
Holistic principle, 229, 377

I-Thou relationships, 125, 126
Imagery, 321–322, 326. *See also*
    Twilight Imagery
    in Period Log, 49–51
    personal, 326
    quietness and, 320

regrouping of images, 325
similes and metaphors as, 51
symbolism in, 320, 321–322
transpersonal, 326
Imagery Extension, 29
Immortality, 3
Inner experience
    four dimensions of, 27–30
        (*see also* Depth Dimension;
        Dialogue Dimension; Life/
        Time Dimension; Meaning
        Dimension)
    mini-processes of, 22–23,
        26–30
    reconstructing development of,
        236–239
Inner meaning
    of interior events, 258
    recognizing events with,
        258–259
Inner Process Entries, 241–246,
    302, 373, 374–375, 378
    importance of, 241–242
    as source for Peaks, Depths,
        and Explorations exercises,
        304–306
Inner Process Meditations
    entries in, 243–245
    preparing for, 242–243
    steps leading up to, 242
    use of, 246
Inner Wisdom Dialogue, 29, 197,
    267. *See also* Wisdom, inner;
    Wisdom figures
    concluding, 284–285
    and Meaning Dimension, 197
    and Peaks, Depths, and
        Explorations, 308–309
    role of, 270
    and Steppingstone Periods, 98
    wisdom figures in, 282–285
    writing, 281–285
Integration process, 13, 64,
    366, 368
Intensive Journal method/
    process, 5–7

creative development in relation
    to, 22–23
developing self-reliance
    through, 18
development of, 19, 23–25
formulation of, 5–6
how to use, 10–15
as indirect approach to problem
    solution, 8
interplay of, 31
inward dynamic of, 9
as means of using past
    experiences as starting
    points, 12
nonanalytical nature of, 21, 27,
    42–43
Process Meditation as part of, 10
as spiritual discipline, 12–13
transpsychological approach of,
    13–14
working in Journal Dyad, 48
Intensive Journal Workbook
    checklist for, 54–56, 96
    color-coding of, 27
    constructing, 44, 46
    establishing categories for, 19
    establishing structure of, 19–21
    freedom to use, after workshop,
        43–44
    frequency of entries in, 365–366
    function of, 402–403
    gaining familiarity with,
        through Workshop, 17
    more than diary, 20
    naming of, 19–20
    objective of techniques of,
        13–16
    ongoing work in, 368–382, 368
    Process Meditation component
        (*see* Meaning Dimension), 10
    structure of, 6, 7, 19–21, 311,
        339–340, 402
Intensive Journal Workshops, 5–6,
    10, 350
    as basic first experience, 16
    atmosphere of, 33–44

Intensive Journal Workshops
    (cont.)
  Dialogue with Works at,
    152–153
  early experimentation in, 21
  goals of, 16–18
  group atmosphere of, 36–37
  guidelines for methodology
    followed in, 36–37
  honoring integrity of life
    process in, 37–39, 40
  preparing for, 16
  reading Steppingstones in,
    81–83
  repositioning oneself through,
    359–360
  as sanctuary, 17
  techniques used in, 36–37
Intersections: Roads Taken and
    Not Taken, 28, 74, 75,
    102–107, 177, 369. See also
    Crossroad situations;
    Decision making; Roads
    Not Taken
  exploring, 113–120
  making list of, 104
  for retraveling road of life,
    106–107
  Steppingstone Periods and,
    98–99
Intuition, 29, 32, 74, 214, 318, 379
Inward beholding, 60

James, William, 10
Jesus Prayer, 315–318, 335
Journal checklist, 54–56, 96
Journal Consultants, 15
Journal Dyad, working in, 48
Journal Feedback/Journal
    Feedback process, 18, 30–32,
    355–356, 370. See also
    Feedback procedures
  aspects of, 24–25
  beginning work of, 127
  completion of Journal sections
    and, 121

cross-fertilization effect and, 121
cumulative effect of, 21–22
Daily Log in relation to, 65
determination of procedures
    in, 21
Dialogue with Events and,
    173–174, 175–177
Dialogue with the Body and,
    162–163
Dialogue with Works and, 146
Dialogues with Persons and,
    133–134, 138
Dream Enlargement and, 221
Dream Log and, 216
events in context of, 168,
    169–170
as force for change, 31–32
Holistic Depth Psychology as
    basis of, 31
Journal checklist and, 54, 55
momentum developed in,
    268–269
perspective on life and, 16
reintegration through, 53
Relationships with Persons
    and, 133–134
Steppingstones and, 79, 91
working with, 375–382
Journal Workshops. See Intensive
    Journal Workshop(s)
Judgment, freedom from, 35
Jung, Carl G., 10, 212–213

Knowledge beyond under-
    standing, 270. See also
    Wisdom, inner

Language of spirit, 15
Lao Tse, method of, 313, 343
Life Correlation, 219–221
  discerning, 61–64
  as inner life-balancing process,
    220, 221
  Twilight Imagery and, 61–64
Life history
  reconstructing, 120–122

of the body, recreating, 155–157
  developing perspective of, 365
  of events, 172–173
  of other person's life, 137
Life History Log, 28, 74, 75, 177
  contents of, 90
  pages for Steppingstone Periods
    in, 93
  entries in, 93–99, 121–122
  Remembrances section in,
    99–100
  Steppingstone Periods in,
    90–101, 109–113
  subsections (see Remembrances;
    Steppingstone Periods)
Life-balancing, 219–220
Life-integration process, 13, 64,
    366, 368
Life/Time, units of, 80, 90–92 (see
    also Steppingstone Periods)
Life/Time Dimension, 27, 31,
    74, 361
  continuing work in, 369
  contents of, 28
  essence of work in, 77
  entries in, 122
  past/future, 100–101, 103
  qualitative experience of, 75, 77,
    79, 91
  sections of (see Intersections:
    Roads Taken and Not Taken;
    Life History Log; Now:
    The Open Moment;
    Steppingstones)
  Steppingstones as units of, 90
  Time Stretching and, 74, 75
  working simultaneously in
    main sections of, 75
Log sections, 25–26. See also Daily
    Log; Dream Log; Life History
    Log; Meditation Log; Period
    Log; Twilight Imagery Log
  brevity of entries in, 53
  as fact gatherers, 307
  informational data of lives
    gathered in, 25–26

Mandalas, 329
Mantra(s), 315–318, 328–330. *See
    also* Mantra/Crystals; "Prayer
    that prays itself"
  effects of, 317
  use of, 329–330
Mantra/Crystal Index, 337
Mantra/Crystals, 30, 299, 310,
    313, 328–349, 374
  breathing rhythm and,
    331–335, 341, 343, 347
  characteristics of, 330–335
  choice of, 347–348
  effects of, 343–344
  inner wisdom and, 333
  levels of inner space and, 335,
    336–337
  meditations, 310, 338–349, 371
  number of syllables, 330–331,
    334–335
  as "prayer that prays itself," 342
  quality developed by, 346–347
  segments of (*see* Mantra/Crystal
    Index; Workings)
  use of phrase, 328–329
  working with, 335,
    337–340, 349
  workshop samplings of,
    392–396
Meaning Dimension (Process
    Meditation), 10
  arriving at, 223–224
  continuing work in, 373–375
  first steps following, 354–355
  as fourth dimension of Intensive
    Journal workshop, 10, 27, 30,
    223–311, 371, 404
  inner level of meaning
    and, 9–10
  Inner Wisdom Dialogue
    and, 197
  Intensive Journal as key to, 8
  introduction to, 223–231
  meaning of life dealt with
    in, 224
  ongoing, 354–358

sections of (*see* Connections;
    Mantra/Crystals; Meditation
    Log; Peaks, Depths, and
    Exploration (PDE);
    Testament)
Meaning of life. *See also* Meaning
    Dimension
  exploring, 9
  importance placed upon, 224
  quest for, 372
Meditation, 226–228, 330,
    376–377. *See also* Meditation
    Log; Process Meditation
  acknowledgment of life
    experiences and, 227
  atmosphere for, 228, 229,
    230–231
  defined, 226
  essence of, 229
  forms of experiencing, 226–227
  Intensive Journal work as,
    8, 372–373
  Mantra/Crystal and, 333
  techniques for, 321
Meditation Log, 30, 371, 373–374
  subsections (*see* Entrance
    Meditations; Inner Process
    Entries; Spiritual Positioning
  expanding role of, 306–308
  ongoing use of, 300–306
Meditation phrases, 315–318.
    See also Mantra/Crystals
Memories, 99–100
Metaphors, 50–51, 94–95, 234
  "muddy water," 319–323, 343
Mini-processes of inner
    experience, 22–23, 30
  clusters of, 27
  coordination of, 23
  of Depth Dimension, 28–29
  inner movements of, 26, 27
  movement of, 24
Mirroring effect, 20
Molecules of thought and
    imagery, 323–327, 377–378.
    See also Imagery

creative self-combining in,
    325, 326
  Holistic Depth Psychology
    and, 326
  Mantra/Crystals and, 348
Mourning, spontaneous, 38–40
  as necessary internal ritual,
    39–41
Movement, of images and
    thoughts, 324, 325
MTIs. *See* Molecules of thought
    and imagery
"Muddied water" metaphor,
    319–323, 343
Muddy water principle, 303
Myth, inner, 14

New experiences
  imagery as source for, 321–322
  modalities for, 312–327
Now: The Open Moment, 28, 74,
    359–363
  maintaining silence about,
    362–363
  Twilight Imagery and, 362
Now moment. *See* Now: The
    Open Moment; Present
    period

Objectivity, in Log sections, 26
Occam's Razor, 353
Operational feedback, 24–25

Passivity/activity, cycles of,
    319–323
  recognizing rhythm of, 322–323
Past experiences, discovering
    purpose of, 14
PDE. *See* Peaks, Depths and
    Explorations
Peaks, Depths and Explorations
    (PDE), 30, 300–311, 380–381
  creativity and, 311
  focus of, 301
  Meditation Log as source for
    work in, 301–302, 304–308

Peaks, Depths and Explorations
(PDE) *(cont.)*
ways of using, 308–309
Period Image, 59–61
dating, 59–60
Period Log, 46–56
approaches to gathering data
for, 54
beginning Journal Workshop
session with, 53
brevity of entries in, 49, 52–55
entries in, 49–54
life periods in, 91
using Twilight Imagery
with, 117
Perspective, interior, 350. *See also*
Testament
continuity feedback and, 24
Journal Feedback and, 16
of integrative principle, 64
knowledge of transitions
and, 17
on relationship to events, 14
renewing, 14–15
reshaping, 87, 89
using Intensive Journal
workbook to gain, 20
Philokalia, 315, 316, 318
Physical experience,
Steppingstones of,
156–159
Political events, relationship to,
185–186
Potentials of our life, 104–107
dreams and, 205–206
"Prayer that prays itself" (Jesus
Prayer), 315–318, 335, 345
Mantra/Crystal as, 342, 343
Present period
approaching through Twilight
Imagery, 57–61
beginning Intensive Journal
work with, 46–49
elasticity of, 46–48
images of, 49–51
specific events in, 51–52

Problems of life, indirect solutions
to, 8–9
Process Meditation. *See* Meaning
Dimension (Process
Meditation)

Quietness. *See* Silence; Stillness

Re-Openings of Spiritual Roads
Not Taken, 262–263,
286–299
entries in, 287–289, 291–299
example of steps involved in,
294–299
Recapitulation, in Daily
Journal, 67
Relationships between persons,
127–130. *See also* Dialogues
between Persons; Dialogue
relationships; Family
relationships
body and, 155
charismatic elements, 185
close, 129
describing, 131–134
extending in Dialogue with
Persons, 129
listing, 130–131
possibilities for future growth
and, 128–129
Religious institutions, relationship
with, 186
Remembrances, 99–100
Renewal, personal, 14–15
Rhythmic relationships, of
activity/passivity cycles,
322–323
Road of life
image of, 102–103
in perspective, 103
retraveling, in Intersections
section, 106–107
Roads Not Taken, 113–116. *See
also* Intersections: Roads
Taken and Not Taken

exploring through Twilight
Imagery, 115–116
remedying void left by, 113
Russian Pilgrim, methods of,
313–318, 335, 343, 345

Salinger, J. D., 313
Self
language of, 15
vital force of, 32
Self-balancing principle, 366, 368
Self-reliance
experiencing, through Intensive
Journal process, 18
Sexuality. *See* Dialogue with the
Body
Silence, respecting validity of,
40–44
Similes, 50–51, 94–95, 234
Situations, 169. *See also* Dialogue
with Events, Situations, and
Circumstances
Sleep, thought and images during,
324–325. *See also* Dreams
Smuts, Jan Christian, 229
Society. *See also* Dialogue with
Society; Family relationships
renewing, 15
use of term, 183
Socrates, 228
Solitary work, in group
atmosphere, 33–37, 43
Spiritual contact
defined, 5
silence of privacy and, 5
Spiritual life, 232–235, 267–285.
See also Spiritual Positioning;
Spiritual Steppingstones
history of, in Connections
section, 257–266
postponing deeper meeting
with truth in, 296
themes of, 302
Spiritual Positioning,
232–240, 302

entries, 232–235
metaphoric entries in, 234
purpose of, 303
reconstructing development
of inner life, 236–239
as source for Peaks, Depths,
and Explorations exercises,
302–304
subsection in Meditation Log
for, 232
use of, 245
Spiritual Steppingstones, 374
adding persons' names to,
279–280
chronological ordering of,
276–277
continuing to work with,
277–278
entries in, 268
examples, 397–401
focus of, 268, 286–287
limitation on number of, 274
listing, 271–272
making entries in, 272–277
reading, 274–275, 279
Re-Openings and, 287,
288–289, 290
working with, 272–278
from workshops, 397–401
Stalemate, breaking through, 6
Steppingstone Period(s),
90–101
additional recall of, 100
as base for Time Stretching, 109
checklist descriptions of,
95–99, 109
defined, 90–91, 112
describing memories of, in Life
History Log, 109–113
and Dialogue with Persons, 131
Dialogue with Society and,
188–193
exploring, 92–93,
94–96
life period in, 91–92
selecting, 93–94

Steppingstones, 28, 74, 75,
76–101. See also Spiritual
Steppingstones; Stepping-
stone Period(s)
continuity of life and, 77, 81,
83–84, 88
defined, 76, 81, 90
Dialogue with Works and,
144–146
first listing of, 77–81, 85
of other person's life, listing,
134–136
of physical life, 156–159
privacy of details of, 83
reading, 81–83
recapitulating, for Dialogue
with Events, 179–180
second listing of, 85
selecting Steppingstone Period
from, 93–94
spontaneous selectivity in
listing, 78, 80, 81, 89
in relation to Steppingstone
Periods, 91
subjective feelings about, 84, 85
transitions in life and, 83–84,
88–89
ways to use, 83–89
of work(s), 148–150
Stillness, 131, 320–323
creativity and, 326
Structure of Intensive Journal
Workbook, 6, 7, 402
establishing, 19–21
freedom within, 311
principal underlying, 339–340
Subjective experiences. See also
Inner Process Entries
inner process of, 241–242
interrelatedness of, 25
making tangible, 25
uniqueness of, 243
Symbolism
ambiguity of, 214, 216
of Depth Dimension, 28, 197
of dreams, 105

of Twilight Imagery, 57–59,
61–62, 320
of "underground stream,"
34, 58
of "well," 33
Synchronicity, 171–172

Testament, 30, 350–358
crystallizing statement in,
353, 354
essence of, 352–354
writing, in twilight state,
351–352, 353
Tillich, Paul, 300
Time. See also Life/Time
Dimension
chronological, 74–75, 79
continuity of, and self-
balancing principle, 166
holistic units of, 229
qualitative, 74, 75, 79
subjective experience of, 28
Time Stretching exercises, 74, 75,
80, 108–122, 269, 369, 370
beginning, 108–110, 120
Life/Time Dimension sections
and, 74, 75
purpose of, 110, 111–112
Tolstoy, Leo, 234
Transcendence, 258
Transfer of entries, from Daily
Log, 66–67
Transformations, inner,
255, 256, 325
Transitions of life
help in navigating through, 74
Intensive Journal work and, 7
knowledge of, and perspective
on life, 17
spiritual, 256
Steppingstones and, 83, 86,
88–89
Transpersonal, 7–8,
379–380
creativity, 311
imagery, 326

Transpersonal *(cont.)*
  personal material enlarged
    to, 224
  exploration of, at personal level,
    300–311
  wisdom figures, 280–281
Transpsychological approach
  defined, 13–14
  of Intensive Journal method,
    13–14
Twilight Dreaming, 197, 207–208,
  209–221
  recording additional reactions
    to, 210–211
  recording method, 209–210
Twilight Imagery, 60–61, 270,
  370. *See also* Twilight state
  as bridge between Depth and
    Life/Time Dimensions, 119
  defined, 57, 58
  Dialogue with Events,
    Situations, and Circum-
    stances and, 179–180
  Dialogue with Works and,
    146, 150
  key to, 57–58
  Life Correlation and, 61–64
  Period Log and, 117
  Roads Taken and Not Taken
    explored with, 115–117

spontaneous, 369–370
Steppingstones of other person's
  life and, 136–137
Steppingstone Periods explored
  with, 95
technique of, 59–61
time-guidance of, 105–106
using in decision-making,
  117–120
Twilight Imagery Log, 29, 59, 197
  Period Image in, 59–61
  Steppingstone Periods and, 98
Twilight state, 58, 253, 298. *See
  also* Twilight Dreaming;
  Twilight Imagery
  imagery during, 324–325
  Mantra/Crystal meditation and,
    336–337, 343–345
  writing Testament in, 351–352

Unconscious mind, 28. *See also*
  Depth Dimension
  dreams and, 203
  psychic energy from, 118–119
  wisdom of, 105

Validation, 335
Visionary capacities, evoking
  of, 12
Vital force, 32

Waiting stance, 321
Whitman, Walt, 3
Wisdom, inner, 12, 171–172,
  270–271, 377. *See also* Inner
    Wisdom Dialogue
  of depth dimension, 105
  evoking of, 12
  Process Meditation as key to, 8
  quest for, 270, 271
  of the body, 154–155, 163–164
Wisdom figures
  dialogues with (*see* Inner
    Wisdom Dialogue)
  listing, 281
  personal, 280–281
  transpersonal, 280–281
Work(s). *See also* Dialogue with
    Works
  concept of, 142–143
  current, 152–153
  describing, 147–148
  listing, 145–147
  recapitulating steps in
    development of, 148–150
  Steppingstones of, 148–150
Workings, 337, 339, 340

Yoga, 331

About the Author
and The Intensive Journal Program

Since the 1950s, Dr. Ira Progoff has been exploring psychological methods for creativity and spiritual experience with social applications. He is a leading authority on the psychology of C.G. Jung, humanistic and transpersonal psychology as well as journal-writing.

Dr. Progoff completed his doctoral dissertation in the psychology of C.G. Jung from the New School of Social Research in New York City, and published it in 1953 as *Jung's Psychology and Its Social Meaning.* Also in 1953, as a Bollingen Fellow in Switzerland, Dr. Progoff studied privately with C.G. Jung.

The conceptual base of Ira Progoff's holistic depth psychology can be found in a trilogy of earlier books. *The Death and Rebirth of Psychology* (1956) crystallizes the cumulative results of the work of Freud, Adler, Jung, and Rank to build the foundation for a new psychology. *Depth Psychology and Modern Man* (1959) presents a holistic view of evolution as a foundation for a nonanalytic method in depth psychology. *The Symbolic and the Real* (1963) discusses the significance of these concepts for modern society and demonstrates the personal use of twilight imagery.

As Director of the Institute for Research in Depth Psychology at the Drew University Graduate School from 1959 to 1971, Dr. Progoff conducted research on life cycles and their relation to spiritual and creative experience. Drawing on the principles of these books and research at Drew University, he developed the *Intensive Journal* method in 1966 as a system of nonanalytic integrative techniques for drawing-out and interrelating the contents of an individual life. He founded Dialogue House in 1966 as a means of organizing *Intensive Journal* workshops.

In 1977, as the public use of the Method increased, Dr. Progoff formed the National *Intensive Journal* Program. It now supplies over 100 trained and certified leaders to conduct *Intensive Journal* workshops in the United States and other countries in cooperation with local sponsoring organizations. While conducting numerous workshops for a variety of organizations, Dr. Progoff continued to develop the *Intensive Journal* method.

Dr. Progoff's writings include numerous articles that have been published in journals. He has also been a frequent lecturer at leading universities, religious, and cultural organizations.

In addition to his writing, Dr. Progoff is currently Director of the *Intensive Journal* program at its Dialogue House headquarters in New York City. For further information about the Progoff *Intensive Journal* Program, please write to Dialogue House Associates, Inc., P.O.B. 1225, Old Chelsea Station, New York, NY 10113-1225.